STREET DESIGN

STREET DESIGN

The Secret to Great Cities and Towns

John Massengale and Victor Dover

WILEY

For general information about our other products and services, please contact our Customer Care Department within the United States at (800) 762-2974, outside the United States at (317) 572-3993 or fax (317) 572-4002.

Wiley publishes in a variety of print and electronic formats and by print-on-demand. Some material included with standard print versions of this book may not be included in e-books or in print-on-demand. If this book refers to media such as a CD or DVD that is not included in the version you purchased, you may download this material at http://booksupport.wiley.com. For more information about Wiley products, visit www.wiley.com.

Library of Congress Cataloging-in-Publication Data:

Dover, Victor, 1962-
    Street design : the secret to great cities and towns / Victor Dover, John Massengale.
      pages cm
    Includes index.
    ISBN 978-1-118-06670-6 (cloth); ISBN 978-1-118-41594-8 (ebk); ISBN 978-1-118-41859-8(ebk).

    1. Streets. I. Massengale, John Montague. II. Title.
    TE279.D68 2014

    713—dc23
                                                                        2013007089

Printed in the United States of America

10 9 8 7 6 5 4 3 2 1

CONTENTS

I am delighted that an evolutionary change in thinking seems to be underway worldwide about how best we can make and sustain our villages, towns and cities. Streets are meant to be places for people and this is most evident in our historic centres – where comfortable streets have made it possible for neighbourhoods to adapt again and again, even as culture and technology have continually evolved. On the other hand, the harsh and unwelcoming streets of urban sprawl were made for moving cars at high speed; their very geometry is car-based and, not surprisingly, these streets are often unsafe for pedestrians.

A handful of fundamental principles seem to separate the streets where communities flourish from those that do not. These principles form the central message of this book.

Learning from observing is one of those fundamental principles. Observation is perhaps the street designer's most powerful tool. At Poundbury, in Dorset, where I have attempted to put these principles into practice for more than 20 years, we have applied lessons learnt from other market towns and villages. For example, we realized that if we wanted to create a walkable town, we would need to insist that the car was not the focus in the physical design, but rather that the street is a pedestrian space through which cars are permitted to move, albeit slowly and safely. There are virtually no traffic signs or painted lines on the ground; instead there are spatial changes and physical and architectural features in a sequence along the streets. These sorts of spatial sequences were normal features in historic towns. Designing the streets this way has lent safety to the town, but it has also created a built environment that relates to the human scale and to the local identity. It is certainly encouraging that all the efforts at Poundbury, in Dorset (England), and my Foundation for Building Community's work elsewhere, have been cited as models in the British Government's new manual "Designing Streets".

Learning from observing is at the root of all living traditions, especially art – and street design is indeed an art; it is the art of place-making and that can only be acquired through study and application. The best streets in the world's villages, towns and cities – whether modest or grand – continually remind one that *simplicity* is part of the recipe for success in this art. The advice of Victor Dover and John Massengale, their historic examples and their own designs, reflect that simplicity.

Great streets define great cities; great cities establish harmony with Nature, continually improve societies and stimulate economic progress in a genuinely sustainable way. There is a real urgency to apply these principles in street design. The rewards will be worth every bit of effort.

PREFACE

WE—JOHN AND VICTOR—have been looking at and thinking about streets for decades. We've logged our favorites in sketchbooks and debated their many differences. At the same time, we've come to understand that what makes a good street is not as subjective or as complex as some might think. In fact, making good streets comes naturally to people, and has for thousands of years.

Studies show that when people are given maps of a town or city and asked to walk around and mark on the maps the places they like and don't like, their choices correspond to a great degree. Yes, some people have more formal tastes than others, and there are other preferences that might distinguish one person's favorites from another's. But increase the sample size, and the preferences become part of a predictable range with a lot of overlap. There is always a consensus about which places are the best and which are the worst, regardless of personal preferences. Practically everyone will say that the Piazza San Marco in Venice and the streets on the Left Bank in Paris are beautiful. Similar reactions are found in cities, towns, neighborhoods, and villages around the world.

If there is so much consensus on what makes a good street, why are we still building so many bad and ugly ones? The reasons can be identified and addressed. Today, too few people bother to think about what makes them feel at home on the street in the first place. Take the time to look, and anyone will begin to notice the patterns of buildings, trees, and comfortable spaces that set the better streets apart from the rest.

For this book, we made lists of our favorite streets, and then examined what made them special. We asked our colleagues to tell us about the streets they admire, and we went into the library and looked online to find other lists of great streets. Then we went out to reexamine many of the streets in person—photographing them, taking measurements, and observing the way people behave and interact on them. We had the pleasure of visiting many great streets, and we were able to see how the experience of visiting the streets today compared to our memories or our colleagues' recommendations. We could see if there had been changes, and if those had made the street better or worse.

A problem we found everywhere was that the automobile has taken over our streets. Writers like Peter D. Norton have shown how Organized Motordom pushed everyone but the driver and his car to the side of the road—and then sometimes took the sidewalk, too.[1] Well-meaning authorities redesigned roads for "throughput" and removed obstacles like pedestrians, who were getting in the way of the cars. This emphasis on driving frequently undermined public spaces that were once wonderful for walking. Some of our favorite streets, when revisited, were no longer agreeable places to be: spending a few hours on the Boulevard St. Germain in Paris was exhausting, because of the never-ending noise, smell, and energy of the cars racing along it (Figure 0.2). The formerly pleasing broad High Street in Marlborough, England, no longer felt like the town center, due to the sheer volume of cars and trucks passing through it on their way from somewhere else to yet another place. Newer streets were often even more disagreeable.

Along with the success stories, therefore, we saw problems, and we also looked at new and old examples of streets commonly regarded as failures. We recorded some of those too. Our hope is that every reader will come away with a sharper sense of the elements that contribute to making a street a place that people seek out or avoid.

The good news is that today, all across the United States, we are in a period of rediscovering our old towns and cities and rebuilding our streets, and more and more people are seeing the need to curtail the radical influence of the car on our physical surroundings. One rallying term for this new vision of community is the Complete Street[2]—one where the pedestrian, the driver, the cyclist, and transit users all have a stake.

Figure 0.2: Boulevard St. Germain, Paris, France. Once the center of Bohemian life in Paris, the boulevard St. Germain is now overwhelmed by traffic. *Flâneurs* today walk on other streets.

The bad news is that Americans are frequently ignoring the basic rules of placemaking in our attempts to create complete streets. Professionals of all stripes—often with competing agendas—are designing and building streets with specialized standards and criteria, which is one of the main reasons why our streets get worse and worse. The formulaic, seemingly ubiquitous use of yellow pedestrian crossings, red bus lanes, green bicycle tracks, ugly bumpouts, and uglier white plastic sticks make sense in the narrow focus of the specialist, but look at the world's best streets, as we have, and you will find they don't have these special things. What they do have is a limited palette of materials in the roadbed and on the sidewalk. When you visit them, what you notice is the beauty and the harmony of the place, not the details like the crosswalks or the bench selection.

In the following chapters, we will look at why streets matter. We will examine historic streets, retrofitted streets, new streets, and street networks. Our hope is that our readers will come to see that we can all envision better places—and then fix our streets, by design. We *must* make the most of the glorious new opportunities to build more walkable towns and cities by creating streets that are places *where people actually want to be.*

NOTES

1. Peter D. Norton, *Fighting Traffic: The Dawn of the Motor Age in the American City* (Cambridge, MA: The MIT Press, 2011). Also see Tom Vanderbilt, *Traffic: Why We Drive the Way We Do (and What It Says About Us)* (New York: Vintage, 2009).

2. "Now, in communities across the country, a movement is growing to **complete the streets.** States, cities and towns are asking their planners and engineers to build road networks that are safer, more livable, and welcoming to everyone. Instituting a **Complete Streets policy** ensures that transportation planners and engineers consistently design and operate the entire roadway with **all users** in mind—including bicyclists, public transportation vehicles and riders, and pedestrians of all ages and abilities."—from the website of the National Complete Streets Coalition at http://www.smartgrowthamerica.org/complete-streets.

ACKNOWLEDGMENTS

FIRST AND FOREMOST, we thank our wives, Maricé Chael and Melanie Hoffman, for their guidance and infinite patience: Melanie was also an indefatigable proofreader. We are deeply grateful to Emily Glavey and Kenneth Garcia at Dover, Kohl & Partners, who tirelessly performed indispensable research, drawing and editorial tasks. And we thank our editor, Alice Truax, who somehow got us to rewrite most of the book. Lauren Poplawski and Kerstin Nasdeo at Wiley brought us along step by step, and graciously let us tinker with the book at every stage.

Richard Driehaus and the Driehaus Charitable Lead Trust gave us a crucial, generous grant to research the book. Paula McMenamin, Carol Wyant, Eric Alexander and Vision Long Island signed on early to support this. Many others helped with information on specific places or tours on our travels. Robert Russell and Macky Hill taught us Charleston history, Christian Sottile and Thomas Wilson expanded our understanding of the Savannah grid, and Chris Gray at the Office for Metropolitan History in New York was, as always, a font of information about his city. Stephane Kirkland knows all there is to know about the history of streets in Paris. Matt Shannon introduced us to street types in Chicago. In two of our favorite towns—Great Barrington and Nantucket, in Massachusetts—David Scribner, Andrew Blechman, and Andrew Vorce helped us.

Besides the enormous debt we owe our guest essayists for broadening the insights in this book, some of them helped us in other ways as well. Hank Dittmar at the Prince's Foundation gave crucial guidance at the earliest stage. Paul Murrain took us on an astounding day-long walk in London. Gabriele Tagliaventi helped us see Bologna in new ways. Douglas Duany not only showed us Orvieto and the medieval streets of Rome, he put up with us for two weeks. We are also in debt to Rebecca Martin, Jim Evarts, Thomas Massengale, Elizabeth Plater-Zyberk, and Laura Heery Prozes for putting us up in Barcelona, London, Miami and New York.

Our colleagues in the Congress for the New Urbanism contributed their wisdom in many discussions. Peter Katz coached and prodded. Rick Hall shared his insights and unflagging enthusiasm about engineering (and engineers). Billy Hattaway, Norm Garrick, Dewayne Carver, and Gary Toth also pitched in their engineering wisdom. Bob Gibbs shared his great knowledge of the rules of successful retail. Elizabeth Plater-Zyberk and Rusty Bloodworth pointed out London streets we didn't know, and the pro-urb, Urbanists, and Trad-Arch listservs helped us kick ideas around. Fred Kent, Dan Burden, Mike Lydon, Richard Layman, Michael Ronkin and others did the same in extensive email discussions. Aaron Naparstek and Benjamin Fried led us to the latest news and opinions about bicycles, while the CNU's Project for Transportation Reform under Marcy McInelly established a thought provoking foundation for this work. At Smart Growth America and the Complete Streets Coalition, we owe a debt to Geoff Anderson, Ilana Preuss, Barbara McCann, and Roger Millar. Beth Osborne at the US DOT and the DC Director of Planning Harriett Tregoning are two of the wisest voices in Washington when it comes to street design. In New York, Janette Sadik-Khan and Jon Orcutt have been smart, inspiring, and generous.

Many people contributed original or historic photographs. Several deserve at least a mention here as well: Sandy Sorlien, Steve Mouzon, Steven Brooke, Joseph Ip, Peter Pennoyer, Anne Walker, David Dixon, David Fishman, and James Mercer. Stephanie Sayre at the Iowa State University Library, Marie Henke at the Nantucket Historical Society, Robert Peterson at the Ingham County DOT, Nilda Rivera at the Museum of the City of New York, Todd Gilbert at the New York Transit Museum, Larry Gould at the Metropolitan Transportation Authority, the staff at HistoryMiami, James Labey at the Royal Borough of Kensington and Chelsea, and Tallulah Morris at the Crown Estate in London all made our work easier. James Dougherty, Kenneth Garcia, Megan McLaughlin, and Andrew Georgiadis at Dover, Kohl & Partners contributed photographs, and James worked on our designs for the Yorkville Promenade, Jane Jacobs Square and Winslow Homer Walk, along with our collaborator Zeke Mermell. The entire crew at Dover-Kohl persistently helped, especially Kristen Thomas, Justin Falango, and, of course, Joseph Kohl.

CHAPTER ONE
INTRODUCTION

> Our streets and squares make up what we call the public realm, which is the physical manifestation of the common good. When you degrade the public realm, the common good suffers.
>
> —James Howard Kunstler

THE DESIGN OF CITIES begins with the design of streets. To make a good city, you need good streets, and that means streets where people want to be. Streets need to be safe and comfortable, they need to be interesting, and they need to be beautiful. They need to be places.

◄ **Figure 1.1:** Broad Street, New York, New York. Looking north on one of the main streets in New York City's financial district around 1905. *Library of Congress, Prints and Photographs Division, Detroit Publishing Company Photograph Collection, LC-D4-33881*

We often think of *buildings* when we think of urban design—as we should. Great streets require great buildings. Good streets can get by with merely good buildings; great or merely good, the art of architecture is clearly indispensable. But streets are the spaces between the buildings, and those spaces need the art of *placemaking*. Placemaking makes the street spaces into settings where people want to be. A place is not a place until there are people in it.

We'll look at great streets in this book and explore what made them great places. Most of them are beautiful, and so it is important to point out that the cliché about beauty being in the eye of the beholder is wrong: we all intuitively know beautiful places when we experience them. If we walk through an arcade in Venice and come out in the Piazza San Marco, no one has to tell us that this is a profound and uplifting experience. There can also be a great deal of beauty in everyday experience, as we see on many "ordinary" Main Streets

Figure 1.2: An "auto sewer" arterial that, except for the palm trees, could be Anywhere, USA. "The road is now like television, violent and tawdry. The landscape it runs through is littered with cartoon buildings and commercial messages. We whiz by them at fifty-five miles an hour and forget them, because one convenience store looks like the next. They do not celebrate anything beyond their mechanistic ability to sell merchandise. We don't want to remember them. We did not savor the approach and we were not rewarded upon reaching the destination, and it will be the same next time, and every time. There is little sense of having arrived anywhere, because everyplace looks like noplace in particular." — James Howard Kunstler, *The Geography of Nowhere.*

Figure 1.3: A placeless cul-de-sac: a residential auto sewer in Anywhere, USA. *Image courtesy of Megan McLaughlin*

in American small towns. When the buildings and trees lining the street give it a sense of enclosure, and the proportions and details form a harmonious whole, Main Street becomes a place where we want to linger, sharing a common experience with our neighbors and fellow citizens.

Tragically, we rarely build streets like that today. The overwhelming majority of the streets in America have been built since World War II, and most of them were built for cars rather than people—like the six-lane arterial road in the middle of nowhere lined with strip malls, shopping malls, big box centers, and the other detritus of modern suburban life (Figure 1.2). These cheaply built, poorly designed sites and buildings do not feel like authentic places to us: there is no there there.[1] The roads are what the writer James Howard Kunstler calls "auto sewers"—suburban "thoroughfares" sized by engineers to make the traffic flow like water in a pipe. Sometimes it seems more like sludge in a sewer pipe.

Not surprisingly, the streets that result look as though they were made for cars. No one walks on them if they can possibly avoid it (Figure 1.3). The problem with these streets is not just their location, far from anything except other shopping centers and big box stores. Their design and construction are bad for people, too. The scale is vast and frightening, speeding cars roar by, there are large swales where the sidewalk should be, and crossing the street is difficult, with long expanses between traffic lights. Even when you get to your destination, you still have to cross a large parking lot that has no sidewalks or shade trees. It's all ugly, and it's all depressing.

Fortunately, after decades of fleeing cities and old towns, Americans have embraced walkable towns and neighborhoods again. There's a common understanding that the automobile-based patterns of building made a physical environment inferior in many ways to the old pedestrian-based one, and that we need to remake our cities, towns, and streets for people. Accordingly, the Federal and local governments are appropriating billions of dollars in a well-intentioned—yet scattered and intermittent—effort to rebuild the nation's roads.

Less encouraging is that many of the professionals involved in remaking our streets bring with them the criteria and biases of their specialties, and that frequently prevents them from designing streets where people want to be. Bicycle specialists, pedestrian specialists, transit specialists, and even Complete Street specialists may understand the need to add a bike lane or a streetcar, but they often don't understand placemaking or the importance of the public realm. The professionals in charge usually continue the late-twentieth-century pattern of allocating most of the square footage there primarily to the motor vehicle and its movement—now with the movement of bicycles and buses added. They introduce innovations that make the street safer for those riding bikes or even traveling on foot, but at the same time they repeatedly diminish the space and beauty of the street for the walker. And when you diminish the public realm, you diminish the common good.

THE TRADITIONAL STREET

The history of urban design and street design in Western civilization has its roots in ancient Rome and Athens. For the Greeks and the Romans, the city was the place where men and women came together to make a good and civilized life. The words "civil," "civilization," and "citizen" come from the Roman word for city, "civitas." From the ancient Greek word for city, "polis," we get "polite," "political," and "police," which reflect the classical idea that the city was a political body of citizens, as well as the place where they politely came together to create civilization. For centuries, the first job of the architect when designing a new building was to make or reinforce the public realm (Figure 1.5).

Ancient Romans talked about the public realm, which they called the *res publica,* as the place where the citizens came together in the *polis.* It was shaped by the buildings in the private realm (*res privata*). In *The Architecture of Community,* the architect and urban designer Léon Krier uses diagrams to show that each realm is incomplete without the other, while the two combine to

make the complete city (Figure 1.6).[2] In addition to open space (streets and squares and parks), the public realm also includes public buildings such as churches and town halls. Much of the art of traditional urban design and town planning consists of two things: shaping and programming the public realm into a place where pedestrians want to be, and strategically placing public buildings (such as a market or place of worship or theater) so that they are understood to be more important than the private buildings (Figure 1.4).

Figure 1.4: Old New York Police Headquarters, 240 Centre Street, New York, New York. Hoppin & Koen, 1905–1909. "The boldest conception of civic art makes it embrace not merely individual groups of buildings with their approaches and gardens but even entire cities. It is one thing to distribute fine groups of public buildings over the area of a city and to connect them effectively. It is a much more difficult thing to relate the entire city to such a scheme."—Werner Hegemann and Elbert Peets, *American Vitruvius: An Architects' Handbook of Civic Art.*

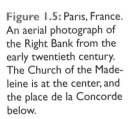

Figure 1.5: Paris, France. An aerial photograph of the Right Bank from the early twentieth century. The Church of the Madeleine is at the center, and the place de la Concorde below.

In the modern world, we also have the semipublic domain of stores, businesses, and places of entertainment, such as movie houses, restaurants, and nightclubs. Office buildings now frequently tower above the church steeples that used to be the tallest structures, and corporate headquarters like the Chicago Tribune Tower or the Woolworth Building in New York are distinguished from speculative office buildings by their monumental-

ity and ornate architecture. All these buildings play a large part in making urban places where people want to be. Some of these spaces were meant to inspire a sense of grandeur; others were designed to be intimate. Most important, whether we are strolling through the ruins of the Roman Forum or exploring the streets of Back Bay, Boston, all of these environments were built to a human scale.

Figure 1.6: The True City. Léon Krier, 1983. To be complete, the city needs to have both a public realm and a private realm. *Image courtesy of Léon Krier*

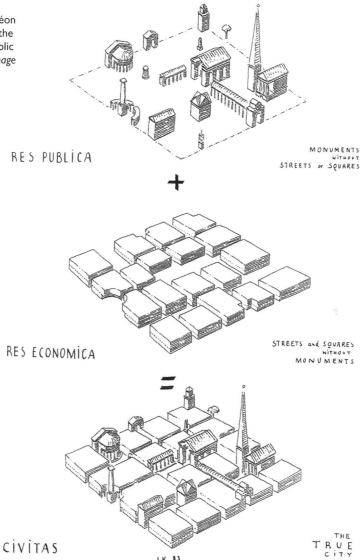

THE GRID

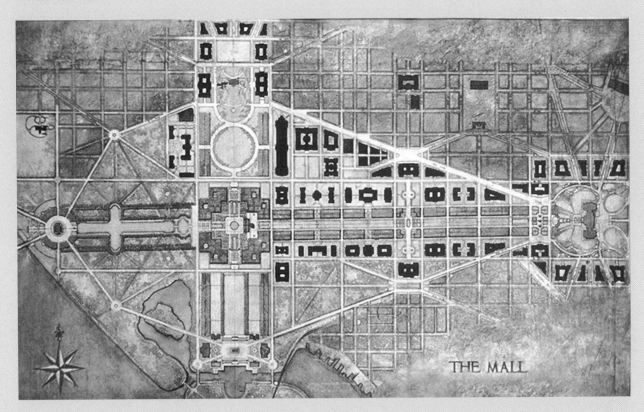

Figure 1.7: McMillan Plan, Washington, DC. Senate Park Commission (Daniel Burnham, F. L. Olmsted, Jr., Charles F. McKim, et al), 1901. At the peak of the City Beautiful movement, the Senate Park Commission hired leading architects and landscape architects to restore the clarity of Pierre Charles L'Enfant's 1791 plan for Washington. The Senate Park Commission was better known as the McMillan Commission, in honor of Senator James McMillan, whose Chief of Staff led the effort.

An American book about street design must mention the grid, however briefly. The rectilinear grid has been used in the planning of towns and cities since at least the fifteenth century BC, when the Chinese started a tradition of gridded plans that they still employ today. In the Western world, the use of rectilinear grids for town plans goes back to at least 2600 or 2500 BC, and the Romans institutionalized a standard gridded plan for the places colonized by the Roman Empire. Roman cities, fortified garrisons, and colonial outposts were designed around the famous *cardo* and *decumanus. Cardi* were north–south streets, and *decumani* east–west streets: the two central axes were the largest streets, known as the *cardo maximus* and the *decumanus maximus*. Where they crossed at the center of the town, there was normally a forum, or public square. The most important streets in many European, Middle Eastern, and North African cities and towns today are still where the Romans built their *cardo maximus* and *decumanus maximus*.

Many early towns and cities in America were laid out by commercial interests that saw the grid as an efficient, simple way to divide open land into rectangular lots with clear boundaries that allowed the easy establishment of title. The seventeenth- and eighteenth-century settlements typically had level sites, often by a river or along the coast. There was not much topography on the flat sites to impede easy implementation of the plans, which frequently ended raggedly along the uneven shorelines. The grandest versions of these plans were in Philadelphia (1682) and Savannah (1733).

Figure 1.8: Philadelphia, Pennsylvania. William Penn, 1682. A plan of Philadelphia published in 1802. An early and influential American grid.

Philadelphia's influential plan (Figure 1.8) started a tradition for American gridded plans: the north–south streets were numbered, while the east–west streets were named after trees.

Savannah and Philadelphia started by the edge of rivers and took many decades to grow into their expansive plans. The plans for Philadelphia and Savannah (Figure 3.1) included regularly repeated squares; in Philadelphia, one square was rented to a lumberyard until the city grew up around it. Savannah had a rich and varied plan, which also made it easy for the city to grow over time (see "The Streets of Charleston and Savannah" in Chapter 3).

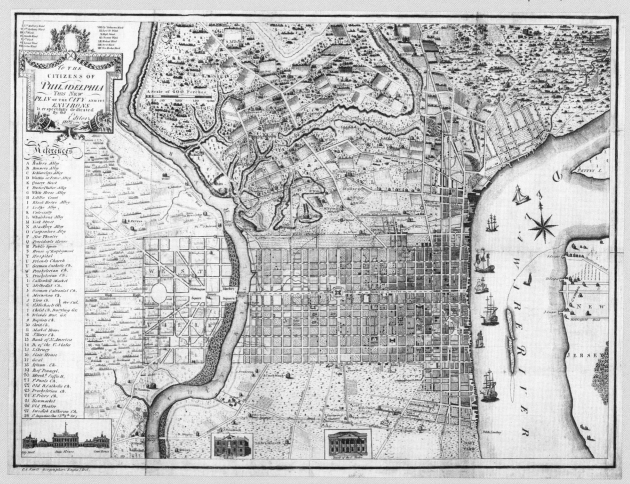

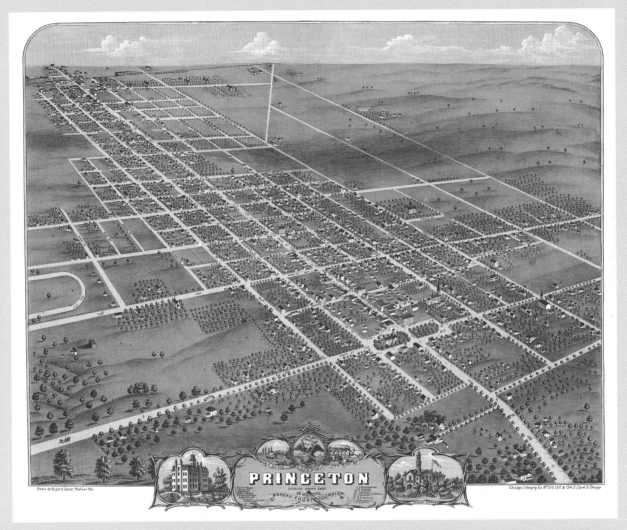

Figure 1.9: Princeton, Illinois. Bird's eye view of Princeton in 1870. A perspective map looking northeast, not drawn to scale. Bird's eye views like this were commonly made for American cities and towns in the nineteenth century. *Library of Congress, Geography and Map Division, Ruger Map Collection, g4104p pm001800*

The predictability of how the grid will shape development is another of its advantages. In 1811, New York's city fathers platted a grid across the island of Manhattan, which was still mainly covered by farmland, woods, and wetland. As in the American towns established by commercial interests, the grid made surveying and selling lots with clear title simple and straightforward. Land speculation started immediately, and the population of Manhattan alone multiplied almost fourteen times before the end of the century. Speculation and growth were helped by the fact that the Commissioners' Plan of 1811 continued block sizes already in use in lower Manhattan, so that building types developed there could be easily used in new parts of the city. "A city is to be composed principally of the habitations of men, and that strait sided, and right angled houses are the most cheap to build, and the most convenient to live in," a Commissioners' Plan report said.[3]

Grids were not only used in planning cities and towns. In 1785, the U.S. Congress passed a land ordinance that expanded on a similar one drafted by Thomas Jefferson the year before. The 1785 Land Ordinance drew a rectilinear National Grid across the entire country, dividing it into six-mile-square "townships." These squares were further divided by thirty-six square sections of 640 acres each. Those sections could be sliced into half-sections, quarter-sections, etc., down to a dimension of sixty feet across (Figure 1.9). Congress established a plan for surveying and laying out the grid, and then sold much of the land for a minimum of $1 an acre.

Satellite views of the Midwest and the Great Plains today clearly show the National Grid laid across the land. New towns and cities like Chicago were planned within the framework of the grid, and modern suburban and exurban arterials frequently follow the National Grid. In the west and southwest, however, the grid sometimes ran into conflict with development patterns in lands formerly belonging to Spain. New towns there were planned according to the Law of the Indies, the royal regulations for Spanish colonies. These included directions for siting and laying out towns with central squares in a rectilinear grid of twelve streets.

Santa Fe, New Mexico, was planned under the Law of the Indies. It is one of the places in America where market demand for second houses for the rich has driven house prices ridiculously high, because of the beauty of the town. Like many classic American small towns, it has a simple grid. Wiscasset, Maine; Easton, Maryland; Marshall, Michigan; and Virginia City, Nevada, are a few of many exemplars across the country. Mayberry, North Carolina, and Bedford Falls, New York, are two fictional examples on television and in the movies. They all have good Main Streets where people enjoy walking surrounded by simple grids with comfortable single-family houses on tree-lined streets (Figure 1.10).

Not all small towns with grids are classic places where we want to be, of course. In *American Notes*, Charles Dickens said Philadelphia is "a handsome city, but

Figure 1.10: Old South Road, Southport, Connecticut. Looking east from the intersection of Old South Road and Pequot Avenue. This classic American street near the Southport train station and the village center has large front yards and a single sidewalk on one side of the road.

distractingly regular. After walking about for an hour or two I felt that I would have given the world for a crooked street."[4] A grid built without thought and attention to detail can be a rigid, unpleasant gridiron, but there are simple ways to soften the grid.

Taming the Grid:

1. A beautiful tree canopy over a street is one of the easiest ways to soften a grid. When New Haven, Connecticut, was the Elm City, it had a more beautiful downtown.

2. A variety of street types and street widths combined with short blocks and squares enriches a grid. Savannah is the supreme example (see figure in Chapter 3).

Figure 1.11: Capitol Street, Charleston, West Virginia. The grid surrounding Capitol Street is almost orthogonal, but the streets bend slightly here and there, always in accordance with the city's gentle topography.

3. In a town or city with gentle slopes, slightly bending the streets to follow the topography softens the grid (Figure 1.11). A traditional design technique for city streets is to change the slope or the direction of the street only at an intersection with another street. As seen on Nassau Street in New York between Fulton Street and Wall Street, this produces a beautiful spatial effect.

4. When a town or city has dramatic hills, like San Francisco, running the grid up and down the hills with little deformation can be visually and experientially interesting. Even in Manhattan, where many hills were shaved down as the grid was built, the most pleasant parts of the long avenues are frequently where hills and plateaus combine to draw attention away from long, unterminated vistas. Madison Avenue in the 90s and Lexington Avenue in the 70s are examples.

5. Shifting the grid, so that some streets are only three or four blocks long, adds variety and richness to the grid. Sidney Place in Brooklyn, discussed in Chapter 2, is an example.

6. Laying diagonals across a grid, as in Pierre L'Enfant's plan for Washington, DC, adds interest if the plan skillfully includes important buildings or monuments on the prominent sites created by the diagonals (Figure 1.7). Diagonals in a grid can also be disorienting, however, and add awkwardly shaped lots that require custom building designs.

7. Streets that open to the surrounding area can draw the landscape into the town. Examples are streets in Santa Fe that point at the mountains and the crosstown streets in Manhattan that open to the Hudson and East rivers.

THE FORMAL, THE PICTURESQUE, AND THE HYBRID

City plans and street designs have historically fallen into three main types: formal plans, picturesque plans, and hybrid designs that combine the two. Preferences for the formal and the picturesque have alternated throughout history. As we have seen, use of the simple grid goes back to at least the fifteenth century BC, but before the classical world of the ancient Greeks and Romans, many human settlements were planned and built in informal ways. In ancient Rome and Greece, Classical buildings were frequently used in both formal plans and informal plans, and we now know that during "the Dark Ages" between the fall of the Roman Empire and the beginning of the Italian Renaissance, planning was not exclusively what is now often called "medieval." Design tendencies became more formal as the Renaissance spread around the Western world, but in the nineteenth century there was a swing towards eclecticism, romanticism, and the picturesque. And yet the nineteenth century also had formal designers, planners, and architects who consciously combined the two, as we shall see.

In the mid-nineteenth century, eclectic designers like the great landscape architect Fredrick Law Olmsted used formal designs and picturesque designs, depending on the context. Olmsted's plans for the streets of Llewellyn Park, New Jersey, and Riverside, Illinois, were winding and romantic, and his plans for Ocean Parkway and Eastern Parkway in Brooklyn, New York, were more formal nineteenth-century American interpretations of the great French boulevards. His designs for Prospect Park in Brooklyn and Central Park in Manhattan contained both informal and formal designs, like the great Central Park Promenade. The formal elements of the Promenade, now known as the Mall or the Poet's Walk, include the long, straight, and level walk lined by a majestic allée of elm trees. The widest walkway in Central Park, it terminates with a grand stair that descends to the Bethesda Terrace and Fountain. The stair is on axis with the Mall, another measure of formal design, and the statue of an angel that crowns the fountain is too. From afar, the angel visually "terminates" the axis, which is another hallmark of formal planning (Figure 1.12).

The Formal

The simple American grid was the work of the surveyor and the engineer. The grid has an obvious rectilinear formality, but it is frequently untouched by many of the principles of formal urban design. And as we've seen, these Classical principles—order, harmony, balance, legibility—shaped the form of great cities and buildings for thousands of years. In the late nineteenth century, the City Beautiful movement set out to reshape American towns and cities with the type of formal order found in the history of Classical architecture and urbanism in Europe. Most of the founders of this movement studied architecture and urbanism in Paris at the École des Beaux-Arts, where they saw firsthand the city's great avenues and boulevards from the eighteenth and nineteenth centuries. The students also studied and visited the landmarks of ancient Greece and Rome, the cities and buildings of the Italian Renaissance, and the Baroque of Western Europe.

They brought all of this back to America in the form of what they called Civic Art, which combined urban design, street design, building design, and the design and placement of monuments and sculpture in the city. They liked the American grid as a starting point, but they wanted to enrich it with a hierarchical range of streets and importantly sited civic buildings.

Figure 1.12: The Mall, Central Park, New York, New York. Frederick Law Olmsted and Calvert Vaux, 1858. Once known as the Promenade, and also called the Poet's Walk, the Mall has the largest stand of American elm trees in the world. Together with the Bethesda Fountain and Terrace that terminate the long axis, the Mall is the most formal spot in Central Park.

CITY BEAUTIFUL

The first full-blown expression of the City Beautiful movement was the World's Columbian Exposition, built in Chicago in 1893 with temporary white plaster buildings that transformed America with a Beaux-Arts-influenced Classical revival. In urban design, the City Beautiful movement included ideas about social and economic justice that allied it with the Progressive movement in American politics. Master plans for American cities, like the 1909 Plan of Chicago, included housing reform and the planning of public parks, as well as formal interventions in simple grids, with new squares and tree-lined avenues visually terminated by important civic buildings.

Daniel Burnham—one of the founders of the City Beautiful movement, the organizer of the World's Columbian Exposition, and author of the 1909

Chicago plan commonly known as the Burnham Plan—famously said, "Make no little plans." Many of the best American cities owe much of their present character to work built during the City Beautiful movement. In New York City, for example, that work includes Grand Central Terminal; the Metropolitan Museum of Art; many of the great skyscrapers, like the Woolworth Building and the Municipal Building (Figure 1.13); the New York Public Library on 42nd Street and many of the branch libraries; the great public schools, parks, and playgrounds; and swaths of rowhouses and apartment buildings in all five boroughs.

Since this is a book about street design, however, it must be said that many of the street designs in the most ambitious City Beautiful plans were never executed, except in small parts here and there, even though American cities were undergoing enormous growth and had tremendous wealth. Of the great diagonals Burnham planned for Chicago, only one was constructed, while the City Beautiful streets designed for Manhattan by America's greatest architects exist only on paper. Notable exceptions are the streets around the Mall in Washington, DC, which were redesigned as part of the McMillan Plan, and the Benjamin Franklin Parkway in Philadelphia, designed by the French landscape architect Jacques Gréber. The goals of the parkway design were broad enough to encompass slum clearance and the creation of sites for new civic buildings, including the Philadelphia Museum of Art and a new city library.

The construction of individual City Beautiful buildings and civic centers around the country (San Francisco and Cleveland have prominent examples) was more

Figure 1.13: Manhattan Municipal Building, 1 Centre Street, New York, New York. McKim, Mead & White, 1907. Painting by Colin Campbell Cooper, 1922. Chambers Street, which is visually terminated by the Municipal Building, once continued through McKim, Mead & White's grand colonnade and arch.

common. In retrospect, the City Beautiful civic centers were often bad for street life, because they concentrated civic buildings around large plazas that drew pedestrians from the streets without filling the plazas. And almost a century after the Franklin Parkway was built in Philadelphia, the wide boulevard still has very little street life most of the time, because seldom-visited parks separate it from the low-density neighborhoods surrounding it, and the cultural institutions along the parkway don't draw much foot traffic. New Urbanists frequently advocate locating civic buildings in different places around the city in order to increase pedestrian traffic and maximize the use of civic buildings as civic monuments on important sites.

A story about three of the most influential founders of the City Beautiful movement demonstrates their fondness for the formal. In 1901, the U.S. Senate authorized the hiring of Burnham, Charles McKim, and Frederick Law Olmsted, Jr. (the son of Frederick Law Olmsted, who with his half-brother continued their father's landscape architecture practice under the name Olmsted Bros.) to study the deterioration of the Mall in Washington, DC, and to make recommendations about how to address it. With a Senate aide, the three set off on a six-week tour of Europe to study "French planning" and "Italian architecture." After touring Paris and Versailles they traveled to Venice, where McKim was unhappy because there was so little of the axial planning he enjoyed in Paris. Wandering the small, meandering passages of Venice, McKim became separated from the group. When Olmsted asked how they would find him, Burnham replied, "We will go to the Piazza San Marco and find him on the axis."[5] They did, and McKim was there.

The Picturesque

The canals and *calli* of Venice that failed to satisfy McKim epitomize medieval and picturesque planning. The father of modern picturesque planning, Camillo Sitte, said about the Piazza San Marco, "So much beauty is united on this unique little patch of earth, that no painter has ever dreamt up anything surpassing it." After describing the elements and details that make the piazza, he continued, "However, it is the felicitous arrangement of them that contributes so decidedly to the whole arrangement. There is no doubt that if all these works of art were disposed separately according to the modern method, straight in line and geometrically centered, their effect would be immeasurably decreased."[6]

Sitte studied medieval towns and cities for his book, *City Planning According to Artistic Principles,* published in 1889. From his studies of medieval urbanism he developed underlying principles of design for what we call picturesque urbanism (Figure 1.14). This was not medieval design but, rather, design based on the spaces that Sitte found pleasing in medieval streets, towns, and cities. He presented his ideas in words, plans, and perspective drawings, emphasizing that the goal was not to reproduce old places but to make new places with experiences as good as those produced by the best medieval designs. He also emphasized that understanding how to produce engaging three-dimensional spaces was the key to creating picturesque urbanism. Irregular medieval squares and streets, he said, were more pleasing than the geometrical designs in later cities. He was particularly critical of contemporary engineering and formal designs like those favored by the City Beautiful movement.

Important to Sitte was the idea that the apprehension of one's surroundings was continuous through both space and time. In a discussion of medieval street design in the Etruscan hill town of Orvieto, Douglas Duany talks about the vernacular mind of the medieval period, which understood streets as a sequential experience (see the essay "Orvieto, Italy" in Chapter 2). For his own era, Sitte developed his designs as a series of picturesque compositions, drawn in perspective at different points along the way.

Figure 1.14: Marché aux poulets, Brussels. Drawing by Camillo Sitte, circa 1885. The composition of the gently curving street makes a space that deflects the view rather than formally terminating the vista with an object. The walk down the street presents a series of pictures and dynamic, unfolding events rather than a single static one.

Thus, they were "picturesque" in two ways: as painterly compositions and as compositions that were asymmetrical and dynamically balanced rather than static, centered, and regular. But it is important to remember that his individual drawings were meant to be seen almost like a flip-book. Picturesque designers today frequently "walk" their plans block by block, picturing the views at street level and adjusting angles and elements in the view to make them more pleasing and picturesque (Figure 1.14).

The Hybrid

In 1909, the influential English architect and planner Sir Raymond Unwin wrote what became one of the most important urban design books of the twentieth century, *Town Planning in Practice*. After a discussion of plans from different cities and towns, he commented on the formal and the informal:

> We can hardly have examined the many different town plans referred to in the last chapter

without realizing that in spite of their great variety they fall into two clearly marked classes, which we may call the formal and the informal, and that there are to-day [sic] two schools of town designers, the work of one being based on the conviction that the treatment should be formal and regular in character, while that of the other springs from an equally strong belief that informality is desirable. From the views given of both types of town we should almost certainly agree that a high order of beauty has been obtained by each method, for although our personal preference may lean strongly to one or the other type, there will be few who will not admit great beauty in many of the examples of its opposite.[7]

Unwin was one of the town planners involved with the Garden City movement, which combined the formal and the informal in hybrid plans—usually for new towns

Figure 1.15: Avenue de l'Opéra, Paris, France. Georges-Eugène Haussmann, 1864. The opera building is known as the Palais Garnier, in honor of the architect. It is an archetypal French version of the axial terminated vista, by an important graduate of the École des Beaux-Arts.

Figure 1.16: High Street, Oxford, England. William Wordsworth praised "the stream-like windings of that glorious street," one of the most beloved streets in England—and a wonderful example of a deflected vista. Contributing to the beauty of "The High" are the lean-in tree on the left and The Queen's College (Nicholas Hawksmoor, 1708–1710), which sits on a bend just beyond (for a plan of Oxford and the High Street, see Figure 2.105). The planner Thomas Sharp described the sycamore as "one of the most important in the world: without it, the scene would suffer greatly."

with formal centers and streets that became increasingly informal as they radiate outward. The Olmsted Bros. plan for Forest Hills Gardens is an American example of the hybrid type (see Figure 3.59). As used there, the hybrid plan illustrates what New Urbanists today call a Transect (discussed in Chapter 3 in "The Transect Observed"), and it's quite common for New Urban designers to make similar, Transect-based hybrid designs. New Urban firms might also choose to do either a formal *or* an informal plan—on the basis of the context or the client's preference.

> To quote Duke Ellington, "There are two kinds of music. Good music, and the other kind." The same can be said about design.

Formal, picturesque, and hybrid designs can all be well or badly done, and *Street Design* does not advocate one over another. Some might prefer the music of Wolfgang Amadeus Mozart to Richard Wagner or vice versa, but they are both musical geniuses. To quote Duke Ellington, "There are two kinds of music. Good music, and the other kind." The same can be said about design.

Many people believe that beauty is in the eye of the beholder and that there can be no way to accurately define what individuals find beautiful. Recent studies,[8] however, show that if individuals walk a prescribed city route with a map in hand and mark the places they like and don't like there will be a high degree of correspondence in their preferences: the results show a consensus about what is beautiful, what is ugly, and how we respond to beauty and ugliness. If the group sample is large enough, there will also be distinct patterns—some people will prefer more formal spaces and some will like more picturesque places, for example, but the favorite and least favorite places will still be consistent. For the purposes of urban design, street design, and this book, what is of greatest importance is that *all* the groups show a preference for the places made according to the principles of placemaking illustrated here, whether formal or informal.

EAST 70TH STREET: A BEAUTIFUL NEW YORK BLOCK

Legend has it that Woody Allen calls the block of East 70th Street between Park Avenue and Lexington Avenue on Manhattan's Upper East Side the most beautiful block in New York.[9] That's interesting, since the block is one of 150 or so very similar blocks between Park Avenue and Lexington Avenue. Looking at what makes it better than many of them illustrates some basic principles of urban design. We're going to examine East 70th Street (Figure 1.17) the way that one would do that in person: by standing on the sidewalk, gazing up and down the street, and observing what it feels like. By the time we finish, we'll also be considering the size of the block and how the block fits in the neighborhood and the city grid.

East 70th Street is a quiet street. Standing under the trees on the sidewalk is comfortable. The width of the sidewalk allows plenty of space for the number of people customarily walking there, and the width of the sidewalk and the height under the branches arcing over the sidewalk are similar, so that the ratio of the horizontal dimension to the vertical is approximately 1-to-1—a proportion that human beings find comfortable, as we shall see.

The parked cars and trees along the edge of the sidewalk shield us from cars and trucks driving by. That's also reassuring; these vehicles are often noisy and smelly, and they weigh four thousand to twenty thousand or more pounds, which can be both a physical and a psychological problem as they rush by at thirty to forty miles per hour. When we're on a sidewalk without any sort of barrier, we know that a car could easily injure or even kill us if it were to veer onto the walk.

When the traffic is quiet and we step out into the road—to cross it or to walk down the street—we find ourselves under a beautiful canopy of trees (Figure 1.18). The trees on East 70th Street, which are all in a line and regularly spaced, were used like architectural columns to provide visual order to the street—another quality

Figure 1.17: East 70th Street, New York, New York. Looking west towards Park Avenue, in the section of the block that has the biggest setback and the largest houses. 720 Park Avenue is visible above the Asia Society building at the end of the block (also see Figure 2.35).

Figure 1.18: East 70th Street Canopy, New York, New York. Farther east on East 70th Street, looking back towards Second Avenue in the spring, with the trees in bloom. *Image courtesy of Noel Y. Calingasan*

humans find comforting. We say the trees "*were* used like architectural columns" because in the last two or three decades they have been significantly changed. Originally, the trees were all American sycamores. Sycamores are traditional American street trees that reach high and form a canopy. Today there are six or seven tree species on the short block, including gingko and locust trees that make breaks in the canopies over the sidewalk and the street (Figure 1.23). The breaks and different tree types stand out like sore thumbs, diminishing the beauty of the street. If Woody Allen did, indeed, call this the most beautiful block in New York, he may have been talking about the old street, when it had a fuller canopy. He once famously said that everything in New York used to be better (a belief we don't share). In any case, the role of trees in street design is of critical importance.

East 70th Street is sixty feet across, like most of Manhattan's cross streets. That is to say, the distance from the property line on the north side of the street to the property line on the south side is 60 feet. The height of most

of the buildings on the block averages 4½ to 5 generously sized stories, so that the height-to-width ratio of the street is also approximately 1-to-1 (Figure 1.19). Traditional principles of urbanism say that the most comfortable streets are 1-to-1 or 1-to-1½, width to height.[10] Many Italian piazzas are 1-to-3 (where the building height is one-third the width of the piazza). Once the proportions of an open space go beyond 1-to-5 or 1-to-6, though, it can lose its sense of spatial enclosure.

The surveyors who laid out the Manhattan grid thought of it as a utilitarian network for future development, so many of the block's elements are very simple. The question is: What was done that made the block feel better than other, similar blocks? We've looked at some of the ways the street trees help. Urban designers also use trees to help define the space between the buildings on a block as an "outdoor room." In terms of the spatial experience of the block, the canopy of the mature trees gives a "ceiling" to the room and limits how far we see in each direction, so that the space is visually contained. The slight slope of

THE SEVEN ROLES OF THE URBAN STREET TREE

1. Define the space of the street.

This particularly applies to streets that are too wide for the height of the buildings, streets with holes in the street wall, or suburban streets with buildings too far apart to contain the space of the street. Mature trees provide a canopy.

2. Define the pedestrian space.

A mature canopy hides the tops of tall buildings, giving the sidewalk a consistent human scale.

3. Calm traffic and protect the pedestrian from cars.

The tree is aided in this by on-street parking.

4. Filter the sunlight.

Deciduous trees, unlike evergreen or palm, serve different functions in the summer and winter. Trees also lower city temperatures in the summer and change carbon dioxide into oxygen through photosynthesis.

5. Bring order to the street.

Trees should be laid out with regular geometries, repetition, consistent sizes, and alignment. On long, straight streets, trees that form canopies over the street limit the visual length of the street.

6. Visually soften the streetscape.

At some times of the day, the shadows are as beautiful as the trees.

7. Introduce the beauty of nature.

Living plants contrast with the buildings, and in many parts of the world introduce seasonal change, color, and fragrance.

what is called Lenox Hill also helps, by bringing the canopy down into our view as we look towards Lexington Avenue.

Many of the elements of the block laid out by the surveyors are simple–but many of the principles of good street design can be simple. For example, the north and south "streetwalls" are parallel, and so are the sidewalks, the street trees, and the roadbed. A street can certainly be more complex in shape, but simple and straightforward work well, if the details are right.

The construction and the composition of the facades on the buildings that shape the street also affect the feeling of enclosure. The harmonious order of the whole and the solidity of the streetwall—the almost unbroken line of buildings—contribute to the making of an outdoor room where the pedestrian is comfortable. Part of the beauty of the block comes from the fact that it boasts an unusually high number of architecturally distinguished early-twentieth-century houses. Built in traditional styles with good natural materials—brick, stone, iron, wood, real

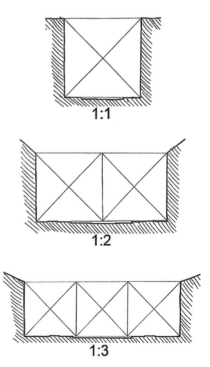

Figure 1.19: Street Sections with Harmonic Proportions.
© 2007 Dover, Kohl & Partners

Figure 1.20: Thomas W. Lamont House, 107 East 70th Street, New York, New York. Walker & Gillette, 1920. One of the large houses on the north side of the block affected by a covenant mandating a 10-foot setback.

horizontal perspective. The windows are deeply set in the walls, increasing the play of light and shadow in a manner that adds a layer of visual interest. The houses themselves are taller than they are wide, which also sets up a pleasing counter rhythm. Good streets, and good cities, require a balance of order and richness. The vertical rhythms, the beautiful ornament, and the play of light and shadow all add richness to the parallel rows of the buildings, the sidewalks, the trees, and the street.

The early twentieth-century houses on the block were designed in accordance with the traditional principles of urbanism, which held that one of the first responsibilities of an architect or builder was to create or reinforce a good public realm (Figure 1.20). We've looked at the primary ways they did that. A building on East 70th Street that interrupts the pattern is a Modernist-style house at number 124 designed by William Lescaze in 1940, with large horizontal windows (Figure 1.21). Looking back at the traditionally designed facades on the block, we see that they appear to respect the forces of gravity. For example, openings in brick walls are spanned by lintels that visually hold up the bricks above them, regardless of whether or not they actually support them (the real structure might be a steel frame). And the exposed depth of the wall gives a mass that makes the wall seem to stand on its own, whether or not that is actually true. In contrast, the brick on the Lescaze facade is cut like wallpaper, and the thinness of the wall is emphasized. If there were any doubt that the brick is in effect glued on, Lescaze cantilevered the wall and pulled back the glass entry wall of the first floor, so that we see from below how thin the brick veneer really is. Finally, the lightly framed glass wall across the width of the first floor visually creates a void, so that as far as we can tell, nothing holds up the weight of the house above: the narrow corner column at one side is obviously not strong enough to bear the four-story wall that sits on it, even if it is just a light curtain wall.

Modern architectural theory argues this is more honest construction: the design reveals that the brick is a veneer rather than load-bearing, while the real structure is inside the house. But in terms of placemaking, the degree to which Lescaze focused on the expression of construction and the creation of a unique object weakened the

stucco—they were designed by some of America's leading architects. The facades are well proportioned and, on the whole, simple and symmetrically composed. They have a layer of detail and ornament that also gives scale and visual interest. As a group, the buildings are varied, and yet they achieve an overall harmony through their similarities in size, massing, proportion, scale, and windows.

Most of the houses have similarly sized double-hung, vertical windows. Because the houses sit on a street, rather than in a piazza, we primarily see them obliquely, and the vertical openings set up a contrapuntal rhythm with the

Figure 1.21: Edward A. Norman House, 124 East 70th Street, New York, New York. William Lescaze, 1941. The thin column, the wide, horizontal openings, and the shallow brick veneer of the Lescaze house all emphasize that the facade is a curtain wall rather than a structural, load-bearing wall. That is one of the reasons why the house has a different effect on the streetscape than the neighboring houses.

emphasis he gave to the larger context of the public realm and the making of a comfortable outdoor room.

The facade designed by Lescaze has a higher percentage of glass and a lower percentage of masonry wall than the other buildings on the block; by itself, the twenty-foot-wide building does not break the street wall, but a block of buildings like Lescaze's would feel less contained. Some other blocks between Lexington and Park avenues have all-glass street walls: consequently, they feel less enclosed and are less pleasant to be on. The mechanical

repetition of the glass curtain over a large area is boring, and therefore detracts from the experience of the street in that way, as well. Only two blocks to the south, on 68th Street between Park and Lexington avenues, the architects of a large modern apartment building and the designers of a new synagogue across the street ignored some of the most basic principles about making the streetwall, so that a block that could be just as beautiful as the parallel block on 70th Street instead feels like an alley.

In comparison to the other buildings on the street, the Lescaze facade has plenty of order, but little richness. That's not a problem on East 70th Street, because the other buildings offer so much richness. In fact, the Lescaze house provides interesting variety. But on a street where there are only boring glass facades, or when the very simple building becomes bigger and more boring, the street suffers.

The Lot and the Block

Rigid and autocratic, the Commissioners' Plan of 1811 was at the same time loose and entrepreneurial. Its grid cut across hills and property lines while leaving unanswered the question of how the blocks would be filled. Coming a little more than one hundred years before New York City introduced the first zoning in America, the plan relied on New York precedent and consensus among real estate developers, builders, buyers, and renters to answer the question of what to build. On the Upper East Side around East 70th Street, developers and builders decided that the area between Central Park and Third Avenue should be filled with single-family rowhouses and mansions for the rich. (A loud elevated subway on Third Avenue made that a natural boundary for the wealthy neighborhood.) New York City's builders already had standard rowhouse plans that could be built with or without architects. By consensus, these were initially built in brownstone, 3½ to 4½ stories tall, with stoops that required setting the house back from the property line so that there was room on the sidewalk to get by the stoops. The setback was six feet, even though there was no regulation that specified that dimension. At the top of the stoop was the main entrance and the main public floor, with the highest ceilings in the rowhouse. The service entrance was under the stoop, and the kitchen was in the raised basement. By the late nineteenth century, this became known as the "American Plan."

In the early twentieth century, many New Yorkers remodeled their brownstones, using the new "English Plan." English Plan houses had ground floor entrances and no stoops, and frequently the new owners replaced the brownstone facades with limestone or brick elevations, and at the same time brought the front of the house a little closer to the street, since they no longer needed a setback for a stoop. Unusually, the houses on the north side of the block on lots perpendicular to 70th Street had restrictive covenants mandating 10 foot setbacks.[11] The sidewalk on that side of the street, therefore, is wider than the sidewalk on the southern side of the block. As a result, the limestone and brick mansions on the northern side get a little more light and air than most New York houses, giving the street a subtle luxuriousness.

The Commissioners' Plan specified that the avenues and the periodic wide cross streets like 72nd and 79th Street would be one hundred feet wide. Over time, larger buildings replaced the houses on the larger streets. Today, an urban designer preparing a form-based code begins by designing the street network and the streets, but he or she also chooses the building types to line each street. Variables in making that decision include the forms, sizes, and uses of the different building types involved. Smaller buildings, like rowhouses, still go on the narrower streets like East 70th Street. Larger buildings, like apartment houses, still go on the wider streets like Park Avenue and East 72nd Street.

All the blocks, including the ones between the wider streets and the narrow streets, are two hundred feet wide because that was the standard in New York by 1811. The two-hundred-foot block can be split down the middle to form back-to-back one-hundred-foot lots, each with its own street frontage, and a variety of building types had been developed to fit on those lots. A small house might have a lot sixteen feet wide by one hundred feet deep. A large house or an apartment building might have a lot twenty-four to forty-eight feet wide by one hundred feet deep. A very large apartment house might have a lot taking the entire two-hundred-foot length of the end of the

block along the avenue. When a block fronted on both a wide cross street and a narrow cross street, larger buildings could go on the wider street, and smaller buildings on the narrower street. For example, apartment houses might sit on the lots along East 72nd Street, one of the wide streets, backing up to lots on East 71st Street with rowhouses on them. An important point for urban design and street design is that the larger buildings face each other across the wide street, appropriate to the shaping of that street, and smaller buildings face each other on the narrower street, appropriately sized for that street. In urban design, this is known as the principle of "like faces like."

Thus we have rowhouses of different widths but similar heights on the north and south sides of our block on East 70th Street and different building types on the east and west ends of the block. At Park Avenue, there is a large institutional building—the Asia Society headquarters and museum—on the north corner and a large postwar apartment building on the south side. On the east end of the block, at Lexington Avenue, is a house the architect Grosvenor Atterbury designed for himself: it has a storefront facing Lexington Avenue, which is the main retail street for the block.[12] Across the street, on the southwest corner of Lexington Avenue and East 70th Street, is a brownstone-faced rowhouse that preceded the fancier houses on the block (Figure 1.22). There were once a number of brownstones on the block, but most were torn down and replaced by more fashionable designs or were thoroughly rebuilt with new facades. Because it faces the busy retail street, the brownstone on the corner of Lexington was given a storefront and converted to apartments instead.

The new apartment buildings at the Park Avenue end of the block share materials with the smaller houses; if they shared double-hung windows as well—an architectural element that unites many other streets in the city—the block would have more unity. One can also argue that it's appropriate that the Asia Society, a civic building, be distinguished from the residential buildings by a more monumental scale or larger windows.

The final element that makes the block of East 70th Street between Park and Lexington Avenues more pleasant to walk on than many blocks in Manhattan is that it is

Figure 1.22: Lexington Avenue and East 70th Street, New York, New York. The brownstone on the northwest corner of the intersection was renovated by the architect Grosvenor Atterbury for his own use in 1909.

Figure 1.23: East 72nd Street, New York, New York. Looking west from Park Avenue. The current fashion for planting multiple types of trees and choosing species that will never grow very high or have a wide spread prevents majestic allées like the old ones in Figures 1.12 and 2.72.

shorter than most east–west blocks in the city. For reasons known only to themselves, the Commissioners varied the length of the east–west blocks in their plan. The blocks between Third Avenue and Sixth Avenue were 920 feet long, while Third Avenue to Second Avenue was a dis-tance of 610, and the next block was 40 feet longer. For the purposes of street design, what's most relevant is that pedestrians like short blocks, and that the blocks between Park Avenue and Lexington Avenue are short, because of an historical anomaly.

For many decades, railroad trains ran in a trough at the center of Fourth Avenue, the original name for Park Avenue. The trains belched thick coal smoke that drove people away, but in the original plan, Fourth Avenue was the only north–south street between Fifth Avenue and Third Avenue, which are more than half a mile apart. To make walking in the neighborhoods around the railroad tracks more pleasant, two new avenues were cut in between Fifth Avenue and Fourth Avenue and between Fourth Avenue and Third Avenue, Madison Avenue being the former and Lexington Avenue the latter. What this means for pedestrians is that the east–west blocks between Fifth Avenue and Third Avenue are half the length of Manhattan's standard east–west blocks, which brings more sunlight and more freedom of movement to the experience of walking through the grid. As Jane Jacobs discusses in *Death and Life of Great American Cities,* long blocks can be visually and even psychologically disagreeable.[13]

Eventually, the trough in Fourth Avenue was covered and capped with planted medians, and the unusually wide street was renamed Park Avenue. On the Upper East Side, Lexington Avenue is primarily commercial, while Park Avenue is predominantly residential. This contrast further increases the pedestrian's feeling of options, which always makes walking more pleasant.

A BRAVE NEW WORLD

For street design in America, everything changed after World War II, reflecting great changes taking place in American business, society, and culture at the time. The way we used streets, the way we built streets, and the way we built our communities were all transformed.

In the early twentieth century, America had walkable towns, cities, and neighborhoods connected by an excellent network of streetcars, trains, and boats; before the Depression brought so much hardship, most Americans could have a comfortable life without owning a car. After the war, living in the suburbs—which required owning a car—was frequently seen as the American Dream. Since then, we have exchanged the town for sprawl, by some estimates

constructing three-quarters of the roads and buildings in America. Today, most Americans have to drive everywhere for everything: living, working, and shopping are all separated by roads built for the use of cars.

Several factors brought this about. Soldiers coming home from America wanted better lives than the ones they had left behind. Most Americans lived in cities before 1940, but by 1945 cities were frequently seen as dirty and crumbling, and old neighborhoods as socially constricting. There was a new sense of possibility and social mobility; after the war, the GI Bill encouraged veterans to go to college and aim for white-collar jobs instead of accepting the same blue-collar jobs their parents had. And when they graduated, low-cost loans that could only be used for buying single-family houses in the suburbs were easily available.

Cars for the new life in the suburbs were also more affordable after the war. Detroit switched from the manufacture of war planes and tanks to cars and produced hundreds of thousands of inexpensive automobiles. At the same time, the flight from the cities was just beginning, so suburban roads were empty, convenient to drive, and often beautiful. In addition, having won the war with technology and industry, we had faith in technology and industry. In 1956 the former Supreme Commander in Chief of the Allied Forces, President Dwight D. Eisenhower, signed the Federal Aid Highway Act, which funded the largest public works program in the history of the world: our interstate highway system. The highways were the centerpiece of a new road system explicitly focused on the free-flowing movement of traffic. The work begun in the 1920s by Organized Motordom, a lobby of automobile interests headed by the American Automobile Association, had won the day.

> Don't honk your horn. Raise your voice. We fought, and we won, our right of way. But now, two miles of road are wearing out for every one being built. Write your hometown officials and postcard your newspaper editors. Demand better highways and more parking space…. Give yourself the green light.
>
> —General Motors propaganda film *Give Yourself the Green Light,* by Handy Jam Productions, 1954

City roads were changed to make it easier for sub-urbanites to drive in and out from the suburbs, while transportation engineers successfully convinced cities that if they failed to build modern roads they would be unable to successfully compete in the twentieth century. In the suburbs, planners developed a new system of automobile-based zoning that separated uses, creating single-use housing developments, shopping centers, and office parks. It was all part of a new world in which President Eisenhower's secretary of defense said, "I thought what was good for our country was good for General Motors, and vice versa."[14] Famously misquoted as "What's good for General Motors is good for the country," and frequently attributed to President Eisenhower, the remark expressed the dominant ethos of the era.

Specialization was seen as one of the reasons why Detroit was able to produce all the planes, tanks, and munitions that beat the Nazis, and specialization became central to the creation of the new automobile-based way of life that promised economic and social mobility. Traffic engineers specializing in auto movement invented new road systems. Developers stopped building mixed-use towns, and built single-use "products." Loan officers at banks became specialists in lending for single-use products: a housing lender would not lend money for a shopping center, for example.

Architects and urban designers, too, participated in this reinvention of the way we live. Three decades earlier, the most influential architect and urban designer in the Western world, Le Corbusier, had written, "The street wears us out. It is altogether disgusting. Why, then, does it still exist?"[15] His solution was to invent a new type of urbanism without normal streets. In the famous "Plan Voisin," Corbusier proposed demolishing most of central Paris north of the Seine and building a new city with sixty-story towers in large parks. Surrounding the parks would be multilevel, multimodal streets (called "machines for circulation"[16]) with cars, buses, trains, and even planes. "The cities will be part of

the country," Corbusier wrote in a paean to technology and futurism:

> I shall live 30 miles from my office in one direction, under a pine tree; my secretary will live 30 miles away from it too, in the other direction, under another pine tree. We shall both have our own car. We shall use up tires, wear out road surfaces and gears, consume oil and gasoline. All of which will necessitate a great deal of work... enough for all.[17]

It was only in the 1940s, however, that Le Corbusier's ideas became standard in American architecture and urbanism. Supersized blocks (superblocks) with towers in parks became so accepted in professional thinking that the federal funding incentives to construct them were impossible to pass up—as Robert Moses learned.

While Moses was working with New York University on a postwar plan for the redevelopment of Washington Square South in Greenwich Village, he saw renderings by Eggers & Higgins—the successor firm to the office of the Classical architect John Russell Pope—that showed two sides of Washington Square rebuilt with Georgian-style buildings. Moses was so impressed that when the university subsequently chose to build only one Georgian building (the NYU Law School), he wrote a letter of complaint to the university's chancellor. During this same period, Moses oversaw slum clearance plans funded by the Federal Housing Act of 1949, for a forty-acre site southeast of the square to be developed as Washington Square Village (Figure 1.24). He asked Eggers & Higgins to design a Georgian-style development, but Eggers soon came back to Moses, reporting that the federal program overwhelmingly favored superblocks with residential-only towers in parks. The authors of the Slum Clearance section of the Housing Act, known as Title I, explained that an "unwise mixture of residential and commercial uses of land" and the "frozen patterns of street layouts" like the Manhattan grid were among the causes of slum conditions.

AERIAL VIEW

EGGERS AND HIGGINS
ARCHITECTS
NEW YORK CITY

Figure 1.24: Washington Square Village, New York, New York. An early site study for Robert Moses by the architects Eggers & Higgins. Committee on Slum Clearance Plans, *Washington Square South Slum Clearance Plan Under Title I of the Housing Act of 1949*.

FUNCTIONAL CLASSIFICATION

Functional Classification is a system transportation planners and traffic engineers use today when designing roads. The system has only three road types (known as "facilities"): "Arterials," "Collectors," and "Local Roads." A fundamental reinvention of how we look at roads, the system was first developed in the United States by planners and engineers in the early part of the twentieth century; it was mandated by law in 1960s and 1970s and enshrined in the 1968 Federal-Aid Highway Act, which required the classification of all roads in the country in order to establish funding priorities. Functional Classification tells planners and engineers what types of roads to design and how they should connect (or not).

Functional Classification exemplifies the philosophy behind the automobile-dependent road system used first in America and later in other countries. It goes hand-in-hand with the automobile-based planning theory that separates uses to create a world in which it is necessary to drive to work, to stores, and to home. It favors the car over all other modes of transportation, including walking, and judges a road's effectiveness by its "Level of Service" (LOS), which measures the free flow of the automobile: How easy is it to drive from one place to another?

PROBLEMS WITH FUNCTIONAL CLASSIFICATION

As shown in Figure 1.25, Functional Classification is based on a philosophy of "mobility" versus "land access." As the urbanist Laurence Aurbach has pointed out, "mobility" generally describes traffic flow and speed, while "land access" generally refers to the frequency of intersections and curb cuts for driveways and parking lots along a road. Local roads deliver traffic to collector roads, which deliver traffic to arterials, which deliver traffic to limited-access highways. The table shows that when land access increases, mobility decreases, and vice versa. This leads to three guiding principles of Functional Classification:

1. The longer the trip, the faster the travel speed should be.

2. The faster the road speed, the more isolated the road should be from its surroundings.

3. Isolated roads are considered bottlenecks, so they must grow wider as "Vehicle Miles Traveled" (VMT) grow.

Thus, highways have limited access, arterial roads have fewer intersections and curb cuts than collector roads, and local roads are considered optimal when they are cul-de-sacs (Figure 1.26). In theory, Level of Service evaluations demonstrate which roads and intersections are creating bottlenecks and lead to their redesign. In reality, growth and density frequently make the Functional Classification system fail on its own terms, because when everyone drives everywhere for everything it is impossible to build roads large enough to handle peak concentrations of cars. And while Functional Classification is designed to increase safety and lower traffic fatalities, studies by rogue transportation engineers show that wide roads frequently have more fatalities than narrower streets, and that increasing the number of intersections rather than minimizing intersections also lowers fatalities.[18] In other words, two of the fundamental principles of Functional Classification—increasing road width and limiting access—can increase deaths caused by traffic accidents.

Unfortunately, Functional Classification and Level of Service standards also conflict on many levels with the making of streets where people want to be (Figure 1.27). In their efforts to make the car's journey ever more efficient, engineers design large, barren, noisy places that pedestrians avoid whenever they can. The level of alienation from ordinary human experience that has crept into this field is reflected in its language: transportation engineers refer to trees as Fixed Hazardous Objects, or FHOs. Even worse, pedestrians are referred to as Moving Hazardous Objects (MHOs) that lower the Level of Service, and are actually banned from many roads. The criteria for Functional Classification obviously do not include making a public realm where people want to be.

In a hopeful development, the Congress for New Urbanism worked with the Institute for Transportation Engineers in 2006 to create the CNU ITE manual *Designing Walkable Urban Thoroughfares: A Context Sensitive Approach*. In contrast with the Functional Classification system, the CNU ITE manual emphasizes connectivity and placemaking. Intersections are encouraged; narrow traffic lanes and on-street parking are called for. Walkable, mixed-use streets are favored over LOS.

Functional Classification & New Urban Street Names

Transportation Engineering	Urban Design
Highway	Parkway
Arterial	Boulevard
Collector	Avenue* and Connector
Local	Street and Road
Cul-de-sac	Close
Driveway	Alley & Lane

*This is an approximate correspondence because an avenue is visually terminated.

"The Functional Classification System needs to be entirely reevaluated," says CNU President John Norquist. "In certain rural contexts, it sometimes makes sense, but applying it to urban contexts doesn't. For example, Greenwich Village is rated F (lowest), based on congestion. It's congested with people who want to be there! They're buying stuff, and creating jobs, and creating art. It's an F that all good urbanism gets."

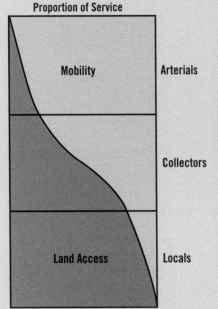

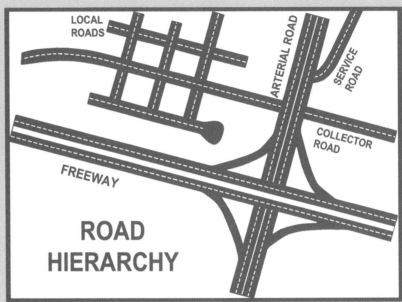

▲**Figure 1.25:** Proportion of Service Diagram for the Functional Classification System. *Image courtesy of Dover, Kohl & Partners, redrawn from the 1969 Federal Aid Highways report*

◄**Figure 1.26:** Road Hierarchy Diagram. *Image courtesy of Dover, Kohl & Partners, redrawn from a Wisconsin DOT manual*

►**Figure 1.27:** I-95 and I-395 Interchange, Overtown, Miami, Florida. Hundreds of houses, businesses, and institutions were displaced to build I-95 and the interchange, in a disastrous urban renewal scheme motivated by racism and auto mania. The city was left more divided than ever. Aerial view, Pictometry. *Image courtesy of Pictometry International Corp. Copyright 2013*

Having built a way of life dependent on the car, we must respond to peoples' needs and desires to use their cars. It's always important to be practical when building in the public realm, particularly in times when public budgets are small. On the other hand, over a third of Americans are too young, too old, or too poor to drive, and most live in places where this inability to get around is a real hardship. At the same time, in the name of practicality, people have created auto sewers all over the world that greatly diminish the use of the public realm for everyone but drivers. Formerly great places where cultural life once flourished have passed a tipping point and become auto sewers.

Functional Classification contributes to climate change and works against the design of walkable, sustainable places. Our lives no longer work without gasoline, and dependence on foreign oil continues to be a serious political and economic challenge. So far, biofuels have caused more problems than they've solved, and the hydrofracking process for extracting natural gas from shale appears to be even worse. Electric cars may be good for the future of the planet, but Americans will be trading oil sources they don't control for battery material sources they don't control (China controls the rare earths needed for batteries). As the world's population grows, it is only going to become more important that our energy sources are renewable.

In the course of writing this book, we've visited Western European towns and cities that have much lower carbon footprints than ours—and that still support a wonderful quality of life. In Amsterdam, enormous numbers of people rely on their feet, bicycles, streetcars, and railroads for roughly 95 percent of their daily travel. The average Dutch citizen has a carbon footprint that is approximately one-half the size of the footprint of the average American, even though some Dutch rely on cars much more than Amsterdammers, who have an exceptionally good quality of life.

Ninety years ago, before World War II and the Great Depression, Americans lived in a time of prosperity when they, too, relied on railroads, streetcars, and bicycles. The countryside had not been spoiled, and people didn't sit in traffic jams on Interstate highways and strip roads. In many ways, they had a better quality of life than most of us have today.

CONTEMPORARY CHALLENGES TO PLACEMAKING

Starting in the 1970s, several well-intentioned streetscape fads have led towns and cities to pile on features like benches and bulbouts (curb extensions) to sidewalks in an effort to improve the street space. Traveling around the country, one can almost always spot the tax-increment-financed, overdone Main Streets tarted up in hopes of revival. While none of these initiatives are necessarily bad (although many *are* bad), in retrospect they are costly and typically do little to improve the vitality of the street. Instead of adding fancy improvements at great expense, governments could achieve a larger and more lasting impact on the public realm by recruiting a mix of uses and shaping the street space with buildings (and street trees, when appropriate). Are the basic rules of successful retail, such as encouraging common hours of operation among storekeepers, being followed? An overblown streetscape will draw attention *away* from storefronts, which is problematic if retail revitalization is the goal. And since a clean sidewalk matters more to retail customers than a fancy one, is there a workable plan for regular cleaning and maintenance? Last but not least, conspicuously overdone streetscapes work against the authenticity characteristic of genuine livable streets.

Today, municipalities add bike lanes with similar fervor. Getting cycling to go mainstream is an important goal, and in some cases striped bike lanes are the best solution. But most municipalities are defaulting to highway striping and dividing up the road space without asking the right questions first: If the design speed of the street were simply lowered, would a separate bike lane even be necessary? Does the bike lane say to motorists that cyclists are to stay in their own space, when they customarily have rights to the whole road space on an urban street? Are those tawdry-looking reflective plastic sticks buffering the bike lane proposed only because some other fundamental aspect of a flawed street design was left unaddressed? Was killing off stores, shops, and restaurants by removing on-

SEVERAL SCENES OR ONE?

There is more than one way to design a street. Some streets are monumental—long and straight, and often visually terminated by a monument or a monumental building. The French masterfully plotted streets like this, coding the architecture precisely, so that the background buildings that make up the urban fabric have a majestic presence enhanced rather than diminished by repetition. In extreme cases like the rue Royale in Paris, all of the facades between the place de la Concorde and the place de la Madeleine were designed by the Royal Architect Ange-Jacques Gabriel and built before the lots were sold (Figure 1.28). In addition, trees and light fixtures repeat regularly in long, straight rows. Cut a cross-section through one location and the drawing will look much like a cross-section cut in any other spot—as if the street were extruded from a mold or rolled out like a steel beam. Some will tell you that using one architect for multiple blocks or having so much repetition kills good urbanism, but few people come back from Paris saying, "Paris, how boring and ugly!" Of course, the architect and the architecture must be good in this scenario.

Less monumental streets can be built up from a series of individual segments laid end-to-end, with their own fine-tuned spatial recipe. The segments might be only a block long or a few blocks long. With each segment, the character can vary, as the total width and building-height-to-street-width proportion changes, the details adjust, and the mixtures of older and newer buildings unfold as we travel along the road. When these spatial segments are defined at their ends by intersections, terminated vistas, curves, cranks, or offsets, each segment reinforces the sense that it is a legible, self-contained piece of the town. The sections establish an impression of "local-ness" and intimacy, and every address along the street is unique.

Figure 1.28: Rue Royale, Paris, France. A hand-tinted view from the place de la Concorde, looking towards the Church of the Madeleine.

street parking to jam in a bike lane really worth it—just to demonstrate that the city was finally doing something about cycling?

Urban designers must be generalists, able to bring together expertise and ideas from many fields, including engineering, retail, finance, law, architecture, and city planning. The city-planning field, notably, has come to be dominated by regulators who do not design; many contemporary municipal-planning departments should probably be renamed "permitting departments." To make our streets places where people want to be, we must focus on what planners call "physical planning," designing or coding the physical form of the city, town, or neighborhood. Distilled down, this is the most crucial professional leadership work involving the built and natural environment today: configuring beautiful, durable, and sustainable places for people. If the urban designer successfully does all those things, his or her design will necessarily include information from many different specialized areas of expertise.

For more than half a century, we steadily increased our extravagant dependence on the car. In the present era our task is to modify, and in some cases reverse, this financially and environmentally costly experiment. Our job now is to pay closer attention to the lessons of history, to see what works and what doesn't. Unlike the global sprawl project and the transformation of ordinary city streets into auto sewers, the New Urbanism must take its cues from five thousand years of human experience in building successful, robust human settlements.

> There should be no reason, finally, why the decisions taken by elected authority cannot be larger ones, disciplining anarchy in order to make the city what it has always been, the ultimate work of human art: making possible the effective action not only of the group but the individual citizen, so liberating what Sophocles called "the feelings that make the town."
>
> —Vincent Scully, "The Death of the Street"

WORK OF MANY HANDS

An urban design cannot be an artist's personal vision, unless that vision is sufficiently broad and meaningful to attract the general public now and in the future. The public realm is forever for all citizens. Every architect or developer who designs a building that shapes the public realm should recognize his or her responsibility to contribute positively to the common good. Urban design and the design of urban architecture are public arts. They share little with the work of a painter or sculptor whose work is designed to be displayed in a collector's private home or in a gallery—where one may choose to look at it or not.

The city is an assembly of public works of art that are never finished, produced by many hands collaborating over time. That said, there are many opportunities for personal vision in the art of placemaking. One distinction between the urban designer and the painter or sculptor working alone is that the urban designer never starts with a truly blank canvas or plain piece of marble; there are always existing conditions that constrain and unlock the artistic response, as each successive round of work builds upon the layers that precede it. In one of the best-known examples, Michelangelo took hold of the incoherent public space of the Campidoglio in Rome and used geometry and a common architectural vocabulary to establish a legible order. The masterpiece is an intervention of finite size that is connected to the surrounding spaces and the fabric of the whole of the city (Figure 1.29).

Figure 1.29: Piazza del Campidoglio, Rome, Italy. Michelangelo, 1536–1546. Plan from Paul Letarouilly, *Edifices de Rome Moderne* (1840).

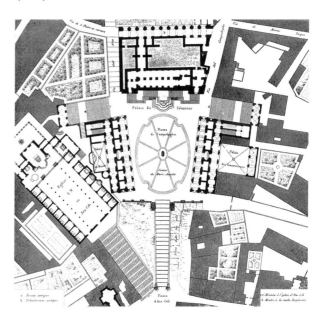

Figure 1.30: Carrer Avinyó, Barcelona, Spain. Streets can be thought of as segmented spatial experiences, perfected independently and stitched together.

This way of seeing good city form—as a complex family of spaces emerging over time from a series of discrete interventions and refinements—stands apart from the view that dominated city planning and architecture in the second half of the twentieth century. The habit of drawing up simplified, ideal cities was many centuries old by then. But with the new futuristic enthusiasm, technological power, and building booms, the postwar Modernists took grandiose utopianism to new levels (low and high). Some assumed that excellence in city form would best be achieved by making the city plan the work of a single master. If the tangled and contradictory city of the past could only be unified under one hand, some thought, maximizing the influence of the soloist's grand personal vision, perhaps it could be succeeded by a one-artist utopia. Predictably the approach instantly racked up many failures, glaringly in Chandīgarh and Brasilia.

Colin Rowe and Fred Koetter helped guide urbanism back to a happier path with their critical writing in *Collage City*; they dismissed the idea of the city as an authoritarian, single-authored, supersized, "perfect" utopian vision and suggested instead that the many scenes of a city can be built up from the juxtaposition of bite-size utopias.[19]

This is a useful way for the urban designer to see the street spaces of a contemporary metropolis—as a series of interconnected spatial experiences that are stitched together and perfected independently and gradually (Figures 1.30 through 1.32). These scenes are simultaneously the beneficiaries of personal artistic vision and collaborative art, as the urban designers lay down lines that guide a collaboration whose participants may never meet: engineers and architects and landscape architects who do their work in small and large projects spread out over centuries.

> Rowe and Koetter dismissed the idea of the city as authoritarian, single-authored, supersized, "perfect" utopian vision and suggested instead that the many scenes of a city can be built up from the juxtaposition of bite-size utopias.

Figure 1.31: High Street, Dumfries, Scotland. A beautifully informal series of public spaces. *Library of Congress, Prints and Photographs Division, Detroit Publishing Company Photograph Collection, LC-DIG-ppmsc-07574*

Figure 1.32: Main Street, Galena, Illinois. The city is an assembly of public works of art that are never finished, produced by many hands collaborating over time. Galena is discussed in a case study in Chapter 2.

CONTEXT MATTERS

Street designers must work in context. A winding road out in the country should not look the same as an urban street inside the loop in Chicago, and a small-town residential street should have a different character than a Parisian boulevard. Today, most New Urban designers and developers use the Urban to Rural Transect developed by Andrés Duany and Douglas Duany. The Transect has six "transect zones": at one of end of the scale is T1, wilderness like Yosemite National Park or the Amazon rain forest, and at the other is T6, the metropolitan core. T2 is rural land, like farmland. Zones T3 through T5 describe different densities and forms of building, adjusted to local conditions, so that T4 would be different in a small country town than in Manhattan. Some choose to modify the Transect by adding T-zones or subzones, especially to differentiate the area where high-rise development should be allowed (Figure 1.34).

People not familiar with the Transect sometimes have a hard time visualizing how this works. It can help to think of the Transect in relationship to how we dress for different places. A banker making a presentation in a corporate boardroom on Wall Street (T-6) in Manhattan wears a dark suit and black leather shoes with laces. The farmer harvesting the wheat on his farm (T-2) might wear blue jeans, a flannel shirt, and brown work boots. The third grader walking to his elementary school from his family's house (T-3) has khaki pants and Jordan Aero Flight sneakers, while the writer in her home office in Park Slope, Brooklyn, puts on her heels to go out to lunch in Manhattan.

Dress is like style, so it's important to emphasize that the Transect is about much more than style. The size of a building, the massing of a building, the relationship of a building to the street, and indeed the way the street is made are all part of the Transect. An office building on Wall Street in Manhattan (T-6) is taller than a farmhouse in T-2, and it has a different relationship to the street. The office building sits at the edge of a large sidewalk, with no setback, while the road in front of the farmhouse probably has no sidewalk, and the house may be far from the road. The rural road in the country (T-2) has no curbs, but a main street in T-4 might have granite curbs and certainly has sidewalks. The traffic lanes in T-4 and T-6 should be narrow, so that cars will drive slowly in the space they share with pedestrians.

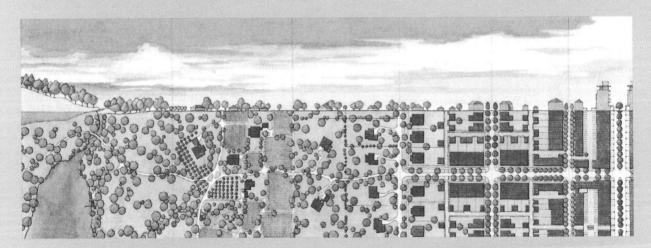

Figure 1.33: Urban to Rural Transect. Plan and section illustrating the six T-zones in the Urban to Rural Transect (also known as "the Transect"). Duany Plater-Zyberk & Company, 1996–2013. *Image courtesy of Duany Plater-Zyberk & Company*

The buildings lining the streets and sidewalks on Wall Street are stone buildings, while the village stores might be in buildings with wood clapboard. A fence in T1 might be a split-rail fence or a stone wall, but you wouldn't use the split-rail on Wall Street, where an iron railing is more appropriate. This is unlike the prevailing trends in contemporary architecture, where a mirror-glass tower is used on Wall Street, in a semirural office park, and in every T-zone in between.

The Transect figures prominently in the best new form-based codes. New Urbanists use these codes to regulate "the relationship between building facades and the public realm, the form and mass of buildings in relation to one another, and the scale and types of streets and blocks" rather than to simply separate activities and land uses.[20] This is a great improvement over the use-based and automobile-centric zoning that contributed to the physical degradation of our towns and cities. To give one example, parking requirements in those auto-centric zoning regulations called for suburban amounts of parking—numbers that were often met by tearing down buildings on Main Streets, leaving unwelcome gaps in the scene. Form-based codes, on the other hand, typically emphasize the importance of continuous streetwalls in commercial areas and call for filling in the gaps on important streets—or at least arranging buildings so that the parking is behind them (Figure 1.34).

Figure 1.34: Urban to Rural Transect. Some choose to modify the Transect by adding T-zones or subzones. This rendering illustrates two T-5 zones. Dover, Kohl & Partners, 2006. © *2006 Dover, Kohl & Partners*

WALKABILITY

> Restore human legs as a means of travel. Pedestrians rely on food for fuel and need no special parking facilities.
> —Lewis Mumford

Until recently, settlements have always been walkable. Note that we use "walkability" as an indicator of a community's livability and completeness, not simply its friendliness toward pedestrians. The walkable streets tend to be the environments where households and businesses and institutions prosper. They tend to be the ones where cyclists are most comfortable, and the ones that make public transit most practical. They tend to be the ones where investments in infrastructure and property are rewarded with revenue. They tend to be the safest, most beautiful, and sustainable. Perhaps most important—because these streets allow for human interaction face to face instead of through windshields—they tend to encourage the social bonds between neighbors and strangers that help solve problems and let democracy flourish.

Walkability is the baseline in street design for a sound city. From there we add the other ingredients in the amounts necessary for each street segment's individual recipe: cycling, motoring, deliveries, garbage pickup,

Figure 1.35: Red Road, Coral Gables, Florida. White plastic sticks are everywhere in modern streets. We are so used to them that we subconsciously discount how alien and alienating they feel to the pedestrian.

Figure 1.36: Grant Avenue, San Francisco, California. Walkable streets are like comfortable outdoor rooms, places where we want to get out of our cars and enjoy the public space.

emergency response, utilities, parking, and other considerations can be incorporated in a balanced way once walking is established as the foundation of the design.[21] To return to the time-tested model of successful mixed-use cities and towns, the pedestrian's needs must come first: vehicles should be accommodated but not at the expense of the citizen on foot.[22]

PRINCIPLES OF WALKABILITY

As we saw in our visit to East 70th Street, the basic principles of making streets where people want to walk are simple. To put it another way, these places are shaped, comfortable, safe, connected, interesting, and memorable.

Shaped

Walkable streets have spatial enclosure. This results from the arrangement of architecture and trees in a way that forms a recognizable outdoor room, in which the "walls" of the room are the facades of the buildings and/or the column-like trunks of street trees, and the "floor" is the surface of the sidewalks and roadway. The proportional relationship between building height and street width and the continuity of the streetwalls are the prime determinants of the sense of place and street character. When the space between the buildings is too wide to give a sense

of enclosure, or when there are gaps in the wall, street trees can be used to shape the space.

Comfortable

In hot places, pedestrians want shade. In cold places, pedestrians like access to sunlight. In the subtropics, people seek protection from sudden storms. Street trees are a most common form of climate adaptation, but awnings, marquees, arches, colonnades, galleries, and other architectural devices also work well. On shopping streets, adaptation to climate can be especially important. Awnings over storefronts make walking more comfortable and protect the interior from glare. Architectural features that control the effects of the climate can be a crucial ingredient in local distinctiveness. For example, in the Middle East or Central America, the close placement of buildings on the narrowest village streets keeps more of the street space in shade during the hot part of the day. In Bologna and Turin, arcades over the sidewalk became signature features of the two cities.

Safe

As pedestrians, we choose to return to places where we feel reasonably free from danger. Without necessarily stopping to think about it, we quickly size up the risks in our environment and steer toward the safer routes as we move about a city. Streets that seem to be watched over by windows, doors, storefronts, or balconies feel safer than streets lined with blank walls; this impression of "natural surveillance" has been shown to reduce street crime. Having other people around going about their business is additionally reassuring because we feel more secure. Safety also means having the confidence that if we were to fall ill or have an accident, a call for help will be heard.[23] Finally, pedestrians want to feel safe from the dangers posed by cars. The best defense against mayhem in pedestrian–auto collisions is to keep motoring speeds low, by design. Studies show that as speeds increase just slightly, injuries and fatalities rise dramatically. Any excessive width in the area devoted to motoring—whether in the number of lanes or their dimension—pushes speeds higher and discourages walking.

Connected

Walkers choose the paths that take them where they want to go. Walkable streets are almost always part of an integrated network—ideally, one with small blocks, so that there are many possible routes. The best street networks offer the pedestrian not only choices about which path to take but also a variety of experiences. When street vistas are arranged to create a sequence of legible segments, marked by landmarks that help with wayfinding and orientation, walkers have a sense of how the street space is knitted into the fabric of the surrounding neighborhood. Not surprisingly, studies undertaken to analyze "space syntax" consistently show that city streets with the most connections to the rest of the network tend to be streets where stores get the most traffic and business.[24]

Interesting, Memorable

Pedestrians are easily bored. We are attracted to places that are beautiful and distinctive. The need can be satisfied with overt design, such as a formal axis framing a ceremonial building on a main street, or with something as subtle as a canopy of leafy autumn color on a quiet and ordinary street. We are drawn to the places that have richness, texture, and character; we tend to return to the places where the three-dimensional geometry of urban design and architecture is employed, in conspicuous or subtle ways, to create street scenes that unfold in some theater-like progression. We naturally want the backdrop of daily life to be agreeable, not drab. Beauty is not something extra to be added in after all of the other decisions about a street have already been made; it's the one ingredient without which no street is ever "complete" (Figure 1.37).

Figure 1.37: Rue de Seine, Paris, France. We are drawn to places that have richness, texture, and character, where street scenes unfold in a theater-like progression.

PLACEMAKING'S POTENTIAL FOR RETURN ON INVESTMENT

Redesigning streets to make places for people may seem like a frivolous, irresponsible way to spend public money, especially during tight financial times. Some will inevitably argue that the zero-investment scenario for automobile-oriented streets is the best way forward—or that, if precious infrastructure funds must be spent, then redesigning streets to be wider and faster is the more practical choice.

Despite being seen as mere "enhancements," however, public investment in retrofitting automobile-oriented streets to make them more pedestrian friendly has been proven to have economic benefits for the communities around them. When streets are transformed into desirable addresses, they attract and concentrate demand for the construction and rehabilitation of the buildings along them, resulting not just in higher property values but also in new housing, increased sales, increased employment, or all three. The municipality benefits directly from the resulting increase in property taxes, hospitality taxes, and sales taxes. The revived street also offers the government at all levels potential cost-savings, which flow from the concentration of activity, especially compared to the cost of delivering municipal services to far-flung sprawl. Other benefits include increased transit use and job creation.

It is critical that we recognize the economic value of real placemaking. Otherwise, retrofitting auto-centric streets will be mistaken for a superficial frill rather than a sound investment in the health of the community. Cities and towns considering the cost of building streets have to weigh the benefits of faster-moving traffic with the economic and social costs of spending money on infrastructure that only serves the car. Beyond the dollars spent on construction, road building affects future land-use patterns and the all-important character of the surrounding community. An important test is whether property values go up or down after public monies have been spent. Regional demands for highways have to be balanced against the needs of the immediate neighbor-hood. Much harm has been done in cities and towns to speed things up for commuters headed elsewhere, which can make the streets worse for pedestrians, shoppers, and residents. When traffic concerns are leavened with placemaking, infrastructure improvements can improve property values considerably.[25]

Sometimes poor development choices are guided by the wrong financial considerations—penny-wise, pound-foolish decisions that favor short-term gains over long-term development goals. At other times, however, the smarter economic and aesthetic choice is also the least expensive over both the short term and the long term, but leaders still may choose poorly; in these instances, the fault lies with hidebound practices and a lack of imagination. Johnnie Dodds Boulevard in South Carolina and Columbia Pike, in Virginia, provide two contrasting—and illuminating—examples of the choices policymakers face.

Two Case Studies

In Mount Pleasant, South Carolina, the segment of Highway 17 known locally as Johnnie Dodds Boulevard is an arterial commercial strip that aged in a graceless way. As sprawl increased traffic, property values declined and blight spread. In 2005, the late economist Don Zuchelli compared the economic costs and benefits of two possible retrofit strategies for Johnnie Dodds Boulevard. The first scenario, embraced by government traffic specialists, favored the conventional approach of increasing automobile capacity (Figure 1.38). The second scenario, put forward by a nonprofit planning council, argued for a traditional multiway boulevard, making places where pedestrians want to be (Figures 1.39, 1.40, and 1.41).

Zuchelli's comparison found that the placemaking alternative would cost approximately $62 million, but in the first twenty-five years, the property value would increase by $207.3 million and annual retail sales would increase by $156 million. Bottom line: the municipality's return on investment would be approximately 145 percent in the first twenty-five years. The government-endorsed alternative, on the other hand, would cost approximately $104.3 million to construct, while Zuchelli predicted that over the

Figure 1.38: Johnnie Dodds Boulevard, Mount Pleasant, South Carolina. A simulation of the Highway Overpass scenario, 2005. © *2005 Dover, Kohl & Partners / UrbanAdvantage*

Figure 1.39: Johnnie Dodds Boulevard, Mount Pleasant, South Carolina. Existing Conditions, circa 2005. © *2005 Dover, Kohl & Partners / UrbanAdvantage*

Figure 1.40: Johnnie Dodds Boulevard, Mount Pleasant, South Carolina. A simulation of the Multiway Boulevard scenario preferred by local residents, Dover, Kohl & Partners, 2005. © *2005 Dover, Kohl & Partners / UrbanAdvantage*

Figure 1.41: Johnnie Dodds Boulevard, Mount Pleasant, South Carolina. Aerial Rendering of the Multiway Boulevard scenario designed by Dover, Kohl & Partners in 2005. © 2005 Dover, Kohl & Partners

same period the property value would eventually increase by just $33.8 million and annual retail sales would slowly increase by $14.8 million. Bottom line: the government's return on investment for their preferred strategy would be negative, at approximately *minus* 113 percent. Unfortunately, the government chose that strategy; unthinkably, it will cost the taxpayers more than the competing design in both the long term *and* the short term.

The Mount Pleasant saga contrasts with the very successful return-on-investment story still unfolding on Co-lumbia Pike in Arlington County, Virginia, where strategic moves by the local government are already paying off handsomely for taxpayers. After a long period of public and private disinvestment, in the late 1990s the community made revitalizing the Pike a priority by committing to placemaking—the opposite of the Johnnie Dodds highway approach. Rather than starting with a road-widening (or by rushing to redecorate by installing pavers and benches), Arlington County began by rewriting the land-development regulations. That unlocked a wave of new private investment in street-oriented buildings along the Pike. The results of the effort are highly visible, which inspires confidence in the community.

According to Arlington County Board member Christopher Zimmerman, the first six developments sparked by the changes to regulations on Columbia Pike are worth a combined $400 million and annual tax revenues of more than $5 million per year. The next wave of infill development, already in the permitting stages, is expected to raise that revenue figure to $10 million—every year. Now the revitalization effort has moved on to a more ambitious phase, including plans for a new streetcar line matched with a push to simultaneously build both affordable housing and luxury housing, so that a mixed-income community will emerge now that prosperity has returned to Columbia Pike. For their investment, residents of Arlington County are getting more jobs, more housing options, a corridor in which it will be easier to move around, and a better quality of life. Columbia Pike will generate great wealth for its investors *and* sustained revenue for public needs.[26]

From an economic-development perspective, the best street design is one that blends land-uses that produce tax revenues with street connectivity without placing undue stress on commuter traffic. Connectivity and placemaking foster alternative forms of transportation and create environments that add value and uniqueness to the street. Car trips and local public service costs drop if residential land use is integrated with good commercial and public services. Property values tend to be higher in areas supported by roads that include pedestrian and bicycle traffic and where buildings are pulled up to the sidewalk rather than set back behind parking lots.

ATTRACTING THE CREATIVE CLASS

The creative class, defined by sociologist Richard Florida, is that restless group of talented artists, writers, scientists, professors, and entrepreneurs characterized by imagination and innovation. When members of the creative class come together in sufficient numbers, they generate economic growth and boost local and global wealth. According to Professor Florida, the creative class is attracted to settings with a lively public realm that feature talent, technology, and tolerance. Drawn to historic cities by the grit and authenticity found there, they seek out places with a good supply of potential mates, and are generally repelled by sprawl. The power of placemaking defines these locations; the creative class chooses where they want to live before they decide what work to take (or create). When employers follow them to "creative centers," the economic result is impressive. Supporting the places that attract the creative class is crucial to advancing financial success, and that is one reason why agreeable street scenes are actually an economic development tool.

COMPLETE STREETS AND THE ENVIRONMENT

Building better streets can be an effective way to address climate change. An agreeable street design encourages people to replace driving trips with walking, cycling, or transit use, reducing greenhouse gas emissions and the consumption of fossil fuels. According to Reid Ewing and the researchers behind *Growing Cooler: The Evidence on Urban Development and Climate Change*, the potential impact of this "mode shift" is vast.[27] Their analysis of vehicle miles traveled shows that a well-connected street network with good public transport can decrease auto use and have a positive effect on the environment. They observe that increased density results in lower levels of VMT and that compact urban development promotes freedom from dependence on the car.[28] And they discuss the work of Peter Newman and Jeff Kenworthy, who conclude that higher-density neighborhoods lower VMT numbers and reduce fuel consumption far better than any other method of cutting fuel consumption.[29] Those who drive less also get more exercise.

Good streets help the environment on another, more subtle level. Walkable streets with bike lanes and mass transit reinforce a variety of broad environmental goals such as controlling sprawl, reducing regional energy consumption, protecting watersheds, and stemming the loss of farmland and wilderness. They do this by encouraging growth in the right places.

On the other hand, no one wants to walk on the arterials and collectors built under the Functional Classification system. Combined with the vast interstate highway system, these roads advanced the sprawl process they were part of by inducing the building of more and more roads. As generations of Americans used the roads to move farther and farther out to get away from it all, the increased driving had the perverse effect of making the traffic still worse—and, yes, inflating demand for still more and wider roads.

A good street where people want to be is naturally more marketable, so it sets up its adjacent places for perpetual use and reuse. This is the ultimate recycling process: reoccupying previously settled land more densely and giving historic buildings new life also accommodates population growth and economic change. Without this, population growth and economic evolution lead inexorably to the development of raw land in far-flung locations, skipping over the previously built-on land. To discourage sprawl, we have to make the real cities and towns attractive to the large number of homebuyers and businesses who have a choice about where to locate. They'll choose the locations that balance beauty, comfort, and convenience with privacy and safety. Better design is the tool that allows compact neighborhoods to fulfill their ecological promise. This is why Michael Busha of the Treasure Coast Regional Planning Council says, "New Urbanism is the operating system of smart growth."[30]

Figure 1.42: Koningsplein, Amsterdam, the Netherlands. Walkable, bike-friendly streets with mass transit can be great, "green" places. Amsterdammers use very little energy for cars, because they prefer to walk, bike, or ride the tram.

ENVIRONMENTAL BENEFITS OF COMPLETE STREETS / Emily Glavey

Carbon neutral. Renewable. Eco-efficient. Green. These words and phrases fill the pages of books, websites, and the blogosphere. Each one references a great initiative. But, while solar panels and recyclable coffee cups are innovative and necessary, they are only a small solution to a complicated environmental problem. A solution with a larger impact? Design and develop better streets, to produce better neighborhoods and cities.

Sustainable development starts with the street. If a person can walk or bike to a destination, decreasing fossil fuel use and reducing daily Vehicle Miles Traveled, then her or his commute becomes more efficient. Driving fewer miles reduces greenhouse gas emissions. Since people don't like to walk on streets that are dominated by car traffic and they don't like to cycle on a road that was designed for only the automobile,

accommodating these alternative forms of transport is a logical priority. It turns out that this logic is actually part of a rising trend—automobile ownership per household peaked in 2001 in America and has been steadily decreasing ever since. Fewer people are driving, and the resulting reduction in VMT is huge.

Designing walkable communities that allow people to be less dependent on fossil fuels is both smart and sustainable. "There can be no sustainable development while fossil and nuclear power prevail as the drivers of urban growth, the very definers of city culture," Peter Droege says. "The by-product of fossil fuel burning is skyrocketing atmospheric CO_2 concentrations. These are now at 390 parts per million, a full third above the proven stable level of 280 ppm."[31] Streets that connect work to home, and home to school (or entertainment), prompt urban growth that leaves a lighter imprint.

More than any singular energy-efficient policy or initiative, great streets and great street networks have large and lasting environmental effects. What if Amsterdam had not developed to be a city with narrow streets that encourage cycling, but instead had a system of streets that were wide and overrun with only car traffic? It could never have become the cycling mecca that it is today. The urban form of a community can be a catalyst for a thriving metropolitan ecosystem. Climate-responsive design can reduce the "urban heat island effect," create a verdant habitat for native plant species and animals, and accommodate local weather patterns by providing shade trees, arcades, and awnings. Great streets have defined the environmentally responsible cities of the past and will define the best cities of the future.

GREEN STREETS

A new Green Streets movement uses a combination of modern and time-tested building materials and methods to make streets green. The movement focuses on creating localized storm water systems and habitats, and using renewable building materials and energy production. Notable experiments are underway in the Midwest in Chicago, through the green alleys program, and in the northwest in Portland, Oregon, through a comprehensive program that includes rain gardens in planting strips, and an increased use of permeable pavement types (Figure 1.43).

Figure 1.43: SW 12th Avenue. A "green street" in Portland, Oregon. *Image courtesy of Kevin Robert Perry, City of Portland*

Figure 1.44: Strandvagen, Stockholm, Sweden. Placemaking achieves utilitarian ends, like accommodating bikes, with beautiful means that transcend mere utility.

Figure 1.45: A new Complete Street in Fort Lauderdale, Florida. The green bicycle lanes are the only hint this street wasn't built in the 1950s, when the car was king. This unpleasant, pedestrian-repellent space needs to be a Completer Street.

The green streets built so far, like the bike lane "demonstration projects" in New York City, suggest a need for a design vocabulary that integrates new technology and desires into the traditional language of street design (see Color Plate 21 and Figure 1.43). In the early rain-garden-cum-street projects the experimental vocabulary is heavy with conspicuous reminders of the technical means for collecting rainwater. Like architecture schools today, landscape schools teach that form should express function, not just follow it. The Green Street designers wanted to communicate that something revolutionary is going on, but the expression of the idea becomes more important than the design of the street: the green streets have much to say about stormwater and its collection, but not much about placemaking.

Making the street design into a conspicuous advertisement for stormwater management may have been worthwhile on the first few technologically innovative projects. The same might be said about the contemporary streets repainted for bikes (Figure 1.45). Now, however, is the time to figure out—or remember—how to make these ideas more beautiful and more elegant, with less overdesign (Figure 1.44). For an analogy, think of the arrival of electrified street lighting—first in Wabash, Indiana, and not long afterward in New York City, where the conspicuously overlit segment of Broadway was nicknamed "The Great White Way" by 1880. Designers eventually took on the task of de-signing electric lamps that fit the streetscape, and gradually the lamppost became an integrated element of street design.

Once the novelty of a useful new technology wears off, its technical and utilitarian conspicuousness can recede. A natural role for civic art is to absorb various elements of the design into context-specific placemaking. The technology's new components should evolve and be integrated into the rest of the street design, so that they add to, rather than subtract from, community character—ideally, to the point where life without them would be hard to imagine. For example, in 1906, a scant generation after electrified street lighting appeared, the much-admired lampposts on the Passeig de Gràcia in Barcelona were introduced by Pere Falqués, the municipal architect (Figure 1.46).[32] Today, they are a famous signature of the street. Miami architect and professor Ramon Triàs, planning director of the City of Coral Gables and a longtime Barcelona scholar, points out that "while almost every other detail of the boulevard has changed since then, the beloved lampposts and benches remain. Barcelona's fixtures were commissioned designs, created by professional artists and architects, not by lamp experts. They were designed to be permanent parts of the civic world."[33]

The job ahead for advocates of healthy streets, green streets, and complete streets is to achieve a level of artistry in the designs that will engender loyalty and love among their everyday occupants.

Figure 1.46: Passeig de Gràcia, Barcelona, Spain. Electrified street lights were once a new and novel technology that challenged designers to find appropriate forms. In time, the designers learned how to combine function, construction, and beauty in new forms like this one. *Image courtesy of Paolo Rosa*

NOTES

1 Gertrude Stein said about Oakland, California, that there is no there there, in *Everybody's Autobiography* (New York: Random House, 1937), 289. Gordon Cullen, the noted advocate of picturesque Modernist planning, thought the concept of "Here and There" (or here versus there) was an important one. Cullen, *The Concise Townscape* (New York: Architectural Press, 1961), 182.

2. Léon Krier, *The Architecture of Community*, ed. Dhiru A. Thadani and Peter J. Hetzel (Washington: Island Press, 2009), 28.

3. Michel Pauls, "111 the american grid," *Recivilization*, http://recivilization.net/UrbanDesignPrimer/111theamericangrid.php. Quoted by Paul Knight, "The American Grid," The Great American Grid, http://www.thegreatamericangrid.com/2012/07/25/the-american-grid-2/, July 25, 2012.

4. Charles Dickens, *American Notes for General Circulation* (New York: Harper & Brothers, 1842), 39.

5. John W. Reps, *Monumental Washington: The Planning and Development of the Capital Center* (Princeton: Princeton University Press, 1967), 97.

6. George R. Collins and Christiane Craseman Collins, *Camillo Sitte: The Birth of Modern City Planning* (New York: Rizzoli, 1986), 195–196.

7. Sir Raymond Unwin, *Town Planning In Practice: An Introduction to the Art of Designing Cities and Suburbs* (New York: Princeton Architectural Press, 1994), 115.

8. Yodan Rofè, "The Meaning and Usefulness of the 'Feeling Map' as a Tool in Urban Design and Architecture," in *The Oxford Conference: A Re-evaluation of Education in Architecture*, ed. Susan Roaf and Andrew Bairstow (Southampton, United Kingdom: WIT Press, 2008), 243–46.

9. Allen once owned one of the houses on the north side of the block: see Christopher Gray, "Streetscapes, East 70th Street, Along Millionaires' Row, at the Crest of Lenox Hill," *New York Times*, September 17, 2006, http://travel.nytimes.com/2006/09/17/realestate/17scap.html. The article also says, "In 1939, *Fortune* magazine called it 'probably New York City's most beautiful residential block,' and Paul Goldberger, in his 1979 book, *New York: The City Observed* (Random House), described it as having 'a perfect balance between individuality and an overall order.'" http://travel.nytimes.com/2006/09/17/realestate/17scap.html. Also see Gray, "Streetscapes, 107 East 70th Street, The Best House on the Best Block," *New York Times*, July 9, 2009. http://www.nytimes.com/2009/07/12/realestate/12scapes.html. Architect and urban designer Léon Krier reportedly prefers the block in Greenwich Village where Barrow Street and Commerce Street come together to form a picturesque intersection. Krier would not like the way that the NYC DOT recently filled the space with bold striping, destroying some of the quiet charm of the irregular space.

10. Charles G. Ramsey and Harold Reeve Sleeper, *Graphic Standards*, 10th ed., ed. John Ray Hoke Jr. (Somerset, New Jersey: John Wiley & Sons, Inc., 2000), 93.

11. Gray, "Along Millionaires Row," *op. cit.*

12. Gray, "Streetscapes, 131 East 70th Street, Architect's Own Brownstone Doesn't Fit the Mold," *New York Times*, April 23, 2006, http://www.nytimes.com/2006/04/23/realestate/23scap.html.

13. Jane Jacobs, *The Death and Life of Great American Cities* (New York, Random House, 1962), 150–51. Jacobs wrote, "To generate exuberant diversity in a city's streets and districts four conditions are indispensable:

   1. The district, and indeed as many of its internal parts as possible, must serve more than one primary function; preferably more than two. . . .

   2. Most blocks must be short; that is, streets and opportunities to turn corners must be frequent.

   3. The district must mingle buildings that vary in age and condition, including a good proportion of old ones so that they vary in the economic yield they must produce. This mingling must be fairly close-grained.

   4. There must be a sufficiently dense concentration of people, for whatever purposes they may be there. . . ."

14. The Secretary of Defense, Charles Erwin Wilson, was the former CEO of General Motors.

15. Le Corbusier, *Oeuvre Complète*, 1910-1929 (Erlenbach: Editions d'Architecture Erlenbach-Zurich, 1946), 129 ff. According to Stanislaus von Moos, *Le Corbusier: Elements of a Synthesis* (Rotterdam: 010 Publishers, 2009), 188.

16. Le Corbusier, *Urbanisme* (Paris: Crès, 1925), 113. Translated by Frederick Etchells as *The City of Tomorrow* (London: J. Rodker, 1929). According to von Moos, *op. cit.*, 188.

17. Le Corbusier, *La Ville radieuse: Eléments d'une doctrine d'urbanisme pour l'équipement de la civilisation machiniste* (Boulogne-sur-Seine: Editions de L'architecture d'aujourd'hui, 1935). Translated by Pamela Wright, Eleanor Levieux, and Derek Coltman as *The Radiant City: Elements of a Doctrine of Urbanism to Be Used as a Basis of our Machine-Age Civilization* (New York: Orion Press, 1967), 74.

18. Road width study: Peter Swift P.E., Dan Painter AICP, and Matthew Goldstein, "Residential Street Typology and Injury Accident Frequency," http://massengale.typepad.com/venustas/files/SwiftSafetyStudy.pdf. Intersection study: Norman Garrick, "Traffic Safety, Travel Mode Choice and Emergency Services," http://www.slideshare.net/CongressfortheNewUrbanism/norman-garrick-cnu-2009.

19. See Colin Rowe and Fred Koetter in *Collage City* (Cambridge, MA: MIT Press, 1984).

20. According to the Form-Based Codes Institute, "Form-based codes foster predictable built results and a high-quality public realm by using physical form (rather than separation of uses) as the organizing principle for the code. They are regulations, not mere guidelines, adopted into city or county law. Form-based codes offer a powerful alternative to conventional zoning." http://www.formbasedcodes.org/what-are-form-based-codes.

21. The AASHTO Green Book states that the transportation officials should first determine the function(s) of the street, then assign the design appropriate for the function(s). If walking is identified as a function of the facility from the beginning, the design will be different; walking ought to be one of the typical functions, but rarely is.

22. Also see Victor Dover's street design essay "Twenty-three" in Emily Talen, Ed., *Charter of the New Urbanism* (New York: McGraw-Hill Professional, 2nd Ed., 2013), 211. "It's time to reunite architecture and the creation of public spaces into complementary and seamless tasks. The details of the right-of-way and the design of adjacent buildings should work together to comfort, satisfy, and stimulate pedestrians. People will walk through areas where they are provided with precise orientation, visual stimulation, protection against the elements, and a variety of activities. Moreover, they must feel safe—both from fear of crime and from fear of being hit by a vehicle."

23. See also CPTED (Crime Prevention through Environmental Design) document, or *Defensible Space* by Oscar Newman (New York: Macmillan, 1973).

24. Some of the best studies on the subject are done by the company Space Syntax. Many are available at http://www.spacesyntax.com/downloads/.

25. See also "Tactical Urbanism in New York City" and the "Madison Square Property Values Study" in Chapter 3.

26. Christopher Zimmerman (Arlington County Board member), interview by Victor Dover, November 14, 2012.

27. Reid Ewing, Keith Bartholomew, Steve Winkelman, Jerry Walters, and Don Chen, *Growing Cooler: The Evidence on Urban Development and Climate Change* (Washington DC: Urban Land Institute, 2008).

28. Ibid., 54–55. "Compact development has the potential to reduce VMT [vehicle miles traveled] by anywhere from 20 to 40 percent relative to sprawl." Reducing VMT reduces the carbon footprint.

29. See also Peter Newman and Jeff Kenworthy in "The Transport Energy Trade-Off: Fuel-Efficient Traffic versus Fuel-Efficient Cities," 1988, http://www.sciencedirect.com/science/article/pii/0191260788900349.

30. Jean Scott, "An Overview of New Urbanism in South Florida," http://www.cnuflorida.org/nu_florida/south_florida.htm.

31. Peter Droege, *Sustainable Urbanism and Beyond: Rethinking Cities for the Future*, ed. Tigran Haas (New York: Rizzoli, 2012), 31.

32. Luis Permanyer, *Un Passeig per la Barcelona Modernista* (Barcelona: Ediciones Poligrafa SA, 1988).

33. In conversation.

CHAPTER TWO
HISTORIC STREETS

BEYOND FUNCTIONAL CLASSIFICATION: A REINTRODUCTION TO ELEVEN ESSENTIAL STREET TYPES

FUNCTIONAL CLASSIFICATION'S meager catalog of street types—arterial, collector, and local roads—is insufficient to produce walkable towns, cities, and neighborhoods. It is urgent that engineers and urban designers establish and promote a richer menu of choices.

History shows that sorting streets according to their form, rather than their Level of Service and Function-

⊠ Les Rambles, Barcelona, Spain. See Figure 2.48

al Classification, will help establish a common language for street design. History also teaches that expanding the range of choices increases the number of possible designs—that human ingenuity, once unleashed, will offer up customized street solutions in response to the needs of each place.

This chapter reintroduces eleven essential street types with case studies and commentary to explain how each type fits into a larger urban system. A goal now should be to use consistent terminology for the items on this bigger and more complex menu to rebuild our civilization's capacity for making great streets, despite ongoing resistance from some engineers and transportation planners. Happily, it is hard to argue against success and successful examples.

Figure 2.1: Multiway Boulevard and Multiway Avenue. © *2013 Dover, Kohl & Partners*

Figure 2.2: Boulevard and Avenue. © *2013 Dover, Kohl & Partners*

Figure 2.3: Promenade and Rambla. © *2013 Dover, Kohl & Partners*

Figure 2.4: Main Street. © *2013 Dover, Kohl & Partners*

Figure 2.5: Downtown Street. © *2013 Dover, Kohl & Partners*

Figure 2.6: Neighborhood Street. © *2013 Dover, Kohl & Partners*

Figure 2.7: Yield Street. © *2013 Dover, Kohl & Partners*

The historic street types we discuss are:
- Boulevard & Multiway Boulevard
- Avenue & Multiway Avenue
- Promenade & Rambla
- Main Street
- Downtown Street
- Neighborhood Street
- Yield Street
- Garden Street
- Pedestrian Street
- Pedestrian Passage & Step Street
- Parkway

AVENUES & BOULEVARDS

Before the era of the automobile, broad streets symbolized progress, prosperity, and public order for their cities. Society occasionally excelled at producing wide streets that served many purposes, not the least of which was instilling civic pride. For the last fifty or sixty years, however, traffic engineers have focused almost exclusively on increasing traffic flow—often by widening traffic lanes, increasing the number of lanes, and eliminating parking and sidewalks. As a result, America now finds itself with too many wide, dangerous streets, few of which can be said to boost civic pride. To fight the excessive widths, traffic calmers working in suburban conditions the last ten years or so have focused on gimmicks like painted "Road Diets." When a street is given the road-diet treatment, highway-scale markings are painted on the street to "narrow" the road, sometimes with space allocated for parking and bicycle lanes. These superscaled stripings are meant for cars and may, in fact, help slow motorists somewhat. Road diets do nothing to supply a human scale for the pedestrian, however, and they rarely do much to make the road more comfortable for walkers: road diets are like tightening your belt a notch instead of losing weight.[1] A more meaningful, enduring kind of road diet changes the nature of the street from a "traffic facility" or vehicular street to a place. This dilemma in part explains why avenues and boulevards, two of our widest street types, have recently become a hot topic in street design: when designers are faced with retrofitting supersized streets, historic avenues and boulevards can suggest a range of previously successful solutions.

Boulevards and avenues are wide, tree-lined streets that come in a variety of forms. The earliest and best examples are in Paris, where by definition an avenue is visually terminated at one or both ends, while a boulevard is a through street. The Lexicon of the New Urbanism continues that useful distinction, which we endorse, but it should be noted that there are a few streets in Paris called avenues that are not terminated. An example is the avenue de New York, a short street that is actually part of a long continuous boulevard along the Seine that regularly changes name. In Amer-ica, we frequently don't make this semantic distinction between avenues and boulevards. The north-south streets in the New York Commissioners' Plan of 1811 that were called avenues are actually boulevards.

"Boulevard" and "avenue" are both French words. Paris's boulevards and avenues do the jobs assigned to them well and are among the most beautiful in the world. The success of these streets stems in part from their adherence to principles that have been a part of French design for centuries. We think of them as having been built by Baron Georges-Eugène Haussmann for the Emperor Napoleon III in the nineteenth century—and many of them were—but a number were built much earlier, during the reigns of Louis XIII and Louis XIV.

The long French tradition of formal, tree-lined roads goes back to planted allées in grand French gardens like the ones at Vaux-le-Vicomte and the Sun King's palace in Versailles. That tradition also led to the design of rural allées that extended from the ramparts of Paris out into the countryside: these avenues ("approaches") are the forerunners of the urban allées within the city walls. Trees were also planted on the tops of the old city walls, in double rows that followed the path of the ramparts as they angled around the city. The original French meaning of boulevard is "top of the bulwark."

As Paris grew up around the rural roads and ramparts, rows of trees in pairs on each side of the avenues and boulevards became the custom. As one still sees in French parks, the trees were planted in regular geometric patterns, carefully proportioned. Typically, four trees would form a perfect square (1-to-1), but sometimes the ratio of width to length would be 1-to-1½ or 1-to-2. All of these dimensions are pleasing. Sadly, thousands of the country's trees have been eliminated in recent years to widen roads. The French traffic engineers didn't cut them all down, as their American counterparts frequently did (leaving Elm and Maple Streets with no elms or maples), but by cutting large gaps in the allées they did diminish the beauty of the streets—particularly for the pedestrian.

There are three primary types of boulevards and avenues. The first is simply a wide, tree-lined street, which can be either one-way or two-way. Examples include the boulevard Haussmann in Paris and most Manhattan avenues.

The second has a median in the center and tree-lined traffic lanes and sidewalks on both sides, like Park Avenue in New York, or Commonwealth Avenue in Boston. The third is what Allan Jacobs, a co-author of *The Boulevard Book*, has dubbed "the multiway boulevard." The multiway boulevard has center traffic lanes and side traffic lanes, designed to separate local and through traffic. Often, but not always, there are tree-lined pedestrian malls or promenades in the center or to one side, but the medians may be as narrow as planting strips. Wide medians are sometimes also used for bicycle lanes and streetcar routes.

In the 20th century, when traffic engineers became the dominant street designers, they frequently eliminated multiway boulevards, for three reasons: medians and trees ("Fixed Hazardous Objects") were sacrificed to widen the traffic lanes; multiway boulevards didn't fit in the single-use functional classification system engineers adopted; and the engineers thought that the intersections where pedestrians, bicycles, cars, and streetcars came together were too complicated and dangerous.

Subsequent studies have shown, however, that properly designed multiway boulevards are not dangerous, and recent interest in both narrowing lanes to slow traffic and designing "multi-modal Complete Streets" calls for what multiway boulevards do best. As we will show, multiway boulevards come in a variety of forms, for different situations: some handle high traffic volumes well, some provide many parking spaces, while others have places for various forms of transportation. New boulevards are also good for stitching back together rips in the urban fabric left by highway removal.

Paris has the highest concentration of multiway boulevards in the world (Figures 2.8, 2.9, and 2.10), but boulevards were imported to America in the nineteenth century, when a parks movement blossomed across the country. Multiway boulevards were used by Frederick Law Olmsted and later became popular with the City Beautiful movement, which included many designers educated in Paris. Frequently, multiway boulevards were part of developing streetcar networks and City Beautiful plans to promote urban expansion.

Figure 2.8: Champs Élysées, Paris, France. Photograph looking northwest towards the Arc de Triomphe around 1900. When vehicles traveled more slowly, lampposts could be in the street, and pedestrians had a place to stand in the wide roadbed. The completion of the Arc de Triomphe and the commencement of the construction of the Champs Élysées came under the administration of Claude-Philibert Barthelot, the Count of Rambuteau, who was the Prefect of Paris and the surrounding region from 1833 to 1848. He laid much of the groundwork for the work carried out by Georges-Eugène Haussmann under Napoleon III. *Library of Congress, Prints and Photographs Division, Frank and Frances Carpenter Collection, LOT 11459-2*

Figure 2.9: Rue de Castiglione, Paris, France. Perhaps by Percier and Fontaine, 1801. A hand-colored photograph from around 1900 looking towards the place Vendôme and the column erected in the center of the square by Napoleon to commemorate the victory of his troops in the battle of Austerlitz.

Figure 2.10: Champs Élysées, Paris, France. André Le Nôtre, 1667. Originally a hunting road in the country, the avenue des Champs Élysées was improved and urbanized during the reigns of Louis XVI, Napoleon I, and Napoleon III. View from the top of the Arc de Triomphe, looking southeast towards the place de la Concorde and the Louvre Museum. Also see Color Plate 11.

MULTIWAY AVENUES & BOULEVARDS

Avenue Montaigne, Paris, France

Bureau de la Voirie Parisienne, 1850

Multiway Avenue

The avenue Montaigne extends from the traffic circle at the Champs Élysées to the place de l'Alma at the edge of the Seine. Wide sidewalks and formal Parisian architecture share a simple palette of materials and colors along the avenue. The combination of a mix of uses, proportional street space, and effective street trees creates a balanced relationship between walkers, cyclists, and drivers.

The avenue Montaigne fits the definition of an avenue—it is a free-moving thoroughfare with a finite length, visually terminated at both ends.[2] The grand avenue is 126 feet wide, which is compact for a Parisian multiway avenue or boulevard: Montaigne efficiently moves traffic but remains a comfortable place for pedestrians. Three travel lanes and a parking lane make up the central roadway. One of the travel lanes today is a counter-flow lane for buses, taxis, and cyclists. The side-access lanes have one lane of traffic and parking on both sides. At several points along the street, one of the side access lanes becomes slightly wider, expanding to approximately twenty-four feet and accommodating an additional row of parking.

Traffic moves well on the avenue Montaigne, despite the fact that it is narrower than many Parisian avenues and boulevards. According to studies published by Allan B. Jacobs, Elizabeth Macdonald, and Yodan Rofè,

Figure 2.11: Multiway Boulevard. © 2013 Dover, Kohl & Partners

Street-oriented Buildings

Transit Lane

Through-going Lanes

Median with Tree Line(s)

Slow side access lane with parallel parking and sharrow markings

850 vehicles per hour use the three central travel lanes and 42 vehicles per hour use the side access lanes. At the same time, a remarkable number of pedestrians are strolling along the street—more than 1,330 people can be counted on the sidewalk within an hour.[3] Roughly half the width of Barcelona's Passeig de Gràcia (Figure 2.21), the avenue Montaigne is just as efficient. It embodies the characteristics of a great street by effectively transporting local patrons without excessively wide travel lanes. The story of this grand avenue begins and ends with its proportion, variety, and beauty (Figures 2.12, 2.13, and 2.14).

Figure 2.12: Avenue Montaigne, Paris, France. Bureau de la Voirie Parisienne, 1850. Looking towards the avenue Montaigne from the rue François 1er. Note the harmonious, muted color palette, with soft grey asphalt sidewalks (rather than stone) on this fashionable and expensive street.

Figure 2.13: Avenue Montaigne, Paris, France. Bureau de la Voirie Parisienne, 1850. What later became the avenue Montaigne was originally a country path or lane that was given an allée of trees in 1770. The aligned rows of trees are key elements in multiway boulevards and avenues. A plan would show that in France their placement is carefully considered, following the traditions started by landscape architects like André Le Nôtre in royal gardens and rural allées.

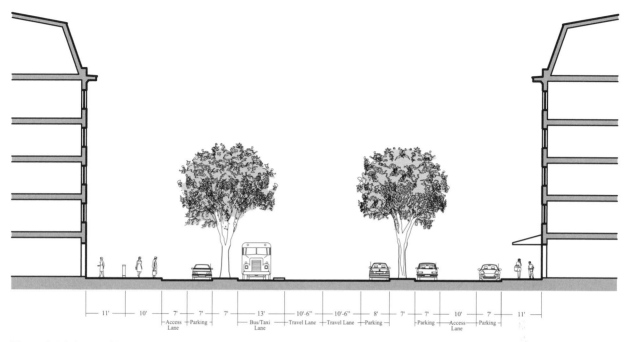

Figure 2.14: Avenue Montaigne, Paris, France. Bureau de la Voirie Parisienne, 1850. Section. © *2013 Dover, Kohl & Partners*

AVENUE D'IENA: THE MOST BEAUTIFUL PARKING LOT ISN'T A PARKING LOT...IT'S A STREET

Avenue d'Iena, Paris, France

Bureau de la Voirie Parisienne, 1858

Multiway Avenue

The avenue d'Iena extends south from the Arc de Triomphe, then deflects southwest toward the Trocadéro gardens (Figure 2.15). Like many of the other grand avenues in Paris,[4] the avenue d'Iena has parallel rows of plane trees symmetrically dividing the center lanes from the side lanes, the ensemble flanked by graceful buildings. But the avenue's chief distinction may lie in the sheer number of automobiles that can be parked on it without harming the public realm. This couldn't be more different, of course, from the American parking lots where we find generous amounts of surface parking,

even on the day after Thanksgiving at the mall (Figure 2.16). But on the avenue d'Iena, six rows of parking along one block of the avenue provide storage space for an astonishing 208 cars and more than 20 motorcycles (Figure 2.17).

This significant feat was accomplished simply by coupling two rows of parking in the side access lanes with two more rows alongside the through lanes (Figure 2.18). The example shows, among other lessons, how important the regular alignment of the trees can be in the overall design of the street space. Standing on the street, a pedestrian is acutely aware of the tree canopies high overhead, of the trunks arrayed like columns marching down the avenue, and of the architecture on either side—but not very aware of the parked cars. The limited palette of materials and colors also unifies

Figure 2.15: Avenue d'Iena, Paris, France. Bureau de la Voirie Parisienne, 1858. Looking south from the top of the Arc de Triomphe. The most beautiful parking lot in the world.

Figure 2.16: Strip Shopping Center, Miami-Dade County, Florida. The avenue d'Iena makes this typical approach to parking look ugly and wasteful.

the space three-dimensionally. The roadway is paved with gray Belgian blocks that are complementary to the colors of the tree trunks, the curbs, the building facades, and the Arc de Triomphe in the distance.

The avenue d'Iena was constructed in 1858, so its designers did not envision this as a street for the movement of cars, much less for their storage. It was the fundamental elegance of the urban form—of the multilane, multiway avenue—that allowed it to be adapted for new needs. The avenue accommodates parking efficiently and stealthily, indicting more conventional solutions.

Figure 2.17: Avenue d'Iena, Paris, France. Bureau de la Voirie Parisienne, 1858. Looking north towards the Arc de Triomphe. A stealthy parking lot: pedestrians are very aware of the aligned trees and the architecture on either side—but hardly notice the parked cars.

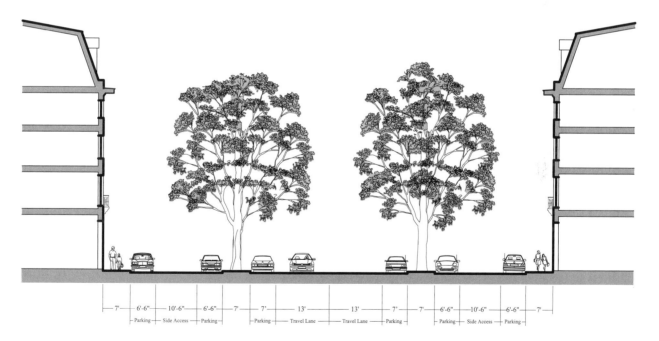

| 7' | 6'-6" | 10'-6" | 6'-6" | 7' | 7' | 13' | 13' | 7' | 7' | 6'-6" | 10'-6" | 6'-6" | 7' |
| | Parking | Side Access | Parking | | Parking | Travel Lane | Travel Lane | Parking | | Parking | Side Access | Parking | |

Figure 2.18: Avenue d'Iena, Paris, France. Bureau de la Voirie Parisienne, 1858. Section. © 2013 Dover, Kohl & Partners

Gran Via de les Corts Catalanes, Barcelona, Spain

Ildefons Cerdà, 1859

Multiway Boulevard

One encounters many spectacular streets in Barcelona, but none are more spectacular than the Gran Via de les Corts Catalanes, the city's spine.[5] Designed in 1859 as a crucial part of Ildefons Cerdà's plan for the Eixample (a large, gridded expansion of the city), Gran Via intersects the Passeig de Gràcia and the Rambla Catalunya one block north of Plaça de Catalunya. The street connects the great addresses and famous streets of Barcelona, tying them together and extending them into an accessible system. Gran Via is a place where people want to be—all 13.1 kilometers of it. It is the route that pedestrians, cyclists, public transit patrons, and drivers use to get to school, to go to work, or to go out for lunch. The ground level of the boulevard is lined with shops, offices, and cafeterias, while hotels and residences occupy the levels above the commercial spaces. One part everyday street for locals and another part traditional boulevard, Gran Via conveys huge numbers of people in multiple modes of travel (Figures 2.19 and 2.20).

The space dedicated to the pedestrian on Gran Via—including the sidewalks and the large medians—measures

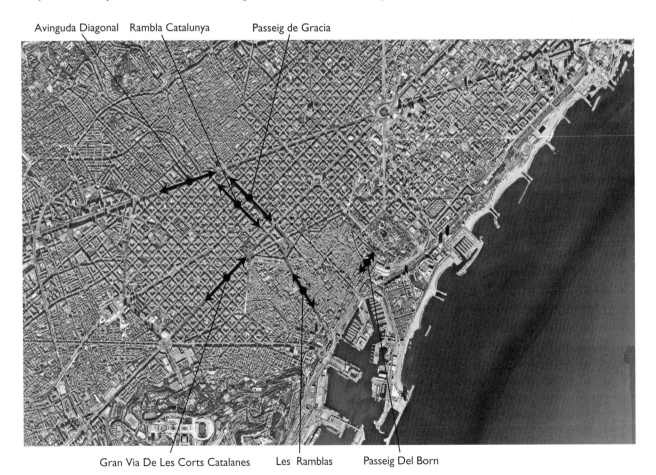

Avinguda Diagonal   Rambla Catalunya   Passeig de Gracia

Gran Via De Les Corts Catalanes   Les Ramblas   Passeig Del Born

Figure 2.19: Barcelona, Spain. Satellite view. *Image courtesy of Google Earth,* © *2012 Institut Catogràfic de Catalunya*

Figure 2.20: Gran Via de les Corts Catalanes, Barcelona, Spain. Ildefons Cerdà, 1859. The Gran Via is the spine of the city. This photograph shows the rows of mature trees, the recently-altered side lanes discussed in the text, and the chamfered corners characteristic of blocks in the Eixample, the extension to Barcelona designed by Cerdà.

approximately eighty-four feet across. The combined paved surfaces dedicated to buses and vehicles measure approximately eighty-two feet, giving a ratio of automobile-occupied space to pedestrian-occupied space that is nearly 1-to-1. This proportion makes crossing Gran Via more comfortable than crossing streets with different ratios of roadbed to pedestrian space but similar traffic volumes and overall widths. Other important characteristics of the boulevard include:

- The approximate dimensions of the multiway boulevard include a fifty-two-foot-wide central carriageway with travel lanes, bookended by medians that are thirty-two feet in width. Side lanes are located on each flank. Ten-foot-wide sidewalks on both sides of the boulevard complete the right-of-way.

- A buffer of hedges lines the side of the median adjacent to the five travel lanes. The hedges provide an additional layer of protection from the moving traffic in the center.

- The medians have parking for bikes and mopeds.

- Bici, a Spanish bike-share initiative, shares locations with metro stops along Gran Via.

- Mature trees symmetrically line each side of the median, spaced at approximately fifty feet on center and creating a canopy that partially shades the boulevard.[6]

- In an unfortunate recent development, the arrangement of the side lanes has been changed by the city in places from a slow local lane and a parking lane to two traffic lanes: these become express lanes right next to the pedestrian on the sidewalk.

Passeig de Gràcia, Barcelona, Spain
Multiway Boulevard

Passeig de Gràcia begins at Plaça de Catalunya, crosses Gran Via de les Corts Catalanes, and ends just after intersecting with Avinguda Diagonal (Figures 2.21 and 2.22). It makes the important connection between the old,

Figure 2.21: Passeig de Gràcia, Barcelona, Spain. Looking southeast from an apartment in the Casa Milà, designed by Antonio Gaudi in 1906. The four rows of aligned trees, the wide sidewalks, and the distinctive lighting fixtures (foreground) are hallmarks of the street design. *Image courtesy of Gianni Longo*

Figure 2.22: Passeig de Gràcia, Barcelona, Spain. Throngs of pedestrians use the Passeig de Gràcia's wide sidewalks, passing some of Barcelona's most popular addresses.

Gothic part of the city and the nineteenth-century Eixample section. Several notable components contribute to this old-world complete street:

- Mature street trees form a canopy for both pedestrians and motorists, offering shelter from the weather and creating visual consistency along the multiway boulevard.

- The sidewalks are approximately thirty-six feet wide and are paved with a patterned hardscape similar in color to the architecture that surrounds it. Typically, they are full of people dining and shopping, making the multiway boulevard both a destination and a travel route.

- Unique lampposts made with elaborate ironwork cantilever above the street. Installed under municipal architect Pere Falqués in 1906, they satisfy the utilitarian need for lighting with a delightful, artful solution (see Figure 1.46).

- Medians range from six feet to twenty-two feet wide and are frequently used by pedestrians as they cross the street, allowing people to easily and comfortably navigate the wide road.

Avinguda Diagonal, Barcelona, Spain

Ildefons Cerdà, 1859

Multiway Boulevard

Ildefons Cerdà first proposed the Avinguda Diagonal in 1859 as part of his plan for the expansion of the city. Fifty meters wide, the avenue begins at the Ronda de Dalt and runs to the Mediterranean, traveling diagonally across the city and crossing Gran Via de les Corts Catalanes and Avinguda Meridiana at Plaça de les Glories Catalanes (Figures 2.23 and 2.24). Diagonal is a boulevard with a heavy volume of traffic that can be exhausting. It nevertheless handles high levels of traffic better than most roads of similar volume and dimension.

Figure 2.23: Avinguda Diagonal, Barcelona, Spain. Ildefons Cerdà, 1859. Looking east towards the Passeig de Gràcia. The multiway boulevard stretches across the Eixample askew to the rest of the city pattern, uniting the city, shortening trips, and relieving the monotony of the grid in a monumental way.

Figure 2.24: Avinguda Diagonal, Barcelona, Spain. Ildefons Cerdà, 1859. Looking west from the Plaça de Francesc Macià. The streetcar line runs in a broad grassy median, a welcome axis of green amid the crowds and concrete of the busy street.

Eastern Parkway, Brooklyn, New York

Frederick Law Olmsted and Calvert Vaux, 1870–1874

Multiway Boulevard

The influential European examples of multiway boulevards were soon followed by a generation of North American experimentation with the form, with memorable results.

Brooklyn's Eastern Parkway, designed by Frederick Law Olmsted and Calvert Vaux during the early 1870s, was one of the first of its type to be constructed in the United States.[7] More than 210 feet wide, the multiway boulevard has six central travel lanes, redesigned in the past half-century to include turn lanes. Wide medians separate the central lanes from narrow local access lanes on each side lined with rows of parallel parking. Each median accommodates pedestrian and bicycle paths, as well as park benches (Figure 2.25).

Figure 2.25: Eastern Parkway, Brooklyn, New York. Frederick Law Olmsted and Calvert Vaux, 1870–1874. The paired trees on the medians are part of a design where pedestrians are comfortable in spite of the extraordinary volume of automobile traffic.

Figure 2.26: Eastern Parkway, Brooklyn, New York. Frederick Law Olmsted and Calvert Vaux, 1870–1874. The through lanes are paralleled by wide medians with paths for cycling and walking, and by slow, narrow access lanes with on-street parking.

Figure 2.27: Eastern Parkway, Brooklyn, New York. Frederick Law Olmsted and Calvert Vaux, 1870–1874. Looking west from Washington Avenue. Recent improvements to the cycle track make Eastern Parkway an important link in New York's expanding network of bicycle routes. *Image courtesy of Kenneth Garcia*

Shaded by mature trees, the medians create a park-like atmosphere along the high traffic throughway (Figure 2.26). Rowhouses and apartment buildings make a continuous street facade that is typically three to five stories tall (Figure 2.27).

The results of a livability study[8] conducted by Peter Bosselmann and Elizabeth Macdonald demonstrate that residents of streets like Eastern Parkway live comfortably despite the high volume of traffic. Bosselmann and Macdonald also concluded that air quality and noise levels along the boulevard are either the same or better than on typical residential streets.

Eastern Parkway is therefore refreshing proof that streets with extraordinary levels of automobile traffic do not have to be placeless spasms of asphalt. According to Bosselmann and Macdonald's study, at least 42,000 vehicles travel through the Brooklyn neighborhood every day. (In contrast, Tamiami Trail in Miami-Dade County, Florida, transports a similar amount of daily car traffic without providing much dedicated space for anything other than cars and buses: it is therefore not a place where people typically like to be.) A remarkable reality on Eastern Parkway is that a resident can comfortably sit on a bench in the median while commuters by the thousands simultaneously navigate their way home.

A sense of place is an essential part of the street design puzzle that contributes to the design of a city as a whole. When a street scene fails to incorporate distinct cultural references, it fails to be attractive—even to the motorists who have to use it. On Eastern Parkway, the traditional rowhouses not only create a solid urban wall; their shape, size, and placement give the street its distinctive, local feel (Figure 2.28).

Figure 2.28: Eastern Parkway, Brooklyn, New York. Frederick Law Olmsted and Calvert Vaux, 1870–1874. Satellite view. *Image courtesy of Google Earth*

Other features include:

- The median on one side of the road functions as part of the Brooklyn-Queens Greenway, a route for cyclists traveling through places like Prospect Park and extending to the neighboring Ocean Parkway.

- Mature elm trees provide protection from weather for more than 50 percent of the street space. The organization and spacing of the trees establish visual order and define the public realm within the large medians (Figure 2.29).

- Front yards as large as twenty-five feet by thirty feet make it possible for families to socialize without interruption as pedestrians pass by on the sidewalk.

- Wide sidewalks next to the large yards also provide enough room for interaction when it is desired.

Eastern Parkway is a unique American street with an architectural style and urban character that evokes a sense of place. Although cities like San Francisco also have streets lined with rowhouses, when you arrive on Eastern Parkway, you know you are in New York.

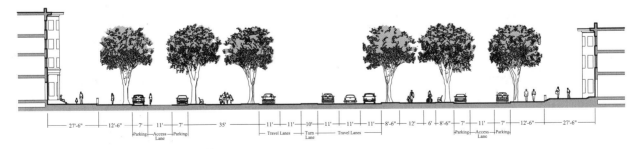

Figure 2.29: Eastern Parkway, Brooklyn, New York. Frederick Law Olmsted and Calvert Vaux, 1870–1874. Section. The traditional rowhouses and apartment buildings give Eastern Parkway its distinctly New York feel; the six rows of trees tame the sizable boulevard into a comfortable place for people. © *2013 Dover, Kohl & Partners*

Ocean Parkway, Brooklyn, New York

Frederick Law Olmsted and Calvert Vaux, 1874–1880

Multiway Boulevard

Frederick Law Olmsted and Calvert Vaux proposed both Eastern Parkway and Ocean Parkway in the 1860s. Eastern Parkway was built between 1870 and 1874, while

Ocean Parkway was constructed from 1874 to 1880. The later road is nearly five and a half miles long and was modeled on the avenue Foch in Paris (Color Plate 10).[9] Ocean Parkway has seven central travel lanes, including a striped median in the center that alternates as a left turn lane. Unlike Eastern Parkway, the street facade is not entirely continuous—detached housing and apartment buildings define the edges rather than rowhouses (Figures 2.30 and 2.31). Pedestrians going to work or using the medians as

Figure 2.30: Ocean Parkway, Brooklyn, New York. Frederick Law Olmsted and Calvert Vaux, 1874–1880. Looking north from Cortelyou Road. The Eastern and Ocean parkways grew from an 1867 proposal by Olmsted to connect Manhattan's Central Park to Brooklyn's Prospect Park and Coney Island with parkways. *Image courtesy of Kenneth Garcia*

Figure 2.31: Ocean Parkway, Brooklyn, New York. Frederick Law Olmsted and Calvert Vaux, 1874–1880. Satellite view. *Image courtesy of Google Earth*

parks benefit from wide spaces between the roads. Other notable features include:

- Apartment buildings and houses with small setbacks from the street, which create a stable streetwall.
- Bike paths in the medians, which cyclists use to travel from Prospect Park (also designed by Olmsted) to Coney Island.
- The greenway, which exemplifies the grace a continuous tree canopy can bring to a pedestrian mall. It is enjoyable to walk or ride in a place sheltered from sun, rain, and snow.

Both Ocean Parkway and Eastern Parkway are successful boulevards that easily accommodated their neighborhoods' changing needs over the past century. Ocean Parkway, however, is slightly larger, and that makes a remarkable difference in its quality. The six central travel lanes on Eastern Parkway have an average total width of sixty-five feet, whereas the seven travel lanes on Ocean Parkway add up to an average width of seventy feet. The five-foot differential makes Eastern Parkway noticeably more compact, easier to navigate as a pedestrian, and visually more agreeable.

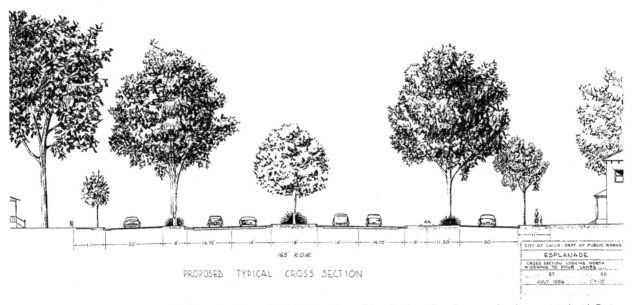

Figure 2.32: The Esplanade, Chico, California. Fred Davis, 1956. Section. The multiway boulevard tradition, so closely associated with Paris, Olmsted, and the City Beautiful movement, occasionally resurfaced during later decades. With the Esplanade, the form was adapted to northern California and predominately single-family neighborhoods. Although the Esplanade is one of Chico's widest streets, it is also the perennial local favorite.

AVENUES & BOULEVARDS

Park Avenue, New York, New York

Avenue

In the Commissioners' Plan of 1811 that laid a street grid over Manhattan Island, the north–south streets were called avenues. What later became Park Avenue was called Fourth Avenue. Like all the new avenues, it was one hundred feet wide. Despite being on the east side of the island, where most of the development took place after the Commissioners' Plan, Fourth Avenue remained unfashionable because of the railroad tracks that ran up its center—first from a terminal at 23rd Street and later from 42nd Street. The moving railroad cars and the noise and smoke from the locomotives made the avenue unpopular for development during most of the nineteenth century. Eventually, however, the tracks south of the new Grand Central Station on 42nd Street were removed, and the tracks north of Grand Central were buried until they came above ground north of Carnegie Hill at 96th Street. In 1903 New York State required that all trains to Grand Central have electric locomotives, and the street was widened to 140 feet and renamed Park Avenue.

That same year, a Park Avenue property owner persuaded the society figure Senator Elihu Root to build a large house on the avenue, designed by the architects Carrère & Hastings, and the wide street became attractive to the rich. Within a decade, the once sparsely-inhabited Park Avenue had become a long street of grand mansions. The west side of Park between East 68th and East 69th streets illustrates the scale of the avenue at the time. The four Georgian-style houses on the block were built between 1909 and 1926—two designed by McKim, Mead & White, one by Delano & Aldrich, and one by Walker & Gillette.

In 1911, however, Senator and Mrs. Root moved to 998 Fifth Avenue, an apartment house thirteen blocks north on Fifth Avenue that was the first apartment building to break the wall of mansions on Fifth Avenue above 59th Street opposite Central Park. 998 Fifth Avenue was designed by McKim, Mead & White and was managed by Douglas Elliman, who convinced Root to move there in return for a 50 percent reduction on his rent. The New York

▲▲ **Figure 2.33:** Park Avenue, New York, New York. Looking south from 87th Street in 1929. Because of the Great Depression and World War II, the brownstones on the west side of the avenue between 85th and 86th streets stayed standing for decades. The median in 1929 was almost twice as wide as it is today, and the sidewalks were wider too, so that each roadbed is now almost twenty feet wider. *Image courtesy of NYC Vintage Images*

▲ **Figure 2.34:** Park Avenue between 85th and 86th Streets, New York, New York. A view of the Reginald De Koven House (John Russell Pope, 1911), sandwiched between two 1920s apartment houses. Until relatively recently, the pedestal mount traffic signal was the only traffic signal used on Park Avenue, but the city has now added redundant mast arm traffic signals. Washington, DC, still uses mostly pedestal mount signals on downtown streets.

middle class had lived in large apartment buildings since the 1870s, but people with the social aspirations of the Roots had previously lived only in houses. Soon many of the mansions on Park Avenue were torn down and replaced by the apartment buildings that still set the character of the broad avenue today (Figures 2.33 and 2.34).

Figure 2.35: Park Avenue, New York, New York. Looking north from 68th Street in 1930. The large apartment house on the west side of Park Avenue at 70th Street is 720 Park Avenue, designed by famous New York apartment architect Rosario Candela in 1929. Older buildings on Park Avenue were limited to a 150-foot height by fire regulations. The City's 1929 Multiple Dwelling Act allowed taller buildings, if they set back above 150 feet. Several wonderful examples of what could be done were quickly built on Park Avenue around 70th Street (some still under construction in this photo). Compare this to Figure 2.33, which shows a slightly less wealthy section of Park Avenue, where development took longer to recover. *Image courtesy of the Museum of the City of New York*

Figure 2.36: Broadway at 85th Street, New York, New York. A view looking north in 1900, showing an informal promenade down the center of the boulevard that preceded the "cut and cover" construction of the West Side IRT subway in 1904, when the median was frequently used for venting the subway platforms. *Image courtesy of New York Transit Museum*

Three elements in the new apartment houses on Park Avenue combined to make a sturdy streetwall that defined the space well: they had stone or brick facades, boxy massing, and a common twelve-story cornice line imper-

ceptibly taller than the avenue was wide. In the boom years of the Roaring Twenties, some of the buildings—like 720 Park Avenue, designed by the noted apartment house architect Rosario Candela (Figure 2.35)—rose above the cornice with setbacks that evoked fantasies of romantic European architecture, simultaneously holding the cornice line and enriching the view down the avenue. On the ground, broad sidewalks, planted medians above the railroad tracks, and a prohibition against trucks and buses gave the sunny street a generous feel.

One of the most appealing things about Park Avenue is the way it goes up and down hill. That breaks up the views along the long, straight street, so that the unterminated vista—the Achilles heel of the American grid—is avoided. The broad medians reinforce the space of the street and make crossing it more comfortable for the pedestrian, as bumpouts rarely do. Until recently, Park Avenue's stoplights were only lights on poles, but more standard hanging traffic signals have unfortunately been added. The traffic lanes on the street are wide enough that some drivers drive over fifty miles per hour, in order to go ten blocks (half a mile) or more between light changes. The speeders reflect the changes that the New York City DOT made to the street in the 1950s, when they narrowed the median and the sidewalks to make wider traffic lanes. In theory the speed limit on Park Avenue is thirty miles per hour, but there is little or no enforcement, even after speeding cars collide at the cross streets.

Monument Avenue, Richmond, Virginia

Begun by CPE Burgwyn, 1887

Avenue

Richmond's Monument Avenue is an axial, tree-lined street, defined along its edges by distinguished houses and apartment buildings. Wide sidewalks that measure between ten feet and twenty feet are next to the front yards and porches, establishing a quiet pedestrian realm within the neighborhood. Despite its overall width, the street space

dedicated to plantings or pedestrian use has nearly a 1-to-1 proportion with the area dedicated to auto use.

When compared to an iconic Parisian street like the avenue Montaigne, the difference in street character is immediately apparent. Monument Avenue is slightly larger, but it is also primarily residential (Figures 2.37, 2.38, 2.39, 2.40, and 2.41). Detached houses and apartment buildings of various sizes and styles create a less enclosed atmosphere that contrasts with the homogenous facades and mix of uses found on the avenues of Paris and Barcelona. All have some similar attributes and terminated vistas, but the American adaption of the European type is a unique evolution.

The parts of the new American type built in Richmond are simple. Wide sidewalks made for strolling combined with broad medians and street-oriented, freestanding buildings define the avenue. Trees are planted approximately forty feet apart. Houses and apartment houses of various sizes account for a range of incomes along the avenue. Modest details—like asphalt paving blocks and hardscape in neutral tones—make Monument Avenue seem grand and approachable at the same time.

Figure 2.37: Monument Avenue, Richmond, Virginia. Begun by CPE Burgwyn, 1887. The grand avenue was gradually adapted to American urban form.

Figure 2.38: Monument Avenue, Richmond, Virginia. Begun by CPE Burgwyn, 1887. When a median is sized generously enough for paired rows of trees, the effect is that of a linear park, a green axis joining the city together rather than dividing it. Compare this with the meager concrete "traffic separator" that runs down the middle of the average suburban arterial. *Image courtesy of Christopher Podstawski*

Figure 2.39: Monument Avenue, Richmond, Virginia. Begun by CPE Burgwyn, 1887. The front porches facing Richmond's avenue are slightly elevated above the sidewalk level, establishing privacy and dignity.

Figure 2.40: Monument Avenue, Richmond, Virginia. Begun by CPE Burgwyn, 1887. Equestrian statue of Robert E. Lee by Antonin Mercié, 1890. At key intersections, eponymous monuments commemorate historical figures ranging from Confederate generals to African-American tennis star Arthur Ashe. *Image courtesy of James Dougherty*

The economical and durable asphalt blocks also give a texture to the street that would improve the look of many wide streets. The monuments give a distinctive character, and here and there street arrangements like the cross-axis at North Davis Avenue—where the Metropolitan Community Church visually terminates the axis of the small green perpendicular to the avenue—give variety and richness.

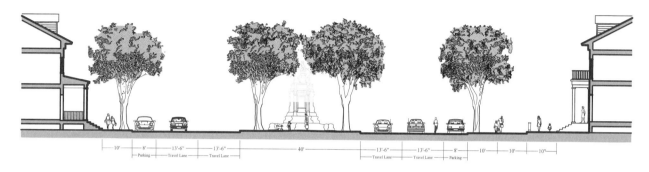

Figure 2.41: Monument Avenue, Richmond, Virginia. Begun by CPE Burgwyn, 1887. Section. Close inspection reveals that the avenue is not completely symmetrical, that its lanes are inadvisably wide, and that the building heights and widths vary substantially. However, the broad median and the parallel rows of majestic trees have a powerful unifying effect. © 2013 Dover, Kohl & Partners

Queens Road West, Charlotte, North Carolina

John Nolen, 1911

Boulevard

Queens Road was designed in 1911 as part of John Nolen's plan for the leafy streetcar suburb of Myers Park, in which he sought to blend town and country. The street is a key through route with substantial daily traffic; at the same time, it showcases the grandest houses on some of the largest lots in Myers Park. Queens Road proves that it is possible for addresses that are part of a continuous, connected street network to retain—and even acquire—prestige, postwar prejudices notwithstanding. Houses in Myers Park have steadily appreciated in value and are among the most sought-after in the Charlotte region. In large part this is a result of Nolen's brilliant yet simple tree-planting plan for Queen's Road, which creates the feeling of moving through a mature forest, under a high canopy of native oak, elm, and tulip poplar trees (Figures 2.42 and 2.43).

Nolen experimented by transplanting one hundred mature trees in Myers Park in the first year of development; after a year, only one of the trees had died.[10] Nolen concluded that the high survival rate of the transplanted trees was due to his use of native species, and thereafter he enthusiastically encouraged the planting of native trees. He directed developer George Stephens to plant large numbers of trees throughout Myers Park, including the street trees following the alignment of Queens Road, and he provided design advice to individual lot owners. He also demanded a specific number of trees in front of and behind each house at a time when this was not common practice.

Figure 2.42: Queens Road West, Charlotte, North Carolina. John Nolen, 1911. Today, the trees planted by Nolen feel like a majestic forest—but one that easily accommodates houses and yards, and that we comfortably drive through.

Figure 2.43: Queens Road West, Charlotte, North Carolina. John Nolen, 1911. The houses on Queens Road have substantial front yards.

Figure 2.44: Queens Road West, Charlotte, North Carolina. John Nolen, 1911. Section. © 2013 Dover, Kohl & Partners

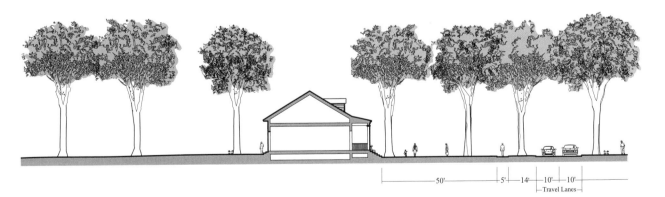

The streets in Myers Park range in width, depending on their type and their proximity to the large public park that is integrated into the neighborhood layout. Some of the streets are as narrow as forty feet. Queens Road West is the widest of the designs, with a right-of-way of 110 feet. A central median thirty-two feet wide is a source of open space along the urban arterial, while wide planting strips frame the sidewalks on each side. Nolen was a landscape architect by training and felt free to depart from orthogonal grids, instead applying gently rounded forms such as those observed in nature. Queens Road has a curving, picturesque design, fitted to the rolling topography, and Nolen's fine-tuned plan allowed for differentiating the sizes (and costs) of houses, lot depths, and front yard setbacks.

> To plan a residential area in a shape that respects the lay of the land obviously necessitates blocks of irregular shapes and sizes, and consequently varied building lots.
>
> —John Nolen, *New Towns for Old* [1]

If one looks only at the cross-section of the street between the curbs, Queens Road shares some characteristics with Commonwealth Avenue in Boston and St. Charles Avenue in New Orleans: all three have wide central medians and tall trees planted in rows (Figure 2.44). However, the effect on Queens Road is radically different from what one sees at the other two. To be-

gin with, Queens Road lacks the central promenade and the attached buildings only slightly set back from the sidewalk that knit Commonwealth Avenue together and lend it urbanity. Unlike the immersive environment of consistent architecture on Commonwealth—the result of a strict design code—Queens Road has an eclectic mix of Colonial Revival, Arts and Crafts, and Tudor Revival house designs. The median on Queens Road was originally intended to provide space for a streetcar, which might have given the street a character reminiscent of St. Charles Avenue. In the end, however, very little of the streetcar line was built. In the absence of tracks, the broad lawn on today's Queens Road lends the corridor a more suburban feel. The great depth of the front yards accentuates this impression; whereas the fronts of many buildings on St. Charles Avenue are within conversational distance of the sidewalks, the fronts of houses on Queens Road can be as far as eighty feet away. Finally, both Commonwealth Avenue and St. Charles Avenue are flat and have long segments of arrow-straight formality. Queens Road winds and dips and rises in a streamform pattern; the effect is more picturesque, but also more highwaylike than Nolen probably intended.

On the other hand, one of the many attributes of a well-designed street is that it gracefully accepts revision, adapting to changing times. Nolen's foresight in reserving the land for the broad median means that someday, when Charlotte fully restores its once-robust streetcar system, Queens Road will be ready for it.

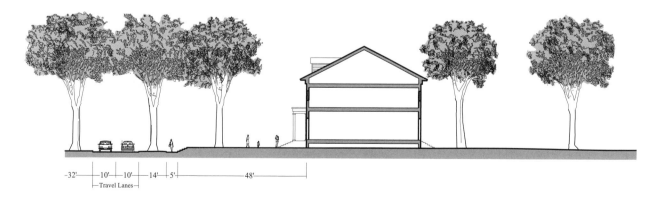

−32' |—10'—|—10'—|—14'—|—5'—|————48'————|
       |—Travel Lanes—|

SUBURBS: THEY DON'T MAKE 'EM THE WAY THEY USED TO

Figure 2.45: Elmwood Village, Buffalo, New York. The classic American streetcar suburb was designed to create a walkable, dignified public realm and to support civic pride.

Figure 2.46: Doral, Florida. In the sprawl era, garage doors and wide driveways supplanted front porches and street trees, leaving the streets unwalkable *and* unloved.

PROMENADES & RAMBLAS

Promenade Streets

A *promenade* is a place for strolling, usually tree-lined. A number of street types and park designs incorporate a form of the promenade. On some of these, like the famous *Rambles* in Spain, the promenade is the signature element. These examples belong in a category of their own: Promenade Streets.

Some classic streets contain promenades as part of a larger ensemble. Commonwealth Avenue in Boston has a central promenade that offers a pleasant alternative to the sidewalks shaded by buildings on a cold but sunny winter's morning. The boulevard de Rochechouart in Paris has a bustling central promenade, too. But when one compares these to Barcelona's Rambles (the Catalan spelling, "Ramblas" is the plural

in Spanish), the Spanish roads have a far smaller proportion of their cross-section devoted to moving and parking vehicles and a wide median devoted to places for walking, dining, and vendors rather than planted beds or lawn.

The *promenade* street is a sibling of the boulevard and the avenue. All three are important streets in the urban scene, and they are usually arranged in a grand manner—the promenade street might be visually terminated like an avenue or open at its end like a boulevard, for instance. Like them, it might be a favored location for stores and restaurants, because it serves as an organizer and attractor of pedestrian activity. A promenade street is not typically the fastest route across town for motorists, though. Its travel lanes are few and narrow, and the flow of auto traffic in many instances tends to be impeded by an almost continuous crossing of pedestrians from the flanking buildings and side streets.

The promenade street is like a park, too, in that it brings a wide swath of public space and tree canopy into the heart of the city, but its linear form makes it more of a spatial *connector* rather than just a green exception to the built-up blocks that surround it. The promenade street is like a square or plaza, as well, in that it assumes a role as the neighbors' shared public space, apart from their homes, yards, and ordinary streets. Like a square, the promenade street is a space where people are drawn to gather and socialize and eye one another—but unlike a square, which condenses this activity, the promenade street stretches it out and sets it in motion. Our favorite examples offer a daily parade of people of all sorts.

The case studies that follow clearly show there was a golden era of building promenade streets, perhaps culminating in the Paseo del Prado in Havana. This is also a highly relevant street type for today, as we talk about reducing auto use to lower our carbon footprint. Not only are the built examples beloved—more popular now than ever—but they offer solutions to modern problems. Today's parks departments are under budgetary siege, struggling to maintain their existing manicured acreage, whereas a promenade is a kind of public space that generates money, with phenomenal economic activity flowing out of its cafes, flower markets, and shops. A *rambla* address has magnetic appeal for tourists, who favor hotel rooms nearby, and for the leaders in creative industries, who know that their designers and thinkers and visitors want to step out into that scene at the day's end. A promenade street is also a practical way to introduce a great open space into the city without acquiring vast tracts of land; its linear form makes it a natural replacement for an obsolete elevated freeway or formerly oversized arterial road, for example. What a trade!

The promenade street is one of the street types that quietly dropped off the professional street-design menu in the twentieth century, but it should be back on our menu for the twenty-first.

Figure 2.47: Promenade Street. © 2013 Dover, Kohl & Partners

Central Promenade

Tree Lines

Narrow, Slow Traffic Lane

On Street Parallel Parking

Small Corner Radii

THE RAMBLA TYPE / Stefanos Polyzoides

Dedicated to Gabriel Garcia Aragon

The rambla is a multimodal street type, distinguished by a large and central pedestrian island, limited narrow carriageways, and a monumental streetscape (Figure 2.48). It is common to Catalonia and the regions of Valencia and the Balearic Islands that share the Catalan language and culture, from whence it spread to other parts of Spain and Spanish colonies. As a design solution, it was born of the need to sanitize cities in response to the pollution and congestion resulting from the early Industrial Revolution. As a design opportunity, it was presented by the demolition of city walls, which began in this part of the world at the end of the eighteenth century and lasted until the 1860s.

The kinds of residual land located outside these urban fortifications were of two possible topographic patterns. The first kind was made up of irregular, abandoned flat fields left open for defensive purposes and often used for open-air commerce. The second kind was made up of dry riverbeds, residual parts of natural landscape, which channeled the surface water of surrounding agricultural lands into the sea. Close to dense cities, these areas had become unsightly and unhealthy places. Yet, they offered all the necessary ingredients for potentially generating a new kind of constructed urban landscape.

The rambla at its origin was introduced as a large-scale linear park, a promenade providing badly needed recreational and civic space for urban dwellers. At the same time, it was a grand element of hydrological infrastructure that solved the twin civil engineering challenges of conducting water runoff and channeling vehicular traffic through cities. After two hundred years, such ramblas have become the single most prominent, iconic, and beautiful public places in Palma de Mallorca, Barcelona, Tarragona, Vilanova i la Geltrú, Figueres, Sant Feliu de Guixols, Arenys de Mar, Sabadell, Tarrassa, Lleida, Girona, and Igualada—the Catalan cities where the prime examples of the type are located.

Figure 2.48 Les Rambles, Barcelona, Spain. Looking north from the waterfront, where the Ramblas begin. The great London Plane trees unify the space which, like the riverbed it once was, flows to the sea. *© 2012 Oh-Barcelona.com / Creative Commons Attribution 2.0 Generic license*

The most prominent design element of the rambla is its central and dimensionally imposing median island. These islands are now paved. (They were originally finished in decomposed granite.) Pedestrian circulation is channeled there, to mark the dominating presence of walkers over vehicles, and to provide a place for a variety of temporary commercial activities and ritual annual events. A single, narrow traffic lane, parking lane, and sidewalk are placed symmetrically on either side of the central island to complete the typical rambla plan configuration.

The cross-section of the rambla is also a distinctive ingredient of this type. Alamedas[12] of large, mature plane trees are typically laid out rhythmically and symmetrically along the central median. When in full foliage in the spring and summer, the trees fill the entire right-of-way and completely shade the median. In this part of the world, plane trees are native to creek and river beds. Their planting pattern produces a spatial effect that recalls the memory of a natural watercourse in the middle of a busy metropolitan street.

LES RAMBLES, BARCELONA, SPAIN / Stefanos Polyzoides

Promenade Street

Les Rambles of Barcelona is located on the central north–south axis of the city. It is one of the most formally complex and vital streets anywhere. The name Les Rambles, plural, refers to the division of the famous promenade into six interconnected sections. These have been identified throughout history with adjacent institutions or activities: Rambla de Canaletes, Rambla dels Estudis, Rambla de Sant Josep, Rambla dels Caputxins, Rambla de Santa Monica, and Rambla del Mar.

But in fact, the form of Les Rambles is more easily understood and experienced as a three-part composition, each part enriched by some of the greatest historic buildings and places in the city, such as the Mercat de la Boqueria, the Plaça Reial, and the Dressanes. A long, straight space dominates the middle part of the street and establishes its dominant character. The alameda planted along the entire length produces the effect of a cathedral nave. To the north and south, two funnel-shaped residual spaces, more open and less planted, transition to the rest of the city, leading to the Eixample and the harbor, respectively.

The collective architectural character of Les Rambles was established in the late eighteenth century. The juxtaposition of buildings previously attached to the demolished western medieval wall with the irregularly plotted suburban buildings in the Raval across from them initially produced a heterogeneous architectural fabric. In the last two centuries, this pattern has become dominant. The addition of buildings diverse in type, style, scale, height, profile, materials, and decorative details has resulted in Les Rambles being defined by an extremely varied built edge (Figure 2.49).

Pedestrian traffic along the street is constant and very high in volume, the result of its privileged location along the central movement axis of Barcelona. This high pedestrian volume generates a powerful retail economy. Stores occupy the ground floors of almost all buildings, and a variety of picturesque, temporary retail activities are accommodated in pavilions on the central island. All kinds of public spectacles also take place along its length. The experience of continuous waves of energy and vitality washing over the place produce a sense of great joy and conviviality (Figure 2.50).

Figure 2.49: Les Rambles, Barcelona, Spain. The buildings along the edge of the Ramblas are diverse and frequently highly articulated. Building heights, widths, facades, and ornamentation change from one end to the other.

Figure 2.50: Les Rambles, Barcelona, Spain. We walk down the center of the street, which is a rare but comfortable vantage point for pedestrians. The constant flow of strolling people under the great canopy is marvelous.

Figure 2.51: Les Rambles, Barcelona, Spain. Section. © *Moule & Polyzoides, Architects & Urbanists*

Figure 2.52: Les Rambles, Barcelona, Spain. Figure-ground drawing. Les Rambles is actually several segments laid end-to-end, rising from the funnel-shaped end at the harbor, through the semi-straight central section, and widening again as it nears the Eixample. © *Moule & Polyzoides, Architects & Urbanists*

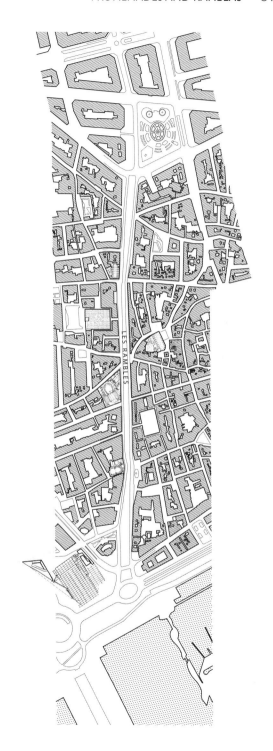

Yet, the single most important formal ingredient of Les Rambles is in the geometric definition of its plan. The place is a virtual symphony of diverging dimensions, an ode to asymmetry and irregularity. The variation of the combined right-of-way, sidewalk, carriageway, and pedestrian island dimensions is extreme. The right-of-way varies between 75 feet at its narrowest to 190 feet at its widest. In places, sidewalks can be as narrow as 4 feet and as wide as 41 feet. The carriageway measures between 15 feet and 33 feet. The pedestrian median squeezes down to 32 feet and opens up to 101 feet. Nowhere in the kilometer length of Les Rambles are the dimensions of the four elements described above ever repeated singly or in combination (Figure 2.51).

The visual effect is as extraordinary as it is unique. Moving on foot from the unusual vantage point of the center of the right-of-way, surrounded by a vertically and horizontally varied architectural enclosure, following in the vector of a lightly sloping ground, through a constant dimensional variation in plan and section (Figure 2.52) and the shifting light of the sun, produces a rare sensation: the ground, buildings, trees, vehicles, pavilions, people, animals, and inanimate objects seem to be engaged all together in gentle motion. This is the magic that is experienced on Les Rambles, and the foundation of its reputation as one of the most famous streets in the world.

RAMBLA CATALUNYA, BARCELONA, SPAIN / Stefanos Polyzoides

Ildefons Cerdà, 1859

Promenade Street

The Rambla Catalunya is one of Barcelona's most distinctive and elegant urban streets. Together with the Passeig de Gràcia it occupies the geographic center for the Eixample, the heroic nineteenth-century regional enlargement of the city designed by Ildefons Cerdà. This rambla was built along ten new, uniform, repetitive city blocks. Conceived as an extension of the historic Les Rambles, it connected the medieval core of the city with the village of Gràcia.

As with all the other street types that Cerdà designed throughout the Eixample, the Rambla Catalunya has a dimensionally stable plan along its entire length. The right-of-way measures 98 feet in width; the pedestrian central island, 42 feet; both sidewalks, 11 feet each; and both the single, one-way traffic and parking lanes, 16 feet each. The small sidewalks are particularly noteworthy as they force most pedestrians to circulate on the central island. There are elegant retail stores lining the ground floors of the buildings along most

of the rambla's length. Many of these ground floor businesses are cafes and restaurants. Their tables are often located under umbrellas in the shade of the alameda of the central island, and are served by waiters who cross the moving traffic to reach their customers.

The dimensions of the two carriageways are tight for traffic movement and parking, and as a result, they appear diminutive compared to the width of the pedestrian island (Figure 2.53). Pedestrian traffic is favored by the continuous slope of the ground plane and various physical and functional impediments to the speedy flow of traffic. These include continuous lines of tree trunks at both edges of the pedestrian islands, the constant and random street crossing by pedestrians, the vibrant store graphics, the merchandise in the storefront windows, and the distracting decorative detail of most of the buildings.

The sectional configuration of the Rambla Catalunya is also very distinctive, just under 1-to-1 in proportion of street width to height (Figure 2.54). The visual effect it conveys is one of intense enclosure and memorable urbanity. The continuous and rhythmic sequence of street trees planted as an alameda, the light poles, and the street furniture further contribute to the stable visual character of the place. But the formal signature of this rambla is the quality of the buildings defining its edges.

The immense Eixample project, extending over three-hundred-plus blocks, was built out over approximately a century through architectural designs operating on two lot and building types only: stacked flats in rectangular lots and stacked flats in triangular corner lots. How could such a rational, repetitive, relentless degree

Figure 2.53: Rambla Catalunya, Barcelona, Spain. Ildefons Cerdà, 1859. Narrow traffic lanes allow deliveries, neighborhood traffic, and parking without interfering with the coming and going of waiters for the café and restaurant tables in the center.

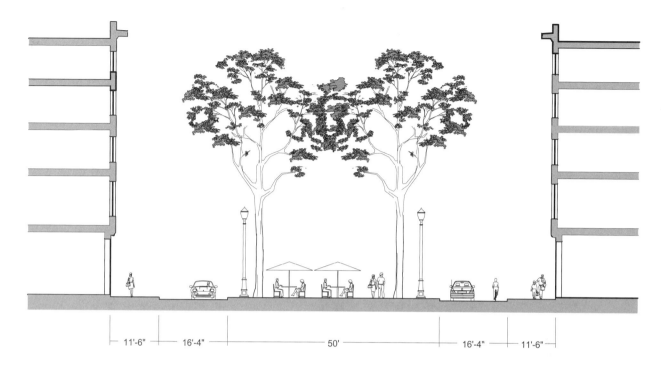

11'-6"   16'-4"   50'   16'-4"   11'-6"

Figure 2.54: Rambla Catalunya, Barcelona, Spain. Ildefons Cerdà, 1859. Section. © *Moule & Polyzoides, Architects & Urbanists*

Figure 2.55: Passeig del Born, Barcelona, Spain. View from the steps of the Church of Santa Maria del Mar, looking northeast. The rambla form appears in shorter, less well-known examples around the region as well, such as this particularly delightful one on the Passeig del Born.

of typological repetition ever produce such a unique and distinguished built environment?

It is because mixed-use buildings of spectacular individual design relieve each block face. There are six fifty-foot-wide lots on the orthogonal portions of every block side facing the Rambla Catalunya. Each of these lots is occupied by a separate building designed by the hand of an accomplished architect. Some of the best examples of Catalan *Modernismo* (Art Nouveau) are to be found there. The stone facades, rich architectural details, and deeply projecting frontages of these buildings form an architectural fabric that animates and enriches the public realm of the Rambla, providing a theatrical stage for the common and the ritual events that unfold day after day along this spectacular urban promenade.

PASEO DEL PRADO, HAVANA, CUBA / Andrés Duany

Begun, 1772; rebuilt, 1834; redesigned by Jean-Claude Nicolas Forestier, 1928

Promenade Street

Paseo del Prado (El Prado) in Havana is the last of those great streets, like the Ringstrasse in Vienna and the ramblas of Barcelona, that replaced demolished fortifications. El Prado was redesigned by Jean-Claude Nicolas Forestier, the Beaux-Arts planner of the 1920s, as part of his overall plan for Havana. This included the waterfront Malecon, as well as two other avenues—one that leads to the university and one dedicated to the Presidents. These are excellent, but neither, and perhaps no promenade in the world, is as accomplished a design as El Prado (Figure 2.56).

The Prado leads from the sea to the new Capitolio, which is from the same period. The Capitolio together with that other great Beaux-Arts ensemble, the Universidad de La Habana, are superb. The Prado itself is special not only because of its section but also for its detailing. The floor is interior-quality terrazzo, and there are masterfully integrated bannisters, steps, benches, and lamps (Figure 2.57). El Prado deploys a unique section: the promenade portion is elevated so that it lifts the pedestrian above the traffic on the side streets. The integral seating faces not only inward to the tree-lined promenade as would be expected but also outward—so that the edge of the elevated area is not a socially impervious "hull." Beyond the promenade, the flanking buildings are required by code to have a continuous arcade. They have a uniform height, but the buildings are by various designers. This produces just enough contrast between the private realm and the uniform civic architecture of the central promenade.

One termination of the Prado is the Capitolio—actually, its slim dome, perfectly framed. The walkways and entourage of the Capitolio (and an intermediary square) are designed in an integral way with the Prado, forming a single unified ensemble. While this is brilliantly handled, the other termination is the great flaw of El Prado. Instead of a building (the Palacio Presidencial could have easily been located there instead of nearby), it is open to the sea. Winds have always swept up the length of El Prado. As a result, about a third of the trees that were integral to the Prado's design are dead and another third are damaged. Only the trees farthest from the sea are sufficiently protected to show the original intention (Figure 2.58).

The ocean can be destructive to urbanism. This lesson of what not to do is visible in El Prado, as it is along Havana's great drive by the sea, the Malecon, which is constantly besieged by the ocean, weather, and neglect. Havana has lessons on the good and the bad on offer, not to be ignored.

▲**Figure 2.56:** Paseo del Prado, Havana, Cuba. Jean-Claude Nicolas Forestier, 1928. Satellite view. The Prado stretches from the sea to the Capitolio. *Image courtesy of Google Earth, © 2012 DigitalGlobe*

◄**Figure 2.57:** Paseo del Prado, Havana, Cuba. Jean-Claude Nicolas Forestier, 1928. The promenade is elevated above street level, with a terrazzo finish worthy of any luxury interior, and benches and lampposts fully integrated in the design. *© 2013 Stephen A. Mouzon, Photographer*

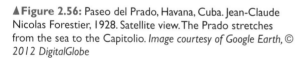

►**Figure 2.58:** Paseo del Prado, Havana, Cuba. Jean-Claude Nicolas Forestier, 1928. The dramatic tree canopy intended for the Prado is seen in the foreground, but the damaging effects of the sea winds on the trees closest to the waterfront are clearly visible in the background. *© 2013 Stephen A. Mouzon, Photographer*

Boulevard de Rochechouart, Paris, France

Service des Promenades et Plantations, 1864

Boulevard

Located at the base of the Montmartre hill, the boulevard de Rochechouart has a compelling street section with a wide median that accommodates walking, cycling, and entrances to the *Métro*. An intricately constructed boulevard, Rochechouart varies slightly in total width as it crosses the Parisian city fabric. The large, central median with four rows of trees gives the street its unique visual signature.

The boulevard is named after a seventeenth-century abbess of Montmartre. It was fashioned into its current form in the nineteenth century, following the alignment of a section of the notorious Wall of the Farmers-General, where tax collectors infuriated the populace with their levies just prior to the French Revolution.[13] Today, it anchors a notably happier neighborhood, just far enough from haunts more overrun by tourists to remain relaxed and popular with ordinary Parisians.

Rochechouart is a mixed-use *tour de force* that puts to shame our contemporary "multimodal" designs (Figure 2.59). Two vehicle lanes travel in each direction, four in total, with two of the lanes dedicated to buses and taxis. Thus, an ample proportion of the right-of-way is given over to public transportation. Beyond the travel lanes, on each of the outer sides, is a row of on-street parking and then a twelve-foot sidewalk typical of major streets in Paris. The storefronts along the sidewalks are virtually continuous and define the outer edges of the street space. Offices and apartments overlook the scene from the upper floors.

The *Métro* runs below the boulevard. Within the median, entrances to the subway are instantly identifed by the famous Art Nouveau entrances designed in 1900 by Hector Guimard.[14] The median is slightly raised above the level of the travel lanes—not dramatically, as with the Paseo del Prado in Havana, but just enough to allow pedestrians on the central promenade to sense their command of the street space. Hedges, benches, and plantings define the median, subtly demarcating the space for pedestrians and cyclists without an excessive amount of striping or signage. Cycle tracks within this median travel in each direction, providing a consistent and protected space for cyclists on the boulevard (see Figures 2.60 and 6.5).

Typically, a curb and hedges form the edge of the median; at specific intervals, however, the curb is replaced with two or three steps. As on the recently retrofitted Cours Mirabeau in Aix-en-Provence, the stepped edge naturally slows the flow of auto traffic. The detail changes the psychology of the space: the steps give a visual impression that pedestrians would and should feel welcome to step out into the travel lane or cross to the center median at many points along the block, and they reinforce the feeling that the buses and cars are moving through pedestrian-dominated space, not vice versa (Figures 2.61 and 2.62). Crossing the street as a pedestrian is not difficult—in fact, all modes of traffic seem to operate with ease.

Figure 2.59: Boulevard de Rochechouart, Paris, France. Service des Promenades et Plantations, 1864. The famed *Métro* entrances (H. Guimard, 1900) are within the median, as seen here at the Anvers station.

Figure 2.60: Boulevard de Rochechouart, Paris, France. Service des Promenades et Plantations, 1864. The cycle track is slightly elevated above the roadway and is framed by rows of bushes and shade trees.

Figure 2.61: Boulevard de Rochechouart, Paris, France. Service des Promenades et Plantations, 1864. View of the broad, planted promenade.

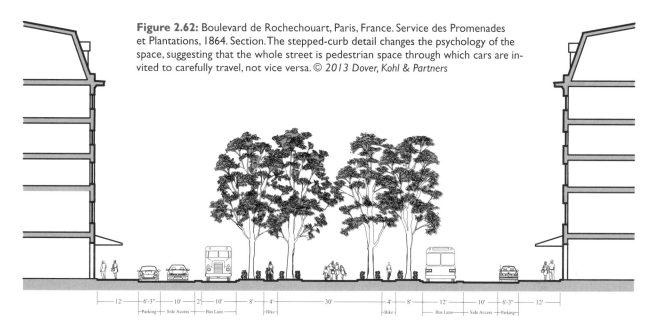

Figure 2.62: Boulevard de Rochechouart, Paris, France. Service des Promenades et Plantations, 1864. Section. The stepped-curb detail changes the psychology of the space, suggesting that the whole street is pedestrian space through which cars are invited to carefully travel, not vice versa. © 2013 Dover, Kohl & Partners

One block south of the Anvers *Métro* station, the avenue Trudaine parallels the boulevard de Rochechouart. Only four blocks long, the quiet street has a narrow median in the center, and trees planted in both sidewalks. In between the two avenues is the green place d'Anvers, which is attached to the block on the western side, with a narrow road on its eastern side. The place and the avenues create a set of green gathering spaces, making prestigious addresses along their edges for local institutions.

The boulevard de Rochechouart extends seamlessly at each end to connect with the boulevard de Clichy in the west and the boulevard de la Chapelle in the east. Together these form a major east–west route across the city, yet Rochechouart is not bloated with motoring lanes. This multimodal balance offers a lesson for many other cities.

Commonwealth Avenue, in Boston and Newton, Massachusetts

Arthur D. Gilman, 1856

Boulevard

Commonwealth Avenue is a formal boulevard that adjusts to the surrounding fabric of the city as it travels through different neighborhoods. The most pleasing section of "Comm Ave" today begins at Boston Common and then crosses through the flatlands of Back Bay, where the city filled in a bay between 1857 and 1882 to create a new neighborhood (Figure 2.63). That part of the boulevard is straight and unusually wide. Sitting in the rectilinear nineteenth-century grid, it brings variety to the street plan with a promenade down the middle. Called the Commonwealth Avenue Mall, the promenade is approximately one hundred feet wide, with two parallel rows of trees on each side of a central walk (Figure 2.64). The trees sit in wide lawns, and the walk is periodically interrupted by monuments along the central axis. Most of the time, Commonwealth Avenue has less traffic than the surrounding streets, and a walk down the center can be peaceful and relaxing.

Figure 2.63: Commonwealth Avenue, Boston, Massachusetts. Arthur D. Gilman, 1856. Satellite view. *Image courtesy of Google Earth*

Figure 2.64: Commonwealth Avenue, Boston, Massachusetts. Arthur D. Gilman, 1856. Wide-angle view showing the promenade flanked by rows of trees. *Image courtesy of Christopher Podstawski*

The Mall falls apart when half the lanes dive under Massachusetts Avenue and the other half join the perpendicular avenue at grade. After another multilevel crossing at Kenmore Street, the greenway drops off altogether, and the center of Commonwealth is taken over by streetcars. This section is the spine of Boston University, but the trolleys and cars dominate the street, and the heavy hand of an engineer is evident. Comm Ave then runs for approximately a mile and a half before turning up the hill and becoming a wide, twisting road that goes up hill and down through the town of Newton. Like the flat, straight portion of the boulevard at Boston University, this section has suffered at the hands of car-focused transportation officials over the years.

Ill-considered improvements for the benefit of the car on and around Commonwealth Avenue not only damaged the boulevard but also the city as a whole. Originally Commonwealth Avenue was part of Frederick Law Olmsted's Emerald Necklace, a seven-mile-long greenway that ran from the Common and through the Fens to Brookline.[15] That connection was severed at Charlesgate by the construction of the Massachusetts Turnpike, and to a lesser degree by entry and exit ramps for Storrow Drive. The Turnpike and Storrow Drive also cut the Emerald Necklace's meeting with the Charles River Esplanade.

MAIN STREETS

Main Streets are both a street type and a metaphor. They have played prominent roles in Hollywood movies like *It's A Wonderful Life,* where they symbolize the All-American Main Street we all have in our mind's eye. Physically, they have shops on both sides of the street with offices or apartments above them. The buildings might be two or three stories tall and only go for a block or two, or they might be eight to twelve stories high and be part of a large downtown. Wall Street versus Main Street is a current political trope to describe the interests of the super-rich and global capitalism versus Middle America, but until

auto-based planning and development killed our downtowns, every city of a certain size had what was known as the Main-Main Corner, where the two most important streets intersected and where the most profitable stores, like the local department store, wanted to be.

Main Street is usually a spine, or what Douglas Duany calls the armature, of the town or city plan (Figures 2.65, 2.66, 2.67, 2.68, and 2.69). They aren't all the same. In our smaller towns and cities, a single street in a downtown neighborhood typically functions as *the* main street, like the ones we write about in the Massachusetts towns of Nantucket and Great Barrington. Main streets are the mixed-use heart of town, and lo-

Figure 2.65: King Street, Alexandria, Virginia. A classic American main street: the mixed-use heart of its community.

Figure 2.66: High Street, Chelmsford, Essex, England. Note the cyclists—originators of the "good roads" movement—in this historic photograph.

Figure 2.67: Main Street, Rhinebeck, New York. A classic downtown in the Hudson River Valley, with small storefronts in two- and three-story brick and granite buildings.

cals living nearby meet many daily needs there. In the largest and most complex cities, on the other hand, certain main streets take on a regional role; for instance, Manhattan has continuous retail along its avenues yet rarely a location one can identify as *the* neighborhood center. London has many neighborhood High Streets (the British equivalent of Main Street), but in the center of London, certain regional shopping streets like Oxford Street or regional entertainment streets like Shaftesbury Avenue take on the dominant role.

While main streets vary, one thing is constant: a successful main street in a sustainable, walkable town or city is a place where people want to get out of their cars and explore. There are many factors that contribute to that, including things to do (like shopping or going to a concert), interesting sights to look at (including people—we like to people-watch), and a level of physical and psychic comfort. As we walk along, we like to feel safe and secure. Beauty is also important to making a place where we want to be.

Figure 2.68: Main Street, Georgetown, Colorado. At two stories, the mining town's main street was modest in scale but designed with human delight in mind: deep corbelled cornices, high ceilings, and storefronts face the space.

Figure 2.69: Main Street, Springfield, Massachusetts. A view from around 1905 of a small New England city rich with manufacturing and rich with architectural detail. *Library of Congress, Prints and Photographs Division, Detroit Publishing Company Photograph Collection, LC-D4-18049*

MAIN STREET

Onstreet Parking

Street-oriented Mixed-use Buildings

Awnings, Marquees, Arcades, or Galleries

Wide Sidewalks

Narrowest Possible Traffic Lanes

Small Corner Radii

Crosswalk

Figure 2.70: Illustration of a typical Main Street. © 2013 *Dover, Kohl & Partners*

Anatomy of a Main Street Building

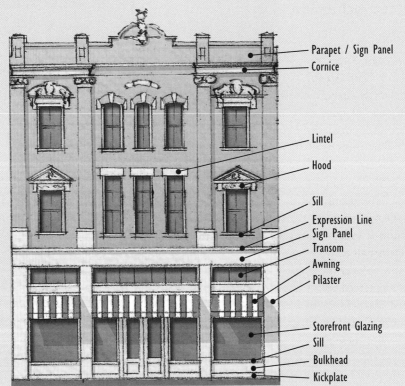

Parapet / Sign Panel

Cornice

Lintel

Hood

Sill

Expression Line

Sign Panel

Transom

Awning

Pilaster

Storefront Glazing

Sill

Bulkhead

Kickplate

Figure 2.71: Anatomy of a Main Street Building.

Main Street, Nantucket, Massachusetts

Main Street

Nantucket's Main Street looks like the archetypal coastal New England Main Street. It has a well-proportioned public realm with a canopy of mature trees and a strong street wall made of quintessential New England storefronts in quintessential New England buildings (Figure 2.72). It has good materials: a cobblestone roadbed bordered by brick and bluestone sidewalks with granite curbs. In the middle of the street is a green metal fountain that could only be historic, because the Massachusetts Department of Transportation (massDOT) wouldn't allow it today—and yet people love the fountain, and against all conventional DOT wisdom manage to avoid running over it.

Every commercial building on the street is more than one hundred years old. Nantucket, an island thirty miles off the coast of Cape Cod, was once the whaling capital of the world, but these durable and well-loved buildings

Figure 2.72: Main Street, Nantucket, Massachusetts. Looking west from Union Street. A view of Lower Main Street around 1920, before Dutch elm disease had arrived in America. Upper Main Street, the residential section of the street, still has many of its old American elm trees. This glorious streetscape can still be created today. *Image courtesy of the Nantucket Historical Association*

were mainly built after both the whaling trade and the island's economy went into a severe decline. From before 1900 to the present, in fact, tourism has been the main economic driver on this small island. Today Nantucket is one of the favorite places for the rich and the super-rich to buy vacation homes, with the result that Nantucket has the highest average house price of all American counties, by a significant margin. The effect of all that on the form and uses of Main Street is a story of many parts, but it's a story worth telling—one that touches on main street retailing, street design, historic preservation, placemaking, its place in development today, and the effect of supply and demand on real estate prices.

Lower Main Street

Main Street is the spine of a small downtown that is the commercial and residential center of the island. The commercial section of the street is called Lower Main Street (Figure 2.73). It's a three-block wide stretch that begins near the harbor at South Water Street and runs uphill to Center Street. Because Nantucket is an island, the downtown is the heart of the community in a way that few American places are today. No one can drive to the next town for shopping or a movie, so the islanders and the summer residents value what they have. There is some modern retail outside the town, but the citizenry has limited its expansion: in 2006, the town not only restricted all future commercial development to areas on the island that already had it but also cut back the areas zoned for commercial uses in 1972.

Nantucket's love for its Main Street, and its debate about what that Main Street should be, goes back to the nineteenth century. After losing 50 percent of its population between 1850 and 1870, the townspeople resolved to make Nantucket one of the most popular resorts in America. They succeeded well enough that when the town fathers wanted to pave over the cobblestones on Main Street in 1919, organized resistance from the summer residents stopped them. In 1937, a summer resident named Everett U. Crosby wrote a book called *"95% Perfect": The Older Residences at Nantucket* that documented Main Street buildings, Nantucket houses, and their architectural details; Crosby's book led, in turn, to an informal consensus in the island's development community about how to build on Nantucket.[16] A second study by Crosby two years later suggested restricting the modernizing of the business district. Passage by the town of Historic District Legislation in 1955 is sometimes credited to Crosby's efforts.

In the late 1950s, S&H Green Stamp heir Walter Beinecke Jr., another summer resident, saw the potential of Nantucket's rundown waterfront at the foot of Main Street and started investing in it, buying waterfront properties, fixing them up, and filling in the holes with tradition*ish* Nantucket buildings. Before long, he owned a lot of the downtown, and he formed the Sherburne Trust for his holdings. Because of the size of his investment, he became king of all he surveyed, with a strong influence over Nantucket's planning.

Beinecke was famous for an elitist yet profitable view that favored those with money to spend over those with less money. "Instead of selling six postcards and two hot dogs," he told *Time*, "you have to sell a hotel room and a couple of sports coats." In the end, Beinecke sold tourists t-shirts and trinkets too, which wasn't always popular with the locals.

"Not everyone saw eye to eye with Mr. Beinecke's plan at first," *Time* reported in 1968, after Beinecke had built a new grocery store and a marina. Buttons circulated on Nantucket that said, "No man is an island" and "Ban the B" because of the amount of power he held over the town. As he hoped, however, his efforts raised the value of his buildings, many of which he had bought for as little as $30,000. In 1987, he sold the entire portfolio to a Boston Real Estate Investment Trust for $55 million.

Since 1990, the United States has seen an enormous increase in the wealth of the super-rich in the country. One result is that many of our most beautiful places like Nantucket, Aspen, Santa Fe, and Charleston have been bought up at prices that only a few can afford. Aspen was just one place that had to institute affordable housing programs that included residents with $150,000 in income, because skyrocketing real estate prices had led not only to a local shortage of low-income workers but doctors and lawyers, as well. Nantucket had a problem attracting veterinarians, among other professions. From the point of view of development and placemaking, unbalanced markets like these tell us, among other things, that there is a shortage of great places like Nantucket and Santa Fe.

The Success of Lower Main Street

Many great individual buildings were built around the world in the last half-century, but few if any new streets built during the period rival Nantucket's organically produced Main Street. That is because in most other places architects, builders, developers, and planners emphasized auto-centric development, isolated buildings and a separation of uses, "unprecedented invention," and an "architecture of our time," viewing traditional architecture as kitsch. But making great streets is about making places people want to be, not about ideological architectural expression. Current theories that limit architecture to the "autonomous" self-referential creation of buildings that don't play well with others can harm old streets and prevent the construction of good new streets. Contemporary development patterns and formulas that produce throwaway architecture and unwalkable suburban Power Centers are bad placemaking. This architecture of time and invention does not add up to good streets. That requires an architecture of *place*.

The successful construction of a place like Nantucket's Lower Main begins with the making of the street. The buildings lining Lower Main Street reinforce one's sense of the street itself—the space between the buildings—by making a solid streetwall. None of the buildings are individual masterpieces, but they all have the urban virtues of traditional materials, composition, rhythms, and beauty (Figure 2.74). "Traditional composition" means that they have distinct bottoms, middles, and tops; that their design involves the use of principles like centering, symmetry, the appearance of obeying the laws of gravity (their walls have substance, with light and shadow, vertical openings, and openings spanned by lintels); and that they have architectural scale and ornament that relates to human scale, human culture, and even the human body. "Traditional composition" does *not* mean that they are in any particular style, or that they cannot appear modern.

These traditional architectural motifs are urban virtues that contribute to the making of a place where people want to gather (Figure 2.75). Lower Main Street is a comfortable place to be and even to park, lined with interesting things to look at. It sits on a slope, which tilts the square up in a way that puts it on display for those coming up from the harbor. This highlights the beauty of the cobblestones, which also slow traffic. So does the horse fountain in the middle of the street as you enter the square (Figures 2.73 and 2.74).

Figure 2.73: Main Street, Nantucket, Massachusetts. Looking west on Lower Main Street in December 2010. In the center of the street, bothering no one and pleasing many, sits a horse fountain commemorating the only Nantucket resident to die in the Spanish-American War. In 2013, the Nantucket Preservation Trust honored the Nantucket Garden Club for maintaining and beautifying the fountain with flowers and wreaths. See Figure 2.79 for a view of another Fixed Hazardous Object on Main Street.

Figure 2.74: Main Street, Nantucket, Massachusetts. Commercial buildings on the north side of Main Street between Union Street and Coal Alley, with the horse fountain in the foreground.

Figure 2.75 Main Street, Nantucket, Massachusetts. Looking west on Upper Main Street from the corner of Federal Street. Many of the expensive stores cater to tourists, but residents look for reasons to come to Main Street.

The end result is one of the most beautiful places in America. The space, the streetwall, the trees, the quality of the materials, and the island light all contribute. So do the consistently Classical proportions of the quiet background buildings, which sing to us in harmony. The best building visible from the square is the Methodist Church's Greek temple on Centre Street, which angles towards Main Street, but which urban designers might put in place of the residential-looking Pacific Bank at the head of the square.

At night, the storefronts light the sidewalks and create a warm glow behind the trees. The pity is that so few of the stores still provide the daily necessities of life. Studies in Copenhagen by Jan Gehl show that buildings with active storefronts have more people in front of them than immediately adjacent buildings with blank walls, even though many of the people in front of the shop ignore the store and just hang out there. We are social beings, and we need other people to socialize. When Main Street was a normal town center, people would go there every day to buy what they needed and socialize with their neighbors.

Today, most of the stores are oriented towards tourists, but islanders still visit Main Street without a hardware store or a barbershop to draw them. Main Street remains the social center, even in a modern, expensive Nantucket that caters to tourists.

Nantucket caters to tourists well. Lower Main Street is the same width as the contemporary "Market Square Center" model that the urban retail consultant Robert J. Gibbs calls one of the best layouts for retail development. The author of the book *Principles of Urban Retail Planning and Development,* Gibbs recommends a maximum width of 85 feet and an optimum length to width ratio of 2.5 to 1, or approximately 212 feet by 85 feet.[17] Lower Main, once called Market Square, is 85 feet wide but 495 feet long. However, the beauty of the space combines with the interesting storefronts to draw the pedestrian in. Retail studies show that Americans do a lot of their shopping while on vacation, even though other studies show that shopping is a stressful activity. Gibbs advises his retail clients that one of the best antidotes to this stress is a beautiful shopping street.

Moreover, the tilt of the street showcases the beautiful space, making it seem inviting rather than long. From the bottom you can survey the square easily, while from the top you see the harbor and, during the winter, the surrounding church steeples. The street is wide enough to provide a sense of place, as a square does, but narrow enough for pedestrians on one side of the street to see the stores on the other side. It has enough space for easy, head-in parking convenient to the stores, and even accommodates without problem the large SUVs that dominate Nantucket today. When the drivers of the parked cars back out, other drivers watch out and slow down.

Gibbs advocates the use of street trees, citing studies that show trees like those on Nantucket have an economic value for merchants because they create a calming sense of place and, like the solid brick buildings on Lower Main, give a feeling of quality. (Also see *The Seven Roles of the Urban Street Tree* in Chapter 1.) Cars park in the shade under the trees, and their visual presence on the street is softened. A photograph of Lower Main Street from the 1920s shows a magnificent allée of elm trees that arc over the street in a full canopy (Figure 2.72). They majestically roof the space, but at the same time their limbs rise above the storefronts, showing off the stores and the buildings. Some of the elms survive, mixed with sweet gums and oaks. The sweet gums and oaks are beautiful, but they will never form a canopy quite like the old one (Figure 2.73). See the discussion of Great Barrington's Main Street in Chapter 4 for a description of why it would be better to slowly phase in modern elm hybrids or American sycamores.

The buildings facing the square also work well with principles of urban retail. One of the most important of these principles is that at least 60 percent of a store's street frontage should be glass. It's important to show potential shoppers what the store is selling, because of what retailers call the Eight Second Rule: the storeowner typically has only eight seconds to interest the passerby enough so that he or she will walk in, which doesn't allow much time for distractions.

Gibbs tells us that the division of the traditional facade helps focus the walker's attention on the lower part of the building, aided by the sign band between the storefront and the upper facade that most traditional buildings have. Merchants want pedestrians to look at their storefronts rather than at fancy new sidewalks or exciting, "unprecedented" architecture.

In other parts of the book, we are critical of the formulaic application of brick sidewalks with granite curbs in the standard Main Street renovation. Gibbs's comment emphasizes one of the reasons why: streets should have a simple harmony that emphasizes the street as a whole. "'Streetscape' is a dirty word," says the nonprofit Project for Public Spaces. What they mean is that formulaic streetscape designs—fancy benches, new street lights, and colored pavements—draw attention away from the experience of the street itself, encouraging us to focus instead on its individual parts. But Nantucket's brick and stone buildings harmonize with Nantucket's brick and stone sidewalks. The red bricks of the sidewalk are muted versions of the red bricks in the buildings, and there are no multicolor bikeways, bus ways, or pedestrian crossings.

These retail rules are not a matter of personal taste. They come from the experience and experimentation of national retailers—first in shopping malls and later on city streets. The retailers can tell you precisely how changing the variables can affect sales price. They know that if one of their stores has a particular light bulb with a cold light, sales per square foot will go up X percent if they change to a particular warm light bulb, and they know that an empty lot next to their building on Main Street will cost them Y percent in sales per square foot. The *Secrets of Successful Retail* break-out box in this chapter has a short list of some of the main rules for urban retail.

Beinecke's Sherburne Trust owned approximately half the commercial buildings on Main Street. Between Main Street and the water are several blocks of shingle-covered shacks, many of which Beinecke built. They were probably intended to be modest, like fisherman's shacks. They all have minimal trim and minimal trim details, no evident composition, and are all painted gray. Despite what Beinecke said about his target audience, they look cheap and attract stores that sell inexpensive items like t-shirts.

With the exception of an attractive movie theater and a supermarket with a well-landscaped parking lot that Beinecke built for the locals to use, the stores in these shacks mainly appeal to the tourist.

Chain stores, also popular with tourists, are another matter, however. There will be no Starbucks café on Nantucket's Main Street, for example, despite the fact that the company's name was taken from the first mate on the Pequod in *Moby Dick*, who was inspired by a Nantucket whaler of the same name. In 2006, Nantucket passed a bylaw that limits stores and restaurants in downtown to companies with fewer than fourteen outlets and fewer than three standard features among items like trademarks, menus, and employee uniforms.

Residential Main Street

At the top of the square, the Pacific National Bank, built in 1818, sits on axis, visually terminating Lower Main Street. But instead of stopping, Main Street narrows there and passes to one side of the bank building, continuing up and then down the hill, and becoming one of the most beautiful residential streets in America. Many of the houses were built by Quakers and are in a modest New England Classical Vernacular (Figure 2.76). The highest points on the street have many of the grandest houses, built by whaling captains and merchants. That includes the famous Three Bricks, three superb Greek Revival houses built in 1837 by the Quaker whaling merchant Joseph Starbuck (Figure 2.77). By today's McMansion standards, these large and grand houses are modest. They don't go for the architectural composition that New Urbanist Andrés Duany calls "the House of Twenty-Seven Gables," which evokes "an entire village in a house." Instead, all the houses have simple, box-like massing and consistent Classical Vernacular details and proportions. By the standards of modern suburbia, the houses also have small setbacks and narrow side yards. Many of the houses come right to the sidewalk, so there is no room for a fence or wall along the street. But a number of the houses are set back three to five feet and have white wooden fences, while the Three Bricks have black wrought-iron fences.

The elements of upper Main Street are simple, similar to those on Lower Main: a cobblestone roadway; brick sidewalks with granite curbs; simple Classical or Classical Vernacular buildings close to the street; and a regular rhythm of majestic, mature trees (many of them American elms) that form a canopy over most of the street. Built before the time of earth-moving equipment, the road follows the path of least resistance along the contours of the island, sometimes curving with the contours of the hill and changing directions slightly every time the grade of the hill changes. At the top of the hill above the square, Main Street angles towards the south. The street then goes downhill and turns again at the lowest point, where a street crosses. The Three Bricks and two large Greek Revival houses stand at a leveling off where another road comes in and the street angles slightly once again (Figure 2.78).

> Built before the time of earth-moving equipment, the road follows the path of least resistance along the contours of the island, sometimes curving with the contours of the hill and changing directions slightly every time the grade of the hill changes.

The highest point on Main Street has an intersection where Main, Milk, and Gardiner streets cross. Here there is a beloved object in the middle of the road, a Civil War memorial with a small but heavy granite obelisk (Figure 2.79). Very effective for traffic calming, it is but one of many similar monuments and fountains in the middle of New England streets. Any town that built one today would risk being sued, though, and if they *were* sued, engineers and lawyers would testify against the town. Sometimes it seems as though it would be better to take away the licenses of drivers who are incapable of avoiding the monument but, as we shall see in the book's Conclusion (and Figure 6.13), slowing the cars down makes it easy for drivers to avoid hitting things.

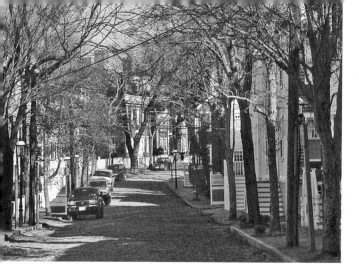

▲ **Figure 2.76:** Main Street, Nantucket, Massachusetts. Looking west on Upper Main Street. The beautiful cobblestone roadway follows the contours of the land.

▲ **Figure 2.77:** Main Street, Nantucket, Massachusetts. Looking east, back towards Lower Main. The Three Bricks are on the left. The cobblestone street follows the gentle contours of the island.

▲ **Figure 2.78:** Main Street, Nantucket, Massachusetts. A pair of Greek Revival mansions sits across the street from the Three Bricks.

▶ **Figure 2.79:** Civil War Monument, Main Street, Nantucket, Massachusetts. Looking east on Main Street from the intersection with Milk Street. Erected in 1875, the obelisk commemorates the 69 islanders who died in the Civil War. Most Departments of Transportation would call the heavy granite memorial a Fixed Hazardous Object, but the rough cobblestone street makes drivers go slowly enough that they avoid hitting it without the need for reflectors and colored striping. The residents of Nantucket love their beautiful streets and work to keep what they have. The result is a great public realm and one of America's most beautiful streets, rather than a place for vehicular throughput.

The Future of Main Street

Nantucket and its downtown are beloved places, and people want them to remain that way. Those who live in Nantucket have chosen either to stay there (often a difficult choice, in light of local incomes and expenses) or to move there, despite the inherent problems. Those who summer in Nantucket have intentionally chosen a beautiful New England island, and they want to preserve its character. As we've seen, resorts are where Americans do much of their shopping these days, and national retailers make more money than local shops, so in most locations the chains can drive out the locals. In Nantucket, year-round and summer residents want to keep a sense of where they are and not lose it to Starbucks, The Gap, Lady Gap, Baby Gap, and Junior Gap.

In 1972, Nantucket worked to continue the preservation of the buildings that had begun with *"95% Perfect,"* the creation of the Historic District, and more controversially, Beinecke's Sherburne Trust, by bringing out *Building with Nantucket in Mind: Guidelines for Protecting the Historic Architecture and Landscape of Nantucket Island.*[18] A set of guidelines for renovation and new construction written by J. Christopher Lang and Kate Stout Lang, it did not address retail issues but, like the architectural pattern books recommended by Gibbs, it supported the creation of a place where retailers wanted to be.

The book was expanded in the 1990s, and in 2003 the town created a special downtown commercial zoning district tailored to existing character, with smaller lots and setbacks than in the previous zoning. That was followed in 2009 by the adoption of a new master plan that expanded the area covered by the downtown commercial district and described implementation plans for the development of key downtown sites. The result was an amalgamation of the pattern books and the form-based codes that Gibbs recommends. A single form-based code that combined all the regulations and guidelines in one document would be even stronger. An advantage of a good form-based code over a pattern book is that much of the judgment involved in interpreting pattern book guidelines becomes simple enforcement of the clear rules in a good form-based code.

An important point in coding Main Streets is that while uses come and go, if we build and code well, our much loved places can keep their physical character over time. Nantucket has been rich and poor and rich again, but the buildings on Main Street are the same buildings that were there 100 years ago, and that is something the community values. Nantucket may have been built when it was the whaling capital of the world, but it has been a resort for almost 150 years. There are now 10,000 residents on the island in the winter and 50,000 people in the summer, and the majority of them want to keep Main Street a real street where they can live their daily life, whether they are there to work or vacation. A problem, of course, is that Nantucket's great success as a resort has threatened the economics of Main Street and full-time residence.

The newest chapter in the story of Nantucket's Main Street is that another summer resident, Wendy Schmidt, has stepped into the ongoing effort, and with the help of Google money has formed ReMain Nantucket. Focused on Main Street and the downtown, it uses both philanthropic funds and private investment to keep the old buildings and local uses of Main Street thriving. ReMain Nantucket has bought buildings, saved a local bookstore, and founded a new downtown bakery. It has an emphasis on adapting buildings to deal with problems of climate change and peak oil, and supporting businesses that keep the downtown strong and lively.

The American Planning Association named Main Street one of the Top Ten Great Streets of 2011. We can't disagree with that, but we can point out that if we made more great places, Nantucket wouldn't be so expensive. From the time in 1919 when the summer residents of Nantucket preserved the cobblestones on Main Street until now, the population of the United States has grown from 104 million to 314 million, more than tripling in size. By some estimates, more than 90 percent of the buildings in America have been built during that period. But a billionaire is willing to pay $20 million for a 150-year-old house on Main Street because of the rarity of the house, the street, and the network of streets that make the downtown.

SECRETS OF SUCCESSFUL RETAIL

Retail design expert Robert Gibbs knows how to help traditional Main Streets compete with shopping malls and strip shopping centers (Figure 2.75). Some of Gibbs's advice is about management, like promoting common hours of operation. However, much of Gibbs's advice is about design. Here are some of the highlights regarding streetscapes and street design, all based on studies that show these produce greater sales per square foot.[19]

- Storefront design
  - Retailers want predictability and quality on the street. A form-based code or pattern book can give that.
  - Storefronts should appear open; at least 60 percent of the storefront should be glass.
  - In a mixed-use building, the ground floor should be distinguished from the rest of the building facade.
  - A top-to-bottom curtain wall in a tall building causes the upper levels to dominate the building's appearance and minimize the curb appeal of ground-floor retail.

- Signs
  - Sign bands above the storefronts are essential to hold the pedestrian's view.
  - Sign bands make it easier to change storefronts over time.
  - Nothing contributes to strong retail sales and an attractive downtown as much as well-designed and properly scaled signs.
  - A single background color on all signs is bad, because it eliminates the sense of unique stores and goods.
  - Rule of thumb for size: One square foot of sign for each linear foot of street frontage.
  - Maximum letter height should be eight to ten inches.
  - Lighting should be external only. Backlighting solid letters or signs should be allowed, but not internal illumination.
  - Some regions have their own sign patterns: New Englanders like painted wooden signs with gold-leaf lettering, but these may be inappropriate elsewhere.
  - The base of the sign must be at least eight feet above the sidewalk and should extend no more than three feet over the sidewalk.
  - There should be at least fifteen feet of separation between signs for different stores.
  - Some businesses, such as cinemas, require bigger signs.

- Awnings
  - Awnings define the storefront and the brand.
  - Awnings should be made of canvas, cloth, metal, or glass.
  - Cloth in an awning should be or look like natural fabric and be limited to two colors (no plastic).
  - Awnings should not have internal illumination.
  - Logos and letters should be limited to eight inches tall and should only be on the front flap, not on the slope of the awning.
  - Shed-type awnings without side panels appear lighter, which is generally beneficial.
  - Awnings should complement the building facade.
  - Awnings should not hide architectural elements.
  - Awnings should have no more than a 25-degree pitch.
  - When every storefront has an awning, the effect is dreary or monotonous.

- Sidewalks
  - Sidewalks provide the first and last impression the shopper sees.

- Sidewalks should be designed with materials and on a scale that harmonize with their location.
- Sidewalks should be wide enough to allow shoppers to pass each other.
- Major urban centers like Michigan Avenue in Chicago call for sidewalk widths of twenty to twenty-five feet.
- Small hamlets or villages need sidewalks at least five to eight feet wide.
- In hot climates, shady sidewalks or the shaded side of the street are the most popular; in cold climates, sunny sidewalks are sought.

- Street Furniture
  - Trendy, "cutting-edge" furnishings will go out of date; buy medium-cost items that will wear well until they are replaced every five to seven years.
  - Planters or merchandise along the sidewalk at the street's edge can distract shoppers away from the stores.
- Lighting
  - Illuminate sidewalks with light from the store windows until 11p.m.; supplement with streetlights where necessary.
  - Use color-corrected light sources for warmth.

In this book, we show how simple it is to make streets where people want to be, if one has the will and the permission. In New Urbanism, we work on making both the streets and the networks. If we judge success by market demand, then New Urbanism has had many successes.

> The challenge for America is to build again in our neighborhoods, towns, and cities in a way that produces great places we all can afford. Then we can concentrate less on preservation and more on making the future better.

New Urban developments always sell for higher prices than neighboring developments, because they are selling something that the market in most cases has not supplied. The average house price in the New Urban resorts on the Florida panhandle is almost as high as the average house price on Nantucket. That's not because the resorts are elitist, as is sometimes said, but because they sell beautiful communities where people want to be, much like Nantucket, Aspen, Charleston, and Santa Fe. The challenge for America is to build again in our neighborhoods, towns, and cities in a way that produces great places we all can afford. Then we can concentrate less on preservation and more on making the future better.

Main Street, Galena, Illinois

Main Street

Galena, Illinois, presents a classic American type. Located in the rolling landscape of the Mississippi River Valley, Galena has brick-clad buildings along its Main Street, with quaint storefronts on the ground floor and offices and apartments on the two or three stories above. The town's topography defines its streets—some with very steep slopes and winding corners—making it an interesting place to walk, bike, or drive. Visibly the densest development in the city, Main Street is clearly *the* center of Galena, and the heart of local economic and social life (Figures 1.32, 2.80, 2.81, and 2.82).

Galena's character is a result of a glacial shift that occurred in the last ice age that flattened most of the surrounding land but missed the hills and valleys that define the city itself. By the early 1800s the land was known to be rich in lead, and the community that grew up there quickly became an active part of the Upper Mississippi Lead Mine District. Named Galena after the technical term for the sulfide of lead, the settlement became a town in 1826 and was chartered as a city in 1841.[20] Until the middle of the nineteenth century, the buildings on Main Street were constructed of wood. After several fires in the 1850s, most of the buildings were rebuilt out of brick or stone—which comprise most of the main street fabric today.

Figure 2.80: Main Street, Galena, Illinois. The relatively flat street is aligned with a natural "bench" in the topography; behind it, the town rises on a steep slope.

Figure 2.81: Main Street, Galena, Illinois. The height of the buildings and the width of the street combine in a nearly perfect proportional relationship.

Figure 2.82: Main Street, Galena, Illinois. The little curve or "crank" produces a gently deflected vista, tipping storefronts into view, and making the space feel finite and intimate. Note that the white building is an intentional focal point; the building itself is bent to match the crank, making for upstairs rooms with unique views in both directions from the bay windows.

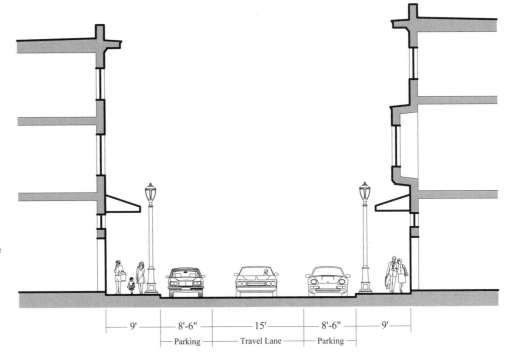

Figure 2.83: Main Street, Galena, Illinois. Section. The design changes substantially segment by segment, like several streets laid end to end. This segment has parallel parking.

9' ⊢ 8'-6" ⊢ 15' ⊢ 8'-6" ⊢ 9'
⊢ Parking ⊢ Travel Lane ⊢ Parking ⊢

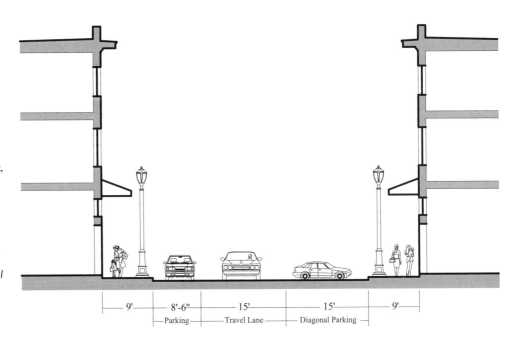

Figure 2.84: Main Street, Galena, Illinois. Section. This segment has diagonal parking. Still other segments have two-way travel, the riverfront floodgates, or other features that differentiate them. © 2013 Dover, Kohl & Partners

9' ⊢ 8'-6" ⊢ 15' ⊢ 15' ⊢ 9'
⊢ Parking ⊢ Travel Lane ⊢ Diagonal Parking ⊢

Figure 2.85: Galena, Illinois. Figure Ground. Main Street (center) curves to match a natural "bench" in the topography, with most of the town behind it (upper left) sloping up away from the riverfront (lower right). © 2013 Dover, Kohl & Partners

Like many of the best streets, Galena's Main Street changes shape and dimensions as it stretches across the town. At one of its narrowest points, the street is approximately fifty feet wide with a one-way travel lane, flanked by a row of parallel parking and nine-foot-wide sidewalks on each side (Figure 2.83). The cross-section changes as the street alignment cranks, maintaining traffic and accommodating diagonal parking spaces (Figure 2.84). The overall width becomes slightly larger at this point, but mostly remains the narrow, historic dimension that it had during the town's industrial boom in the early 1800s.[21] On the original plat for the City of Galena, a fifty-foot-wide curb-to-curb dimension is shown at both the beginning and the end of Main Street (Figure 2.85).

The slight curve or "crank" on Main Street is an excellent urban feature in central Galena. The crank provides a sequence of changing vistas for the user of the space. Although the curve matches the topography, the result of a natural event, the effect is often purposely replicated by urban designers. The deflected vista makes the street feel as though it has an end rather than appearing to extend far into the distance. This vista is also good for business: the storefronts down the street tip into view, showcasing the variety and quality of goods and services. Main Street has an understated color palette established by the brick facades and concrete hardscape.

ORVIETO, ITALY / Douglas Duany

Main Street

The Passeggiata

Every evening in Orvieto, people gather along a long and narrow street—talking, clustering and dispersing, and only slowly moving. They do so as a community, and they do it daily.

All over the world, this quintessential urban behavior occurs spontaneously. It becomes a custom, a ritual, a pleasure. This greeting and gathering helps to unite the community. It's not an abstract notion; it's how a town takes possession of its public space, and how individuals take possession of themselves at the end of the day.

The Corso in Orvieto

The two main streets are the Corso Cavour and the Via del Duomo. The Corso Cavour runs uphill from the Piazza della Repubblica, intersecting with the Via del Duomo at a three-way crossroad that leads from the lower town. The Via del Duomo then leads to the Piazza del Duomo, where one encounters the city's magnificent cathedral. Taken together, these streets and their anchoring end-squares constitute the pedestrian armature of the town's public realm (see Figure 2.99 at the end of this case study). I will call both the Corso, a name redolent of its most important function, which is to serve as the social gathering place of the town in the early evening.

The Piazza della Repubblica is an interesting square with a town hall and an ancient church (Figure 2.86). The best feature of the space is a beautiful Renaissance-era loggia—modest in appearance but one of my favorites—that closes the entrance to the piazza. Its placement is as elegant as its architecture (Figure 2.87).

Figure 2.86: Piazza della Repubblica, Orvieto, Italy. Looking east towards the Piazza della Repubblica, approaching the loggia on axis.

Figure 2.87: Orvieto, Italy. In the Piazza della Repubblica, looking east towards the loggia and the Corso. The tower appears on the Corso.

As one leaves the civic piazza behind to stroll along Corso Cavour, one finds oneself in the heart of the old city's armature, the shops interspersed with restaurants, cafes, craft and food shops, as well as stalwarts like hardware stores.

The Furlong as a Unit of Pedestrian Life

The Corso is a miracle of balance, an ancient market street anchored at the edges by the cathedral, a municipal theater, and the city hall. The distances between them measure about 660 feet, and this is a critical dimension: the furlong. Why a furlong? Because it seems to be a distance that measures excellent short walks, a measure of pedestrian engagement and of retail activity. It's the distance between centers of interest, one that grounds our hyperactive minds and propels our bodies to the next one, irrespective of whether we're engaging in a good country walk in the south of England or rushing between avenues in Manhattan. Shorter than the traditional half-mile diameter that defines a neighborhood, furlongs remind designers of the smaller or overlapping scales of pedestrian life.

> Why a furlong? Because it seems to be a distance that measures excellent short walks, a measure of pedestrian engagement and of retail activity.

Street as Place

When we see a wide street on a map in the center of town, we assume it's important. While that often holds true, the narrowness of the Corso contradicts this. People simply enjoy the closure and intimacy of narrow streets. Across the world, streets that are sixteen to twenty-four feet wide are considered "sweet" for the way they contain space and aid shopping. You can see the goods on both sides very easily. Further

exploration in cities will reveal that this narrowness marks the best market concourse in many cultures, from shambles to bazaars to malls, and this is something to remember.

Both the curves and the range of widths of the Corso add visual closure to the corridor space of the street. The curves and alternating counter-curves (the Classical Cyma) are marked with small building jut-outs that emphasize the shift from one to another. The unfolding vista has a rhythm that reminds us that the experience of streets can pleasantly involve time. People respond by moving more slowly, and time slows down with slowing movement. At end of the day, they meet and form groups to talk, and the enclosed space now becomes a public drawing room.

Organic Geometry

It's unorthodox to say this in America, but parallel curves are actually hard to lay out without modern surveying equipment! Urban planners have reduced geometry to just a few options, and streets are all parallel, all either curved or straight, and all intersections are four-way. How can there be any other way, if we've lost the ability to imagine it?

In organic streets, geometry is open. Straight parts alternate with curves, and you can mix straight and curves, or have different curves on either side. One beauty is to have a straight segment on one side, while still curving on the other! But organic geometry is not simply about variety; it has an objective, a general rule that was once stated as: "open before closing, close before opening." So a series of visual spaces are created and streets become a series of places.

Orvieto's narrow meander is ideal in the way it responds visually to the slow pedestrian movement. One architectural element after another dominates the visual field and then "disappears" as another comes in to hold the visual attention (Figures 2.88, 2.89, and 2.90).

Figure 2.88: Orvieto, Italy. Looking east at the central part of the Corso Cavour, with the orienting central tower.

Figure 2.89: Orvieto, Italy. Looking east. The central tower beginning to disappear as one approaches from the Piazza della Repubblica.

Figure 2.90: Orvieto, Italy. Looking east. Approaching the intersection of the Corso and the Via del Duomo, the tower has disappeared, replaced by the palazzo in the center of the photograph.

We associate the sequencing of visual events with "medieval streets." This is a rubric that covers everything that is not "planned" or "designed." A standard explanation is that this sequencing is the result of organic processes, of functional paths that were improved, and of architecture responding and exploiting the visual space. What is extraordinary in Orvieto is how quickly the visual events follow one another, and how they differ. Good medieval streets best respond to the fourth dimension, which is time. In comparison with other superb examples of streets that unfold events, Orvieto's Corso makes sequences like the Governo Vecchio in Rome or the central armature of Montepulciano seem a bit slow.

The Magic Tower

Old Italian cities were full of towers. They formed a clustered skyline from afar and when one walked the streets, the towers appeared and followed one another sequentially. We know that from the only remaining complete example, the small *citta* of San Gimignano.

In San Gimignano the towers do a perfect dance of appearing and disappearing magically in response to the pedestrian movement in the winding streets. Was this "planned"? We can assume that the medieval aristocracy wished to show them off as centers of power and prestige, but there is a more functional reason that is overlooked. The towers had to be defended, and that required that shooters in the tower could survey the streets as completely as possible, both near and far. The towers sited defensively work well aesthetically and make perfect landmarks. What this means is that in urbanism there are two ways of "seeing" a building: from within the building itself and from the street.

The Corso in Orvieto has that same visual responsiveness to movement as San Gimignano, but it has only one tower marking its central intersection, the Torre del Moro. When you visit Orvieto, this tower is eminently worth tracking as you walk the passeggiata. It will open up the world of dynamic street making, a lesson that you can then apply to the other elements that unfold.

The Torre del Moro is simple and not very high, but it is visually impressive. It is seen in tripartite: in a level approach from the Piazza della Repubblica (Figures 2.88 and 2.89), during the descent from the Piazza del Duomo (Figure 2.96), and in ascent from the lower town. It is stable through much of the ascent from the lower city, pulling people into the passeggiata, then engaging the rooflines of the winding street beautifully before disappearing behind an irregular palazzo, to be replaced immediately by a small campanile (Figures 2.97 and 2.98). From the Via del Duomo, it appears centered on the road at the beginning, and then disappears, only to reappear with a different face and sink slowly, while from the passeggiata in the Corso it descends to the left before disappearing.

The effect is magical. The moment it disappears from the cone of vision, another object—a palazzo or a nearby simple campanile—catches your eye, and then, just as that is passed, the tower reappears, always marking the central intersection.

So what lesson can one learn from medieval towers? Well, there is always the old one suggested by the great historian, architect, and urban designer Camillo Sitte: When you blow the budget on a single building, frame it in as many ways as possible in order to exploit its potential.

Figure 2.91: Orvieto, Italy. Looking south. Going uphill from the central tower towards the Duomo, passing the café in the Largo Luigi Barzini, a piazzeta on the Via del Duomo.

Figure 2.92: Orvieto, Italy. Looking south. At the end of the Largo Luigi Barzini, the facade of the Duomo first appears.

Figure 2.93: Orvieto, Italy. Looking south, near the end of the Via del Duomo. The first bracketing of the Duomo.

But there is also a second, more practical lesson for this secular age. A city of high-rises looks great from the interstate, but in the city their tops can disappear, leaving us with a less impressive base along the street. Not bad, you say, but no longer the magical city one saw from the distance.

In an era of austere budgets, one can learn how to place buildings so that they are worth observing from every angle, in interaction with the surrounding fabric. In plan, one places a halo at some distance from the tower and then one deflects segments of streets towards the tower within the "donut." Steeples, with churches at their base, are perfect for this, which is why good urban designers have a motto, "If churches

didn't exist, we would have to invent them." Very subtle deflections in the streets suffice.

Why not place towers simply, at the end of an axis? Again, not bad—especially over a short distance if the tower has an engaging base. But a perceptually stable object over a long distance gets boring quickly and the mind wanders to the next thing.

Why not make the "next thing" another piece of a beautiful world, instead of another (usually repetitive) thought? We need interesting urbanism to ground us when we shut down our computers and walk outside, and in an increasingly abstract age we need a way back to the concrete. Interesting urbanism turns our walk into a passeggiata, our surroundings into a promenade.

Figure 2.94: Orvieto, Italy. Looking north from the Piazza del Duomo, back to the beginning of the Via del Duomo.

Figure 2.95: Orvieto, Italy. Returning to the Largo Luigi Barzini, walking north. In Orvieto, small trucks navigate the streets in the morning.

Figure 2.96: Orvieto, Italy. Walking north after passing the Largo, the central tower reappears on the Via del Duomo.

Figure 2.97: Orvieto, Italy. Looking west. The tower particularly dominates the uphill approach from the lower town and is beautifully framed by the serpentine street.

Figure 2.98: Orvieto, Italy. Looking west. When the tower disappears, it is immediately replaced visually by a small campanile.

The Visual Angles of Hans Maertens

It's worth decoding the underlying mechanism of this magical dynamic effect. The key is the natural cone of vision of the human eye, the cone that changes what we see when we turn our head or, when we are moving, replaces one thing with another. The urban effects of the cone of vision were worked out by a German, Hans Maertens, but his theory doesn't have to be read or explained. One learns it simply by approaching a good building and noting how our perception of it changes with our distance from it.

Note that, as you get closer, everything becomes more finely textured: instead of seeing the outline, for example, you can read the composition of a building, how its elements hold together. As you get even closer, an impressive building becomes even more

impressive, until from close up (45 degrees from your eye to the top) the cornice and the edges of the building lose importance. But close up the whole doesn't hold together; the elements take precedence, and if you're standing next to the base, it is the door that you see.

This is all a function of the cone of vision. The active cone of vision is less than 33 degrees, and this explains why buildings appear and disappear in the Corso even before you pass them, as another building, an element, or a café, engages your attention.

The cone of vision is universal, a key tool in design, the one that makes the relation between building and space intimate. Imagine designing a square: you cannot simply take a bird's eye view. Instead, you must imagine the perspective of the eye from both the square's edges and from its center; the long view and crosswise. It is the cone of vision that reveals how we will experience the closure of the space.

A Great Masterpiece

The approach to the cathedral is the climax of the visual effects of the Corso. The Duomo is itself a masterpiece—reason enough by itself to go to Orvieto—its many-hued facade a brilliant stage set. Approached from the end of the passeggiata along the Via del Duomo, this facade and its two towers are bracketed and rebracketed in an astonishing manner by the street (Figure 2.93). The street frames and reframes different parts of it in a short distance, each a perfect picture before it shifts again.

The square of the Duomo is at a high point on the edge of the great plateau of Orvieto. Some of the edges of the square are low. After the narrow enclosure of the street, the piazza releases us into the sky and open space.

It is still part of the passeggiata. Baby carriages, grandfathers, mothers, conversations. And, on the other side of the Duomo, teenagers. But the cathedral is also a meaningful counterpoint to the market and the society of the Corso. It calls us into a larger order than society: nature, art, religion, and this, the nonmarket. That which is not every day or mundane is a meaningful component of life in every *citta*—or of every town or village that is balanced, that meets the needs of human habitation.

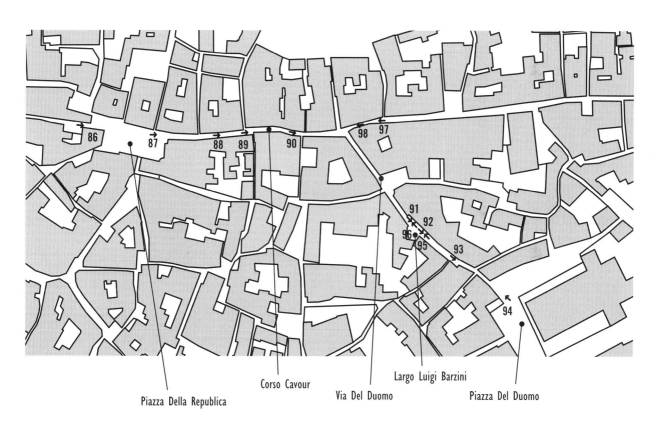

Figure 2.99: Orvieto, Italy. Figure-ground drawing. © 2013 Dover, Kohl & Partners

Quinta Avenida, La Antigua, Guatemala

Main Street

Antigua was established as a splendid Spanish capital for the New World, but devastating earthquakes led to the relocation of the capital in 1776. The result of its near abandonment was that the original Spanish colonial form of the town remained intact and many of its impressive ruins were left undisturbed, enabling a gradual restoration beginning one hundred and fifty years later. Today, Quinta Avenida's yellow arch framing the Volcán de Agua is the city's iconic view. In the other direction, the view also ends dramatically, culminating with the side facade of La Iglesia de la Merced, a massive, brightly colored church with baroque details (Figure 2.100). The arch itself is Antigua's most recognizable landmark; it was built in the 1600s so that nuns from the Santa Catalina convent could cross to a school without using the street.

Other attributes include:

- The cobblestone street operates like a shared space—automobiles drive on the road at slow speeds, but cyclists and pedestrians dominate.

- Colorful building facades form a continuous streetwall (no more than two or three stories tall), establishing a balance between the height of the buildings and the width of the street.

- Sidewalks are narrow—usually only five or six feet wide—and pedestrians often spill out into the space beyond the sidewalks.

- Antigua's oversized grid is emblematic of the pattern followed by many Latin American cities. The resulting streets have nearly identical dimensions throughout each city block.

Figure 2.100: Quinta Avenida, La Antigua, Guatemala. The view looking north culminates at the facade of La Iglesia de la Merced, with green hills beyond. *Image courtesy of Kenneth Garcia*

Figure 2.101: Quinta Avenida, La Antigua, Guatemala. The view looking south, in which the arch frames the distant volcano, is the city's iconic vista.

GINZA DORI, TOKYO, JAPAN / Gianni Longo

Main Street

Ginza Dori, in Tokyo, is the attractive "main street" of a region of thirty-two million people: an eminently walkable and well-scaled street at the center of a shopping, residential, and business district. Following a major fire, the Ginza district was deliberately rebuilt in 1872 as the showcase of Japan's modernization efforts. At its core stood Ginza, a large street lined with two- and three-story-high Georgian brick buildings: a novelty in a city of narrow winding streets and wood buildings.

Ginza (Figures 2.102 and 2.103) is 3,500 feet long and 90 feet wide with 22-foot sidewalks. Building heights range from six to eight stories, giving the street ample yet well-contained proportions. Harumi Dori, a shorter east–west street, divides Ginza into two equal segments. Their intersection is Tokyo's preeminent 100-percent corner, a distinctive meeting and gathering place. Together, they anchor a compact district of 0.2 square miles that is home to an estimated 10,000 shops.

One of the unique characteristics of Ginza's 400-foot-long blocks is that they contain a larger number of buildings than are typically found on major streets. Some of these skinny buildings have frontages as narrow as fifteen feet. They are for the most part anonymous, thirty to forty years old, not particularly beautiful or unique, and typical of most of Tokyo's postwar architecture. They establish the street-level character of Ginza with shop entrances and elegant window displays that change rapidly from building to building. High land values have pushed shops, restaurants, cafés, hotels, and nightclubs to the upper floors of buildings, adding an exuberant mix of uses and a vertical dimension to the street's diversity. Multiple-story retailing is a condition that has rarely worked in other parts of the world; in Tokyo, where it is a necessity more than a choice, upper-story uses succeed without detracting from the already rich street vitality.

Ginza is a complete and complex street that supports and protects a great variety of street uses. Pedestrians and bikes share the sidewalks, as in the rest of Tokyo.

Deliveries, however, take place using the extensive network of service alleys, eliminating all trucks from the street. Speed limits are low and scrupulously respected, leading to what appears to be relaxed and unhurried driving. The most extensive network of public rail transportation in the world drastically reduces the number of private automobiles on the road. Three major subway lines converge under Ginza, and a major underground concourse that is clean, well lit, and elegantly appointed efficiently distributes passengers throughout the district using twenty-one clearly marked exits. These three lines connect Ginza to a system of subways and commuter rails that carries over forty million passengers daily and makes Ginza fully accessible to the region. This system is also what liberates the street from vehicular congestion, creating a dedicated pedestrian environment that is vibrant and safe.

Ginza has rubberized pavement, which reduces noise. Pedestrians can converse at normal speaking levels, and the effect is reminiscent of some of Europe's most successful pedestrian precincts. The street is also impeccably maintained and clean, in spite of its high usage and the complete absence of public trashcans. Its maintenance is the result of efficient public sanitation, the support of organized volunteer groups, and the continuous efforts of individual shop owners. The fact that many people in Japan consider it bad manners to eat while walking in public also reduces a major source of public waste.

Signs, tree planting, and transparent storefronts add to the pleasure of walking along Ginza. Vertical signs are better suited to the orientation of Japanese calligraphy; they also better serve those narrow buildings advertising shops and restaurants on their upper stories. Well-designed graphics, illuminated at night, give rhythm to the street, enhance the anonymous architecture, and keep the walker's eye interested. Trees planted at the edge of the sidewalk alternate with flowerbeds planted flush with the pavement. The trees are evergreens and are kept at a height of seven to eight feet, an unusual arrangement. They are designed to

Figure 2.102: Ginza Dori, Tokyo, Japan. The unusual evergreen tree planting creates a transparent screen separating the sidewalks from the roadway. The planting is not designed to create a canopy but to accentuate the pedestrian progress and to create a secondary surface to contain the space of the sidewalk.

Figure 2.103: Ginza Dori, Tokyo, Japan. The vertical signs along Ginza have a function similar to the prescribed vertical elements of London's Regent Street facades or the flag displays along New York's Fifth Avenue. They enrich the visual environment of the street. *Image courtesy of Gianni Longo*

provide a distinct visual screen to separate the sidewalks from the roadway. Storefronts are often fully open to the street in the Japanese tradition of the merchant townhouses. This merchandising technique gives pedestrians the ability to experience and react to the stores' offerings and to transition from the public to the private realm of the stores.

Ironically, Ginza's extraordinary success has, in recent years, begun to erode its idiosyncratic charms. The combination of anonymous buildings and vertical retailing along Ginza has begun to change as larger buildings by signature architects replace multiple narrow ones, and international brands exclusively occupy space previously shared by many.

116

BROAD STREETS, NOT WIDE STREETS

Since the end of World War II, Americans have made a staggering number of streets that function only as auto sewers or isolated cul-de-sacs. The biggest problem with many of them is that they are too wide. Some were new streets; others were old streets that were widened to add more lanes, or create wider lanes, or both. Sidewalks were narrowed and trees chopped down on the old roads. Many of the new streets never had trees or sidewalks.

Before modern planning and zoning, however, some of our best streets were made by simply widening sections of streets where important activities took place. These are places made less formally than squares and plazas. Broad Street in Oxford is an example that comes from a British market street tradition: streets on the edge of town that were widened for markets hundreds of years ago (Figures 2.104 and 2.105—also see Color Plate 17). As the towns grew, the broad streets were at the center.

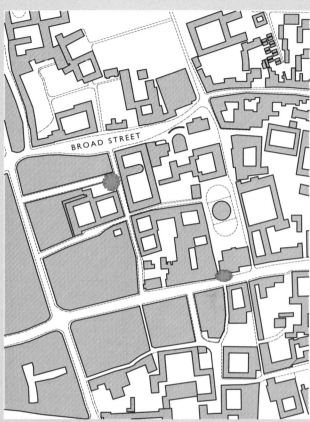

▼ **Figure 2.104:** Broad Street, Oxford, England. English broad streets commonly have parking in the center, which is removed for farmer's markets and street fairs.

▲ **Figure 2.105:** Broad Street and its environs, Oxford, England. Figure-ground drawing, showing the marvelous variety of broad and narrow spaces in central Oxford. Narrow Turl Street runs between Broad Street and High Street. The green circles on Turl Street and the High Street mark the two famous lean-in trees seen in Figure 2.124, Color Plate 8, and Figure 1.16. Color Plate 8 shows the courts around the Sheldonian Theatre and the Bodleian Library, in a photograph taken from underneath the Bridge of Sighs on New College Lane. © 2013 Dover, Kohl & Partners

Figure 2.106: Pitt Street, Mt. Pleasant, South Carolina. "That's not a real town," goes an old Southern saying, "that's just a wide spot in the road." Pitt Street splays slightly to form an extraordinary funnel-shaped space in the Old Village in Mount Pleasant, faced by housing, lodging, the old post office (now a restaurant) and the Pitt Street Pharmacy, arguably the social center of the town. *Image courtesy of James Dougherty*

Figure 2.107: Pitt Street, Mt. Pleasant, South Carolina. Satellite view. Most of the Old Village is comprised of single-family detached houses on spacious lots, but for the briefest of moments, where Pitt Street broadens, more urban buildings are grouped closely together and tightly frame the street. *Image courtesy of Google Earth*

American towns have their own variations on the tradition (Figures 2.106 and 2.107). Broad Street in lower Manhattan is wide because there was a canal running down the center when New York was Nieuw Amsterdam, but when New York started building tall buildings in its financial district, its width made Broad Street a favored location for the new skyscrapers (Figure 1.1).

Marlborough High Street in England is an unusually long broad street, presumably because it was built in an important Wiltshire market town. Each end of the street has a civic building that "plugs" the street and visually contains the space (Figure 2.108). The interesting broad street in another Wiltshire town, Lacock, is not the wide High Street but the end of Church Street near the church,

Figure 2.108: High Street, Marlborough, England. Looking northeast from the tower of St. Peter's Church. When medieval broad streets were on the edge of town, they commonly had a large entrance at the end near the town and split at the far end, with exits to more than one destination. Marlborough's unusually long High Street splits at both ends. *Image courtesy of Neil Goodwin, marlboroughnews.co.uk*

Figure 2.109: Church Street, Lacock, England. Lacock is listed in the Domesday Book that recorded the physical state of England in 1086 for the Norman conquerors. With a variety of old street types and spaces, it is used for the filming of English period dramas.

where the street widens, after being very narrow (Figure 2.109) This follows the medieval street design principle "narrow before widening, widen before narrowing."

Main Street in Northampton, Massachusetts, breaks most of the rules of placemaking and yet is a popular gathering place. The Project for Public Spaces put it on a list of favorite places, and the American Planning Association named it a Great American Street.[22] Its width comes from the annexation of an old New England common that was paved over long ago. Sitting at the top of a hill, the street broadens to the sky as we approach.

The garden streets of London are another type of broad street, some drawing on the city's tradition of private squares (Figures 2.151 and 2.152).

Regent Street, London, Great Britain

John Nash, 1811–1814

Main Street

Oxford Circus, at the intersection of Regent Street and Oxford Street, is the retail Main-Main corner of London. Piccadilly Circus, where Regent Street crosses Piccadilly, is a center for tourists and Londoners looking for entertainment in the metropolis. London is too large to have a Main Street in the small-town sense, but Regent Street serves as a regional Main Street for Greater London and London visitors. Over 7.5 million tourists visit it every year, and the world's most profitable retailer, Apple Computer, chose Regent Street as the location for its first store in Europe. Until Apple opened larger stores in London and elsewhere, the Regent Street store was its most profitable store, as well as the most profitable store in London.

Regent Street's prominence came about by design in 1811 after an act of Parliament gave the Prince Regent full authority to rule for his father, "Mad" King George III. The fashionable son admired Napoleon's urban interventions in Paris, so one of his first decisions was to hire Sir John Nash to push a wide, north–south axis through a maze of narrow streets to create a formal, processional street from Pall Mall to a new park called Regent's Park. Many Londoners had wanted a reordering of medieval London at least since the Great Fire of 1666, but until the Prince Regent and Nash, no one had both the vision and the authority to make it happen.

The Crown owned land to the north that was cut off from fashionable and wealthy London by the narrow medieval streets. Nash laid out Regent's Park on the royal land, surrounded by what looked like Classical palaces that were actually English "terraces" with luxurious apartments where members of the growing upper-middle class could live like kings. The southern end of the street was a broad axis terminated by Carlton House, the Prince Regent's residence on Pall Mall, which is the royal ceremonial route from Trafalgar Square and the Admiralty Arch to Buckingham Palace.

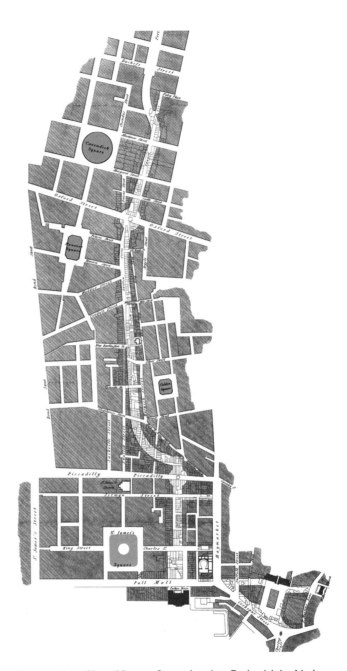

Figure 2.110: Plan of Regent Street, London, England. John Nash, 1811–1814. The classic Regent Street plan, discussed by Edmund Bacon in The *Design of Cities*. The drawing shows the old streets and buildings along the path of the new Regent Street.

In his book *Design of Cities*, the planner Edmund Bacon makes the point that Nash masterfully adapted the form of Regent Street to the functional requirements of the city.[23] Unlike the planners who worked for Napoleon and Napoleon III, Nash did not simply drive great avenues and boulevards through jumbled streets. He used some existing streets by widening them, frequently respected the backs of properties on surrounding streets, and primarily kept within the street grids that floated at different angles between the new park and Pall Mall. That meant that the street could not go in a straight line from Regent's Park to Carlton House but had to shift to the east before it arrived at Pall Mall.

The original design for Regent Street has a smooth curve between Portland Place and the place a little north of where Regent Street crossed Oxford Street (Figure 2.110). Nash changed the plan to preserve the backs of mansions on Cavendish Square. He then persuaded the authorities to hire him to design a church at the knuckle of this armature and used the design for All Souls Church to turn a potentially awkward juncture along the street into a beautiful point of focus and transition. Going south, Regent Street flows around the circular entrance to the church. From the south, Regent Street is visually terminated by the church and its spire.

At the crossing of Oxford Street, to counter the "fashionable objection" of living farther north, Nash blurred the boundary by introducing the circular, omnidirectional Oxford Circus. The size of the circus was determined once again by the backs of neighboring properties. Early plans had a large square south of the Circus, entered at the corners, to allow easy eastward movement. That plan gave too much land to open space, so Nash replaced the square with the beautiful curve of lower Regent Street, an unusual urban space sometimes called the Quadrant (Figure 2.111). The curve ends at Piccadilly Circus, another circle designed by Nash. It terminates the axis to the Mall, redirects the street, and marks the beginning of Shaftesbury Avenue, Coventry Street, and Piccadilly (originally called Portuguese Road).

Figure 2.111: The Quadrant, Regent Street, London, England. Sir Richard Norman Shaw, 1908, Sir Reginald Blomfield and others, 1928. Commerce and business demanded larger buildings than the original designs by Nash, and Shaw gave the Crown Estate an Imperial Edwardian Classicism. © 2009 Jon Curnow / Creative Commons Attribution 2.0 Generic license

Figure 2.112: Park Crescent, London, England. John Nash, 1806. View looking south from Park Square West. A crescent marks the beginning of Regent's Street at Regent's Park (although the northern end of Regent Street is called Portland Place, and there is a small green called Park Square connecting the Crescent to Regent's Park). The Prince Regent said Regent Street would rival Napoleon's Paris, but the Regency architecture of the Crescent is much quieter than the Imperial Classicism built on Regent Street less than 100 years later.

A little over seventy-five years after Nash's plan was made, the son of Charles Dickens wrote, "Piccadilly, the great thoroughfare leading from the Haymarket and Regent Street westward to Hyde Park-corner, is the nearest approach to the Parisian boulevard of which London can boast."[24] Nash cleared a large axis south of Piccadilly Circus, which runs downhill. He further widened the street at the lower end, where Carlton House sat on axis. Flanking buildings designed by Nash on the north side of the square framed the view back to Piccadilly, where another building designed by Nash terminated the view. Between Piccadilly Circus and Carlton House, Nash cleared a cross-axis from St. James Square to Haymarket. He (or perhaps the Prince Regent) persuaded the owner of the Haymarket Theatre to move the theater to the end of the axis and to let Nash design the new theater with a Classical portico and pediment to terminate the vista.

The Prince Regent left Carlton House in 1820, when he succeeded his father as king and moved his residence to Buckingham Palace. That provided the opportunity to open a grand vista from Piccadilly Circus to the Mall and St. James Park. Carlton House was torn down in 1825, and the Duke of York Monument was placed on axis, at the top of stairs leading down to the Mall. One hundred thirty-seven feet, nine inches tall, the monument was a Tuscan column topped by a statue of the Duke, who was the brother of the new king and the commander of the British forces during the French Revolutionary Wars. At the same time, the lower end of Regent Street was renamed Waterloo Place.

Waterloo Place and the nearby Trafalgar Square commemorated British battles on land and sea. Regent Street was a real estate deal for a Prince Regent who was always in debt, but it was also an expression of Britain's modern imperial power and the Prince Regent's position as a leader of architecture and fashion. The imposing curve of Regent Street and the new axes around Waterloo Place tell us that London was a world capital, designed by the leading architects of the day in what came to be known as the Regency Style (Figure 2.112).[25] When commerce demanded more functional spaces for new businesses at the end of the nineteenth century, the Crown Estate built even larger and more imperial buildings. Sir Richard Norman Shaw invented a grand British Classicism so popular that it became characteristic of the Edwardian age, and the Crown Estate acquired neighboring properties so that it could make the new buildings larger. Shaw designed the Piccadilly Hotel, completed at the intersection of Regent Street and Piccadilly Circus in 1908, and Sir Reginald Blomfield was brought in two years later to oversee the completion of the Quadrant.[26] Each block had harmonious Classical facades built in Portland Stone, with a uniform cornice sixty-six feet above the sidewalk (dormers and turrets decorate the mansard roofs above the cornice–Figure 2.113). Impressive rusticated arches and majestic columnar screens pierce the

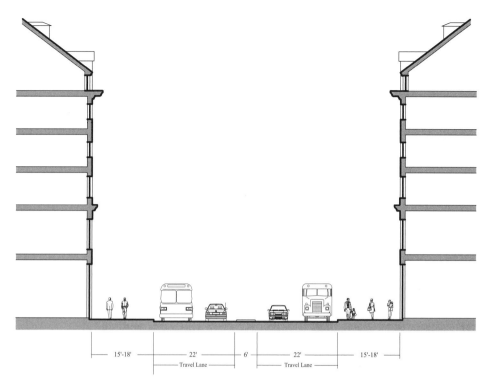

facades but continue the buildings where small lanes cross Regent Street (Figure 2.114).

Regent Street is a British variant of the Grands Boulevards of Paris. Paris would not be the Paris we love if it had only the medieval streets of old Paris, without the grand urban interventions of Louis XVI, Napoleon, and Napoleon III with Baron Haussmann. London would be a very different place without Piccadilly Circus, Regent Street, and Regent's Park.

Large-scale urban interventions got a bad name in the twentieth century, when American planners inspired by Le Corbusier's urban design principles built disastrous urban renewal projects across the country. Corbusier advocated the demolition of the street and the construction of towers in parks, but as Jane Jacobs pointed out we ac-

Figure 2.114: Air Street, London, England. View from Piccadilly, looking north on Air Street. Air Street is one of the old streets that crosses Regent Street. Sir Richard Norman Shaw incorporated it into his grand Edward Classicism with bold arches and columnar screens in buildings along the Quadrant. *Image courtesy of the Crown Estate*

tually built towers in parking lots. She also labeled urban renewal "urban removal," and hand in hand with that went a program of building highways that ran through cities and tore apart neighborhoods. Today we have begun to pull down those highways, leaving us with large swaths of cleared land and badly ripped urban fabric that needs to be reknit in creative ways. Ambitious designs like the ones for Regent Street and the Grands Boulevards are once again relevant, useful precedents for modern designs.

DOWNTOWN STREETS

Railroad Street, Great Barrington, Massachusetts

Downtown Street

Railroad Street, a short shopping street in Great Barrington, Massachusetts, shows how easy it can be to make a good street, because the elements and details of the street are so simple and easy to replicate. It has one medium-length block that goes uphill from Main Street (Figure 4.55) before the street makes a right turn and becomes a service street for a parking lot next to the railroad tracks (Figures 2.115 and 2.118). The sidewalks are poured concrete slabs with granite curbs, and the streetlights are old cobra heads. The buildings along the street are two- and three-story mixed-use buildings, with storefronts on the ground floor and offices or apartments above—all typical of Massachusetts in the nineteenth century. The Western Massachusetts town has enough tourists so that the spaces have a high occupancy rate, but the rents are not expensive, and no one is getting rich owning the stores or buildings.

Let's catalog why it's good. The space is a comfortable "outdoor room" because:

- It is well proportioned; the tallest buildings are approximately three-quarters as tall as the street is wide.

- From wall to wall, the space is 50 feet wide and 350 feet long (1-to-7).

Figure 2.115: Railroad Street, Great Barrington, Massachusetts. Looking west from Main Street, with the Bradford pear trees in bloom. The tree in the bumpout at the end of Railroad Street is gone.

Figure 2.116: Railroad Street, Great Barrington, Massachusetts. Looking back towards Main Street, with one of the green hills of the Berkshires in the background. The Bradford pear tree at the end of the street, discussed in the text, is still standing in this photo.

- The slight upward slope gives the building that terminates the vista more prominence and increases the sense of enclosure.

- The streetwalls that define the room are almost continuous.

- The streetwalls have great "firmness," a solidity that comes from their weighty materials and the light and shadow that show the depth of the facades.

- The materials that make the streetwall, primarily brick and stone, are pleasing to the senses.

- The vertical window openings above the ground floor and the number of individual buildings on the block give a visual counterbalance to the horizontal space.

- The weathered asphalt "floor" is a pleasant grey. The asphalt harmonizes with the building colors and unifies the space.

- The parked cars and the painted stripe alongside the parked cars visually narrow the space.

- The cars, the stripe, and the sidewalks are all parallel to the streetwalls.

- The street plan works well with the block.

The buildings are not great works of architecture, but they are all beautiful in a simple way that reflects the visual principles described by Christopher Alexander in *A Pattern Language* and *The Nature of Order.* The simple compositions of their facades and their natural materials make excellent background buildings, background buildings that can withstand scrutiny and that give a pleasant feel to the street (Figure 2.116).

Streets that don't have good architecture need trees to screen the buildings while providing order and beauty. The buildings on Railroad Street are good enough that the street feels good without trees. The street used to have one tree, in the bumpout on the north side of the street where Railroad meets the town's Main Street, a situation that is worth discussing (Figure 2.117). In Chapter 4, we will see that there has been a lot of discussion about Great Barrington's street trees, related to the fact that Bradford

Figure 2.117: Railroad Street, Great Barrington, Massachusetts. View of the bumpout at the intersection of Railroad Street and Main Street, showing the Bradford pear tree mentioned in the text. Unlike the ubiquitous, one-size-fits-all bumpouts commonly built today, this bumpout is a civic amenity.

Figure 2.118: Railroad Street, Great Barrington, Massachusetts. Figure-ground drawing. © 2013 Dover, Kohl & Partners

pear trees have weak "crotches," and this tree came down in a freak Halloween blizzard (see *Street Trees* in the section about Great Barrington's Main Street).

When it was still standing, the location of the tree on the bumpout was subtle. Trees on both sides of Main Street usually line up along the street and on opposites sides of the street. One of the Main Street trees is directly across from the end of Railroad Street, on axis with its center. The single tree on Railroad Street partially balanced the tree on the other side of Main, while also softening the width of Railroad Street without blocking it, functionally or visually. The bumpout provided a place for a pair of mailboxes on the sidewalk without blocking the narrow sidewalk on Railroad or the wider but busier sidewalk on Main. And it did all this without calling attention to itself as a bumpout. Part of the reason for that is that it does not stick out as far as the parked cars, but partially shields the parked cars on one side of the street in a way that feels like relaxed placemaking, rather than the imposition of a rigid, one-size-fits-all streetscape formula. Unfortunately, the Massachusetts Department

of Transportation has proposed a formulaic makeover for Great Barrington's Main Street, which—exactly as it is today—is one of the best Main Streets in New England (see *Retrofitting a Main Street That's Also a State Highway: A Cautionary Tale* in Chapter 4).

The final bullet point above says, "The street plan works well with the block." To understand what that means, it helps to look on both sides of Main Street (Figure 2.118). Railroad Street is to the west of Main Street, with nineteenth- and early-twentieth-century mixed-use buildings on both sides. Some of these are flexible New England loft-buildings that over the years have accommodated offices, manufacturing space, apartments, hotel rooms, and stores on the ground floor. One building has a large theater called The Mahaiwe behind and beneath the offices and apartments.

The other side of Main Street has similar buildings, but behind those buildings, to the east, are parking lots that were at some point cleared in a typical "urban removal" plan. The lots come out to the sidewalks on both side streets, creating an unpleasant pedestrian experience along the streets as well as a view of the backs of buildings that were never meant to be seen by passersby.

There is parking to the west of Main Street, too, but it is screened by buildings along the side streets. Railroad Street does that well, and also screens the railroad tracks at the top of the slight hill. When you get to the top of the hill, however, where a building with a restaurant and an outdoor terrace blocks the view of the tracks just behind the building, Railroad Street takes a sharp right-hand turn and enters a parking lot along the railroad track. Facing the parking on the right are some inexpensive utilitarian buildings that screen another parking lot behind the buildings on Main Street. Many of the Main Street buildings have rear doors that open onto the parking lot, and just enough work has been done on the lot (there is a mural on a windowless wall, trees, and a small terrace for a coffee shop) that it functions as both parking and public space. One pedestrian alleyway lets you walk back to Railroad, and another pedestrian walk, next to the café, goes out to Main Street. In the center, between the two parking lots, sits a new three-screen movie theater.

The parking to the east of Main is useful but a visual blight. Partly thanks to Railroad Street, however, the parking to the west is a civic amenity.

Aviles Street, St. Augustine, Florida

Downtown Street

One of the oldest American streets, St. Augustine's Aviles Street is generally full of people—dining outdoors, stopping to peer into the windows of storefronts, casually walking and biking through the right-of-way. Although predominantly a street for pedestrians, motorists and cyclists use it, too, and the sidewalk cafes spill out into the right-of-way. The total width of the road varies: at its narrowest, the road measures only a little more than ten feet curb to curb. The dimension widens at intersections, but

only slightly, which accommodates parallel parking at its southern end. The width does not deter cars from using the street, but it does make them move slowly, and this is reinforced by the textured pavers installed in a recent renovation. The hardscape unites the space (Figure 2.119).

Because it is such a narrow road, Aviles Street functions similarly to many of the shared spaces of Amsterdam, such as Tweede Tuindwarsstraat in the Jordaan District. Shared space of that sort is prevalent in many Dutch cities, but it is still quite rare in America—although, ironically, the pattern still works so well on one of our oldest streets.

Figure 2.119: Aviles Street, St. Augustine, Florida. Small is beautiful: a single narrow lane, tightly spaced buildings, and the slight cant combine to make one of the most comfortable "shared space" streets in America.

Formosa Street, London, Great Britain

Downtown Street

There is a debate among urban designers about the best locations for neighborhood centers, particularly neighborhood retail centers. Those who mainly work in places where everyone drives want to put the retail centers on high-traffic roads. Designers working in more urban settings where most people walk, or at least park and walk, want some models for getting away from roads dominated by cars. Formosa Street is an interesting model for the second group.

> There is a debate among urban designers about the best locations for neighborhood centers, particularly neighborhood retail centers.

Formosa Street is a small neighborhood center in the Little Venice section of Maida Vale. The local Underground stop, Warwick Avenue, is two short blocks to the south. From the Underground station, one walks to Formosa Street via Warrington Crescent, which begins at the Underground stop and curves off to the northeast. "The Crescent" is a fancy street, with large "terrace houses" (English for identical or mirror-image rowhouses) that have high ceilings and large, shared private gardens in the center of their large blocks. To the west of Warrington Crescent is Castellain Road, which has smaller houses, with smaller gardens. Formosa Street begins at Warrington Crescent and runs west, crossing Castellain. In between Castellain and Warrington, Formosa bends in the middle so that it is perpendicular to both cross streets. Only the block of Formosa Street between the two has stores (Figure 2.120).

Figure 2.120: Formosa Street, London, England. Looking east on Formosa Street, from Castellain Road. The Prince Alfred pub is on the corner.

Figure 2.121: Formosa Street, London, England. Looking north on Warrington Crescent. The eastern end of Formosa Street is seen on the left, flanked by the decorative arches.

The short block has a travel lane in each direction, with a parking lane on one side. But people park on both sides, sometimes leaving a yield lane in the center that is less than 9 feet wide. Even in the best of conditions, the sidewalks are 9 feet wide on both sides and the parking lane is 6½ feet, leaving 15 feet for the travel lanes, or 7½ feet per lane. Traffic is frequently reduced to one lane in the center of the street that is less than 9 feet wide.

Most of the buildings on the street are two-bay, three-story, mixed-use buildings with small stores on the ground floor. A Victorian pub at one end also has a dining room in the middle of the block. At the other end, on the Crescent, the small mixed-use buildings nod to the formality of the large terrace houses with applied triumphal arches on mainly blank walls (Figure 2.121). But small, understated doors in each facade, as well as a small side window in one elevation, give a quirky informality to the monumental elevations.

Warrington Crescent is wide and lightly trafficked. The few cars there move quickly through the quiet residential neighborhood, on their way to somewhere else. Step off the Crescent onto Formosa, and you are in a quieter, smaller, less formal place. The bend in the road focuses the space on the center of the block. Very few cars enter the block unless that is their destination, and most people on the street arrive by foot. Since there is so little traffic, pedestrians frequently walk in the street rather than on the sidewalks, automatically creating a shared space where cars go slowly. If the locals didn't walk in the street, the narrow sidewalks would be crowded, because several establishments on the street have outdoor tables or stands. Shops include a convenience store, a café, a launderette, a dry cleaner, a small restaurant that serves breakfast and lunch, a bakery and small restaurant, and a large restaurant attached to the corner pub. Some larger neighborhood centers with more stores and variety are within a quarter of a mile walk. When coming from the center of London on the Underground, one can choose to go to the next stop, where there are more stores.

TWEEDE TUINDWARSSTRAAT, AMSTERDAM, NETHERLANDS /
Ethan Kent

Downtown Street

A STREET AS A PLACE

The patterns of activity that occur in one place on this street offer the outcomes for which all streets should be planned.

When wandering through a network of streets we are naturally drawn to its center. On each street we seek out its slowest point—often an intersection—which usually brings us to progressively more engaging and slower streets and spaces.

Amsterdam's Jordaan District offers such a network of streets, where the external thoroughfares feed into progressively more pedestrian-oriented and comfortable spaces. Moving into the district, shops get smaller and increasingly concerned with the street; walking shifts to strolling; conversations grow longer; and people feel justified, and often compelled, to just stop and linger, taking in the scene.

The desire to pause and experience the street peaks in a section of Tuindwarsstraat that happens to be near the center of the district. The nexus of a flower shop, a bar, and a café across the street creates what is perhaps the slowest place in the neighborhood. Each passerby moves through the space with attention engaged, making eye contact and frequently stopping to read a menu, greet a friend, or purchase some flowers.

These patterns of use all beget themselves.

While the pace is slow, the space supports dynamic experiences, exchanges, and interactions for its participants. The vibrancy of these interactions is buttressed through the broad diversity of people, all allowed to feel equal and respected in this space while being brought together by the strong cultural identity of the setting. The greatest indicator of its comfort—and perhaps its greatest achievement—is its sociability, reflected in consistent displays of engaged conversation, picture-taking, and affectionate greetings.

While not technically defined as a "shared space" or "Complete Street," this spot succeeds as both (Figures 2.122 and 2.123). All types of traffic can easily and comfortably access this place and benefit from its qualities. Even a passing truck driver is able to engage in the social life of the street, stopping briefly to talk with café patrons. But because of the strong hierarchy of streets surrounding the Jordaan District, the transit and bike orientation of the city, and the slowness of this street, it does not carry significant traffic.

There are many features of the street to which one can attribute its dynamism, from the affluent neighbors and tourists to the Dutch culture and related scale, density, and style of urban design. Indeed, it is through these contexts that we usually evaluate, explain, and experience such spaces. Yet the experience of these fundamental patterns of social life—of a street performing as

Figure 2.122: Tweede Tuindwarsstraat, Amsterdam, the Netherlands. A film strip showing the constantly-changing activity in Tweede Tuindwarsstraat. Even a passing truck driver engages in the social life of the street. *Images courtesy of Ethan Kent, Project for Public Spaces*

a place—is something infinitely possible and prevalent in human settlement.

Across contexts and cultures, when allowed, people naturally gravitate to participating in and creating street life. And it is this life that is the building block of strong communities, cultures, and local economies. This dynamic street hums along because of a vibrant Dutch culture and context, yet that strength emerged because of a society nurtured around shared places like this. As Chuck Marohn of Strong Towns says, "We did not build places like this because we were rich; we became rich because we built places like this."

It may well be the presence of the flower vendor, who spends time in front of his shop adjusting his display and talking with passersby, that truly anchors the place and embodies what this street makes possible. Retail that competes to contribute to the public experience,

not just benefit from it, is usually the greatest contributor to successful streets, and is what allows public streets to compete with malls and chains. The life and vitality of cities is defined at this human scale of the street, yet no one but pedestrians and those serving them really pay this scale any attention.

Despite our deep affection for scenes like these, few plan a street for the potential of what it can become as a place. Tweede Tuindwarsstraat centers on the daily patterns of social life, business activity, personal mobility, and people being allowed to feel comfortable in the city. While most streets and transportation systems are planning for mobility and attempting to mitigate its negative impacts, what if we planned streets and transportation systems with the goal of supporting settings like this, of planning first for places where people want to be?

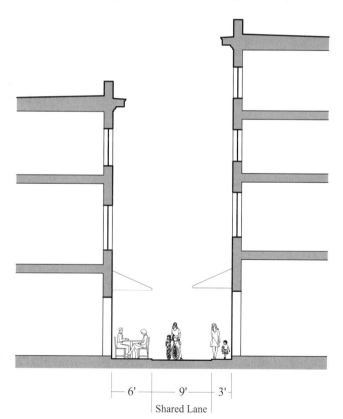

Figure 2.123: Tweede Tuindwarsstraat, Amsterdam, the Netherlands. Section. © 2013 Dover, Kohl & Partners

6' 9' 3'
Shared Lane

THE LEAN-IN TREE: TURL STREET, OXFORD, ENGLAND

Oxford is a place where the city and the university combine in a unique neighborhood fabric. The Gothic, Neo-Gothic, and Classical buildings create a cityscape with a distinguished sense of place. Turl Street is a skinny street that connects Broad Street to the High Street (Figure 2.124 and Color Plate 8). One of its most notable features is the large tree that overhangs from an adjacent courtyard. The "lean-in tree" naturally unifies the street scene. In many American cities and towns, ordinances require trees that lean over the right-of-way to be trimmed or cut back. This Oxford street is an example of how the lean-in tree can instead add comfort and character to an urban environment. An additional element on Turl is the hydraulic bollard—which can be adjusted to let cars travel through Turl Street when desired. When car traffic is not desired, the bollards remain up.

Figure 2.124: Turl Street, Oxford, England. Looking north towards Broad Street.

NEIGHBORHOOD STREETS

Sidney Place, Brooklyn, New York

Neighborhood Street

There are two reasons for including Sidney Place in this book. First, like Railroad Street in Great Barrington (Figure 2.115), it shows how easy it can be to make a good street. Sidney Place is one of the most beautiful streets in New York, and yet it was made almost entirely without the help of architects or urban designers. Second, Sidney Place demonstrates that a shift in a simple grid can contribute a lot to the act of place making.

> Like Railroad Street in Great Barrington, Sidney Place shows how easy it can be to make a good street. Sidney Place is one of the most beautiful streets in New York, and yet it was made almost entirely without the help of architects or urban designers.

Sidney Place (Figure 2.125) is in Brooklyn Heights—one of the oldest parts of Brooklyn, which sits on a bluff across the East River from lower Manhattan. Development of Brooklyn Heights began soon after the start of ferry service between Brooklyn and Manhattan in 1814. In 1818, the Brooklyn trustees wanted to extend two long north–south streets, Columbia and Willow streets, across the estate of Hezekiah B. Pierrepont.[27] The Pierrepont family allowed east–west streets to cross the property but blocked the construction of the north–south streets, which soon leapfrogged over it. When the estate was later sold and then subdivided in 1842, this resulted in the construction of short, discontinuous north–south streets, including Columbia Place, Willow Place, and Sidney Place. Each runs between State Street and Joralemon Street. Each is a tree-lined street with rowhouses, visually terminated by houses on the cross streets. This small change in the Brooklyn Heights grid makes it enough like a plaza that someone appropriately named them "places" rather than "streets."

State Street and Joralemon are not quite parallel to each other, so the blocks between them get longer as the streets go east; Sidney Place is the farthest east of the discontinuous blocks. About seven hundred feet long, Sidney Place has an interruption mid-block on one side, where a new east–west street, Livingston Street, starts. This interruption visually and psychologically breaks down the scale of Sidney Place: even though it's not a through street, Livingston Street prevents Sidney from feeling like a long block. A Catholic church sits on the northeast corner of Livingston and Sidney, and its parochial school is on the other side of Livingston. Livingston Street is now one-way from Sidney Place, which doesn't have much traffic, so that intersection becomes something of an assembly ground for the church and the school.

Lined with rowhouses on standard lots, Sidney Place is architecturally typical of many blocks in Brooklyn (Fig-

ure 2.126). When the Brooklyn Heights grid was platted by Brooklyn's engineers in 1839, before Brooklyn was part of New York City, they used the 200-foot by 400-foot-to-900-foot blocks that were already becoming the standard across the river in New York. All over the two cities, rowhouses were commonly built on 100-foot by 16-foot-to-32-foot lots that went back-to-back on the 200-foot blocks.

Today, great Brooklyn neighborhoods like Park Slope, Fort Greene, Cobble Hill, and Brooklyn Heights have block after block that remain largely intact from the nineteenth century. In 2006, the editors of *Time Out* magazine picked one of the blocks of South Portland Avenue in Fort Greene as the most beautiful block in the city, although there are many other blocks that are almost identical (see Figure 2.144). Their common elements are mature trees and rowhouses with stoops. The rowhouses on both sides of the street will often be

Figure 2.125: Sidney Place, Brooklyn, New York. Looking north from State Street. A house on Joralemon Street is visible at the opposite end of Sidney Place.

Figure 2.126: Sidney Place, Brooklyn, New York. Looking south towards State Street from midblock.

in just one or two styles, either repeated or mirrored. The houses facing each other and on the same side of the block will typically be all brownstone, or primarily brick, and the trees will all be the same genus, planted equidistant apart and all in a row. There is lots of repetition, in other words, but only contemporary architects and landscape architects say the street needs more variety and "creativity." Most New Yorkers just wish they could live there.

Sidney Place has more architectural variety than South Portland Avenue. The rowhouses are a combination of redbrick Greek Revival houses (some have been painted) and Connecticut-brownstone neo-Classical houses of the sort built all over New York during the late-nineteenth-century period that Lewis Mumford called "the Brown Decades." Many have their original stoops; some have been converted to "the English plan" (which means their stoops were removed); and some are apartment house conversions with no stoop. The buildings are unified by their similar heights and widths, Classical details and proportions, masonry fronts, vertical, double-hung windows, and the trees that form a canopy over the street. Locally, the trees are thought to be London Plane trees, but they are actually their American cousins, the sycamore.

Alta Vista Terrace, Chicago, Illinois

J.C. Brompton, 1904

Neighborhood Street

Alta Vista Terrace (Figures 2.127 and 2.128) is a straight, block-long, narrow residential street developed by the prolific builder Samuel Gross in 1904. Gross was fascinated with European urbanism and with the terrace houses of London in particular, so he directed architect Joseph C. Brompton to adapt the type to American conditions in Chicago's Lake View neighborhood. On Alta Vista Terrace, the compact design of both the forty lots and the street allowed substantial development to fit in an unusually shallow parcel while

Figure 2.127: Alta Vista Terrace, Chicago, Illinois. J.C. Brompton, 1904. Satellite view. The shallow lots, compact building type, and narrow street (center) permitted the development of distinctive addresses despite the extremely tight parcel. Compare the shallow houses to the full-size rowhouses nearby (right and bottom). *Image courtesy of Google Earth*

keeping the street framed by matching house types on either side—like facing like—to create a unified street scene. Brompton and Gross then alternated the facade designs diagonally so that identical houses do not line up with each other, which introduced variety and improved privacy. The lots are twenty-four feet wide and forty feet deep.

This skinny street space is open at both ends—knitted into the regular grid of Chicago blocks—and yet intimate and very distinctively its own place. Visitors get a sense of entering the residents' territory. With stoops and bay windows overlooking the street and friendly neigh-

bors coming and going, the scene is very clearly watched over. Alta Vista Terrace feels private and self-policing, but there's no gate or guardhouse here.

This combination of intimacy, sociability, and security is partly accomplished by its narrow width: the street includes just a one-way travel lane, a row of parallel parking, and sidewalks. The sidewalks are approximately ten feet wide and meet the edges of small dooryards in front of each rowhouse.

Unique in Chicago, Gross's block is now a National Historic Landmark, designated the Alta Vista Terrace Historic District.

Figure 2.128: Alta Vista Terrace, Chicago, Illinois. J.C. Brompton, 1904. Like facing like, with a twist: Identical house facades are alternated diagonally, imparting visual variety within the group of rapidly-produced, similar houses.

CHURCH STREET, CHARLESTON, SOUTH CAROLINA

Neighborhood Street

Some of the most memorable and delightful streets unfold in sequences, like a play or novel, and vary dramatically from one scene to the next. Church Street is one such episodic street, changing in width and character as it travels north along the peninsula of Charleston's historic district. The experience of the street breaks down into five short, distinct segments just in the section between White Point Gardens and St. Philips Church. The spatial sequence from south to north changes in formality and scale to match the kinds of addresses rooted along each segment. This sequence accumulated slowly over time, with no single designer or grand, overarching plan. The effect is as if each segment had been treated as its own unique compositional assignment, but the idiosyncrasies are endearing and make Church Street an example of what François Spoerry called "gentle urbanism."[28]

The traditional buildings framing the street easily adapted to the twenty-first century. Meanwhile, although there are many beautiful works of architecture on Church Street, nothing about the road details are particularly fancy or elaborate. In many ways, the street is an ode to simplicity. A visitor will notice the near total lack of roadway striping and signs. Church Street proves that parallel parking does not need excessive amounts of white paint in order to work, and that speed can be controlled without brightly painted objects that detract from the aesthetic quality of a town. Unpretentious local plants and flowers add value and beauty.

From the south, the sequence begins at White Point Gardens, Charleston's formal waterfront square (Figure 2.129). This is not just the edge of the neighborhood; it is the end of the peninsula. Wide vistas across the harbor extend to distant barrier islands and the horizon. The contrast is dramatic once we cross Battery Street to begin the walk along Church Street.

Here, Church Street is at its tightest and most enclosed, and the views are short. On this segment between Battery Street and Water Street, the carriageway

Figure 2.129: White Point Gardens, Charleston, South Carolina. Looking south towards the Ashley River. Church Street begins at Charleston's formal waterfront square.

is paved with red bricks and the curb-to-curb dimension is approximately seventeen feet. Vehicles travel at slow speeds through this single lane, leaving ample space for parallel parking (Figure 2.130). Contrary to what many traffic engineers might expect, motorists and emergency vehicles have no problem navigating the narrow street (Figure 6.12). This portion of Church has few street trees in the conventional sense. Instead, the pattern is that of the satisfactory lean-in tree, reminiscent of Turl Street in Oxford (Figure 2.124 and Color Plate 8).[29] There are sidewalks on both sides, but most people walk in the street.

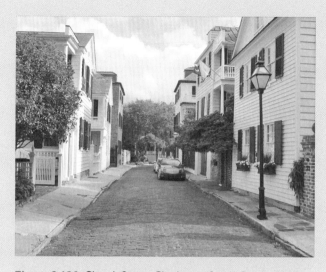

Figure 2.130: Church Street, Charleston, South Carolina. Looking south to White Point Gardens. Here, Church Street is narrow, and trees "lean in" from adjacent gardens.

Figure 2.131: Church Street, Charleston, South Carolina. Looking north towards Water Street. The dogleg at this intersection provides a series of delightful effects, including the shady triangular space and tamer traffic.

The experience changes again when Church Street cranks—it doesn't curve, bend, or arc, it cranks—in a dogleg at Water Street (Figure 2.131). On the west side, the property lines on the Church Street lots continue straight to the corner lot, and the result is a shady triangular space on one side, in which the walls of gardens and houses are no longer parallel to the curbs. We are told Water Street is appropriately named; it used to be a creek, in the early days of the settlement, and—like a lot of special places in Charleston—its urban form emerged gradually as earthquakes and hurricanes knocked down buildings that became the fill material for much of the town's upland. The dogleg, the crank, and the triangular space at the intersection of Water and Church streets are all artifacts of that evolutionary process. The long, straight vista is softly concluded; the space feels enclosed but not claustrophobic, and street trees are introduced. The variation from a regular grid removes the sensation that the street might go on forever. But there is another effect—on the traffic. The cranked street slows down any motorist without being annoying. It's like a giant, invisible speed bump, only better, because it's a place rather than an anti-place.

Figure 2.132: Church Street, Charleston, South Carolina. Looking north towards Stoll's Alley, which is on the right.

Between Water Street and Tradd Street, Church Street is still one-way, but here the lane widens and there is parking on both sides. Narrow one-way streets are okay in this kind of residential fabric, where there is a rich network of streets, blocks are fairly small, and there are plenty of surrounding streets to support circulation (Figure 2.132). This neighborhood is one of Charleston's

▶**Figure 2.133:** Stoll's Alley, Charleston, South Carolina. The neighborhoods around Church Street have a wide range of street types, from broad to tiny.

▶▶**Figure 2.134:** Longitude Lane, Charleston, South Carolina. The narrow passage is both a conversation piece and a practical convenience—one of the most popular tourist spots and a convenient short-cut. Like Stoll's Alley, the lane breaks down Charleston's otherwise oversized blocks.

▼**Figure 2.135:** Church Street, Charleston, South Carolina. In this short, straight segment, Church Street briefly opens up visually and has two-way travel, under the arched canopy of live oaks.

Figure 2.136: Church Street, Charleston, South Carolina. Looking north from Broad Street. The climactic moment comes where the steeple of St. Philip's Church, still nearly three blocks away, becomes visible under the tree canopy.

most beloved and livable, and in part this is because it has a generous menu of street types and widths, including the charming Stoll's Alley (Figure 2.133) and—narrowest of all—Longitude Lane (Figure 2.134).

Between Tradd Street and Broad Street Church widens again and there is a brief, two-way segment. By this point Church Street is a different sort of street from the intimate place seen earlier (Figure 3.4). It is still beautiful, and the oak canopy arches overhead in a spectacular way, but pedestrians keep mainly to their sidewalks. The scene is becoming more citified (Figure 2.135).

The climactic moment in the walk comes just before Broad Street, where the steeple of St. Philips, still

nearly three blocks away, becomes visible under the tree canopy (Figure 2.136). Today this is one of the most celebrated examples of the "terminated vista" in American urbanism, but the church buildings came first and, happily, the street was compromised to match. The present St. Philips church building was completed in 1838 and substantially encroaches on the alignment of the Church Street centerline, as had its predecessors. The steeple, added in 1848, is about two hundred feet tall.[30]

Between Broad Street and St. Philips, the street reverts to one-way traffic, and the giant oaks give way to smaller trees and palmettos to avoid obscuring the steeple. Once the street reaches the church, the roadway skirts around the steeple and porticoes. The pavement on Church Street is perennially cracked, patched, and broken, but hardly anyone notices—it's the view of that steeple that counts (Figure 2.137). As Douglas Duany has pointed out, until modern engineering came along, curving roads were usually edged with straight sections of curb, and that is the case at St. Philips.[31] The whole thing is the opposite of smooth, friction-free, stream-form auto geometry (Figure 2.138). Indeed, Church Street makes demands of the drivers who travel it, and that makes it safer. Almost everything about its design would be labeled substandard by most contemporary engineering manuals, but there it sits, and it works.

Figure 2.137: Church Street, Charleston, South Carolina. St. Philip's Church (J. Hyde, 1838; steeple by E.B. White, 1848) instantly produced a quintessential terminated vista (and the iconic Charleston street scene). The street goes around the steeple in a faceted jog. At more than 200 feet tall, the steeple has long been the skyline's most recognizable feature, and thus it was used as a target during the bombardment of Charleston during the Civil War. Although the sanctuary was damaged by shelling on several occasions, thankfully the steeple survived.

Figure 2.138: Figure Ground of Church Street, Charleston, South Carolina. The street alignment takes a sudden westward jog, allowing the church steeple to step forward into view. *Image courtesy of Dover, Kohl & Partners with data provided by the City of Charleston*

Market Street

St. Philip's Church

Church Street

Meeting Street

LEGARE STREET, CHARLESTON, SOUTH CAROLINA

Neighborhood Street

Many great streets do not comply with the rigid public-works standards in force today. Frequently, the narrowest streets with the most idiosyncratic details are the best places to be. Venerable Legare Street (pronounced "Luh-GREE") is one of Charleston's most popular addresses, but its physical form would be tough to replicate within the current rules. Legare Street (Figure 2.139 and Color Plate 45) provides plenty of evidence to suggest the rules need to change.

Legare Street—which runs roughly parallel to Church and Meeting streets—is a key organizing element of the historic district. The oak trees provide a beautiful, continuous canopy along the street. There are both "lean-in" trees and street trees within the right-of-way on Legare. Some are quite old trees, with large roots

coming out of the sidewalk, and several enter the travel lanes. These trees may not comply with typical regulations, but that doesn't mean that they aren't safe or effective. In fact, their massive presence calms traffic without looking like a "traffic calming device." (Also see Turl Street, Figure 2.124 and Color Plate 8.)

> If typical suburban residential streets were designed like Legare Street, there would be no need for "traffic calming devices."

Legare Street is not quite as narrow as the southernmost segment of Church Street, but it's close. At its smallest, the measured curb-to-curb dimension is just under twenty feet wide—comparable to Twain Avenue in Davidson—expanding somewhat as the

Figure 2.139: Legare Street, Charleston, South Carolina. Legare Street breaks some rules; trees emerge straight from the pavement, for example. The alignment of the street makes a very slight crescent, bent plenty (in two places) to close off the view and create a delightful intimacy, but barely enough to be noticeable as a designer's maneuver unless one is looking for it. Also see Color Plate 45.

road travels north from Battery Street. The narrow dimension accommodates informal parking and effectively slows traffic. Another characteristic that Legare shares with Church Street: the perspectival effect of a deflected vista, rather than a seemingly endless vista. Subtle bends in the street (shown in the plan, Figure 2.140) limit what can be seen by the walker, cyclist, or motorist looking down it.

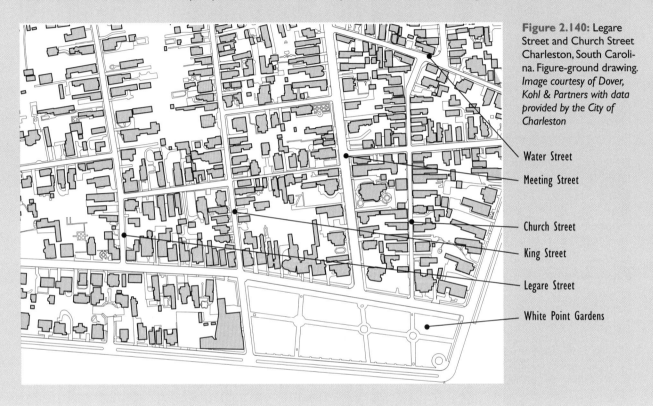

Figure 2.140: Legare Street and Church Street Charleston, South Carolina. Figure-ground drawing. *Image courtesy of Dover, Kohl & Partners with data provided by the City of Charleston*

Water Street

Meeting Street

Church Street

King Street

Legare Street

White Point Gardens

BENEFIT STREET, PROVIDENCE, RHODE ISLAND / David Brussat

Neighborhood Street

The most beloved street in Providence goes by the name of Benefit. It sits midway up College Hill, one of the most beautiful and well preserved neighborhoods in America, looking over the city founded in 1636 by Roger Williams. From between the houses of Benefit you look west across the narrow Providence River at the best-preserved midsized downtown in America.

Some might say that it looks as though time stood still on Benefit. No. In fact, its stretch of simple clapboard houses and grand merchant mansions runs an architectural "Mile of History," from the late Colonial and Federal periods through the Gilded Age, the Classical Revival, and the City Beautiful—even including a bare smidgeon of the Modern era, which then steps back from Benefit with a rare and becoming modesty.

If this sounds paradisiacal, the blessing is magnified by the physical, streetly character of Benefit and its neighboring thoroughfares, such as North and South Main Street, College Street, and Thomas Street—not to mention the recently built Memorial Park along a short stretch of the Providence River. Benefit Street was laid in 1756–58. Originally called Back Street, it is up the hill from and parallel to the town's original main street—first known as the Towne Street and since called Main Street. The buildings on the west side of Main Street ran along the Providence River, which was paved over in the nineteenth century but (as we shall see) uncovered again in the 1990s.

Benefit, which lies generally flat but curves gently along the steep topography, was originally intended for houses displaced by the growing bustle of the Towne Street (its commercial district was called Cheapside), before the construction of the Providence Arcade in 1828 in what is now downtown led commerce to the other side of the river. The great houses are mostly on the south end of the street and on its uphill side, from which mercantile princes might gaze from their rooftop widow's walks downriver toward Narragansett Bay.

The narrower, northern end of Benefit features a large collection of clapboard houses erected between the Revolution and the Civil War, fronting right up to the sidewalk, with facades of soft pastel coloration. The streetwall is largely unbroken except by steep cross streets, many with views of the Rhode Island State House designed by McKim, Mead & White and completed in 1901. Street trees meet overhead, contributing to the feeling of intimacy. The sidewalks are of brick, and period lampposts add to the sense of history. Cars pass gingerly.

This stretch boasts the first Rhode Island State House (1762, add. 1851). Among many buildings of note are the Sullivan Dorr House (1809), where Thomas Dorr, leader of the Dorr Rebellion of 1842, was raised; the John Reynolds House (1785), where poet Sarah Helen Whitman dallied with Edgar Allan Poe; the John Mawney House (1764), the street's oldest and the setting for one of H.P. Lovecraft's short stories, "The Shunned House"; and the Benefit Street Arsenal (1840), with its twin crenellated towers.

To the south Benefit widens, as does the ambition of its architecture. The John Brown House (1786) was described by John Quincy Adams as "the most magnificent and elegant private mansion I have ever seen on this continent." On the very next block is the Col. Joseph Nightingale House (1791). The First Unitarian Church (1816) is one of several buildings on Benefit by John Holden Greene, a prolific practitioner among early Providence architects.

Figure 2.141: Benefit Street, Providence, Rhode Island. Looking north from South Court Street. Victorian rowhouses across the street from an Italianate mansion.

Figure 2.142: Benefit Street, Providence, Rhode Island. Looking east on Power Street, from Benefit Street. A portion of the street that has Brown family mansions uphill from Benefit Street. John Quincy Adams described the John Brown House, just out of sight on the left, as "the most magnificent and elegant private mansion I have ever seen on this continent." *Image courtesy of Diana S. Faria, creator of the blog Long Island Daily Photo*

Between the north and south portions of Benefit stand two blocks of grand civic and institutional architecture. The Providence Athenaeum (1838), a Doric temple by the Philadelphia architect William Strickland, still operates as a private library and is where Poe made love, literally, to Miss Whitman. The Rhode Island School of Design (founded in 1877), with its string of elegant institutional structures, gives Benefit Street an urbane, classical ambience; the Providence County Courthouse (1924–33), by Jackson, Robertson & Adams, steps up in three gabled Georgian stages from South Main. Athenaeum Row's five splendid townhouses sit just south of the Athenaeum itself.

Benefit's fine looks today belie its middle years of dilapidation. The well-to-do left Benefit partly because the center of urban gravity had moved across the river in the nineteenth century and because early motor vehicles lacked the horses to climb College Hill. At the depth of Benefit's decline, urban renewal called for the demolition of much of the street. This was thwarted by a study, in 1961, urging a tepid preserva-tionism. It would only have saved some of the historic houses while embracing, without any apparent reluctance, new multifamily housing, including towers, insensitive to the street's historic appearance.

Thankfully, local worthies led by Beatrice O. "Happy" Chace, advised by early preservationist Antoinette Downing, purchased historic houses, restored their exteriors, and sold them for next to nothing to families willing to finance their own interior restorations or renovations. With these private activities in full swing, talk of demolition evaporated. In the 1970s, the sidewalks were bricked and "faux" gas lamps replaced cobra-head lampposts.

"This is not preservation, this is Las Vegas!" said architecture critic Ada Louise Huxtable of these em-bellishments during a visit around that time. She was wrong. Whether the period lampposts are preservation or beautification, they are equally authentic. A street is for people, for their use and their pleasure. It is not the head of a pin on which experts are invited to dance with theory.

> A street is for people, for their use and their pleasure. It is not the head of a pin on which experts are invited to dance with theory.

Which brings us downhill via College Street, Waterman Street, and Thomas Street. All of the fifteen streets climbing down from Benefit to North or South Main have a different sort of charm, small-grained or high caliber. Many are lined by wood-frame houses of the nineteenth century, modest but of considerable variety in style. Perhaps the most extraordinary of these streets are the major connectors, College, Waterman, and Thomas, which run from Benefit down to where North Main becomes South Main at Market Square, next to the Providence River.

College, a relatively wide avenue of two lanes carrying traffic east and west, opens at Brown University's ornate campus gate a block above Benefit. It widens as it crosses Benefit by the Athenaeum, then dips between the Providence County Courthouse and the RISD College Edifice (1936). Both are by the same firm and of Georgian Revival style, large buildings that seem to bend with the gentle curve of the street (though only the RISD building actually does so). They form a gateway of monumental brick bookends between College Hill and downtown. The new brick vehicular bridge that spans this newly uncovered stretch of the Providence River is flanked by two softly arched pedestrian bridges, also of brick, an ensemble that echoes the gateway.

One block north, Waterman takes traffic headed uphill out of downtown, and Thomas, the next block north, takes traffic downhill into downtown. In between, on the slope, sits the First Baptist Church (1775), America's first of the denomination, by Joseph Brown. Adjacent to Waterman, opposite the church, is the entrance to a tunnel built in 1914 to ease the grade for traffic heading up College Hill. It emerges on Thayer Street, near Brown.

Angell Street, College Hill's main westbound avenue, becomes Thomas Street for one block between Benefit and North Main, then becomes Steeple Street before hopping another elegant new bridge into downtown. Stepping down Thomas are the Providence Art Club's four magnificent townhouses, spanning 1786 to 1885, forming a lovely backdrop for the church. However, vehicles hurtling downhill and around the curve at Benefit have turned Thomas into a danger zone for pedestrians that trumps the block's beauty for many who travel its lovely, slender, unprotected, treeless brick sidewalk. The church railing often bears mangled evidence of Thomas's hazard.

South and North Main both head north by such splendid buildings as the courthouse—with an impressive colonnade on this side—and the church, but many more as well, including the Old Stone Bank (1898) and the ogee-gabled Joseph Brown House (1774). Modernism has been bolder on Main than on Benefit: Old Stone Square (1985), by Edward Larrabee Barnes, and RISD's recent museum addition, by Rafael Moneo, diminish the waterfront's beauty without adding much, if anything, to its interest.

Between South Main and the river lies Memorial Park (1996), dominated by Paul Cret's World War I memorial. The park is the southern terminus of a new riverfront created in the 1990s when the state "daylighted" the river, which had been covered by streets since the nineteenth century. The widest bridge in the world (1,147 feet, as noted in the Guinness Book of World Records), has been replaced by twelve elegant bridges and a river walk terminating at Waterplace Park. The new riverfront's traditional style is almost as much a miracle as its passage through local, state, and federal bureaucracies (pushed by its designer, Rhode Island architect and planner William D. Warner) as an adjunct to an earlier major redevelopment/transportation project.

Miraculous well describes the survival of Providence's urbane beauty during a period when so many other cities mutilated some of their loveliest features. The territory between Benefit and the Providence River may show off the blessings of the T3-T4 transect at its best—please excuse the New Urban nomenclature—but it is only the beginning of this small city's large *civitas*.

LOCAL NEIGHBORHOOD STREETS, REDISCOVERED

Figure 2.143: Main Street, Southport, Connecticut. A classic New England Main Street. "Under a spreading chestnut tree…."

Figure 2.144: South Portland Avenue, Brooklyn, New York. In 2006, voted the most beautiful block in New York by the readers of *Time Out,* although there are many similar blocks in South Brooklyn.

CANYON ROAD, SANTA FE, NEW MEXICO / Stefanos Polyzoides and John Massengale

Neighborhood Street

The people of Santa Fe are justly proud of their rich and heterogeneous cultural heritage. Native Americans lived a thousand years ago where the city now stands; Spain and then Mexico later occupied the area for several centuries before the Americans took the territory in 1846. The history produced several influences: Pueblo, Spanish Colonial, and Territorial. And yet so much has either been built or significantly altered since New Mexico began preparations to become a state in 1912 that almost everything we see in downtown Santa Fe

can be described as new since 1910. That's why we have called it elsewhere "the most beautiful city of the twentieth century."[32]

> That's why we have called Santa Fe "the most beautiful city of the twentieth century."

Even the Palace of the Governors—the "oldest continuously inhabited building in the United States"—was dramatically Victorianized by the United States Army in the nineteenth century while Santa Fe was still part of the New Mexico Territory. In 1910 architects imaginatively recreated it in a form that had never quite existed before, giving us the building we have now.

In 1912, the city fathers prepared a master plan for the city that mandated the use of the regional architectural style we now associate with Santa Fe. When the Palace of the Governors was rebuilt in 1913, it served as one of the style's first examples. Based on both Native pueblo and Spanish Colonial architecture, this combination eventually developed into two official Santa Fe styles: Territorial and Spanish Pueblo. The first was based on the material character of native pueblo architecture with occasional Spanish Colonial overtones, overlaid with a thin white classicism, concentrated mostly in doors, windows, and portales. Spurred by the expectations of tourists and fueled by boosters and promoters, a second style emerged a little later, based more literally on Pueblo architecture precedents, including their volumetric composition, their earth-hugging profiles, deep-wall structure, combination wooden and masonry portales, and spare openings. It has been recognized since as the Santa Fe or Pueblo Revival style. A city preservation ordinance in 1957 mandated the use of one or the other for all construction in more than half the rapidly expanding city.

Old Santa Fe, far away from quarries or forests, was initially built with adobe bricks, covered by earthen mud applied wet over them. Dried mud washes away ever so slowly in the rain, and has to be regularly repaired (which accounts for the rounded forms of the architecture of the native pueblos). Because of the high maintenance required on adobe buildings, once freight trains arrived, most projects in the twentieth century were finished with stucco plaster rather than with local adobe. Stucco is just as malleable as mud, but doesn't dissolve in the rain. Tinted with the colors of the local earth, it is magical in the famous desert light of Santa Fe.

Initially, the stucco was always applied over an adobe brick structure, later over a concrete frame with tile or concrete block infill, and, lately, increasingly over highly insulated wood-frame and plywood structures. This is Santa Fe's default building technology. It provides good thermal mass and thermal gain or loss protection, in a high desert climate where the nights can be cold and the days hot. It is a simple and durable technology, and the resultant architectural forms are well understood and loved in Santa Fe. Good, new interpretations of the Santa Fe Style architecture are characterized by simplicity, honesty of construction, and beauty of materials and form.

Canyon Road is a half-mile-long old country road, leading into Santa Fe's downtown from the east. Built long before earth-moving equipment was available, it gently follows the natural topography, sometimes flat and sometimes sloped, taking the path of least resistance. Its right-of-way roughly parallels the Acequia Madre (Mother Ditch) that flows into the city from a nearby canyon in the Santa Fe Mountains. The overall urban form of Canyon Road is that of a traditional New Mexico Cordillera village. Such linear villages, often one building deep, edge many New Mexico rural roads.

The early houses on Canyon Road are eighteenth-century farmhouses that were later folded into family compounds encouraged by local patterns of inheritance. When New Mexico became a state, a number of American artists moved to Santa Fe, and many settled on Canyon Road. Galleries followed them, and a second generation of artists and galleries arrived in the 1940s, attracted by what was then known as the Santa Fe Colony. In 1962, the city designated the road a "residential arts and crafts zone." Today there are more than one hundred art galleries on Canyon Road.

The most extraordinary characteristic of the urbanism of Canyon Road—and the subject matter of the adjoining sketches—are the frontages of its buildings. A frontage is a threshold device that mediates between the private realm of each house and the public realm of the street it fronts. Any good thoroughfare contains a few distinctive frontages. On a short two-hour visit, no less than twenty frontages were documented by Stefanos Polyzoides on Canyon Road. This is a rare, encyclopedic catalog of an exceptionally rich array of frontage types: essential ingredients in distinctive architectural design and memorable urban placemaking (Figure 2.145).

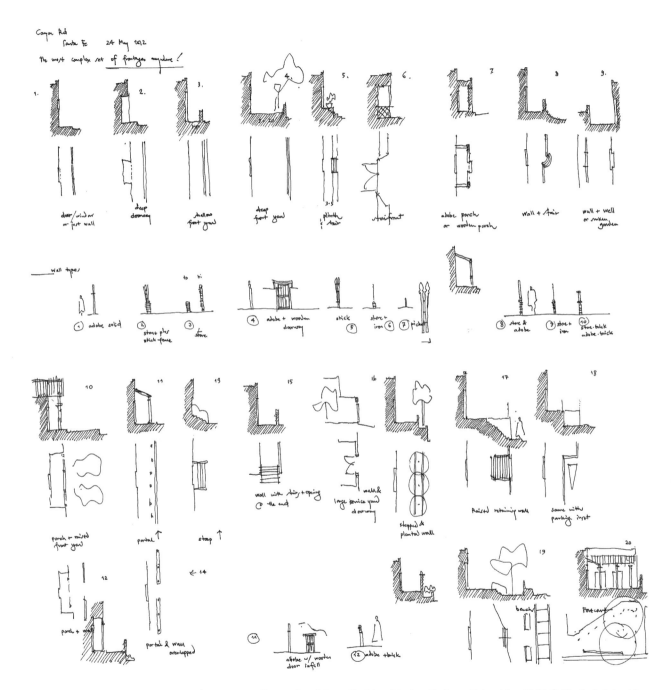

Figure 2.145: Sketches cataloging frontages on Canyon Road, Santa Fe, New Mexico. Stefanos Polyzoides, 2012. © *Moule & Polyzoides, Architects & Urbanists*

The reasons why so many frontages came to be invented and applied here are very instructive for the future of urbanism everywhere, so we will list them here:

- Canyon Road was very sensitively located on a hilly topography. The variety of its frontages results in part from the fact that some houses' designs are responding to flat sites, others to uphill or downhill ones.

- Hispanic New Mexican society has traditionally valued both family privacy and safeguarding community form—thus the definition of a walled residential architecture organized around internal patios and balanced by frontages that deliver an active, pedestrian public realm.

- The climate extremes of northern New Mexico are notable. Many frontage types are designed to provide cover from rain and shade from the sun and to moderate the effects of the local climate through the four seasons.

- Many of the houses on Canyon Road were built either directly by their owners or by builders under the direction of owners. The variety and spontaneity of frontage design is the result of the freedom that these individuals enjoyed in deciding their designs as thresholds between their particular house and their particular place on the street—whether on a flat spot, a terminated vista, an uphill or a downhill site, a large lot, or a tiny one.

- Until the advent of statehood, there was no regulation of use or form in this part of Santa Fe. Frontages were, therefore, initially designed to accommodate residential, local commercial, local-craft, agricultural, and other uses. Over time, and as building uses changed, owners felt free to modify the form of frontages based on their evolving functional needs. The visual complexity, the picturesque composition, and the sheer beauty of Canyon Road must be understood as an essay on successional urbanism: its streetscape is based on the contributions of hundreds of people that had a small hand in making it possible.

- The width of the street and the geometry of its carriageway is a clear reflection of its origins as a thoroughfare that was built to accommodate animal-drawn carts, people on horse, mule, or donkey-back, and pedestrians. The charm of Canyon Road's insistent irregularity reflects not only that the design of its right-of-way evolved over time, based on the ever-changing needs of its residents, but also that the frontages mediate between the form of the street and the fabric of its buildings.

When the city's economy was poor, Canyon Road was one of the hippie capitals of the West, with very inexpensive rentals. Today, Canyon Road is thought of as one of the most beautiful places in America; Santa Fe has a thriving high-end real estate market and a treasured architectural heritage. But Santa Fe's buildings are not valued because they have been preserved in amber; they are valued because the city's inhabitants have developed a disciplined yet organic architectural approach to the region's extraordinary cultural legacy.

Santa Maria Street, Coral Gables, Florida

F. M. Button and Pierson & Skinner, 1925

Neighborhood Street

Santa Maria Street is an example of an appropriately auto-scaled street in a suburban neighborhood (Figures 2.146 and 2.147). The street is not too wide; it measures approximately twenty-one feet across, which is narrow enough to moderate traffic flow. Slow speeds also encourage pedestrian and cyclist activity.

From the perspective of a cyclist, a neighborhood street like Santa Maria that is well shaded by large canopy trees and often has "eyes on the street" (or residents in their front yards, casually monitoring road activity) is ideal for biking. Noticeably absent from this

Figure 2.146: Santa Maria Street, Coral Gables, Florida. F. M. Button and Pierson & Skinner, 1925. Originally conceived by Coral Gables founder George Merrick as a Neoclassical Village, Santa Maria Street is the archetypal American "T3" street.

Figure 2.147: Santa Maria Street, Coral Gables, Florida. F. M. Button and Pierson & Skinner, 1925. Wide swales have permitted the trees to grow massive by South Florida standards, giving year-round shade. The front yard fences define the private space with elegance, as a natural extension of the architecture of the houses.

cycling-friendly street: separate zones or lanes marked with brightly colored paint, designated for bike use only. On an adequately sized suburban street where beauty is seamlessly integrated with function, specialized lanes are not needed as long as cars drive slowly (Color Plate 23). Noticeably present on Santa Maria: sidewalks with an informal appeal. The curbless edges are safer and create a pleasant aesthetic. The sidewalks measure five feet—a typically narrow dimension—but the lack of curbs at the edge of the pavement *and* at the edge of the sidewalks enables pedestrians to casually overflow into the adjacent swale.

La Alameda de Santa Rosa, Antigua, Guatemala

Neighborhood Street

Antigua Guatemala has three *alamedas*, the most exceptional of which is the Alameda de Santa Rosa (Figure 2.148). Like the other two, Santa Rosa is paved with cobblestones. Vehicles and pedestrians co-exist within the space; motorists drive slowly because the surface of the street is not smooth and flat. The street has a steep inverted crown, draining toward its center rather than the sides, and while a bit disconcerting, this undoubtedly also slows down drivers.

While Quinta Avenida is the civic emblem of Antigua, the streets with alamedas in the city are immediately noticed by visitors because of their rarity. Most streets in the historic center do not have trees, so Santa Rosa stands out. Existing within the pattern of the large, regular grid, La Alameda de Santa Rosa has wide swales at each edge of the street. Narrow sidewalks are located next to the swales, and many buildings and garden walls have been constructed immediately adjacent to the sidewalks, interrupted occasionally by *zaguans* or tall, wide gates, as is customary in Spanish colonial towns in the region. Antigua has become famous for its growing number of Spanish-language immersion schools, and at the beginning and end of each day the sidewalks of La Alameda de Santa Rosa are filled with foreign students finding their way to and from all-day conversation sessions.

The mature trees that line the street do not simply add "columns" to the public room with their trunks. The canopy they create provides a sense of "ceiling" enclosure overhead as well, making the wide street feel even more contained.

Figure 2.148: La Alameda de Santa Rosa, Antigua, Guatemala. A rare exception in the city's streets, its formal rows of trees grow in wide swales on both sides of the inverted-crown roadway; high garden walls with *zaguans* line the sidewalks (seen at right).

YIELD STREETS AND GARDEN STREETS

Figure 2.149: Balfour Place, London, England. View looking north toward Mount Street. The 'yield street' is a time-honored way to handle light two-way traffic without an unduly wide roadway.

Yield Streets

Yield streets are two-way streets so narrow that one car must pull over to let a car going the other way pass by. England has many examples, both in old village and city fabric and on narrow country lanes (Color Plate 31). Pictured here is Balfour Place, in Mayfair, London (Figure 2.149). Out in the countryside, many roads between hedgerows are so small that they are barely wide enough for one car, let alone two (Figures 2.150 and 2.159). Pullovers are made by the side of the road every mile or two, or when visibility is particularly bad.

American developers dealing with truculent bureaucracies demanding wide roads have been known to build one-way streets with parking on both sides, taking down the one-way signs after all permits are issued. A more legal approach, when building privately deeded roads, is to use local standards for parking lots and alleys: a yield street can frequently be built by calling it "parking" or "alley," because the regulations for those are frequently less restrictive.

Figure 2.150: Deep Lane, South Hams, England. A yield street in the country just outside the city of Plymouth. The hedgerows occasionally leave space to one side or the other to pull over and wait for a car to pass.

English Garden Streets

▲ **Figure 2.151:** Knightsbridge, London, England. Satellite view. The developers of Georgian London perfected variations on a unique and useful form, in which the streets are stretched and planted with tall trees as lush, elongated parks, faced by terrace houses. The maneuver simultaneously made the city greener and healthier, added shared outdoor open space to offset the scarcity of private gardens on the compact house lots, aided with stormwater management, and created special addresses of enormous value. Beaufort Gardens (center) is an example of these English Garden Streets. The wide street at the end of Beaufort Gardens is Brompton Road. *Image courtesy of Google Earth, © 2012 Bluesky*

◀ **Figure 2.152:** Cornwall Gardens, London, England. Satellite view. Cornwall Gardens is a variation on the private squares of London, showing how flexible the type can be; other examples are bent, mashed, squeezed, and adapted to great effect. Despite some blurring of the usual spatial distinctions between street, square, and park, they remain in the end streets, perhaps owing to the fact that the architecture shaping them is consistently street-oriented and resolutely urbane. In architectural terms, the way the large houses at the western end of the street are "plugged into" the park creates a valuable variety in the character of the gardens. Two houses have private yards on the private park (which in most cities would be public park). *Image courtesy of Google Earth, © 2012 Bluesky*

◀◀ **Figure 2.153:** Beaufort Gardens, London, England. George Adam Burn, architect, Jeremiah and Henry Little, builders, 1861-70. Looking north towards Brompton Road. Beaufort Gardens is just one block long, functioning like a Close. A single row of immense trees hovers over the space, which instead of a green has a beautiful place for parking and walking.

▶ **Figure 2.154:** Beaufort Gardens, London, England. George Adam Burn, architect, Jeremiah and Henry Little, builders, 1861–70. Looking north towards Brompton Road. At four stories plus attics, the street has a height-to-width ratio of approximately 1:1.5. The graceful houses prove that repetitive designs can indeed be agreeable.

PEDESTRIAN PASSAGES AND STEP STREETS

Much of the focus of urban design is on the big, important streets, but there is wonder and promise in the skinny, specialized streets, too. Small laneways, pedestrian passages, canal streets, and staircases are useful exceptions to the rule, defining the networks that bind some of the world's best neighborhoods together. These exceptional streets tend to originate with some problem that needed solving, like breaking down oversized blocks into walkable ones, crossing topography too steep for vehicles, or simply squeezing in a direct route to make things convenient in circumstances where a full-size street just won't fit. A standout little street is at times just the right recipe for an address of distinction; for example, the tony Burlington Arcade, a calmly elegant shopping street in London, is wholly unlike its bustling surroundings, which is precisely the point.

Figure 2.155: Quince Street, Philadelphia, Pennsylvania. One of Philadelphia's Trinity streets, named for the tiny, three-story (Father, Son, and Holy Ghost) houses that line them. Each floor has one room: the three floors combined amount to 400 to 700 square feet. Built as mid-block worker housing, the oldest may date from 1720. *Image courtesy of Paul Murrain*

These streets benefit a city in many ways, besides the practical business of providing a direct route. The skinny streets offer up alternative addresses, expanding the choices in local real estate. They can be used to convey prestige (by setting up especially tranquil home sites) or to enable affordability (by using a low-cost type of infrastructure while getting a few more buildable lots into the block). The urban designer might also employ exceptional little streets to showcase special views, or to overcome a topographic feature that threatens the urban framework's continuity.

But the biggest benefit is variety. The exceptional little streets are inherently human-scaled, and they introduce contrasts into what otherwise might be a relentless or boring set of similar spatial experiences.

The skinniest charming streets make a great argument for a fine-grained grid and tightly wound intersections. Most of these exceptional streets are either pedestrian-only or allow just one-way traffic; neither pattern is recommended as the norm for a whole neighborhood (Figure 2.155). However, when one has a lot of connected streets to work with, one can afford to demote a few links to a less-trafficked status. The result can elevate the quality of the whole urban ensemble.

The Ninety-Nine Steps, Charlotte Amalie, St. Thomas, United States Virgin Islands

Step Street

Charlotte Amalie contains one of the largest collections of stepped streets in the world, forty-five in total. The staircases extend the ordinary streets and were included in the original Danish layout of the town in order to make connections up slopes too steep for vehicles. (Some historians think the pattern originated with designers back in Denmark who specified the street grid without realizing the site was so hilly.) Hardy pedestrians have more options than motorists on the hillsides above the harbor, and as they climb the stairs, long views gradually unfold. Over the past fifty years, many of the stepped streets fell into disrepair and disuse. The Ninety-Nine Steps—now a major landmark in the U.S.

▶ **Figure 2.156:** Ninety-Nine Steps, Charlotte Amalie, St. Thomas, U.S. Virgin Islands. The step street is a practical alternative to full-sized streets where the topography demands it. The houses on the Ninety-Nine Steps boast a landmark address, and pedestrians are rewarded for the cardiovascular workout with panoramic views of the harbor.

▶▶ **Figure 2.157:** Longitude Lane, Charleston, South Carolina. The passage cuts one of Charleston's oversized blocks down to size, making the neighborhood more permeable and more interesting.

Virgin Islands, and a must-see destination for island tourists—became the first of the stepped streets to be restored and is one of the most prominent examples of this unique street type (Figure 2.156).

Developer Michael Ball and designer Felipe Ayala collaborated to restore the Ninety-Nine Steps beginning in 1998 as part of an effort to upgrade the Blackbeard's Castle hotel and its environs, welcoming visitors deeper into the town and showcasing the views from the hillside.[33] They cleared the path, reconstructing the steps where necessary. (Note, there are one hundred three of them, not ninety-nine.)[34] Next, they strategically placed plantings that frame the space with color and texture. On either side, houses were renovated and vacant lots filled in with buildings that open directly onto the staircase. This process continued, house by house, right up to the present. Today the Ninety-Nine Steps form not just a path up the hill, but a place in its own right.

Longitude Lane, Charleston, South Carolina

Pedestrian Passage

Longitude Lane is a street for pedestrians in Charleston (Figure 2.157). Averaging ten feet wide, the narrow passage begins at Bay Street and goes west. Lined with houses and residential compounds, it has a brick and stone hardscape that unify the visually interesting route.

The pedestrian passage complements the well-knit network of Charleston. One of the skinniest streets in America, Longitude Lane is an example of a type that is an integral part of the urban fabric in many cities of the world. Like the narrow passages in Melbourne, the small, compact streets in the Barri Gotic of Barcelona, or the narrow passages in many of the ancient neighborhoods of Rome, Longitude Lane complements the larger network of roads in its city. The narrow passage adds a surprise in the walk around town, a welcome contrast with the full-size streets.

PRINCIPLES FOR DESIGNING BEAUTIFUL RURAL ROADS

- Follow the contours of the land, as though you had no access to modern machinery for grading. Avoid long, single-radius curves.
- Alternate straight lines with natural curves.
- Make edges on one or both sides of the road with rows of trees, hedgerows, stone walls, or rural fences. Walls and rows of trees can be combined.

- When there is a vista, a single edge or a single edge with a low wall on the opposite side can be good.
- When there is no vista, both sides of the road should have a well-defined edge. An allée with a tree canopy over the road is good.
- Coming into a clearing with a vista is good.
- When the road passes through a clearing, put the road along the edge of the clearing or have a good reason for not doing so.
- Alternating clearings with allées in woods or forests is good.
- Alternating clearings with sequences in allées or forests to create a sequence of vistas is good.
- When there are ridges and valleys, put the road on the ridge or at the bottom of the valley, or pass from one to the other.
- Clearing the hillside so that the line of the top of the hill is visible, with or without trees along the crest, can be good.
- Make the roads drain without curbs.
- Minimize the use of signs and interstate-style striping.
- Do not use suburban arterial elements such as Jersey barriers, center turn lanes, large signs, and modern galvanized light fixtures.

Figure 2.158: Streever Farm Road, Pine Plains, New York. The trees date from a Great Depression era program in Dutchess County that paid farmers to plant allées along country roads.

Figure 2.159: Lane, Little-bredy, England. A one-lane yield road in Dorset. *Image courtesy of Ben Pentreath*

Figure 2.160: Strada della Stazione, Orvieto, Italy. The road leaving the Umbrian hill town.

- When rural roads come into hamlets or villages, the buildings should be close to the road.
- When rural roads have very few buildings, individual buildings may be very close to the road. In that case, they should be parallel to the road.

- When rural roads have frequent buildings, the buildings should either be close to the road or distant from the road. Avoid frequent, repetitive suburban-style setbacks (twenty-five to fifty feet), with parking or poorly defined front yards along the road.

PARKWAYS

> Of course I litter the public highway. Every chance I get. After all, it's not the beer cans that are ugly; it's the highway that is ugly.
>
> —Edward Abbey, *The Second Rape of the West*[35]

American highways weren't always ugly. Once a collaboration between engineers, architects, and landscape architects, they were beautiful, by design. A new type of road called a "parkway" allowed city dwellers to escape into the countryside while offering them a rural experience that was pleasurable in itself. Parkways were places.

The first of these parkways, the Bronx River Parkway, was the first limited-access highway in the world (Figure 2.161). The parkway runs alongside the Bronx River in northern New York City and in Westchester County, New York, the county to the north of the Bronx. Construction began in 1907. Originally planned to be 13.2 miles long (the parkway was later expanded to both the north and the south), the Bronx River Parkway opened to traffic in 1922 and was completed in 1925 (Figure 2.162). The beautiful road was set in parkland along a badly polluted river (Figure 2.163). One of the purposes of building the parkway was to remove the sources of pollution along the river and create parks along both sides of it (Figure 2.164).

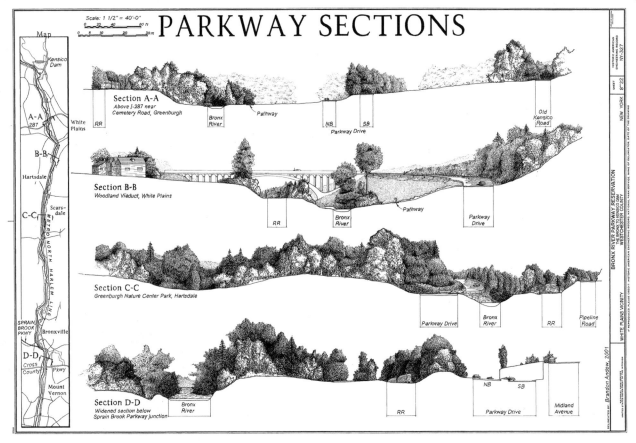

Figure 2.161: Bronx River Parkway, The Bronx, New York, and Westchester County, New York. Gilmore Clarke, Landscape Architect and Civil Engineer; Arthur Hayden, Designing Engineer; and Hermann Merkel, Forester, 1907–1925. Sections of the parkway in the vicinity of White Plains, New York. *Image courtesy of Historic American Engineering Record, National Park Service, Brandon Andow Delineator, 2001*

Particularly important for the design were a German-trained forester named Hermann Merkel and the landscape architect Gilmore Clarke, who went on to design many other early parkways. Clarke also praised the Designing Engineer, Arthur Hayden, saying that his "sensitivity to aesthetic matters" was exceptional among engineers.

The team set the standards for America's early parkways, capturing the public's imagination with this new type of road that combined efficiency and beauty (Figure 2.165). Carefully coordinating landscape design with highway engineering, they created a safe, comfortable roadway that gave its users the feeling of a ride through the countryside, even when town centers were nearby. The parkway helped the environmentalist and planner Benton MacKaye to formulate his idea of "the townless highway,"[36] which was influential before engineers took sole control of the highway building process after World War II (Figure 2.166). But ideas developed for the Bronx River Parkway also continued to influence the design of interstate highways built after the war: the primary concepts were limited access to the main road, using bridges to replace at-grade intersections with grade separations, the elimination of steep grades and sharp curves, and the separation of oncoming traffic with landscaped medians.

Figure 2.162: Bronx River Parkway, The Bronx, New York, and Westchester County, New York. Gilmore Clarke, Landscape Architect and Civil Engineer; Arthur Hayden, Designing Engineer; and Hermann Merkel, Forester; 1907–1925. A 1922 photograph showing an early section of the parkway in Yonkers, New York. *Library of Congress, Prints & Photographs Division, Historic American Buildings Survey/Historic American Engineering Record/ Historic American Landscapes Survey Collection, HAER NY-327-99*

Figure 2.163: Bronx River Parkway, The Bronx, New York, and Westchester County, New York. Gilmore Clarke, Landscape Architect and Civil Engineer; Arthur Hayden, Designing Engineer; and Hermann Merkel, Forester; 1907– 1925. A 1912 photograph documenting the conditions along the Bronx River before construction of the parkway. This "before" view from White Plains, New York, shows privies draining into the river. The "after" view in 1915 is shown in Figure 2.164. *Library of Congress, Prints & Photographs Division, Historic American Buildings Survey/Historic American Engineering Record/Historic American Landscapes Survey Collection, HAER NY-327-80*

Figure 2.164: Bronx River Parkway, The Bronx, New York, and Westchester County, New York. Gilmore Clarke, Landscape Architect and Civil Engineer; Arthur Hayden, Designing Engineer; and Hermann Merkel, Forester; 1907–1925. A 1915 photograph of the Bronx River Parkway Reservation in White Plains, New York, showing the "after" view of the site in Figure 2.163. *Library of Congress, Prints & Photographs Division, Historic American Buildings Survey/Historic American Engineering Record/Historic American Landscapes Survey Collection, HAER NY-327-81*

Figure 2.165: Bronx River Parkway, The Bronx, New York, and Westchester County, New York. Gilmore Clarke, Landscape Architect and Civil Engineer; Arthur Hayden, Designing Engineer; and Hermann Merkel, Forester; 1907–1925. A view of the stone bridge built for the Elm Street access road in Tuckahoe, New York. *Library of Congress, Prints & Photographs Division, Historic American Buildings Survey/Historic American Engineering Record/ Historic American Landscapes Survey Collection, HAER NY-327-20*

Figure 2.166: Bronx River Parkway, The Bronx, New York, and Westchester County, New York. Gilmore Clarke, Landscape Architect and Civil Engineer; Arthur Hayden, Designing Engineer; and Hermann Merkel, Forester; 1907–1925. A 1927 photograph of the Palmer Road bridge over the Bronx River Parkway in Bronxville, New York, designed by Cecil Stoughton. *Library of Congress, Prints & Photographs Division, Historic American Buildings Survey/Historic American Engineering Record/Historic American Landscapes Survey Collection, HAER NY-327-101*

Design precedents for the parkway included English parks and country estates, but the most direct precedent was perhaps New York City's Central Park, designed by Frederick Law Olmsted and Calvert Vaux. Central Park had limited-access roads, informal designs that brought the appearance of wild and rural plans and details to New York City, and innovative grade- and use-separation for the vehicles and walkers in the urban park. Olmsted and Vaux are credited with introducing the term "park-way" with their urban boulevards in Brooklyn, and their design for the Fenway in Boston was also important for the Bronx River Parkway.

The Bronx River Parkway Commission identified a number of key principles for the Parkway's design.[37] These included:

- The roadway should conveniently accommodate the large amount of traffic expected and display to the traveler the principal interesting features without despoiling them.

- Bridges should be carefully designed and built for permanence, with architectural treatment in harmony with their natural surroundings.

- Exposed surfaces of bridges, retaining walls, etc., should be of native stone, avoiding formal, cut-stone effects. Only long-span viaducts would have outside surfaces of concrete.

- Natural features should be preserved, which included taking adequate care of existing trees.

- Reforestation and landscaping treatment should be carried out along natural lines, avoiding exotic plantings.

- "All objects foreign to, or distracting from, the naturalness of the valley must be hidden by natural objects wherever possible."

- "In planning the planting, therefore, as in the rest of the design, a humanized naturalness should be aimed at, sufficiently diversified to create woodland groups and vistas of all of the types that belong; broad enough that he who runs (or rides) may see; with intimate bits for those who wish to pause; with material prevailingly indigenous, but always suitable to the situation and its requirements."

The design of the Bronx River Parkway influenced the design of other parkways. Clarke went on to become the chief designer for the Taconic State Parkway, which begins in northern Westchester County at the Kensico Dam, where the Bronx River Parkway ends.

The Taconic Parkway was originally planned with the idea that city dwellers could use the road to drive upstate to a series of state parks. Franklin Delano Roosevelt, who

lived both in New York City and in the Hudson Valley, was a long-term advocate for rural parkways. He first argued for a road like it when he ran for State Senate in 1910, but when he later lost the full use of his legs to polio in 1920, he relaxed by touring the countryside in his car and therefore became an even stronger advocate. Two years later, he became Chairman of the Taconic State Park Commission, which supervised the construction of the Parkway. (This became the source of long-running friction between Roosevelt and New York highway czar Robert Moses.[38]) Noted critic Lewis Mumford was another fan of the Parkway. Although he frequently wrote about the negative effect highways had on cities, Mumford advised friends and professionals visiting him in Dutchess County, New York, to take the Taconic,[39] which he described as "a consummate work of art, fit to stand on a par with our loftiest creations"[40] (Figures 2.167 and 2.168).

A number of parkways were built in and around New York City in the boom years of the 1920s and the Great Depression that followed. The Grand Central Parkway in Queens, the Hutchinson River and Sprain Brook parkways in Westchester County, the Merritt Parkway in Connecticut that met the Hutchinson River Parkway at the New York–Connecticut border, the Palisades Parkway in New York and New Jersey on the west side of the Hudson River, and the Bear Mountain Parkway that connected the Palisades and Taconic parkways were among the best. The best-preserved of those, well worth visiting today, are the Bronx River Parkway, the Taconic State Parkway, the Bear Mountain Park-

Figure 2.167: Taconic Parkway, Hudson River Valley, New York. Gilmore Clarke, 1925–1949. Looking north on the Taconic Parkway in Dutchess County, New York. Gilmore designed the Taconic Parkway to provide a variety of views and vistas. Sometimes there are large open fields between the north and south roadways, and at other times the roadways go their separate ways in the woods.

Figure 2.168: Taconic Parkway, Hudson River Valley, New York. Gilmore Clarke, 1925–1949. Looking north on the Taconic Parkway in Dutchess County, New York. The roadways are narrow enough that the trees can make canopies over the parkway.

way, the Palisades Interstate Parkway, and the Merritt Parkway. All of these have portions that have been "upgraded," but one can also see stretches in their original state.

Public-works projects during the Depression continued the tradition of great parkways: the Colonial Parkway that runs from Jamestown to Williamsburg, Virginia; the Potomac and Rock Creek parkways in Washington, DC; the George Washington Memorial Parkway in northern Virginia; the Blue Ridge, Shenandoah Skyline, and Great Smoky Mountains parkway system in Virginia, North Carolina, and Tennessee; and the Natchez Trace in Tennessee and Mississippi.[41] These historic roads, now maintained by the National Park Service, are all still cherished.

The interstates and arterials we build are not. And yet cars are still with us and will remain part of our lives in the future. The parkways, boulevards, promenades, and main streets provide inspiration for ways to build in the future to accommodate both cars and pedestrians.

NOTES

1. "Widening roads to deal with traffic congestion is like loosening your belt to combat obesity," the futurist Glen Hiemstra famously said (although it's not clear exactly when and where he said it). Painting a road diet on a street is almost the opposite idea: the stripes are supposed to narrow the road, but the width of the asphalt paving in the roadbed remains unchanged.

2. Duany, Plater-Zyberk & Co., *Lexicon of the New Urbanism,* http://www.dpz.com/Research/Lexicon.

3. Allan B. Jacobs, Elizabeth Macdonald, and Yodan Rofè, *The Boulevard Book* (Cambridge, MA: The MIT Press, 2002), 20–22.

4. Alistair Horne, *Seven Ages of Paris* (New York: Alfred A. Knopf, 2002), 232–240.

5. Joan Busquets, *Barcelona: The Urban Evolution of a Compact City* (Rovereto, Italy: Nicolodi editore, 2006).

6. Jacobs, Macdonald, and Rofè, op cit, pp. 43, 83–84, 101–102, 108–109.

7. New York City Department of Parks and Recreation, "Eastern Parkway," http://www.nycgovparks.org/parks/B029/history.

8. Peter Bosselmann and Elizabeth Macdonald, "Boulevard Livability Study," *Places, A Forum of Design for the Public Realm* 11:2 (1997), 66–69.

9. New York City Department of Parks and Recreation, "Ocean Parkway," http://www.nycgovparks.org/about/history/historical-signs/listings?id=10787 and Jacobs, Macdonald, and Rofè, *The Boulevard Book,* 44–53. Too new to be included in our text is an excellent study of the Eastern and Ocean Parkways by Elizabeth Macdonald: *Pleasure Drives and Promenades, History of Frederick Law Olmsted's Brooklyn Parkways* (Chicago: Center for American Places at Columbia College, 2012).

10. John Nolen, *New Towns for Old, Achievements in Civic Improvement in Some American Small Towns and Neighborhoods* (Boston: Marshall Jones Co., 1927), 104–10.

11. Ibid., 105.

12. An alameda is a formal alignment of paired trees with a public walkway or promenade, found in Spain and former Spanish colonies.

13. Jacques Hillairet, *Dictionnaire historique des rues de Paris* (Paris: Éditions de minuit, 1963), and *France in the Age of Les Misérables,* "Mapping Paris." https://www.mtholyoke.edu/courses/rschwart/hist255-s01/mapping-paris/Farmers%20General%20Wall.html.

14. Maurice Rheims and Felipe Ferre, *Hector Guimard* trans. Robert Erich Wolf (New York: Harry N. Abrams, 1988), *passim.*

15. Charles Beveridge, *Frederick Law Olmsted: Designing the American Landscape,* rev. ed. (New York: Universe, 2005).

16. Everett U. Crosby, *"95% Perfect": The Older Residences at Nantucket* (Nantucket, MA: Tetaukimmo Press, 1937).

17. Robert J. Gibbs, *Principles of Urban Retail Planning and Development* (Hoboken: John Wiley & Sons, 2012), 67–71.

18. J. Christopher Lang and Kate Stout, *Building with Nantucket in Mind, Guidelines for Protecting the Historic Architecture and Landscape of Nantucket Island* (Nantucket, MA: Nantucket Historic District Commission, 1996).

19. Gibbs, op. cit., adapted from pages 81–95.

20. Diann Marsh, *Galena, Illinois: A Brief History* (Charleston, SC: The History Press, 2010), 13–14.

21. City of Galena, Illinois, "Galena History," http://www.cityofgalena.org/history.cfm.

22. The Project for Public Places named Northampton's Main Street one of their Great Public Spaces. See http://www.pps.org/great_public_spaces/one?public_place_id=184. In 2007, the American Planning Association honored the street with one of their annual Great American Places awards: http://www.planning.org/greatplaces/streets/2007/mainstreet-northampton.htm.

23. Edmund N. Bacon, *Design of Cities* (New York: Penguin, 1976), 201.

24. Charles Dickens Jr., *Dickens's Dictionary of London,* http://www.victorianlondon.org/districts/piccadilly.htm.

25. In addition to Nash, two of the most prominent architects were Sir John Soane and Charles Robert Cockerell.

26. World War I delayed construction, and Blomfield continued until 1928, with architects Sir John James Burnet, Arthur Joseph Davis, and Henry Tanner were also involved.

27. Clay Lancaster and Edmund V. Gillon Jr., *Old Brooklyn Heights: New York's First Suburb* (Mineola: Dover Publications, 1979), 74. Also see Max Carr, boxed out (blog), "Ones and Twos: The State of Joralemon West," http://max-carr.blogspot.com/2012/08/ones-and-twos-state-of-joralemon-east.html.

28. François Spoerry, *A Gentle Urbanism* (Chichester, UK: John Wiley & Sons, 1991).

29. Sir Raymond Unwin, *Town Planning In Practice: An Introduction to the Art of Designing Cities and Suburbs* (New York: Princeton Architectural Press, 1994).

30. National Park Service, U.S. Department of the Interior, "Charleston's Historic Religious and Community Buildings." http://www.nps.gov/nr/travel/charleston/stp.htm.

31. Prominent exceptions may have been the designs of the seventeenth and eighteenth centuries that celebrated pure geometry in places like the Circus in Bath. Since those curbs haven't survived centuries of repaving, we don't know.

32. John Massengale, *Veritas et Venustas* blog, "The Most Beautiful City of the Twentieth Century." http://massengale.typepad.com/venustas/2010/07/the-most-beautiful-city-of-the-twentieth-century-redux.html.

33. St. Thomas Source. "Signs of the Renaissance, Haagensen House." http://stthomassource.com/content/business/st-thomas-business/2000/03/23/signs-renaissance-haagensen-house-more.

34. Virgin Islands Now. "Historic Sites in Charlotte an Amalie (Kongen's Quarter)." http://www.vinow.com/stthomas/attractions_stt/attractions_town.php/.

35. Edward Abbey, "The Second Rape of the West," *The Journey Home* (New York: Penguin Books USA, 1991), 158–59.

36. Benton MacKaye, "The Townless Highway," *The New Republic, March 12, 1930.*

37. New York (State) Bronx River Parkway Commission, *Report of the Bronx River Parkway Commission: Appointed under Chapter 669 of the Laws of 1906* (New York: Trow Press, 1907). Also see http://westchesterarchives.com/BRPR/Report_fr.html.

38. In 1929 Roosevelt was elected governor of New York, and Robert Moses was his secretary of state. Moses, expert at obtaining and controlling funding, diverted state funds away from construction of the Taconic to the parkways Moses built on Long Island, beginning with the Northern State Parkway. "Taconic State Parkway," Wikipedia, http://en.wikipedia.org/wiki/Taconic_Parkway.

39. Donald L. Miller, Lewis Mumford: A *Life* (New York: Grove Press, 2002), 480. "[A]nd whenever he was in Leedsville Mumford would tell friends from New York City who were coming by car to visit him to take [the] Taconic State Parkway, a winding ribbon of road through the Hudson River Valley."

40. Harold Faber, "Metropolitan Baedeker; Savoring the Scenic Delights Along the Taconic State Parkway," *The New York Times*, August 14, 1987. http://www.nytimes.com/1987/08/14/arts/metropolitan-baedeker-savoring-the-scenic-delights-along-the-taconic-parkway.html.

41. National Park Service, "Lying Lightly On the Land: Building America's National Parks Roads and Parkways," http://www.nps.gov/history/hdp/exhibits/lll/overview.htm. See also "Highways in Harmony," http://www.nps.gov/history/history/online_books/hih/index.htm.

CHAPTER THREE

STREET SYSTEMS AND NETWORKS

STREETS DON'T FLOAT IN ISOLATION. They are inseparable from the larger city, integrated into a system of other streets and public spaces. Similarly, our understanding of a street can rarely be separated from the particular details of the place where we experience it. That context might be the immediate one of the adjacent streets, or it might be a larger one, such as the history of the city where the street is found, or the form of the city itself.

An urban designer must simultaneously think of the design of the individual street and how that street will operate in its larger setting. In this chapter we explore useful streets, both historic and new, in pairs and in sets, and in grids, patterns, and networks. Here policy and design inevitably intersect. In this holistic way of thinking, removing a damaging inner-city highway to make a new boulevard, inserting a new street to create more routes for walking, rewriting the development rules for groups of similar corridors, or measuring a neighborhood's walkability so that it can be improved are all part of the same work.

THE STREETS OF CHARLESTON AND SAVANNAH

Some of our favorite streets are found in Charleston, South Carolina, and Savannah, Georgia, two southern American cities that are only one hundred miles apart. As we looked at them anew, we realized that these streets characterize their respective cities, which are also two of our favorite cities. Their urban plans help to explain important issues in street design (Figure 3.1).

Charleston and Savannah are beautiful because their historic streets are beautiful, but the streets became beautiful in different ways. Savannah, planned by General James Oglethorpe in 1733, has the most intelligently varied, pure grid in America, perhaps the world. In contrast to that orderly plan, the old streets of Charleston are a ragged agglomeration of more conventional American grids built over time, first by the Lords Proprietors

◀Historic Center, Rome, Italy. See Figure 3.22.

Figure 3.1: Charleston, South Carolina, and Savannah, Georgia. Historic maps drawn at the same scale. Both cities have beautiful streets, but they became beautiful in different ways.

who owned the Carolina colony and later by the developers who came after them. As a result of that piecemeal process, a map of Charleston can look in places like a patchwork quilt (Figure 3.2). And with some notable exceptions, the beauty of the individual streets of Charleston depends more on the buildings that line the streets than the artfulness of the streets. Savannah, on the other hand, has good and sometimes great build-

ings, but the planning of the streets is an essential part of the city's greatness and beauty.

Savannah, planned by General James Oglethorpe in 1733, has the most intelligently varied, pure grid in America, perhaps the world.

Market Street

St. Philips Church

Four Corners of Law

Broad Street

Church Street

Meeting Street

Water Street

Church Street
at Water Street

Legare Street

White Point Gardens

Figure 3.2: Charleston, South Carolina. Figure-ground drawing. *Image courtesy of Dover, Kohl & Partners using data provided by the City of Charleston*

In his book *Architecture, Men, Women and Money, 1600–1860,* the banker and historian Roger Kennedy explains how the different political and economic histories of the two cities affected the ways their physical form evolved. Before the American Revolution, Charleston was the fourth-largest port in the American colonies, and the wealthiest and largest city south of Philadelphia. The port continued to grow after the war, but Charleston had half the population of New York, and for a long time its planters and hunters were content to let the British control the trading and shipping from Charleston to England and its colonies. The city became known for the luxury items its wealthy residents imported from the home country, and a number of its inhabitants were English Loyalists who sat out the Revolution in London.[1]

In the early nineteenth century, Charleston's economy and port grew more slowly than those in Boston, New York, Philadelphia, and Savannah. According to Kennedy, Charleston was led by an oligarchy dominated by a large contingent of wealthy planters who stayed in the city and lived an increasingly patrician lifestyle, with more emphasis on conserving money than making it. The importing of luxury items from Europe continued, and in the War of 1812 many Charlestonians were reluctant to oppose British sanctions.

In contrast, Savannah grew rapidly during and after the War of 1812, and the city's share of the shipping of cotton surged as the market boomed, thanks to new inventions of the Industrial Revolution like the cotton gin and the steamboat. Cotton and other goods flowed down the Savannah River from land previously closed off from easy access to trade. In the first quarter of the century, Savannah raced past Charleston as a center of trading and shipping.

Architecture in Charleston and Savannah

The architecture built in the booming city of Savannah in the early nineteenth century was innovative and adventurous, particularly in the hands of local architect William Jay. The architecture of Charleston at the same time was a conservative continuation of Charleston's unique and beautiful building type, the Single House (Figure 3.3). This was a reflection of its patrician society, a contrast to the more entrepreneurial culture of Savannah.

The image of a row of refined and restrained Single Houses on shaded tree-lined streets became the dominant architectural and urban image of Charleston. The Single House type was built in the city for over one hundred years, and for most of that time it was a built in a tradition that never lost its stylistic connection to eighteenth-century Classicism. That tradition included a long-lasting Classical Vernacular that was related to eighteenth-century Georgian architecture but simultaneously particular to the region. The simple Classical aesthetic also dominated the design of other building types in the city, giving Charleston a character strongly connected to its roots in the 1700s. No other American city has such a consistent collection of outstanding Classical buildings shaping its streets (Figure 3.4).

When we walk around a city we know well, we keep an unconscious connection to other parts of the city. Walking the old parts of Charleston's main commercial street, King Street, surrounded by mixed-use, party-wall buildings with ground-floor stores, we consciously or unconsciously draw connections between the architecture of King Street and the Classical Vernacular we know from the residential streets. The fact that the commercial buildings are rooted in the same cultural past and architectural sensibility as the freestanding Single Houses supports those connections.

Not coincidentally, the buildings on both the residential streets and the commercial streets tend to be on narrow building lots. There is an urban legend that Charleston's lots are narrow because the Lords Proprietors taxed the lot frontage or the number of windows along the street. That is supposed to explain why the Single House has its narrow side, just one room deep, along the street. The architectural historian Robert Russell, former Director of the College of Charleston's Program in Historic Preservation and Community Planning, says there is no historical record to support the legend, however, which was not published until the 1980s.[2]

To explain the narrow lots Russell notes that as the original large lots were subdivided over time, long narrow lots worked best on the deep blocks, because early business owners wanted to be on Broad Street, where there were only a few blocks to subdivide. Supply and demand naturally led to narrow storefronts on Broad.

Figure 3.3: Maiden Lane, Charleston, South Carolina. This 1937 photograph of Single Houses on Maiden Lane shows the characteristic house type and streetscape of Charleston. "Single" refers to the one-room width of the houses: they also have a porch facing a side yard, perpendicular to the street. The regular pattern of yard-porch-house, yard-porch-house along the street establishes a spatial rhythm in Charleston streets. Modern development replaced these particular Single Houses with larger new buildings. *Library of Congress, Prints & Photographs Division, Carnegie Survey of the Architecture of the South, LC-J7-SC-1187*

Figure 3.4: 90-94 Church Street, Charleston, South Carolina. Two Single Houses from the 1760s flanking an 1830s replacement show the continuity over time in Charleston's homegrown building type. *© 2013 Max L. Hill, III*

In other old cities, large blocks were frequently divided over time with alleys and new streets that gave smaller lots and a separation of houses and businesses. But the Lords Proprietors discouraged subdivision of the blocks, so businesses and residences were frequently combined on the deep, narrow lots, with stores in the front and houses behind.

In time, the residents of the growing city built more and more houses away from the commercial streets, while keeping the distinctively narrow and deep lots, and the form of the Single House evolved: a simple building mass, one-room wide for cross ventilation, was turned perpendicular to the street. Each floor (with a minimum of two floors) had two rooms, separated by a stair hall in the center of the block, removed from the street. A porch, called a "piazza" by Charlestonians (who put no T-sound in the word), ran along the side of the house—usually on the south or the west side, where it would block the sun. At the street, a Classical doorway enclosed the piazza, making it a semipublic space; this was unlike the typical Southern porch, where there was more interaction with the street. The back of the deep lots was where the kitchen, the outbuildings, and the slaves and servants were, so the owners of the houses socialized along the side garden, and office space gravitated to the back of the house, at the end of the piazza. Built from the 1780s until the 1890s, these narrow houses—made of brick, stucco, stone, or wood, with Classical columns and ornament—gave a beauty, rhythm, and continuity to the simple streets and blocks of Charleston.

These streets still exist because Charlestonians value their past. Since 1783, the motto of the city has been *Aedes Mores Juraque Curat,* which Charlestonians translate as "She guards her buildings, her manners, and her laws." They built new buildings in their own traditions, which include the Single House and its "northside manners." While not required by law, northside manners were religiously followed: the convention dictated that the northern (or eastern) sides of the Single Houses have small windows, because one shouldn't watch one's neighbors sitting on the piazzas of their nearby house. (Actually you *could* watch, but it was bad manners to talk about what you saw.)

Charlestonians also preserved many buildings constructed before the advent of the large building types of the late nineteenth and twentieth centuries. In 1931 the city passed the first preservation ordinance in America, to protect its "Old and Historic District." The area was declared a National Historic District in 1960, just as the urban renewal that plagued so many American cities was gaining sway. That's another important reason why the city has so many beautiful streets.

Figure 3.5: Branford-Horry House, 59 Meeting Street, Charleston, South Carolina. A Charleston Double House built around 1765. The two-story "piazza" over the sidewalk was added by William Branford's grandson, Elias Horry, around 1830. For many years, there was a bus stop at the house, sheltered from the sun and rain by the private piazza over the public realm. Recent buyers of the house successfully petitioned, unfortunately, to have the bus stop moved down the street.

Civic Art and Street Design in Charleston

The individual streets of Charleston in the different grids downtown are rarely particularly artful in their design, but because they embody the basic principles of placemaking, they provide a good public realm and a good platform for Charleston's buildings. Most of the streets are not wide,

Figure 3.6: Meeting Street, Charleston, South Carolina. Looking north towards the South Carolina Society and St. Michael's Church in the distance. The church stands on the corner of Meeting and Broad streets, at the Four Corners of Law. Just to the south of the vantage point from which this photograph was taken is the Branford-Horry House with its piazza covering the sidewalk (Figure 3.5), similar to the way the porticos on St. Michael's and the Society building span the public sidewalk. This view from 1865 also shows that before Charleston's streets were paved, trees were planted in the roadbed. When the city paved the streets they moved the trees to the sidewalks, which made them very narrow for pedestrians. One way to narrow streets without the expense of moving the drains that run alongside the sidewalks is to create permeable tree-planting strips with bicycle lanes between the trees and the sidewalks. This would also create better conditions for the trees to grow. *Library of Congress, Prints & Photographs Division, Selected Civil War photographs, 1861–1865, LC-B811-3110*

and spatially they are contained by the buildings and trees lining them. (Meeting Street can be very wide, but when it has a canopy of live oaks, as it has south of Broad Street, it feels contained and comfortable.) The basic elements that make up the streets in the simple grids are usually parallel or perpendicular: the streets on most blocks are straight, the sidewalks and the buildings align with the street, the building setbacks are usually consistent, and there is often a regular rhythm established by the buildings.

Charleston's trees are traditionally planted in rows, close enough to each other that the mature trees grow together. Like the buildings, they give a rhythm to the street. Palm trees like the new palmettos on Market Street function as architectural elements, providing a sense of enclosure. Old photographs show that when Charleston had dirt streets, the utility poles and trees were frequently in the roadway, and the sidewalks ran between the trees and the edge of the right-of-way (Figures 3.6–3.7). Unfortunately, Charleston today frequently has sidewalks that are too narrow for more than one person at the points where the trees and utility poles were moved out of the street and into the pedestrian space.

Figure 3.7: Meeting Street south of Broad Street, Charleston, South Carolina. A beautiful mature canopy of live oak trees, only slightly south of the blocks shown in Figures 3.5 and 3.6.

Figure 3.8: Market Street, Charleston, South Carolina. A picture-perfect example of a terminated vista (but notice how much the palm trees constrain walking on the already-narrow sidewalks). The building at the end of Market Street is the Market Hall at the Charleston City Market, designed by Edward Brickwell White in 1841.

The original plan for Charleston had a continuous, orthogonal grid. As the city grew, individual developers platted their private tracts without government oversight. Creeks and swamps on the low peninsula sometimes separated the extensions of Charleston from the old grid, so that when the new neighborhoods were built, there was no direct connection to many of the older streets. One of the earliest extensions was Ansonborough, laid out by the British naval hero, Lord George Anson, who named two of the new streets for himself, George and Anson streets, and three for his ships, the *Centurion*, the *Scarborough*, and the *Squirrel* (these three names were later changed). His land extended to what is now Market Street, which was then a creek bed. When the market was built over the creek, the original Charleston streets Church and State were connected to Ansonborough simply where they fell by chance.

The City Market building was a raised temple that sat on the Market Street axis, providing a picture-perfect example of a terminated vista (Figure 3.8). Market Street has one of only three grand terminated vistas in the lower peninsula's collection of utilitarian grids. The other two are on Broad Street and Church Street. One is the build-

ing from which the Lords Proprietor ruled Charleston: the Old Exchange and Dungeon at the eastern end of Broad Street. The other is the notable exception of St. Philip's Church on Church Street, brought about by felicitous circumstance (see Figure 2.137).

The case of St. Philip's is unusual among Charleston's churches, though. Once called "the Holy City" because of its early religious tolerance and the steeples that dominated its skyline, Charleston has many churches that sit on unexceptional sites on their blocks and don't necessarily have setbacks to distinguish them from their neighbors. Like their neighbors, their primary contribution to the streetscape is usually their high level of classical beauty. A number of them are white Greek Revival temples in a sea of red-brick Single Houses.

Like many of the handsome churches and temples, Charleston's civic buildings have sites with little of the civic importance that urban designers would normally give them. The Four Corners of Law at the center of the city has a unique and interesting plan, but it is stronger in conception than in execution. Four civic buildings stand proudly on the four corners of Meeting and Broad streets, the most important intersection in the city. Gradually assembled from 1752 to 1896, the four corner sites hold the City Hall, the County Courthouse, the Federal Courthouse, and St. Michael's Episcopal Church (representing God's law). The original idea was clearly that the civic buildings should have small setbacks on the corners but appear to sit in a larger park. In reality, the park spaces that remain are small and disconnected. Nevertheless, the combined architectural presence of the buildings is strong, and the long history of commitment to this address on the part of the four institutions has made the Four Corners of Law a crucial anchor in the downtown (Figure 3.2).

Civic Art in the Plan of Savannah

Savannah's more eclectic architecture doesn't consistently rise to the level of beauty seen in Charleston's buildings, and yet Savannah too is one of the most beautiful cities in America. Oglethorpe's plan for the city combines a variety of well-proportioned streets and spaces in an intelligent layout that shows how rich a grid can be: its regular rhythm of squares and streets of varying widths give a hierarchy, order, and majesty to the grid (Figure 3.1).

The original design for Savannah was an expression of Enlightenment ideals in which a rational grid was seen as a manifestation of a correlation between the underlying natural order of the plan and the divine principles of social equality and civic beauty. The planner Thomas D. Wilson documents in his book *The Oglethorpe Plan: Enlightenment Design in Savannah and Beyond* that these included a belief that a balanced and just government depended on the fair distribution of land and the perceived benefits of land ownership: Oglethorpe had a plan for a slave-free society of small farmers owning land in what he called "agrarian equality."

Likely precedents for the plan were many: colonial towns planned by the ancient Greeks and Romans, ideal cities of the Italian Renaissance, English gardens, and Freemason sources in the Old Testament. Oglethorpe was a Mason, and he designed the plan of the city in cubits, a measurement favored by Freemasons because the Old Testament described the use of the cubit for the planning

of ancient cities and Solomon's Temple. Also found in the Classical text *Ten Books of Architecture* by Vitruvius, the cubit was equal to 1½ feet.

Oglethorpe's plan was based on a system of square wards (450 cubits by 450 cubits, or 675 feet square) that were repeated as the city grew—although Wilson argues convincingly that Oglethorpe was an agrarian who never intended that Savannah would grow as large as it has. Whether or not that's true, it's a fact that Oglethorpe intentionally designed a plan with modular units (the Wards) that could easily be repeated. His plan also made all land in a square mile around Savannah common land owned by the city, so that over time, when the city needed to expand or to raise revenue, the city fathers would plat and sell land for the private development of new wards.

Oglethorpe designed six wards and initially built four. Each ward was organized around a central square; the first four built were Johnson Square, Wright Square, Ellis Square, and Telfair Square. North–south and east–west streets on axis with the centers of the squares had 50-cubit, or 75-foot, right-of-ways. When these broad streets bisected the squares, the streets split: the streets that ran around the perimeters of the squares were half as wide, with 25-cubit, or 37½ foot, right-of-ways. Bull Street (Figures 3.9 and 3.10) was the first north–south broad street, and President Street (originally named King Street) an example of the original cross-axial broad streets.

Each square has only one north–south street going through, but the streets along the top and bottom of each square continue as 25-cubit (37½-foot) streets going east and west. This creates an A-B-C-B-A rhythm at each end of the square, if we call A the narrow streets at the top and bottom of the squares, the two equally sized blocks are the Bs, and C is the broad, axial street aligned with the center of the square. Oglethorpe designated the four blocks flanking the square Trust Lots, which were to be reserved for civic buildings. They are small lots for civic buildings, 40 cubits by 120 cubits, or 60 feet by 180 feet.

The other blocks in the ward are four Tything (residential) Blocks, two to the north of the square and two to the south. These are bisected by narrow east–west Lanes that are only 15 cubits, or 22½ feet, wide. These larger

Figure 3.9: Bull Street, Savannah, Georgia. Looking south towards Johnson Square and Wright Square, in a photograph taken in 1901 from the Savannah City Hall. The view clearly illustrates how close the squares are. *Library of Congress, Detroit Publishing Company Photograph Collection, LC-D4-13360*

Figure 3.10: Bull Street, Savannah, Georgia. Looking north towards Wright Square and the Savannah City Hall around 1910. Today the squares are full of lush trees that block all long vistas except at street level. *Library of Congress, Detroit Publishing Company Photograph Collection, LC-D4-70128*

Figure 3.11: Oglethorpe Avenue, Savannah, Georgia. A nineteenth-century view of one of the broad boulevards between Savannah's wards before Organized Motordom turned the central space into a Unique Vegetative Containment Zone where Moving Hazardous Objects (the picnickers) were prohibited.

blocks are 135 cubits by 200 cubits (202½ feet by 300 feet). Originally, each block had ten residential lots that together shared one square mile of farmland outside the city. Today, lots have frequently been divided or combined, and there are a few places where the Lanes were closed in order to combine the 90-foot lots with the 22½-foot alleys to make a single 202½-foot lot across the lot.

By 1851, Savannah had twenty-four wards based on Oglethorpe's model. Some street and block dimensions were modified slightly in the later wards. Oglethorpe himself made Johnson Square larger as construction began, in order to accommodate government buildings and make it the most important square. The next important change came in the building of the roads around the wards. The original plan had a 50-cubit (75-foot) east–west through street between the wards (Broughton Street was the first), and a 50-cubit east–west through street, Bay Street,

between the wards and the river. A north–south through-street between the original wards, Whitaker Street, had a narrower 30-cubit (45-foot) right-of-way. But as Savannah grew, two of the 50-cubit perimeter streets were built as wider boulevards with green medians. The first was Oglethorpe Avenue, which was 110 cubits wide, or 165 feet (Figure 3.11), and the second was Liberty Street, 90 cubits, or 135 feet wide.

This change from Oglethorpe's plan was easy to make because the wide streets were built in the open land surrounding Savannah that the city held for expansion. The boulevards enriched the variety of the plan, supplying another type of green space. Old photographs show people picnicking in the linear parks. Eventually, streetcars were run down the medians, as part of the system that enabled Savannah to develop streetcar suburbs. Today, unfortunately, the road department has planted the medi-

Figure 3.12: Bull Street at Madison Square, Savannah, Georgia. As the wide north-south streets come into the squares, they narrow to half the width and become part of the squares, functioning almost like shared spaces. The fact that they are not designed like roundabouts means that pedestrians feel comfortable crossing the street, while drivers have multiple distractions that force them to slow down to avoid hitting people and other cars. *Image courtesy of Kevin Klinkenberg*

Figure 3.13: Madison Square, Savannah, Georgia. Looking south along one of the walks that continues on axis through the squares. In person, the walker sees the next square ahead, and the stores along the street in between.

Figure 3.14: Jones Street, Savannah, Georgia. Under the state tree of Georgia (the live oak), the wide-but-short street feels almost like a piazza. The gentle undulation of the red brick road surface slows cars down and contributes to the comfortable feel of the space.

ans with bushes that prevent people from crossing the boulevards anywhere except at the intersections, because the east–west avenues carry a lot of the through traffic in the city. The medians still enrich our mental image of the plan, but less than they once did.

Details in the plan highlight its clarity, like the sidewalks that go straight through the squares and the regular repetition of the squares themselves, which always puts the pedestrian close to a square (Figure 3.12). On the broad streets that bisect the squares, the sidewalks on the long straight streets are aligned with the sidewalks that go through the squares, so the walker understands that this walk literally goes on for miles. The long vista is softened by the trees in the square, and the walker feels a longer axis than he or she actually sees. The axiality is powerful (Figure 3.13).

The cool, shady squares have a commanding presence. In the hot, humid climate of Savannah's summer, it's noticeable that the checkerboard plan reverses the pattern of medieval cities. There, narrow streets are frequently in shade, and walkers see sunlight in the distance where the squares open up. Savannah's squares are heavily planted with live oaks that provide restful shade, while the trees on the wide streets are usually too small to provide a canopy overhead. There are noticeable exceptions, like Jones Street—a wide, canopied street where some of the short blocks feel almost like piazzas (Figure 3.14).

With South Carolina to the north, blocking municipal purchase of common land on the far side of the Savannah River, the city grew to the south along the axis of Forsyth Park. The one-way, north–south streets like Whitaker Street, with narrow sidewalks and few trees or stop signs, frequently became raceways. But the traffic on the broad streets that go through the rectangular squares, like Savannah's central axis, Bull Street, are naturally calmed by the conditions around the squares. The narrow streets there are almost shared spaces, and pedestrians feel safe slowly crossing the streets in the Southern heat.

The architect and urbanist Christian Sottile, Dean of the School of Building Arts at the Savannah College of Art and Design and the designer of an extension of the city based on the ward system, says the residents of Savan-

nah are well aware of the elements of the grid and how they interrelate. The squares and the various street types are the dominant image of the city for them. The legibility and clarity of what he calls its "radically clear rationality" is a comfortable part of their daily lives as they move around the city.[4]

Sottile also points out that the building lots created by the small blocks influence the way we experience the city. The modestly sized Trust Lots flanking the squares seem smaller with modern building types on them than they did in the eighteenth century. Now each lot is frequently filled from lot line to lot line by a single church, institutional building, or government building, often raised on a Classical plinth. The effect can be monumental and dignified, giving civic importance to the squares that have these buildings. For the largest or most complex buildings on the civic lots, the streets at the top and bottom of the square become service streets with loading docks, while the larger streets on axis with the squares remain prime pedestrian streets. Away from the center, city residents turned many of the Trust Lots into mansion sites, because as the number of wards grew, there were more Trust blocks than were needed. By today's standards, these are small mansions. Some of them were later converted to civic uses, like the Telfair Museum, which occupies one of William Jay's best designs (Figure 3.15).

The 90-foot lots in the Tything Blocks encourage modest urbanism and build-out. Most of the buildings on these sites extend to the lot lines and go straight up without additional setbacks. When the city allowed some developers to close the narrow Lanes, the discipline was relaxed. One of the most egregious examples is the Hilton Savannah DeSoto hotel, which inappropriately pulls back from the street to make room for guest drop-off. Low terraces along the sidewalk are clumsily detailed and feel out of place in Savannah. Equally out of place is the looming mass of the hotel's minimally detailed concrete tower.

Bull Street and Broughton Street

The Hilton Savannah DeSoto sits on Bull Street, Savannah's central north–south spine. City Hall sits on axis

Figure 3.15: Alexander Telfair House / Telfair Academy of Arts and Sciences, 121 Barnard Street, Savannah, Georgia. William Jay, 1818–1819. Jay was an English architect who brought an inventive combination of the latest Regency Style architecture and the Greek Revival to the booming city of Savannah. At the same time, Charlestonians one hundred miles to the north were continuing to build the traditional Single Houses they had been building for decades. Since 1886, the mansion has housed the Telfair Museum, which also owns another Savannah house designed by William Jay. *Library of Congress, Prints & Photographs Division, Carnegie Survey of the Architecture of the South, LC-J7-GA-1145*

at the northern end of the street, making the only terminated vista in the old part of Savannah as well as the spot where Oglethorpe began construction. To the south, Forsyth Park interrupts the Bull Street axis with a broad, green swath that makes a good juxtaposition to the smaller squares. Bull stops at the park and resumes at its southern end.

Bull Street is not Savannah's main retail street. Long-distance traffic going south to the suburbs moves to north–south streets uninterrupted by squares, making raceways that do not support retail well. There are many stores along Bull Street, but Broughton Street, a wide street perpendicular to the raceways, is more accessible for drivers coming and going south and north, and it has long been the main street for shopping. Broughton Street and Bay Street, which also runs east-west and has many bars and restaurants, show that even in auto-oriented cit-

ies, commercial streets don't have to be on the main traffic routes, so long as they are *convenient* to the main traffic routes.

Forty or fifty years ago, Broughton Street and Savannah itself fell on hard times. Shopping centers, shopping malls, suburban office parks, and white flight moved much of the money in the city to its periphery. But in 1978, four individuals founded the private Savannah College of Art and Design (SCAD), which has grown from 71 students in the first year to more than 10,000 today. The school and its students brought money and investment to Savannah. The old department store on Broughton Street houses the school's library, and the movie theater is one of SCAD's theaters. The college has followed a program of buying and restoring old buildings around the city that has greatly benefited Savannah and shown the durability of good architecture and great urbanism.

Color Plate 1: Via Appia Antica, Rome, Italy. Appius Claudius, 312 BC. "The Queen of the Long Roads." Street design has always defined advanced civilization. Today, visitors who fly into Rome's small original airport can drive into the city along the old Appian Way and then via the Roman Forum. One of the most scenic entries to any large city.

Color Plate 2: Steenstraat, Bruges, Belgium. The design of cities begins with the design of streets. The art of architecture is indispensable, but streets are the spaces between the buildings, requiring the art of placemaking.

Color Plate 3: Mercato di Mezzo, Bologna, Italy. When a street has a sense of enclosure, and the proportions and details form a harmonious whole, it becomes a setting for sharing a common experience with our friends and neighbors.

Color Plate 4: High Street, Lacock, England. The post office, general store, and community center in an English village.

Color Plate 5: New College Lane, Oxford, England. View looking west under the Hertford Bridge (Sir Thomas Jackson, completed 1914) towards the Sheldonian Theatre (Christopher Wren, 1668) and the Bodleian Library, with the Old Bodleian (1600–1619) on the left and the Clarendon Building (Nicholas Hawksmoor, 1715) on the right. Intersections, terminated vistas, curves, cranks, offsets, and spans can divide a street into spatial segments, making each segment a complete scene and a legible piece of the town. The spatial variety creates "local-ness" and orientation, making every address and vantage point unique.

Color Plate 6: Main Street, Cooperstown, New York. Looking west from River Street. The relationship of the buildings to the street shapes the public realm. The sidewalk, tree, and porch are far more important to the character of the street than the traffic lanes.

Color Plate 7: Rue de Bellechasse, Paris, France. The southwest corner at the intersection with the boulevard Saint-Germain. No longer just the hobby of a small body of children, eccentrics, and thrill-seekers, cycling is now mainstream. The benefits to public health and local economies are immense. The best way to make biking and walking safer is to increase the numbers of cyclists and pedestrians.

Color Plate 8: Turl Street, Oxford, England. View looking north toward Broad Street. The "lean-in tree" gently sculpts the narrow, intimate space.

Color Plate 9: Pont Street, London, England. View looking west toward St. Columba's Church. One block has an asymmetrical cross-section, adding the double row of trees on the south side to form Cadogan Square.

Color Plate 10: Avenue Foch, Paris, France. View looking west from the Arc de Triomphe. The broad axial avenue brings the green of the Bois de Boulogne into the heart of the city in a single, unified sequence. Street designs can employ formal geometry and monumental scale to communicate an impression of sublime order, symbolizing the rational workings and dominance of the nation-state.

Color Plate 11: Avenue des Champs-Élysées, Paris, France. View looking southwest from the Arc de Triomphe. Redesign: Bernard Huet, 1994. The famous avenue has been reconfigured numerous times. In the most recent alteration, the city removed the side access lanes to increase pedestrian space and incorporate underground parking.

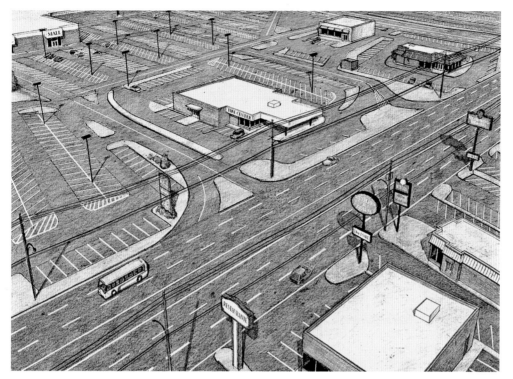

Color Plate 12: North Roan Street, Johnson City, Tennessee. Before: Aerial view, rendering of existing conditions in 2001. The American suburban strip corridors, hastily constructed for the motoring era, have not aged gracefully. © 2001 Dover, Kohl & Partners

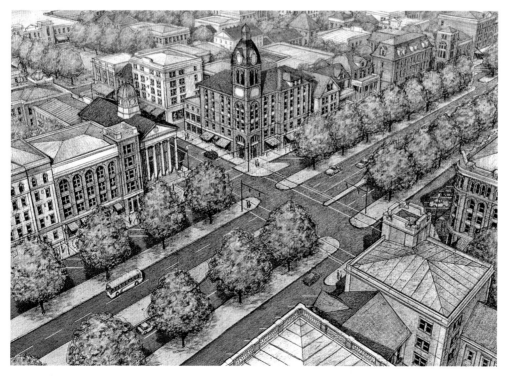

Color Plate 13: North Roan Street, Johnson City, Tennessee. Dover, Kohl & Partners, 2001. After: Reimagined as an urban street, the strip could be transformed into a multiway boulevard and re-established as a transit corridor, an economic engine, a linear park, and a better address, all at the same time. © 2001 Dover, Kohl & Partners

Color Plate 14: Chartres Street, New Orleans, Louisiana. View looking north between Iberville and Bienville streets. Main Streets are both a street type and a cultural metaphor. A successful main street in a sustainable, walkable town or city is a place where people want to get out of their cars and explore. Unlike a mall, a main street gets better with age, too. Well-designed iron bollards add character to the street when they tilt a little, but delaminating, yellowing plastic sticks look cheap when they inevitably begin to lean.

Color Plate 15: Portobello Road, London, England. View looking northwest, towards Denbigh Close. Businesses gravitate to car and foot traffic, sometimes with help from planners and developers. Portobello Road is a former country lane that became an important market street in the mid-nineteenth century, when new neighborhoods were built around it in Paddington and Notting Hill.

Color Plate 16: Mount Street, Mayfair, London, England. Viewing looking west, towards South Audley Street. Real estate developers who build places of enduring quality and value reap ongoing rewards. The Grosvenor family built Mount Street in the nineteenth century and still owns it and much of surrounding Mayfair.

Color Plate 17: Broad Street, Oxford, England. View looking west. Less formal than squares and plazas, market streets were formed by widening a segment of a traditional street, pulling open the space to make room for vendor stalls. Once at the edge of villages, they became centers of the towns that grew up around them.

▶**Color Plate 20:** Ponte Vecchio, Florence, Italy. Taddeo Gaddi, 996 AD. Because of flooding, the bridge over the Arno was rebuilt in 1117 and 1345, and in 1565 Giorgo Vasari designed a second-floor corridor that connected the Uffizi to the Pitti Palace. We are social beings: put interesting things in beautiful settings and we will gather there.

Color Plate 21: North Michigan Avenue, Chicago, Illinois. View looking south. The width of the street is matched by the proportions of the substantial buildings flanking it. Chicago's mayors have made its flower beds symbols of the resurgence of the city. *Image courtesy of Jason King*

Color Plate 22: Tenth Street, Port Royal, South Carolina. Prior to 1995, the road was wide and treeless, and the lots were largely vacant. The town swapped some of the right-of-way for an alley in the back, and now the front porches of cottages face a walkable, tree-lined street.

Color Plate 23: Santa Maria Street, Coral Gables, Florida. F. M. Button and Pierson & Skinner, 1925. In the single-family residential sections of traditional North American neighborhoods, prestigious and valuable streets almost always follow a time-tested recipe: street-oriented architecture, spatial definition, agreeable proportions, slow speed, narrow width, and trees lined up to make a canopy over the street.

Color Plate 24: Eastlake Road, I'On, Mount Pleasant, South Carolina. Dover, Kohl & Partners and Duany, Plater-Zyberk & Company, 1995. A fundamental act of urban design is determining the relationship of the building to the street. A lack of mature trees in this part of I'On made building placement all the more important to define the street space.

Color Plate 25: Leidsegracht, Amsterdam, the Netherlands. View looking southwest towards the Keizersgracht. The city is built on fill and is usually flat, but streets flanking the canals gently rise to meet bridges crossing the canals, setting a regular rhythm and variety from block to block.

Color Plate 26: Lafayette Canal walk, I'On, Mount Pleasant, South Carolina. Dover, Kohl & Partners and Duany, Plater-Zyberk & Company, 1995. View looking west. A network of midblock paths and rear lanes effectively reduce the block size, making the grid more permeable for pedestrians and increasing the variety in walks around the village. *Image courtesy of James Dougherty*

Color Plate 27: Barri Gòtic, Barcelona, Spain. Long lost from the urban design palette, there is wonder and promise in skinny, exceptional streets and tightly wound intersections. They introduce contrasts into what otherwise might be a relentless or boring set of similar spatial experiences.

Color Plate 28: New Row, London, England. View looking east from Bedfordbury. Exceptionally narrow streets might be either pedestrian-only or allow just one-way traffic. Neither pattern is recommended for a whole neighborhood, but when there are many connected streets, some links can be demoted to a less-trafficked status, to great effect.

Color Plate 29: Centre Place, Melbourne, Australia. Melbourne's slender laneways are vital scenes, bustling with art, cafes, and pedestrians. Centre Place is open to vehicular traffic only during limited hours each day. © *2013 Photography by Joseph Ip, All Rights Reserved*

Color Plate 30: Hoffman Lane, Cooperstown, New York. View looking north towards Otsego Lake. Half a block from the center of Main Street, an alley in a residential block near the Baseball Hall of Fame. Large changes in character can take place from street to street.

Color Plate 31: Lane at Little-bredy, Dorset, United Kingdom. The green wall made by the hedgerow highlights the view on the other side of the road. It is precisely because the road has not been widened, straightened, or flattened for the convenience of drivers that speeds are mild and the rural character undisturbed. *Image courtesy of Ben Pentreath*

GLENWOOD PARK

ATLANTA, GEORGIA

for GREENSTREET PROPERTIES
by TUNNELL-SPANGLER & ASSOCIATES / DOVER, KOHL & PARTNERS

◄**Color Plate 32**: Via Castiglione, Bologna, Italy. Beginning in the fourteenth century, the city coded Bologna's famous arcades. The city now has the most extensive network of arcaded streets in Europe, protecting pedestrians from the elements, linking the streets into a system, and narrowing the streets. © *2011 Stephen A. Mouzon, Photographer*

▲**Color Plate 33**: Glenwood Park, Atlanta, Georgia. Dover, Kohl & Partners and Tunnell-Spangler-Walsh & Associates, 2001. Developers from Greenstreet Properties gave the former industrial site a new street pattern and repurposed it with a rich mix of housing, workplaces, and storefronts, plus a new park and a square faced by live/work units. © *2001 Dover, Kohl & Partners*

Color Plate 34: Garrett Street, Glenwood Park, Atlanta, Georgia. Dover, Kohl & Partners and Tunnell-Spangler-Walsh & Associates, 2001. View looking east toward Brasfield Square. The development was directed via detailed regulating plans and a form-based code. Approval of the narrow street cross-sections required extensive arm-twisting with reluctant public officials. *Image courtesy of Christopher Podstawski*

Color Plate 35: Kerr Property, Johns Island, Charleston, South Carolina. Dover, Kohl & Partners, Hall Planning & Engineering, and Kubilins, 2008. The power of networked systems: two two-lane streets have more traffic capacity than one four-lane road. With a network, the streets can be right-sized and nurture placemaking. © *2008 Dover, Kohl & Partners*

Color Plate 36: Madison Landing, Madison, Connecticut. Massengale & Co LLC, Robert Orr & Associates, and Michael Morrissey, 2001. Green suburban infill proposed for the reuse of a small airport scheduled to be closed. Creating inviting streets in a legible network is the design foundation for walkable neighborhoods. *Watercolor © 2000 Michael B. Morrissey*

Color Plate 37: Quinta Avenida, Antigua, Guatemala. View looking south under the Santa Catalina arch. The stone street operates like a shared space; automobiles drive on the road at slow speeds, but motorcyclists and pedestrians dominate. Typical of Spanish colonial streets, colorful building facades form a continuous streetwall, balancing the height of the buildings with the width of the space. *Image courtesy of Kenneth Garcia*

Color Plate 38: First Street, Gainesville, Florida. View looking south toward the Hippodrome State Theatre (Thomas Ryerson, 1911). A terminated street vista is perhaps the oldest, most dependable tool in the urban designer's kit; the axial geometry gives civic importance.

Color Plate 39: Admiralty Arch, The Mall, London, England. Sir Aston Webb, 1912. View looking northwest. The arch—actually three major arches and two small ones—is the backdrop for public ceremonies ranging from coronation processions to the London Marathon finish line. It marks the transition from The Mall to Trafalgar Square. Spanning over streets is a powerful architectural medicine, to be administered in careful doses, but skillful designs can embed the scenes in our memories and define the image of the city or a neighborhood.

Color Plate 40: Lexham Gardens, Kensington, London, England. Rows of nearly identical terrace houses built during successive booms in the Georgian, Victorian, and Edwardian periods prove that repetition and rapid building can be friendly to urbanism. Sight lines are interrupted by attractive deflections and distortions in the grid and the "garden street" type sets the buildings against a contrasting green backdrop.

Color Plate 41: Holland Park, London, England. Attached houses allow for foundations that step down sloping streets, maintaining the building-to-street relationship despite the topographic challenges. In England, the building type evolved with an almost perfect balance between public and private needs: the houses shape elegant, safe streets that adapt to site conditions on one hand, and have livable, practical, tranquil interiors on the other. Gardens behind can be small and enclosed or combined in private parks.

Color Plate 42: Mobile Street, Montgomery, Alabama. Rendering depicting revitalization of the neighborhood, Dover, Kohl & Partners, 2007. The future of our cities depends on putting the top priority on the happiness of citizens and the success of businesses and institutions, not just on "Happy Motoring." © 2007 Dover, Kohl & Partners

Color Plate 43: Cobble Hill, Brooklyn, New York. Rowhouses and their stoops shaping street space. In New York, houses are set back six feet to make room for the stoop, but stoops are allowed to extend beyond that and into the public sidewalk. As one might guess, the word was brought to America by the Dutch, and the type might come from a need to raise the entry floor above flood level. In the nineteenth century, the public space in the house was above the raised basement behind the stoop, where the kitchen and service spaces were. Jane Jacobs praises the stoop for the way it provides a seat for the urban spectacle, giving "eyes on the street."

Color Plate 44: Jones Street, Savannah, Georgia. Savannah's variation on the rowhouse tradition reflects both climate and society. The tops of the stoops are often shaded by a roof, forming a small porch that serves as an intermediary zone between the public street and the private interior. It protects us from the storms and glare when we are entering the house or overlooking the parade of passersby.

Color Plate 45: Legare Street, Charleston, South Carolina. View looking north by the Simmons-Edwards House, built around 1800. The live oaks make the scene and yet break all the rules. Some of the most memorable, prized streets defy the criteria enforced by modern specialists; a traffic engineer, arborist, zoning official, stormwater expert, or utility clerk could all give reasons why a street like Legare is unprofessional—yet there it sits, beautiful, safe, practical, and perennially valuable.

Color Plate 46: Exmouth Market, London, England. View looking southwest toward Farringdon Road. London Plane trees in London. At the southwest end of Exmouth Market, what might have otherwise been an ordinary tangle of intersecting roads becomes a small shaded square, under the high canopy of trees that emerge directly from the pavement.

Color Plate 47: Motcomb Street, London, United Kingdom. Corner Condition: Most of the great streets of the world have an understated, muted palette of colors, materials, and textures, rather than a riot of bright stripes and loud traffic signs. Figure 6.23 has another view of Motcomb Street.

▶ **Color Plate 48:** Wijde Heisteeg, Amsterdam, the Netherlands. View looking south from a bridge over the Singel canal. In the 1960s, Amsterdammers decided not to tolerate the way that the car was taking over the public realm of their beautiful city. Today, the vast majority of intersections there have no stop signs, no stoplights, and few traffic signs. The high quality of life in Amsterdam flows from the design of its streets, offering lessons for many other cities.

Color Plate 49: St. Charles Avenue, New Orleans, Louisiana. The streetcar runs in a broad grassy median, appropriately enough called a "neutral ground" in the local vernacular, setting an example for new transit systems that must fit gently into their mixed-use surroundings.

DESIGNING THE 21ST CENTURY STREET

VIEW LOOKING NORTH EAST DOWN 4TH AVE

Color Plate 50: "21st Century Street," New York, New York. Computer simulation. Steven Nutter, 2011. Looking east on Fourth Avenue in Brooklyn. A winning entry for a competition in New York City to redesign Fourth Avenue in Brooklyn, imagining it as the 21st Century Street. Instead of making a comfortable place where Brooklynites might want to stroll or shop, the design focuses on the roadbed, which it divides into pieces. The bicycle specialist who designed the entry made a special, visually dramatic bike lane that cuts the space in two and forces cyclists to weave dangerously across an anti-urban turn lane. This emphasis on the intersection where the vehicles come together ignores the design of the public realm between the intersections. In all of this, it is representative of the work of specialists in the 21st century. *Image courtesy of Steven Nutter*

Color Plate 51: First Avenue, New York, New York. View looking north from East 6th Street. NYC DOT, 2008. A multimodal Complete Street in Manhattan, it is first and foremost a suburban-style arterial for suburbanites to drive in and out of the city. Like the competition entry in Plate 50, this design divides the public realm into pieces, most of which are given to the car. See "Completer Streets" and the opening image in Chapter 6. *Image courtesy of NACTO*

Color Plate 52: Main Street, Great Barrington, Massachusetts. Computer simulation. Redesign, massDOT, 2011. Looking east in the center of town, showing the variety of trees to replace the Bradford Pear trees that will be removed. A town committee working with massDOT eliminated the ramp shown in the rendering, since the current ramp is functional, simpler, more attractive, and less expensive. © 2012 Fuss & O'Neill, Inc., by permission of the Town of Great Barrington, MA

Color Plate 53: Nieuwe Spiegelstraat, Amsterdam, the Netherlands. "When I see an adult on a bicycle I do not despair for the future of the human race" is a quote often attributed to the science fiction writer H. G. Wells. Today's surge in cycling is no fantasy; it symbolizes a much wider urban transformation urgently underway, in which street design will be the indispensable art.

NETWORKS AND CONNECTIVITY: LEED-ND ANALYSIS

The street corridor exists as a part of a pattern or a web. The level of connectivity within a given street network is a potent indicator of how people move around the neighborhood and how environmentally and economically viable the network is. LEED-ND stands for Leadership in Energy and Environmental Design for Neighborhood Development. A rating system produced by the US Green Building Council (USGBC), the Natural Resources Defense Council (NRDC), and the Congress for the New Urbanism (CNU), LEED-ND assigns a score based on the extent to which a given neighborhood plan incorporates good location decisions, good neighborhood pattern and design techniques, and green building technology. A high score means a project can be "LEED-certified" as sustainable development.

During the creation of the standards for LEED-ND, Dover, Kohl & Partners devised a method for calculating effective thoroughfare connectivity. This tool evaluates the street network within a given area by calculating the number of intersections per square mile and assigning a connectivity score. Under this method, intersections with alleys count, and a percentage of intersections with bikeways and trails count, but intersections that lead only to cul-de-sacs do not. The higher the score, the better connected the network is; the better connected the network is, the lower the vehicle-miles-traveled (VMT) per person are likely to be. Increasing choices for travel routes increases the options for walking or biking and lowers congestion at any one intersection. Not surprisingly, older neighborhoods built with grid plans usually score better on this analysis than auto-centric sprawl neighborhoods.

◀ **Figure 3.16:** The Woodlands, Texas. Satellite view. *Image courtesy of Google Earth*

▶ **Figure 3.17:** The Woodlands, Texas. The suburban cul-de-sac pattern scores poorly on connectivity, forcing longer driving trips and harming walkability. © *2013 Dover, Kohl & Partners*

The Woodlands, Texas

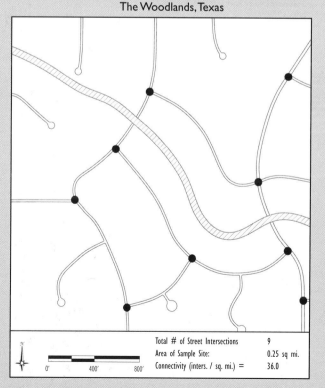

Total # of Street Intersections	9
Area of Sample Site:	0.25 sq. mi.
Connectivity (inters. / sq. mi.) =	36.0

0'   400'   800'

Figure 3.18: Celebration, Florida. Cooper, Robertson & Partners and Robert A.M. Stern Architects, 1997. Satellite view. *Image courtesy of Google Earth*

Celebration, Florida

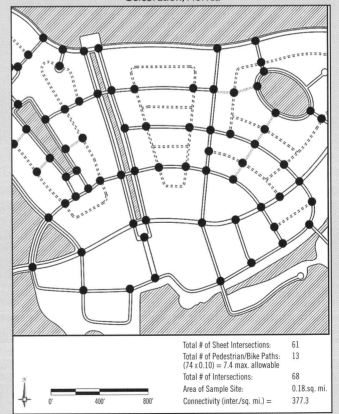

Figure 3.19: Celebration, Florida. Cooper, Robertson & Partners and Robert A.M. Stern Architects, 1997. Block sizes vary, improving the connectivity score. © 2013 Dover, Kohl & Partners

Total # of Sheet Intersections:	61
Total # of Pedestrian/Bike Paths:	13
(74 x 0.10) = 7.4 max. allowable	
Total # of Intersections:	68
Area of Sample Site:	0.18.sq. mi.
Connectivity (inter./sq. mi.) =	377.3

N

0'   400'   800'

Figure 3.20: Miami Lakes, Florida. Lester Collins, 1962. Satellite view. *Image courtesy of Google Earth*

Miami Lakes, Florida

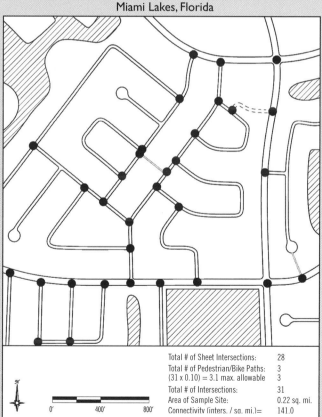

Figure 3.21: Miami Lakes, Florida. Lester Collins, 1962. Oversized blocks result in a poor connectivity score. © *2013 Dover, Kohl & Partners*

Total # of Sheet Intersections:	28
Total # of Pedestrian/Bike Paths:	3
(31 x 0.10) = 3.1 max. allowable	3
Total # of Intersections:	31
Area of Sample Site:	0.22 sq. mi.
Connectivity (inters. / sq. mi.)=	141.0

N

0'   400'   800'

Figure 3.22: Historic Center, Rome, Italy. Satellite view. The Pantheon is in the center of the photo, on the right, and the Piazza Navona is on the left. In the nineteenth and twentieth centuries, broad streets were cut through the fabric: the Corso Vittorio Emanuele II goes east-west, and the Corso del Rinascimento runs parallel to the Piazza Navona. *Image courtesy of Google Earth*

Rome, Italy

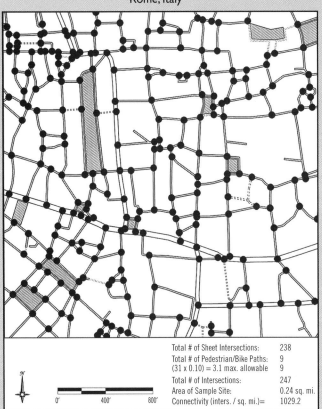

Figure 3.23: Rome, Italy. The full menu of street types, from wider main streets to tiny lanes, is combined with small blocks to result in extraordinarily high connectivity. © 2013 Dover, Kohl & Partners

Total # of Sheet Intersections:	238
Total # of Pedestrian/Bike Paths:	9
(31 x 0.10) = 3.1 max. allowable	9
Total # of Intersections:	247
Area of Sample Site:	0.24 sq. mi.
Connectivity (inters. / sq. mi.)=	1029.2

0'   400'   800'

RUE DE RIVOLI AND RUE DE CASTIGLIONE, PARIS, FRANCE / Javier Cenicacelaya

Rue de Rivoli

Begun by Percier and Fontaine, 1801–1830; extended 1847–1854

Downtown Street

The rue de Rivoli in Paris is located on the north side of the Louvre Museum and runs for more than two kilometers (about a mile and a quarter), going from the district of the Marais on the east (near the place des Vosges), to the place de la Concorde on the west (Figure 3.24). The street was named in honor of the victory of Napoleon's army in the Battle of Rivoli against Austrian troops in 1797.

Conceived by Napoleon I, the street was designed by Charles Percier and Leonard Fontaine, official architects of the emperor. Their architecture, interior design, and decorative arts, known as *le Style Empire*, were influential across Europe. They practiced a radical Neoclassicism that added references from Egypt to the common ones from Rome and Greece to make an eclectic and sophisticated Classical style.

When Napoleon moved the imperial residence from the palace at Versailles to the Tuileries Palace at the Louvre, he commissioned Percier and Fontaine to create a suitable street on the north side of the Louvre. As laid out by Percier and Fontaine, the rue de Rivoli was one of the longest straight streets in Paris. Later rulers extended the street until it reached its present length. The part of the street designed by Percier and Fontaine is the most interesting.

This portion of rue de Rivoli is inexorably straight. To achieve such an alignment on the north side of the Louvre, it was necessary to literally chop off the *cours*, or yards, of different existing *hôtels*; the absence of a continuous alignment of the facades of those hôtels was therefore replaced with a long arcaded facade. The repetitive facade and the long roofline increase the grandeur of the street. The result is a kind of megastructure capable of competing with—or at least standing up to—the long north facade of the Louvre. It is interesting to note the way the roof is treated with a barrel vault that softens the roofline and recalls other significant Classical buildings, such as the Basilica of Vicenza.

Inside the arcades are shops that give the street some of its vitality. Percier and Fontaine opted for arches in the porticos, a choice in tune with their eclecticism. This became popular in later stylistic revivals, both Classical and medieval, as in the *Rundbogenstil* in Germany. If we compare those to the design by Percier and Fontaine, though, the rue de Rivoli appears more restrained—most likely due to the scale of the intervention. In smaller projects like the rue des Colonnes, Percier and Fontaine showed a higher level of sophistication and invention. There we find an exquisite portico with arches, built in the Empire Style but at a different scale.

The arcade of the rue de Rivoli is one of the longest in Europe to have a single architectural treatment, and the street itself served as a precedent for the boulevards Baron Haussmann later cut through the medieval fabric of Paris during the reign of Napoleon III.

Rue de Castiglione

Perhaps by Percier and Fontaine, 1801

Downtown Street

The impressive effect of the rue de Rivoli on the pedestrian can be countered after time by a surplus of repetition. After a certain amount of walking, one feels like turning around the next corner and escaping into a street with more variety. One of those streets is the rue de Castiglione, which runs from the rue de Rivoli to the place Vendôme. Wider than the other streets that start from rue de Rivoli, Castiglione is arcaded (Figure 2.9). It was conceived as a continuation of the longer street; the visual connection to the place Vendôme was the reason for keeping the same treatment of the facades.

The architecture around the magnificent place Vendôme is the work of Jules Hardouin Mansart, conceived as we see it today around the end of the seventeenth century. It is one of the baroque *Places Royales* built during the reign of Louis XIV. The center of this type of square was meant to be occupied by a statue or monument to the reigning king. Such a landmark should be visible from as far away as possible. The effect of perspective was very important, therefore, and this explains the special treatment given to rue de Castiglione, as the anteroom or "entrance" to place Vendôme. The statue of Louis XIV was torn down during the French Revolution and was later replaced by Napoleon with an obelisk modeled after Trajan's Column to celebrate the French victory at Austerlitz.

The rue de Rivoli and the rue de Castiglione are two of the best examples of Neoclassical urbanism. Following baroque precedents, Neoclassicists laid out long perspectives, or allées, with the clear intention of making elegant promenades of some grandeur. The urban designers of the Neoclassical period were also interested in straight alignments in order to get more rational arrangements of all types of infrastructure. In addition, they wanted to improve urban hygienic conditions and create places where people could socialize.

Figure 3.24: Rue de Rivoli, Paris, France. Begun by Percier and Fontaine, 1801, extended 1847. A nineteenth-century view looking west.

THE ARCHITECTURAL AND URBAN CODES OF PARIS

The streets of Paris are among the most regulated and ordered in the world. The standardization of Parisian architecture and streets began with King Henri IV. He brought this urban standardization about by both regulation and example, setting a pattern that lasted for hundreds of years. In 1600, Henri IV made the first of two royal orders that set maximum dimensions for building projections and required urban buildings to follow build-to lines (*lignes d'alignment*) along streets. He also built two developments as king that established the classicizing and regularization of Paris architecture: the place Dauphine and the place Royale (now the place des Vosges). A third unbuilt square, the place de France, would have shared with the other two a common architectural language of repeated, often identical Classical facades. Between the place Dauphine and the place de France, Henri IV planned a new street called the rue de Turenne that was to run straight from one square to the other with rows of repeating facades. This street was not built until the time of Louis XIII, but south of the Place Dauphine Henri IV ordered the private owners of sites by the Pont Neuf to build identical Classical facades for the "beautiful ornament" of the city.

During the reign of Louis XIV (1661–1715), building types were regularized, and the dominant new type—private *hôtels* built by aristocrats—had a Classical architectural style that flowed from the Sun King and the Royal Academy of Architecture he founded. Palaces built by Louis XIV were influential and imitated, while the Royal Academy of Architecture disseminated didactic knowledge, with standards for the design and composition of harmonious Classical facades, as well as for proportions, materials, and details. These trends influenced all building in Paris, in what became known at the time as the *architecture d'accompagnement* (accompanying or supporting architecture). Pierre le Muet's *Maniere de bien bâtir pour toutes sortes de personnes* (*Good Building for All Kinds of People,* published in 1647), documented and supported the *architecture d'accompagnement* and was dedicated to the king. Le Muet presented a series of urban residential buildings that went from small to large while maintaining a consistent Classical taste, with supporting details.[5]

In 1666, influenced by the Great Fire of London, the French Treasury regulated building projections, and the following year the Royal Bureau of Finance set a maximum height (8 *toises*, or 15.6 meters) for the front walls of new houses in Paris and required that exposed timbers of existing houses be covered with plaster. In 1669, the rue de la Ferronnerie—a narrow Parisian street where Henri IV had been assassinated when his carriage was blocked—was widened as part of a speculative real estate venture by the church that owned the buildings along the street. As king, Henri's grandson Louis XIV imposed the first street ordinance in Paris. A fifty-two-bay row of houses was given Classical symmetry, rhythm, and details, with many of the classic elements of later Parisian architecture, such as uniform floor heights, moldings that ran across multiple buildings, an arched *entresol*, repeated elevations, and mandatory balconies. "By 1715," Anthony Sutcliffe writes in *Paris: An Architectural History,* "the triumph of Classicism had launched the belief that Paris was one of the world's most beautiful cities."[6] Contemporary authors identified symmetry, uniform heights, and architectural regularization as critical elements and pointed to the rue de la Ferronnerie and the royal squares built by Henri IV as examples of beautiful places. The trend grew, and in 1755 the Abbé Laugier published the important *Essai sur l'architecture* (*Essay on Architecture*) that promoted urban interventions with new streets lined with buildings made harmonious by regulation. Later authors like Pierre Platte endorsed the creation of urban beauty by code.

By the early eighteenth century, according to Sutcliffe, the Royal Academy of Architecture had firmly established the idea that there was a French national manner of architecture, based on proportion, a high standard of materials and execution, and the correct use of

Classical design. Architecture was a frequent subject of publication, and the tone was usually didactic, with an almost exclusive focus on French examples. Jacques-François Blondel (who was apparently unrelated to François Blondel, the founder of the Royal Academy a century earlier) was the most prolific and influential author. His four-volume *Architecture française* (*French Architecture*) and his nine-volume *Cours d'architecture* (*Architecture Course*) marked a move away from the principles taught by François Blondel and towards the emulation of examples. An important part of his work was an emphasis on the design of houses for the middle class.

It became common for all buildings on a new Parisian street to be designed by a single architect. Individual lots would come with the drawings for the facade, or even with the facade already built. In the eyes of the Crown, one of the most important urban improvements of the eighteenth century was the creation of the place Louis XV, now the place de la Concorde, where the axis of the Champs Élysées meets the royal palace. At the time, the Champs Élysées was a royal promenade on the western edge of the city, designed by André Le Nôtre for Marie Antoinette and Louis XIV. Choosing the site for a statue of Louis XV marked that edge of the city for expansion. A design competition for the site was won by the architect Jacques-Ange Gabriel, who proposed two grand hôtels on the north side of the large square, bordered on three sides by formal plantings of trees. Instead of houses on the north side, Gabriel proposed that hôtels frame a new street to be called the rue Royale. In the early nineteenth century, Napoleon ordered the great vista from the place de la Concorde be completed with the construction of the Church of the Madeleine at the end of the axis (Figure 1.28).

The two hôtels and all the buildings on the rue Royale were designed by Gabriel, with royal approval. There was no use for the hôtels at first, and only the facades were built until uses could be found. For the rue Royale, the Crown imposed an architectural ordinance that precisely coded Gabriel's design. Royal letters of patent required that Paris ensure that any surrounding streets be suitably harmonious if the streets were widened or realigned.

Louis XVI had great interest in the improvement of Paris. In 1783, the royal authorities issued under his name a new set of building regulations for the city. At the same time, Louis XVI ordered an accurate survey of the city as the basis for the revision of the build-to lines established in the seventeenth century. The codes, revised a year later, were the first Parisian codes to relate building height to street width: the maximum height for new buildings was set at 60 feet (*pieds*, or 18 meters), but lower heights were set for streets less than 30 feet wide. The preamble to the code stated that this was in response to the building of apartment houses that, if too tall, were unhealthy for the populace.

> All of the codes operate under the Parisian belief that harmony and good taste are more important for a streetscape than complete artistic freedom, the antithesis of most architectural theory today. And yet how many new streets approach the quality of typical Parisian streets, famous around the world for their beauty?

The primary tactical strategy was a focus on natural light. Maximum heights were determined by a line drawn at an angle of 67.5 degrees from the bottom of a building properly aligned to the top of the opposite building. The maximum cornice height of 54 feet was set for 30-foot streets, including the cornices below attics and mansard roofs built in the place of attics. Formulas for roof heights gave an overall height of 64 to 69 feet, depending on the depth of the building.

Little building took place after the French Revolution in 1789 until Napoleon came to power in the early nineteenth century, but the royal regulations for the city remained in place. Napoleon's imperial ambitions came out in his work on the great axes of Paris, including the Champs Élysées and the rue Royale, where he authorized the construction of the Arc de Triomphe on the former and the church of the Madeleine on the latter. In 1801 Napoleon authorized the construction of the first stage of the rue de Rivoli, which was the most obvious way to extend the east–west axis of the Champs Élysées blocked by the Louvre. The government built the arches and the vaults of the arcade designed by Percier and Fontaine, but had difficulty attracting private investment for the completion of the buildings. What little private construction there was elsewhere in Paris continued under the code of 1783–84, with the exception of a revision in 1823 that changed the regulations for building projections and a height-limit change in 1848.

Apartment construction in Paris revived in the 1830s, but the next significant transformation of Paris didn't take place until the Second Empire. In 1852, the ambitions of Napoleon III, the ideas of Baron Haussmann, and the fruits of the Industrial Revolution combined to form much of the physical city we know today. Important for a book on street design are the *Grands Boulevards* and the Parisian building code of 1859. The roots of the new code lay in the regulations of 1783–84, but the code was adapted to the new scale and scope of construction

in the 1850s, when the *Grands Boulevards* were plowed through the medieval neighborhoods of Paris. Buildings on the wider new streets could be 2½ meters, or roughly one story, taller than before, and the new code emphasized a horizontality desired by Haussmann to reinforce the dramatic perspectives of his long avenues and boulevards.

There were further code revisions in 1882, 1884, and 1902. An expert in the history of the codes can walk the streets of Paris and identify which codes were in place when the buildings were built. The entresol comes and goes, balconies move up and down or in and out, and so the buildings at the east end of the rue de Rivoli are slightly different than the buildings at the western end, because they were built under a different code. The 1902 code was a response to a call for more stylistic freedom, enabling the design of Art Nouveau buildings. At the same time, all of the codes operate under the Parisian belief that harmony and good taste are more important for a streetscape than complete artistic freedom, the antithesis of most architectural theory today. And yet how many new streets approach the quality of the average Parisian street, famous around the world for its beauty?

THE ARCADES OF BOLOGNA / Gabriele Tagliaventi

Bologna is famous for having the largest set of arcades in Europe. Arcades provide multiple benefits, including protecting pedestrians from the elements and adding spatial definition to a street. Arcades also shade the storefronts. In Bologna, the arcades link together a series of commercial streets, forming a web of comfortable and coherent public spaces (Figures 3.25 and 3.26).

Bologna arcades come from a unique urban code. The code dates back to the fourteenth century, when the city began to expand beyond its existing walls to accommodate a rapidly growing population. New walls—that would define the city limits until 1889—encompassed

nearly 456 hectares (about 1,125 acres), making Bologna one of the largest European cities of its time. The growing city, reflecting an urban renaissance that was embracing nearly all of Italy in the 1300s, was planned according to a clear law that required all new buildings to have arcades at the ground floor if they were located along a main street. Today, Bologna has four distinct networks of arcades (Color Plate 32).

1. The first network of arcades, laid out between 1561 and 1563, occurs at the monumental core of the city, along the Pavaglione and connecting to the two plazas around the Basilica of San Petronio.

▲ **Figure 3.25**: Piazza Santo Stefano, Bologna, Italy. The arcades of Bologna, built over the course of centuries, come in many different styles and forms. *Image courtesy of Gabriele Tagliaventi, Photo by Bernard Durand-Rival*

◄ **Figure 3.26**: Via Santo Stefano, Bologna, Italy. Bologna's network of arcades gives the city a unique feel.

2. A second network occurs along the main avenues, including Strada Maggiore, Via Zamboni, Via Santo Stefano, and Via San Vitale. These Renaissance streets were built using the palazzo building type as a reference.
3. A third system of arcades—the vernacular—corresponds to the secondary streets.
4. Lastly, the network of *extra moenia* arcades—the arcades built outside the fourteenth-century walls—are based on the 3.5-kilometer-long arcade that connects Porta Saragozza to the Sanctuary of San Luca on top of the hills surrounding Bologna. The term "extra moenia" also refers to the arcades that connect the Sanctuary with the main Carthusian cemetery and to the Alemanni's arcades, which connect the Porta Mazzini with the hospitals of the 1500s.

The construction of the arcades at the core of Bologna was the largest urban operation during the Renaissance, involving architects such as Vignola and Antonio Morandi (called "Terribilia"). A monumental axis and a series of important civic institutions—such as the Ospedale della Vita and the Biblioteca communale dell' Archiginnasio—define the main commercial venues of the city. This institutional grouping was the first permanent establishment of the University of Bologna. Pope Pius IV initiated the design and implementation of the development to provide the city with a proper public plaza in accordance with new Classical ideals. (The pope also intended to stop the construction of the Basilica of San Petronio in order to prevent Bologna from having the largest church in Christendom.)

The extra moenia arcades of Bologna are part of one of the most successful examples of an intentionally designed peripheral urban neighborhood in Europe. The Masterplan for the Extension of the City in 1889 further reinforced the design when a series of new urban neighborhoods to be built around an arcaded square were planned. The most famous of those, called *Bolognina*, was a new neighborhood built north of the historic center on a typical 1800s grid along a main commercial axis (Via Matteotti). Since Bolognina was conceived as a "little Bologna," it had its own main arcaded avenue and public monuments, including a new cathedral and a new town hall.

SEVEN DIALS, LONDON, ENGLAND / Hank Dittmar

Thomas Neale, circa 1690

Shared Space

> But what involutions can compare with those of Seven Dials? Where is there such another maze of streets, courts, lanes, and alleys?... The stranger who finds himself in "The Dials" for the first time, and stands Belzoni-like, at the entrance of seven obscure passages, uncertain which to take, will see enough around him to keep his curiosity and attention awake for no inconsiderable time. From the irregular square into which he has plunged, the streets and courts dart in all directions, until they are lost in the unwholesome vapor which hangs over the house-tops.
>
> —Charles Dickens, *Sketches*, 1843

My favorite London street is actually the confluence of seven streets near London's Covent Garden into a circular space called the Seven Dials (Figures 3.27 and 3.28). At the center of the Dials stands an obelisk with six sundials (not seven) donated by the Worshipful Company of Mercers—one of London's guilds, and the owner of the area—in the 1690s.

Designed by Thomas Neale, a speculator who took the area on a lease from the Mercers Company, the area has certainly seen its ups and downs. In Dickens's time, it was part of the infamous St. Giles Rookery, an overcrowded slum famous for violence, prostitution, and brawls between the Irish and the English. With the redevelopment of the Covent Garden Market as an attraction in the 1970s, Seven Dials has grown in popularity, and today is loved by residents and tourists alike.

Over the past two years, the clutter has been removed from nearby streets, granite pavers have been restored in the pavement, and the monument has been cleaned and restored. In traffic-engineering terms, the junction operates as a shared space, with the monument serving as a pedestrian haven and the junction itself used equally by cars, cyclists, and pedestrians. Each of the seven streets is similarly a shared space, and the surrounding area boasts one of London's best coffee roasters; a back court called Neal's Yard with London's best *fromagerie*; and many delightfully individual cafes and shops, with wares ranging from rare books to secondhand designer clothing. Each street has its own character (one with market stalls), and no matter where one sets out to go, one ends up in an interesting place.

Incidentally, not two blocks away is Central St. Giles—a celebrated new building covering a city block and designed by Renzo Piano—that is the opposite of Seven Dials. The buildings are made of steel and brightly colored glass, and the public space is internal, irrigated neither by cars or pedestrians. As a result the retail is struggling—less than a year after Central St. Giles opened to acclaim from some design critics for its contribution to the civic realm.

Comparing the two areas is instructive, for it reveals what makes Seven Dials special. It is part of a densely connected network of small streets, bounded by three- to six-story buildings, with continuous retail, mostly on the small side. While there is a traditional delineation between street and pavement, it is made with paving materials and curbs—and without either the bright colors or railings that have become the default positions of the shared spacers and the engineers, respectively. The monument at the center has an inviting shelf upon which to sit and people-watch, and to get there pedestrians have to walk across the intersection. Finally, the area is managed for a mix of small unique shops and larger brands, with residential space above and office space nearby.

Traffic engineering is a small but essential part of what makes this a great street. The junction of seven streets could have easily become a no-go area for pedestrians, but the intimate scale of the streets, the quality of the pavement, the calm and understated detailing and materials, and the fine monument at the center of the junction all contribute to make this a space for people where cars are tolerated, and one of my favorite places to be.

Figure 3.27: Seven Dials, London, England. Shared space in London. *Image courtesy of Emily Glavey*

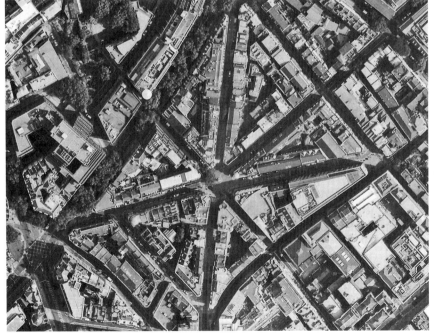

Figure 3.28: Seven Dials, London, England. Satellite view. The wide street with trees is Shaftesbury Avenue. *Image courtesy of Google Earth,* © *2012 Bluesky*

MIDBLOCK PASSAGES

▲ Figure 3.29: Burlington Arcade, London W1, England. Samuel Ware, 1819. The Burlington Arcade cuts through a large block in Piccadilly that was the part of the London estate of a wealthy aristocratic family with many titles and names, including Burlington (the Royal Academy of Arts next door is their former house). The Arcade is a convenient passage that also has a lavish architectural expression, making it a natural home for jewelry stores and other luxury shops. © 2005 Andrew Dunn / *Creative Commons Attribution-Share Alike 2.0 Generic license*

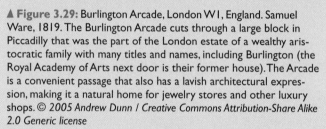

◀Figure 3.30: Sicilian Avenue, between Southampton Row and Vernon Place, London WC1, England. R.J. Worley, 1910. A popular outdoor space in Bloomsbury, the Edwardian interpretation of an Italian street is a diagonal cut between two buildings designed by Worley.

◀◀ Figure 3.31: Lansdowne Row, between Berkeley Street and Fitzmaurice Place, London W1, England. A handy shortcut near Berkeley Square, lined with convenience stores and inexpensive food shops, most of which would be unable to pay the rents on the neighboring streets of Mayfair near Berkeley Square.

▶Figure 3.32 Crown Passage, between Pall Mall and King Street, London SW1, England. A convenient shortcut in a long block, with less expensive stores than the surrounding upscale streets.

▲ **Figure 3.33:** Stratford Studios, off Stratford Street, London W8, England. A quiet, pedestrian cul-de-sac. The cozy space gives variety to the west London neighborhood.

◀ **Figure 3.34:** Galerie Vivienne, between place de la Bourse and rue des Petits Champs, Paris 2, France. A popular Parisian *passage couvert.* © 2011 Groume / Creative Commons Attribution-Share Alike 2.0 Generic license

◀◀ **Figure 3.35:** Cour du Commerce Saint-André, between boulevard St.-Germain and rue Saint-André des Arts, Paris 6, France. An old street, closed to traffic. The large wooden gates at each end lend it the air of a "secret" place—even when it's crowded.

▶ **Figure 3.36:** Galleria Vittorio Emanuele II, between Piazza del Duomo and Via T. Marino, Milan, Italy. One of the grand shopping places of Italy: a place for the Milanese to see and be seen. © 2008 Alterboy / Creative Commons Attribution-Share Alike 3.0 Unported license

▲ **Figure 3.37:** Westminster Arcade, between Westminster and Weybosset streets, Providence, Rhode Island. Known locally as The Arcade. In 2013 a developer is converting the shops and offices on the top two floors of this distinctive passage into small apartments.

◀ **Figure 3.38:** Latta Arcade, between South Tryon and South Church streets, Charlotte, North Carolina. William H. Peeps, 1914. On the National Register of Historic Places, the Latta Arcade is a popular destination in a city working hard to revive the walkability of Uptown Charlotte (its downtown). The arcade brings variety to the pedestrian experience in the regular grid of Charlotte's downtown. *Image courtesy of Steve Minor*

▶ **Figure 3.39:** Warren Place, between Warren and Baltic streets, Brooklyn, New York. A semi-private passage through model housing in Cobble Hill, built in 1878 by the developer Alfred Tredway White, whose motto was "philanthropy plus five percent." The cottages for "working men" originally rented for $18 per month. Today the 14-foot-wide cottages rent for $4,500.

MEASURING WALKABILITY

Hall Planning & Engineering, a New Urban firm in Tallahassee, Florida, created a Walkability Index that uses a fixed set of criteria to measure pedestrian-friendliness (Figure 3.41).[7] Unlike the system at the popular website Walk Score®,[8] Hall's Walkability Index is based on physical attributes such as the frequency of intersections and the character of the block front. Blending transportation planning and engineering with urban design, the Walkability Index uses measures of context and density to determine the pedestrian's sense of freedom, comfort, and safety, block by block.

The Index uses ten criteria to determine the overall walkability:

1. Vehicle speed: Vehicle speed is measured outside of peak traffic times, when traffic is moving freely. Taking at least ten samples with a radar gun is recommended. (Lower speeds are better for pedestrians.)

2. Thoroughfare width: The street width at each pedestrian crossing, measured from curb face to curb face. (Wider streets are more daunting for those on foot.)

3. Street parking: The presence of on-street parking; the percentage of block front dedicated to parking where it is permitted and in use. (On-street parking improves walkability.)

4. Sidewalk width: The full width of paved sidewalk. (The ranges offered vary, according to the urban-to-rural transect, but wider sidewalks are still preferred within each category.)

5. Pedestrian connectivity: The distance between street intersections or midblock crossings; this measures network density. (The more options afforded the pedestrian, the more walkable the street or block is.)

6. Pedestrian features: The presence and quality of pedestrian amenities. (Shade trees, sidewalks in good condition, and the like raise the score.)

7. Street enclosure: The ratio of building height to street width. (A 1-to-1 ratio is considered ideal for pedestrians.)

8. Land-use mix: The presence of different land-use types—retail stores, restaurants, private homes, for example. (Here, also, the Index is sensitive to the urban-to-rural transect—a country road is very different from a bustling town—but variety is valued by the pedestrian in all settings.)

Figure 3.41: Trinity Street, Cambridge, England. Measuring walkability. *Image courtesy of Iulia Colescu*

◄ **Figure 3.40:** Piazzale degli Uffizi, Florence, Italy. Giorgio Vasari, 1560. View from the Palazzo Vecchio looking towards the Arno river. Planned by Cosimo de Medici to house various state offices ("uffizi" in the Florentine dialect), the Palazzo degli Uffizi has two wings. The space between is the main route from the most important square in the city to the Arno. Known as the Piazzale degli Uffizi, it is enclosed but not closed at the southern end by a cross between a triumphal arch and a grand Serliana that screens the river. Two well-lit corridors pass over the arch: one is part of the Vasari Corridor that runs from the Palazzo Vecchio to the Palazzo Pitti, over the top of the Ponte Vecchio. The glorious space is one of the first regularized streetscapes of modern Europe. © *Samuli Lintula / Creative Commons Attribution-ShareAlike 3.0*

9. Facade design: The number of doors and the character of the facade per block face. (A long, blank factory wall would receive a poor walkability rating. A row of townhouses or small shops would receive a much better rating.)

10. Transit/bicycle features: The presence of bus shelters, bus stops, bicycle lockers, and bicycle racks.

The Walkability Index Number Data Sheet, available on the Internet, allows one to evaluate a street, segment by segment, according to these criteria. In the current version of the Index, each criterion has a maximum value of 10, making 100 points the highest possible score. Future versions will allow the user to adjust the weight given to each criterion according to its importance in their situation. The following table shows total scores, graded per street segment.

90–100: High walkability (A)

70–89: Very walkable (B)

50–69: Moderately walkable (C)

30–49: Basic walkability (D)

20–29: Minimal walkability (E)

19 points or less: Uncomfortable / Hazardous for walking (F)

Easy to understand and easy to apply, the Walkability Index Number offers both professionals and concerned citizens an easy way of determining what works and what doesn't for pedestrians in their communities. Its criteria have been used to produce designs for walkable places in over forty community workshops.

BIG BOULEVARDS AND TINY LANEWAYS IN MELBOURNE, AUSTRALIA / Chip Kaufman

Begun by Robert Hoddle, 1837

Multiway Boulevards and Pedestrian Passages

The characteristic big boulevards and tiny laneways of Melbourne, Australia, are wonderful examples of how streets at very different scales can enliven the grid and expedite multimodal movement (Figures 3.42, 3.43, and 3.44). Robert Hoddle, Melbourne's original city surveyor, began the layout of its street network in 1837, making use of both narrow lanes and very broad multilane boulevards that went out to the suburbs.

Melbourne's orthogonal Central Business District (CBD) is admired in part for its tiny, north–south pedestrian streets (both open-air and with glazed roofs), which complement and contribute to its "plaid" street network of north–south streets 30 meters wide and spaced 200 meters apart. The east–west streets are 100 meters apart and alternate between 10 and 30 meters wide. Many additional open-air, 6-meter-wide, north–south service lanes give access for deliveries and

basement parking and have helped keep most single properties small—another key characteristic of Melbourne's highly diverse and attractive CBD.

Heavy rail, most of which is below ground, runs the perimeter of the CBD before radiating outward in several directions. New developments are gradually capping over the remaining at-grade heavy rail lines adjoining the CBD. On-street light rail lines lace through the CBD and then continue out to the suburbs, giving Melbourne the fourth-largest light rail network in the world.

The pedestrian ways, ranging in width from 10 meters to 4 meters and directly fronted by mid-rise heritage buildings, have many amenities that attract small local boutique shops (Figure 3.43 and Color Plate 29). The street-level stores are generally no more than 5 meters wide, and have offices and apartments above. Some of these arcades rival the covered passages (*passages couverts*) of Paris (Figure 3.34).

At the opposite end of the scale, large multimodal, multilane boulevards fan out from Melbourne's Central

Business District. Several of the boulevards have new Copenhagen cycle lanes. The pedestrian experience is heightened by medians planted with trees spaced no more than two lanes apart, which usually means four or six rows of mature trees for each boulevard, and relative ease of crossing for pedestrians.

St. Kilda Road is Melbourne's highest-capacity boulevard. It supports a popular tram line, a footpath, and a bicycle path, as well as traffic lanes sufficient for more than 50,000 vehicles per day. It begins as Swanston Street, the central north–south 30-meter-wide spine of the CBD, and then extends many kilometers southward

Figure 3.42: St. Kilda Road, Melbourne, Australia. View looking north toward the Shrine of Remembrance. At sixty meters wide, the major avenue was readily adapted to multi-modal travel, including the city's famous trams. *Image courtesy of Chip Kaufman*

Figure 3.43: Centre Place, Melbourne, Australia. The city's downtown remains dominant, thanks in part to its pedestrian-oriented, effective street network, devised before the automobile. *Image courtesy of Chip Kaufman*

Figure 3.44: Central Business District, Melbourne, Australia. Figure-ground drawing showing the result of "the Hoddle grid," devised by surveyor Robert Hoddle in the 1830s. Note the range of widths in the streets, service lanes, and tiny north-south "laneways." © 2013 Dover, Kohl & Partners

to the suburb of St. Kilda on Port Phillip Bay as an approximately 60-meter-wide multilane boulevard. Some of Melbourne's most prestigious businesses and apartment buildings are on St. Kilda Road.

Thanks in large part to the government's initiative to establish a well-organized and effective street network long before the advent of the car, Melbourne has matured into a vibrant, attractive, and transit-oriented mixed-use inner city, centered around a still-dominant CBD and close to many popular neighborhoods. It has Robert Hoddle, who first stretched the spectrum of street types and scales, to thank for its renowned urban character.

Corridor Transformations in Jeddah, Saudi Arabia

Dover, Kohl & Partners with Hall Planning & Engineering, 2008

Multiway Boulevards and Main Streets

In 2008, the municipality of Jeddah in the Kingdom of Saudi Arabia undertook the Jeddah Street Improvement Project, hiring urban designers and transportation engineers to produce a heavily illustrated street-improvement manual (Figure 3.45 and 3.46). The municipality had the experts study a number of corridors, addressing in each case the form and regulation of the vehicular realm, the pedestrian realm, and the private realm. Over time, the standards in this manual could help the Kingdom produce one of the most coherent and context-responsive street networks

STREETSCAPE & URBAN DESIGN MANUAL

JEDDAH, KINGDOM OF SAUDI ARABIA

AUGUST 30, 2008

Figure 3.45: Corridor Transformations, Jeddah, Saudi Arabia. Dover, Kohl & Partners with Hall Planning & Engineering, 2008. Jeddah Streetscape and Urban Design Manual cover. © 2008 Dover, Kohl & Partners

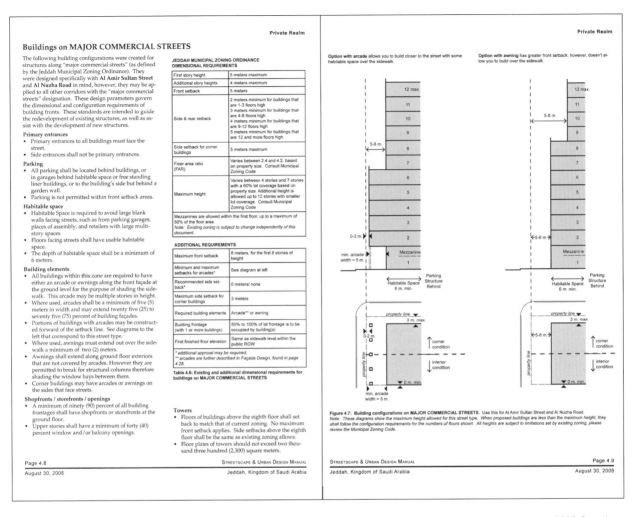

Figure 3.46: Corridor Transformations, Jeddah, Saudi Arabia. Dover, Kohl & Partners with Hall Planning & Engineering, 2008. Sample pages from the Jeddah Streetscape and Urban Design Manual. © *2008 Dover, Kohl & Partners*

in the Middle East. The manual contains detailed *how-to* instructions for architects, engineers, and developers, as well as extensive background material on the reasons why the standards specify certain requirements (Figures 3.47, 3.48, 3.49, 3.50 and 3.51). To make the manual easy to use, it also includes a series of simple question-by-question checklists for confirming compliance.

The story of a legible city is told in its corridors, if they can be made coherent, and in Jeddah the needs are great. The significance of this project is that the most crucial corridors in the city were considered at once, as an ensemble. With a standardized approach to the analysis and a highly customized, context-specific approach to the individual designs, the city can proceed with the improvements in an efficient way.

Figure 3.47: Corridor Transformations, Jeddah, Saudi Arabia. Dover, Kohl & Partners with Hall Planning & Engineering, 2008. Rendering of Old Mekkah corridor. © *2008 Dover, Kohl & Partners*

Figure 3.48: Corridor Transformations, Jeddah, Saudi Arabia. Dover, Kohl & Partners with Hall Planning & Engineering, 2008. Rendering of Al Malik corridor. © *2008 Dover, Kohl & Partners*

Figure 3.49: Corridor Transformations, Jeddah, Saudi Arabia. Dover, Kohl & Partners with Hall Planning & Engineering, 2008. Rendering of a park / plaza along a street corridor. © *2008 Dover, Kohl & Partners*

Figure 3.50: Corridor Transformations, Jeddah, Saudi Arabia. Dover, Kohl & Partners with Hall Planning & Engineering, 2008. Rendering of a corridor interrupted by a neighborhood square. © *2008 Dover, Kohl & Partners*

Figure 3.51: Corridor Transformations, Jeddah, Saudi Arabia. Dover, Kohl & Partners with Hall Planning & Engineering, 2008. Rendering of a regional park and adjacent corridor. © *2008 Dover, Kohl & Partners*

The Cap at Union Station, Columbus, Ohio

Meleca Architecture, 2004

Downtown Street Retrofit: Hiding a Highway

When transportation officials and engineers carved up Columbus, Ohio, for Interstate 670 in the 1970s, they severed an old neighborhood around North High Street from the downtown, leaving behind what the *New York Times* architectural writer Herbert Muschamp called an "engineered gash."[9] Like most postwar, inner-city highway construction projects, this one brought alienation and disruption to the people forced to live next to it (Figure 3.52).

In the early 1990s, in spite of the high value of land in this location—the highway abruptly divides the downtown area from the Short North arts and entertainment district—local officials and the Ohio Department of Transportation (ODOT) proposed to further expand the highway—from a four-lane to an eight-lane freeway. In an effort to appease angry neighbors, ODOT offered to construct a hardscaped "park" on top of the bridge across the interstate in order to offset the unattractive highway expansion.

The business owners and residents of the neighborhoods located just north of I-670, including Short North, opposed the highway-widening and the perfunctory hardscaped bridge-park, pointing out that the existing four-lane freeway and long bridge already discouraged patrons from making their way across. They realized that the widening would only make things worse.

In a political breakthrough, the City of Columbus, the Department of Transportation, developers from Continental Real Estate Companies, and local business owners compromised by agreeing on the "Cap" alternative. Along with the highway expansion, they converted the bridge above it into a walkable street, hiding the freeway and sewing the two parts of the city back together (Figure 3.53). The parties agreed to a complex arrangement in which both the costs and the profits of the development would be divided up and shared. Continental owned neighboring properties and did not want to see its land devalued; the Cap offered them a way to use their own work to improve those values, and to link Columbus's successful arts district with the downtown convention center.

Figure 3.52: The Cap at Union Station, N High Street over I-670, Columbus, Ohio. View looking west, showing the High Street bridge before construction of The Cap. *Image courtesy of David Meleca*

Figure 3.53: The Cap at Union Station, N High Street over I-670, Columbus, Ohio. View looking south on N High Street, showing The Cap crossing I-670. *Image courtesy of David Meleca*

Figure 3.54: The Cap at Union Station, N High Street over I-670, Columbus, Ohio. View showing an arcade at The Cap. *Image courtesy of David Meleca*

Figure 3.55: The Cap at Union Station, N High Street over I-670, Columbus, Ohio. Section. *Image courtesy of David Meleca*

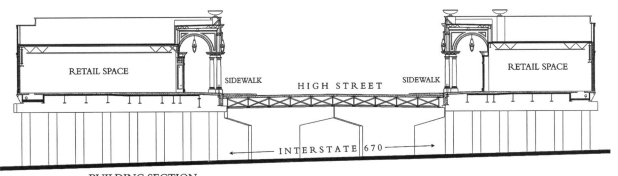

RETAIL SPACE   SIDEWALK   HIGH STREET   SIDEWALK   RETAIL SPACE

INTERSTATE 670

BUILDING SECTION

0   8   16 ft

Completed in 2004, the Cap at Union Station is now a place to go rather than simply one to drive through. David Meleca of Meleca Architecture designed the buildings and public spaces. Arcades and sidewalks in front of the shops are more than twenty-five feet wide and constantly full of people, thanks to the Cap's varied mix of retail and restaurants (Figure 3.54). Lightweight materials were used in the construction of the Cap in order to address the structural challenge of constructing full-size buildings above the wide Interstate (Figures 3.55 and 3.56). The west side of the "cap" is nearly 73½ feet deep and the east side is 53½ feet deep; both span the total distance of the bridge.

Figure 3.56: The Cap at Union Station, N High Street over I-670, Columbus, Ohio. Aerial view, looking north. *Image courtesy of Pictometry International Corp. Copyright 2013*

Figure 3.57: Pulteney Bridge, Bath, England. Robert Adam, 1774, later expanded and altered. Spanning the River Avon, the Pulteney Bridge is promoted in Bath as one of four bridges in the world crossing a river that has shops on both sides. The Cap at Union Station shows that the type has tremendous promise for neighborhoods torn apart by half-buried highways.

FREEWAY TEARDOWNS / John Norquist

The utopian dream of traveling through cities without interruption goes back at least to 1922, when the revolutionary architect Le Corbusier drew what he called the *Ville Contemporaine*. Before that, the movement of railroads on their own right-of-ways must have brought to mind the notion that streets could be designed to speed traffic on its own right-of-way, thus avoiding the hustle and bustle of the city. It may even have occurred to the ancient Romans that roads could be designed like aqueducts, to attain free-flowing cart and chariot movement. Regardless, the new technology of the motorcar created demand for paved streets, all-weather roads, and a taste for higher speeds. Within ten years of Corbusier's drawing, the first autobahn was constructed in Germany and work had started on New York City's West Side Highway. The freeway era had begun.

Freeways proved to have several significant side effects in the urban context. First of all, the roads were expensive to build in cities with higher land values and existing buildings in the way. Some cities tried to build freeways with their own money. In 1949, Milwaukee started the Stadium North Freeway. The city built it through Washington Park, which had been designed by Frederick Law Olmsted. It was the site of the zoo, which had to be relocated at great expense. The Stadium North would probably have been Milwaukee's last freeway if the Interstate Highway Act of 1956 hadn't come along with its high-octane, 90 percent Federal and 10 percent state funding mixture. With free roads on the menu, few cities could resist.

In Western Europe, freeways exist between cities and around the perimeter but rarely intrude on city centers. Our Canadian neighbors, after flirting with urban freeways in the 1960s, have largely confined them to intercity travel. One reason for this may be that Canada has no equivalent of our interstate highway program. The cities and provinces pretty much pay for their own infrastructure—and that means that infrastructure had better add value to the place where it is built. Perhaps, as a result, all major Canadian cities have good transit and only have the roads they are willing to pay for. Vancouver, for example, has no freeways within its borders, but has an excellent system of boulevards, avenues, and streets, along with efficient transit lines. It should be noted that despite the lack of a national highway-financing program, Canadian roads do successfully connect across provincial and even international borders.

Another unanticipated side effect of freeways: the effect they have had on settlement patterns and the flow of commerce. Street networks coupled with streetcars, subways, and commuter trains attracted people to the center of cities. An auto-centric system of expressways has the opposite effect, pushing the distances people regularly travel—"the drive-sheds"—deep into the hinterlands and altering shopping and commuting patterns.

Corbusier's dream of unimpeded traffic influenced the world, especially the Americas. The well-known New York City planner and expressway enthusiast Robert Moses was paid by the Rockefeller family to visit São Paolo, Brazil, in 1949 to draft a new plan for the fast-growing city. In fact, São Paulo already had existing plans, which Moses was seeking to replace; in 1930, the Brazilian architect, engineer, and planner Francisco Prestes Maia had put forward the *Plano de las Avenidas*, which had significant support among designers and civic leaders. This plan envisioned a European-type system of streets with a hierarchy scaling up to boulevards (without the grade separations recommended by Corbusier and Moses). When Maia was the mayor of São Paulo, between 1938 and 1945, he began the implementation.

Maia's boulevards accommodated large traffic volumes, with three moving lanes in each direction,

Figure 3.58: Cheonggyecheon, Seoul, South Korea. Remnants of the highway after its demolition. © *2007 Kyle Nishioka / Creative Commons Attribution 2.0 Generic license.*

but the streets retained their connection to the city fabric.

Throughout the history of urban civilization, major thoroughfares had three important functions: to move people and goods, to provide a place for commerce, and to serve as a social gathering place for the community. Corbusier and Moses sought to restrict the urban thoroughfare's function to movement alone. Moses viewed the Maia Plan's complexity and detailed fabric as an obstacle to fast vehicular movement; in São Paolo, his vision of a city of expressways won over Maia's urban vision. A vast system of expressways was constructed.

In 1961, Maia was elected to a new term as mayor that lasted until 1965. He tried to change the direction established by Moses. If he had lived longer (he died in 1965), he might have enjoyed the commencement of the construction of a metro train system that now exceeds 300 kilometers in length and is projected to reach 500 kilometers, surpassing London's Underground by 2017. Maia would also enjoy São Paulo's recent decision to begin removing some of its freeway infrastructure. First to go will be what is called "the Worm," a giant roadway that travels through the city center.

Urban freeway removal has gained popularity. San Francisco, Portland, New York, and Milwaukee have all deconstructed freeways. Others are considering it. Baltimore's Interstate 83, Buffalo's Skyway, and the Claiborne Expressway in New Orleans are all under consideration for demolition. Cities can undo damage done to them—which points out a prevalent characteristic in Americans: we make huge mistakes, but we also correct them. We are replacing welfare with work, we're ending (or redesigning) federal housing programs, we're reversing environmentally destructive river-channeling programs, and we're changing our attitudes about highways and transportation.

Four American cities have replaced expressways with avenues and boulevards, but perhaps the most spectacular example of highway removal is in Seoul, South Korea (Figure 3.58). An expressway that had originally been built atop a stream called Cheonggyecheon and carried more than 150,000 vehicles per day was later removed and replaced with two surface lanes on each side of the restored waterway. I predict this is just the beginning. With property values skyrocketing near demolished freeways, urban expressway deconstruction could be one of the biggest public works projects of the twenty-first century.

> Americans: we make huge mistakes, but we also correct them.

Rethinking Freeways

It may seem strange, tearing down expressways after fifty years of the greatest road-building binge in world history, but we've been through this rethinking process before. Remember the U.S. Army Corps of Engineers? In the Florida Everglades watershed, the Corps once drained marshes and forced streams into concrete-lined channels in an attempt to tame waterways and make more land available for agriculture and development. Now we know that draining wetlands and "channelizing" streams not only damaged the environment but increased the likelihood of pollution and flooding downstream. Marshes, meadows, swamps, grasslands, and bogs slow down and filter the water that flows through them.

As it entered the twenty-first century, the Corps has begun the process of undoing the damage that many of its twentieth-century projects caused. Having learned that forcing water into concrete-lined channels was foolish and counterproductive, it is now ripping out concrete and restoring marshes. In a similar way, traffic engineers are learning that urban street grids can distribute urban traffic more efficiently than superhighways.

THE TRANSECT OBSERVED: FOREST HILLS GARDENS

Forest Hills Gardens is a railroad suburb in Queens, New York, built by the Russell Sage Foundation in the early twentieth century as a model development (Figure 3.59). The Olmsted Brothers, landscape architects, were the planners, and the primary architect was Grosvenor Atterbury. The streets, which are privately owned but open to the public, connect to the Queens grid around the development. The streets illustrate the Urban to Rural Transect, even though they were built long before designers talked about the Transect. Their arrangement is most formal at Station Square, at the center of the transit-oriented development (Figure 3.60), and most informal and winding at the periphery of the 142-acre site.

Figure 3.59: Forest Hills Gardens, Queens, New York. Olmsted Brothers and Grosvenor Atterbury, 1908. Aerial rendering, drawn by Grosvenor Atterbury, 1910. The drawing shows how the development goes from Transect zone T-5 to Transect zone T-3 as one walks along and away from the axis of the Greenway that extends from Station Square in the foreground.

Figure 3.60: Station Square, Forest Hills Gardens, Queens, New York. Olmsted Brothers and Grosvenor Atterbury, 1908. Looking southeast towards the Greenway. Station Square has apartments above stores, restaurants, and offices.

Figure 3.61: Greenway Terrace, Forest Hills Gardens, Queens, New York. Olmsted Brothers and Grosvenor Atterbury, 1908. Looking back towards Station Square from the intersection of Greenway Terrace and Archway Place. Rowhouses behind stone walls face a sidewalk with brick strips between the concrete walk and the roadway.

As one walks along the Forest Hills Gardens Greenway from Station Square, the Transect changes quickly. As it changes, the details of the streetscape subtly and appropriately change too. The square is hard-paved and shaped by four-and-a-half-story buildings with built-in bridges spanning the streets that lead out of the square.

As the roads leave Station Square, the brick pavers change to asphalt. On the Greenway, the sidewalks enter arcades where the walks have small-scale patterns in the concrete. Coming out of the arcades, the pattern changes to larger concrete panels, and brick strips are introduced between the sidewalk and the road (Figure 3.61).

The park in the center of the street is only a few feet wide close to the square, but at the far end it broadens to a few hundred yards across (Figure 3.59). The roads on each side of the park have gentle curves that follow the topography. A lamppost at the beginning of the square has a family resemblance to the lights in Station Square, but those were mounted on buildings rather than on posts (Figure 3.62). Across from the park, close to the square on both sides, are two-and-a-half-story rowhouses. On the west side of the park, the rowhouses continue up and over an arch that allows a road to go through to Archway Place, recalling the covered roads a few hundred feet away at Station Square.

As the pedestrian moves south along the Greenway and the widening park, the sidewalks change from concrete with brick strips along the road to concrete with planting strips along the road (Figure 3.63). The blocks of rowhouses become shorter, and the setbacks in front of the group houses become larger. The walls separating the front yards of the houses from the sidewalk become more rustic, changing from stone and concrete to stone and brick, but—like the lights—they maintain

Figure 3.62: Forest Hills Gardens, Queens, New York. Olmsted Brothers and Grosvenor Atterbury, 1908. A street light in Station Square, with the silhouette of Dashing Dan, the symbol of the Long Island Railroad. Compare to the lamppost in Figure 3.61.

Figure 3.63: Forest Hills Gardens, Queens, New York. Olmsted Brothers and Grosvenor Atterbury, 1908. A photograph of the west side of Greenway Terrace, looking north, taken just fifty feet south of the vantage point in Figure 3.61. The strips between the sidewalk and the roadbed are wider, as well as planted rather than paved with bricks.

Figure 3.64: Forest Hills Gardens, Queens, New York. Olmsted Brothers and Grosvenor Atterbury, 1908. Looking south towards the intersection of Greenway Terrace and Slocum Crescent. The near side of the street has the block of rowhouses seen in Figure 3.62, while the other side of the street has free-standing, single-family houses. "Like faces like" along Slocum Crescent (see *East 70th Street* in Chapter 1 for a discussion of like faces like).

a family resemblance. The houses themselves get more variation in materials, including more details in wood. Within a few hundred yards of Station Square, the group houses seamlessly morph into single-family houses, and at the end of the park the houses become freestanding in suburban-style grass lawns (Figure 3.64). The sidewalks become narrower with wider grass strips than fifty feet before, and the stone and brick houses turn into stone and stucco houses, or stone and wood houses. Throughout the development, places where roads intersect frequently have group houses that harmonize with the size and massing of the single-family houses just around the corner.

The Spui, Amsterdam, the Netherlands

Shared Space

The corner in Amsterdam where Huidenstraat crosses the Singel canal on its way to the square called "the Spui" is an almost perfect urban place—which is one of the reasons why we put a photo of it on the cover of this book. Solid seventeenth- and eighteenth-century brick houses line both sides of the canal there, most of them in a local Classical vernacular with simple trim and harmonious proportions that relate to the Classical music Amsterdammers love: 1 to 2, 2 to 3, 3 to 4, and so on. The houses are mainly red brick, but some have light-colored brick and some have very dark brick. Most are three bays wide (three windows across), but there are also two-bay houses, and some are four or five bays wide. With the exception of the wonderful shop windows, all the windows are vertical and come from just a few "families" of windows. The window trim and the rest of the trim and moldings are usually, but not always, light stone or wood painted white. All in all, the houses produce a wonderful combination of the order and variety that good urbanism requires.

The similar but different houses line up along the street to make a solid street wall, punctuated by the rhythm of the vertical windows and the vertical houses with "Dutch" gables that make a varied skyline. The brick, stone, and painted wood are pleasing, and the street and sidewalks in front of the houses are a cheaper but also pleasant brick. Stone steps and low stone curbs in front of the houses separate the walks and the narrow street. Amsterdammers don't drive much, but they walk and ride bicycles a lot: the shared-space street is dominated by the bikes, first, and the pedestrians, second. Cars and trucks come last, although their drivers occasionally get impatient with the arrangement (Color Plates 25 and 53).

The trees along the canal and the houses are a similar height, about 1½ to 2 times the width of the street, making a comfortable space ordered by the regular rhythm of the trees. On the other side of the trees from the houses is the canal, which is roughly twice as wide as the trees are tall. The proportions of the space are beautiful, and water in the middle of the city is almost always pleasing (see

Color Plate 48). But what's great about the form of the city is just beginning.

Amsterdam is flat, often built from fill, but where bridges cross the canals they are raised, so that there is a regular rhythm and variety from cross street to cross street as the streets along the canal rise and fall (Figure 3.66). The curves of street where the Singel bends and the Huidenstraat crosses over it are gentle and beautiful, and the subtle rise it makes to span the canal is impressive.

Continuing to the east, the Huidenstraat turns into a passage called Heisteeg, wide enough only for walkers and bicycles. Lined by human-scaled buildings similar to the ones on the canal but with fewer stores, Heisteeg is approximately seventy-five feet long. Each side of the passage opens to well-designed, small-scale cafes and food shops before the passage ends at the northwest corner of the Spui, one of Amsterdam's most informal, most beautiful, and best-used square (Figure 3.65).

Figure 3.65: The Spui, Amsterdam, the Netherlands. Satellite view. The canal on the left is the Singel, shown on the cover and in Color Plate 48. *Image courtesy of Google Earth, © 2013 Aerodata International Surveys*

Figure 3.66: Reguliers-gracht, Amsterdam, the Netherlands. Looking south on the Reguliers-gracht from the Heren-gracht ("gracht" means "canal"). The roads along-side the canals rise up as they approach the bridges, creating an artificial but pleasant topography.

Figure 3.67: The Spui, Amsterdam, the Nether-lands. Cyclists ride along the south side of the square in the late after-noon.

Spuistraat comes into the square at that point. Lined with cafes, bars, and restaurants, it continues along the west end of the square, where there are outdoor tables that are heavily used day and night. The square has lightly trafficked roads along three sides of the square and an important streetcar street (Nieuwezijds Voorburgwal) that cuts through near the western end. Most of the square is paved with stone blocks. The low-traffic streets along the edges have brick pavers, separated from most of the stone areas by low stone curbs. But the higher-traffic street with multiple streetcar lines narrows down to one traffic lane as it passes through the square, before changing from asphalt paving to the same stone paving as the no-traffic areas in the rest of the square.

"Spui" is the Dutch word for a particular type of sluice used in their canals. Where the square is now there was once a body of water at the southern limits of the city. When the Singel canal was built as a moat around the city in the 1420s, the area was inside the city boundary, but the square was not filled in until 1882. The Spui was renovated in 1996, and today it is both a destination and a place one happily passes through on the way to other destinations (Figure 3.67). Some of Amsterdam's primary shopping streets are just to the east of the square, so that if you live on the Singel canal or to the west, you might frequently go through the square. There are also important destinations to the north and south.

The Spui itself has the old library at the University of Amsterdam, and the square has traditionally been a center for bookstores. Every week, book and art markets set up there, and cafes, restaurants, and bars with outdoor tables are on every side of it.[10] On a work day, just a few minutes after five o'clock, every café and bar is full. Unless there is a hard rain or it is bitterly cold, people spill out into the Spui, sitting and standing, enjoying each other's company.

NOTES

1. Roger G. Kennedy, *Architecture, Men, Women and Money* (New York: Random House, 1985), *passim*.

2. Robert Russell, "The Architecture of Politeness: Form and Meaning of the Charleston Single House," Talk delivered for the Center for the Study of the American South, UNC-Chapel Hill in February, 2006. In *Southern Architecture: 350 Years of Distinctive American Buildings* (New York: Dutton Adult, 1981), Kenneth Severans proposes the theory that the Single House originated in Barbados, from where several Charleston planters came. Russell visited Barbados to look into this theory, and found it unconvincing.

3. Thomas D. Wilson, *The Oglethorpe Plan: Enlightenment Design in Savannah and Beyond* (Charlottesville, VA: University of Virginia Press, 2012), *passim*.

4. In conversation.

5. Anthony Sutcliffe, *Paris: An Architectural History* (New Haven and London: Yale University Press, 1993): 48–50. We are indebted to Sutcliffe for his encyclopedic history of the urban codes, architectural texts, and architectural education in Paris. *Paris: An Architectural History* is the best and most thorough book about the architecture and urbanism of Paris that we know of in English.

6. *Ibid.*, 50.

7. For more information about the Walkability Index, see http://www.hpe-inc.com/walkability-index.html.

8. Walk Score® also makes apps for smart phones and tablets. http://www.walkscore.com/.

9. Herbert Muschamp, "This Time, Eisenman Goes Conventional," *New York Times,* May 2, 1993, http://www.nytimes.com/1993/05/02/arts/architecture-view-this-time-eisenman-goes-conventional.html. For a case study from the Urban Land Institute, see "The Cap at Union Station," http://casestudies.uli.org/casestudies/C035010.htm.

10. A bar called Hoppe on the west side of the square, at the intersection of Spuistraat and the tiny lane leading to the Huidenstraat, is reportedly where Freddy Heineken got his start. A simple and unpretentious Amsterdam "brown café," it was called by *Newsweek* one of the ten best bars in the world.

CHAPTER FOUR

RETROFITTED STREETS

THERE ARE TWO TYPES OF PLACES in America where retrofitted streets are most valuable and useful: auto-centric suburban and exurban sites where the residents and their elected representatives have decided to make walkable streets and communities; and walkable or once-walkable places where the public realm has been damaged by the application of engineering principles that favor the car, making the roads worse for pedestrians, cyclists, and public transit users than they once were.

The first description fits almost every American place built since 1945. The second includes most American neighborhoods, towns, or cities built before that: there are few American places that have not kicked the pedestrian to the side of the road and then narrowed the sidewalk. Most in the second group also suffered from the flight of businesses to shopping malls and strip centers—not to mention the self-inflicted damage of tearing down Main Street buildings for parking lots that were supposed to help the downtown compete with those outlying businesses. Experience shows that competing with shopping centers on the shopping centers' terms (convenient driving and parking[1])

rather than playing up the strengths of town centers (walkability and a public realm where people want to be) is a losing strategy.

> There are few American places that have not kicked the pedestrian to the side of the road and then narrowed the sidewalk.

For a variety of reasons, including climate change, dependence on foreign oil, rising oil prices, and a growing desire among many to live in walkable towns, cities, and neighborhoods, the job of retrofitting main streets and neighborhood streets to make them more pedestrian-friendly has begun across the country. At the same time, the nation's population continues to grow, and there is a burgeoning movement to retrofit appropriate places in suburbia with new, walkable centers. We have come to see that our pattern of abandoning old buildings and existing patterns of development in favor of cheaply-built strip buildings with short life spans is inefficient and expensive

◄ Yorkville Promenade, New York, New York. See Figure 4.80.

217

over the long run. And we have discovered that the most energy-efficient building is an old building. Similarly, compact towns and neighborhoods where we can get out of our cars and walk conserve energy, and we have too much invested in the old buildings and infrastructure of those neighborhoods to throw them away. The wasteful days of discarding places and driving farther and farther into exurbia are over. Now we want to maintain, recycle, and refurbish what we already have.

Many arterial strips[2] are ripe for retrofit. Drivers already travel along them during their daily routine, but—unlike the fiercely protected cul-de-sac subdivisions—hardly anyone loves the strip the way it is. Instead, it represents a part of the urban land inventory where investors, already realizing that their current crop of buildings is temporary, await the day when their parcels can be more fully used. What's missing is a sense of place, and in most cases that can only be added by *more* building—changing the strips from suburban roads to urban streets—at least in certain segments. The strips feel like uncoiled, unraveled half-cities, with buildings and signs set apart from one another at just the wrong distance: close enough together to create a jumbled sense of congestion, but too far apart to create cohesion, coherence, and the social contact that main streets bring.

AVENUES & BOULEVARDS

Dexter Avenue, Montgomery, Alabama

Dover, Kohl & Partners and Hall Planning & Engineering, 2007

Retrofit: Repairing an Historic Place

Avenue

Dexter Avenue, the main street of Montgomery, has witnessed momentous events in American history (Figure 4.1). The focal points of Dexter Avenue are the dome on the statehouse at one end and the fountain in Court Square at the other. This was the street where electric streetcars were first introduced in the United States—as part of the city's "Lightning Route." It is the place where Confederate leaders sent off their fateful telegram to Charleston, giving the order to fire on Fort Sumter. Nearly a century later, this was where Rosa Parks caught the bus but refused to sit in the back of it, leading to the Montgomery bus boycott. Thus, the Court Square intersection is both the birthplace of the Civil War and, later, the Civil Rights movement. Dexter Avenue was also the concluding leg of the marches

Figure 4.1: Dexter Avenue, Montgomery, Alabama. Mural by unknown artist, circa 1938. Dexter Avenue has been the site of momentous events in American history, from the Civil War to the civil rights movement.

Figure 4.2: Dexter Avenue, Montgomery, Alabama. Before: Existing conditions, circa 2006. © *2006 Dover, Kohl & Partners / UrbanAdvantage*

Figure 4.3: Dexter Avenue, Montgomery, Alabama. After: Computer simulation of proposed improvements and revitalization. © *2007 Dover, Kohl & Partners / UrbanAdvantage*

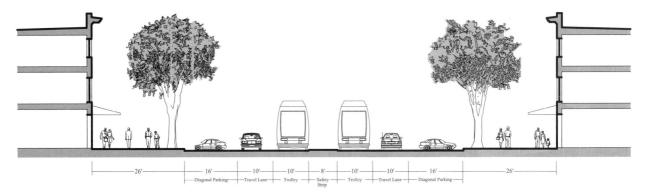

26'
Diagonal Parking — 16' — Travel Lane — 10' — Trolley — 10' — 8' Safety Strip — 10' Trolley — 10' Travel Lane — 16' Diagonal Parking — 26'

Figure 4.4: Dexter Avenue, Montgomery, Alabama. Section showing proposed improvements. © *2013 Dover, Kohl & Partners*

from Selma to Montgomery, with the avenue and state-house becoming the formal backdrops for speeches by the Reverend Dr. Martin Luther King, Jr.

During the long national decline of downtowns and main streets, Dexter Avenue became quiet, then quieter, then moribund. Court Square and Court Street were converted into a bland pedestrian mall, and Dexter Avenue storefronts began to disappear.

The fortunes of Dexter Avenue finally began to improve when the City of Montgomery restored Court Square as a proper plaza, following a design by Rick Hall of Hall Planning & Engineering. The square is paved in Belgian cobblestones with the fountain at its center. Cars, buses, pedestrians, and parades share the space, which has minimal traffic markings. The reconstruction was completed in early 2007, making Court Square the first new urban space of its kind on a major U.S. city street in over fifty years (Figure 4.63).

This transformation marked the beginning of the city's downtown revitalization, in accordance with its 2007 Master Plan, prepared by Dover, Kohl & Partners. Today, historic buildings are being restored and reoccupied, and vacant lots will be filled in according to the new SmartCode. The Plan's visualizations and recommendations are the result of public input from over

850 local residents, business owners, and community leaders. The SmartCode, customized for Montgomery's downtown, is intended to ensure that all future development promotes architecture, civic space, and street design appropriate for the city.

Fundamentally, this meant shifting from an emphasis on land uses and parking requirements to an emphasis on design, especially regarding the relationships between the buildings and the streets. The need for this change was painfully clear. The supersized new buildings developed in downtown Montgomery in the 1970s and 1980s tended to face sidewalks with the blank walls and cold facades one might expect from fortifications, not from office buildings or stores on a main street. Now the rules have been changed to give the flexibility needed for a greater number of normal-sized buildings and to get those buildings to face the public spaces with doors, storefronts, outdoor cafés, balconies, and the like.

The city plan also calls for overhauling the Dexter Avenue right-of-way, correcting the dimensions of the sidewalks, lanes, and parking spaces (Figures 4.2, 4.3, and 4.4). This presents a welcome opportunity to give the avenue a more harmonious geometry where it meets the State Capitol building, and to incorporate elements of the Olmsted Brothers' plan for the capitol campus.

WE SHAPE OUR INFRASTRUCTURE AND IT SHAPES US: WORKING WITH ENGINEERS

Elsewhere in the book, the point is made that since the Second World War engineers have been the *de facto* designers of the public realm. Anyone who takes part in the design of the public realm needs to know whom to talk to, because while it is common to call all engineers who work on road design and planning "traffic engineers," that's a mistake.

Civil Engineers have a Transportation Engineering branch consisting of three parts:

1. Transportation Planner
2. Traffic Engineer
3. Roadway Design Engineer

The Transportation Planner takes responsibility for the big picture: twenty-year plans for metropolitan planning organizations (MPOs), highway planning, rail planning, and the like. The Traffic Engineer is responsible for most things above the pavement, such as trees, signs, signals, and even striping (but not utilities). The Roadway Design Engineer designs everything from the pavement surface down: curbs, drainage, utilities, grades, slopes, etc.

Traffic Engineers and Roadway Design Engineers are Professional Engineers (PE). Transportation Planners can be either PEs or Certified Planners in the American Institute of Certified Planners (AICP). The American Association of State Highway and Transportation Officials (AASHTO) sets the standards, guidelines, and protocols for road design in the United States that are then adopted by local jurisdictions. The American Society of Civil Engineers (ASCE) represents professional engineers. The Institute of Transportation Engineers (ITE) was founded in 1930, sixteen years after AASHTO. Over time, the ITE be-

came more oriented towards cities and urban context than AASHTO.

The U.S. Department of Transportation (U.S. DOT) is a federal cabinet department in charge of transportation regulation. It includes the Federal Highway Administration (FHWA), the division of the U.S. DOT responsible for highways, and the Federal Transit Administration, which is in charge of transit systems. The National Association of City Transportation Officials (NACTO) is a coalition of transportation officials from fifteen of the largest cities in the United States.

In March 2006, the Congress for the New Urbanism and the ITE released the Street Design Manual *Designing Walkable Urban Thoroughfares, A Context Sensitive Approach, An ITE Recommended Practice* to address "the challenges that New Urbanists face in creating streets that match the urban built environment." The 255-page manual gives engineers, planners, and designers guidance for interpreting AASHTO Green Book policy and "demonstrates for practitioners how CSS (Context Sensitive Solutions) concepts and principles may be applied . . . in places where community objectives support walkable communities, compact development, mixed land uses and support for pedestrians and bicyclists." The manual, sponsored by the FHWA and the U.S. Environmental Protection Agency, can be downloaded at www.cnu.org or www.ite.org. In May 2013, John Massengale, Victor Dover, and Rick Hall began a series of meetings with officials at the U.S. DOT to discuss changes to the FHWA Functional Classification System (see Chapter 6).

LANCASTER BOULEVARD, LANCASTER, CALIFORNIA / Kaid Benfield

Moule & Polyzoides, 2010

Retrofit: Arterial Strip to Boulevard

Boulevard

A terrific street redesign is assisting economic recovery in a Southern California community that has suffered from deteriorating economic conditions but is nevertheless seeing significant population growth. This is a story of municipal foresight, excellent recent planning, and green ambition.

Lancaster is a fast-growing city, with a population of a little over 150,000 in far northern Los Angeles County, about seventy miles from downtown L.A. Its population has more than tripled since 1980; it increased by nearly a third from 2000 to 2010. It is racially mixed (38 percent Latino, 34 percent white, 20 percent African American) and, like so many fast-growing western cities, decidedly sprawling. The satellite view on Google Earth reveals a patchwork pattern of leapfrog development, carved out of the desert. It is a city with a very suburban character.

Lancaster's economic condition isn't among the country's very worst, but it has certainly been better. According to City-Data.com, the median price of home sales in the city plummeted by almost two-thirds between 2007 and 2009, from $350,000 to about $125,000—which is more or less where it still stands. As of August 2012, unemployment stood at 15.7 percent, way above the state average of 10.4 percent. Because the city is not far from Edwards Air Force Base and related industry, its fortunes have long been associated with aerospace engineering and defense contractors. In recent years, however, some major employers, including Lockheed-Martin, have been moving their investments elsewhere.

Sprawl and disinvestment in Lancaster have left their scars. Greg Konar writes in the San Diego Planning Journal:

By the late 1980s the City's historic downtown was in serious decline. Most retailers and commercial services had long since migrated to commercial centers and strip malls in other parts of the city. For years big box retailers and regional malls had captured nearly all new commercial growth. Much of it was concentrated along the Antelope Valley Freeway (I-14). Meanwhile the historic downtown deteriorated rapidly. Crime became an increasing problem and the surrounding older neighborhoods were suffering.[3]

That's a pattern all too typical of America in the late twentieth century, but Lancaster moved to do something about it, including the adoption in 2008 of a form-based zoning code for Lancaster Boulevard, a downtown corridor. (Form-based codes encourage walkability by promoting mixed uses and a pedestrian-friendly streetscape.) The city also hired the well-known architecture and planning firm Moule & Polyzoides to capitalize on the opportunities created by the code by redesigning the boulevard to attract businesses and people.

The results—a reinvigorated section of downtown now named The Boulevard—have been spectacular (Figures 4.5, 4.6, 4.7, and 4.8). The project has won multiple awards, including EPA's top national award for smart growth achievement. Moule & Polyzoides describe the design features: "Among the Plan's key elements are wide, pedestrian-friendly sidewalks, awnings and arcades, outdoor dining, single travel lanes, enhanced crosswalks, abundant street trees and shading, and added lighting, gateways and public art. Lancaster Boulevard has been transformed into an attractive shopping destination, a magnet for pedestrian activity and a venue for civic gatherings."

Greg Konar's article, cited above, provides an excellent review of what makes the design features of the project work so well.

Figure 4.5: Lancaster Boulevard, Lancaster, California. Before: Existing conditions, circa 2008. © *Moule & Polzoides, Architects & Urbanists*

Figure 4.6: Lancaster Boulevard, Lancaster, California. Moule & Polzoides, 2010. Illustrative plan. The new promenade is multi-functional, able to accommodate both parking and civic events. © *Moule & Polzoides, Architects & Urbanists*

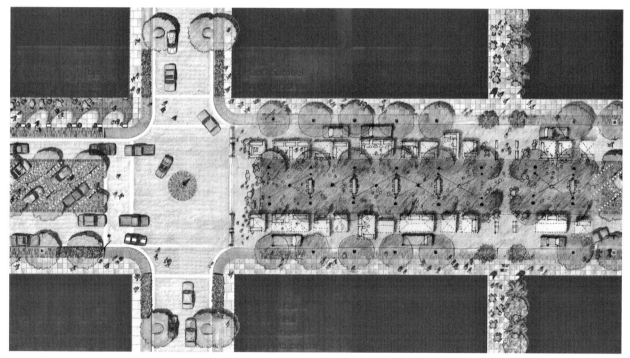

Justly proud of their work, the architects recount some of what's happened in the area since the project was completed:

- Forty-nine new businesses along the boulevard and an almost doubling of revenue generated, compared with just before the work began.

- An almost 10 percent rise in downtown property values.

- Eight hundred new permanent jobs, 1,100 temporary construction jobs, and an estimated $273 million in economic output.

- Eight hundred new and rehabbed homes.

- Dramatically increased roadway safety, with traffic collisions cut in half and collisions with personal injury cut by 85 percent.

223

Figure 4.7: Lancaster Boulevard, Lancaster, California. Moule & Polyzoides, 2010. The design by Moule & Polyzoides transformed the street by removing traffic lanes and installing a central promenade, with aligned trees and lampposts. *Image courtesy of the City of Lancaster*

Figure 4.8: Lancaster Boulevard, Lancaster, California. Moule & Polyzoides, 2010. Lancaster reclaimed its public realm. *Image courtesy of the City of Lancaster, photograph by Curt Gideon Photography*

This is a great example of how the right legal framework and the right design at the right time can help make a difference. It is also a great example of how our suburban communities can be improved. Is Lancaster Boulevard the best or most walkable district in America? Not by a long shot. But the change is tangible. This enterprising redesign gives the city something to build upon and sets an example for similarly situated communities—while at the same time reusing infrastructure and reducing emissions from car travel by taking advantage of a central location that shortens driving distances and encourages walking.

LE COURS MIRABEAU, AIX-EN-PROVENCE, FRANCE

Antoine Grumbach & Associates, 2002

Retrofit: Right-sizing the Roadway

Avenue

Le Cours Mirabeau in Aix-en-Provence is a quintessential "great street."[4] There is no debating its attractions; it dates from an age when public-works officials were heroes. This is what an eighteenth-century road-widening project looks like. By comparison, today's average traffic-capacity "improvement" looks like malpractice.

Two rows of mature plane trees line each side of the street (Figure 4.9). The resulting tree canopy is one of this French avenue's defining attributes. The first row of trees is eighteen feet from the building line. The second row is offset by an approximately thirty-foot-wide pedestrian space. The buildings on each side are fifty to sixty feet tall.

In a city famous for its fountains, the Cours begins with a fountain at the place du General de Gaulle and extends for a quarter of a mile, before terminating at a statue of King René. The Cours Mirabeau has long been known as a wide street with the majority of the street space dedicated to pedestrians, but, in fact, the division of the street into different parts has changed since its original construction. Before its latest incarnation, significantly more space was dedicated to auto traffic. Today, however—thanks to a redesign completed in 2002 by Antoine Grumbach & Associates—more than half of the right-of-way is dedicated to pedestrians (Figures 4.10 and 4.11). The Grumbach retrofit elim-

Figure 4.9: Cours Mirabeau, Aix-en-Provence, France. Antoine Grumbach & Associates, 2002. Public works officials were once heroes, building places of such high quality that they became the postcard-worthy symbols of their towns. *Image courtesy of Jason King*

Figure 4.10: Cours Mirabeau, Aix-en-Provence, France. Antoine Grumbach & Associates, 2002. In its most recent makeover, the amount of space devoted to pedestrians was increased. *Image courtesy of Andrew Georgiadis*

Figure 4.11: Cours Mirabeau, Aix-en-Provence, France. Antoine Grumbach & Associates, 2002. Section. The buildings on each side are fifty to sixty feet tall. Four rows of carefully spaced trees produce a high canopy over the space between the buildings. © 2013 Dover, Kohl & Partners

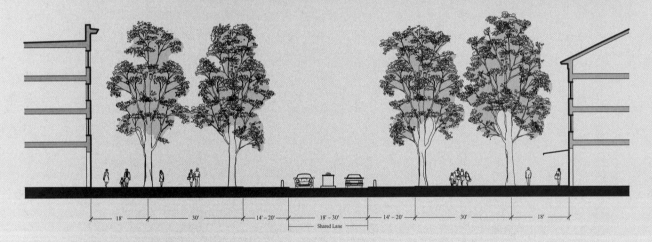

inated two of the four travel lanes and extended the sidewalks by thirteen feet on each side of the street.[5] The larger sidewalks contribute to the transformation of the boulevard from a primary transport route to a space dominated by pedestrians, cyclists, and market carts. Although still a direct route to the center of Aix, the pedestrian is now clearly the king in the new space.

In addition to giving the pedestrian more of the right-of-way, the retrofit also called for the installation of ramps around the fountains, with a slope of 5.6 percent.[6]

A natural traffic-calming device, the ramps and the narrowing of the travel lanes alter the character of the street, but not drastically. Car traffic moves very slowly on the street, so there is very little paint on the roadbed and a noticeable absence of stoplights and stop signs. The combination of these techniques designates the Cours Mirabeau as a true Complete Street, with a regional aesthetic all its own. The Cours provides shelter from the weather and is always full of people visiting local businesses and enjoying a stroll in the city.

Fairfax Boulevard, Fairfax, Virginia

Dover, Kohl & Partners, 2008

Retrofit: Arterial Strip to Multiway Boulevard

Multiway Boulevard

Like most aging traffic corridors with shopping centers and low-density commercial uses, Fairfax Boulevard is a wide arterial dominated by cars that invites high speeds and chases away pedestrians. Built in 1934, it was once the "new bypass" connecting the eastern portion of Lee Highway with the part of Fairfax known as Kamp Wash-

Figure 4.12: Fairfax Circle, Fairfax, Virginia. Before: Existing conditions, seen from within the circle, 2008. The circle is a local landmark as a traffic solution only, not as a *place*.

Figure 4.13: Fairfax Circle, Fairfax, Virginia. Dover, Kohl & Partners, 2008. Watercolor rendering, aerial view. The redesign includes correcting the traffic flow for slower speeds, planting a ring of trees within the circle to make its form more spatially evident, and amending development regulations to require space-shaping, street-oriented buildings. © 2008 Dover, Kohl & Partners

Figure 4.14: Fairfax Boulevard, Fairfax, Virginia. Before: Existing conditions in 2008. © *2008 Dover, Kohl & Partners / UrbanAdvantage*

ington. It became the desired location for the emerging retail model of the time: fast-food chains, strip centers, discount tire stores. The boulevard is still an active commercial street, but it has lost much of its economic value, in part because the old stores and strip centers cannot compete with the newer malls, "lifestyle centers," and revitalized downtowns in the area, where customers would prefer to be. Retail is always changing, and Fairfax Boulevard feels out of date (Figure 4.12).

A comparison with other major roads in mature metropolitan areas is useful. Boulevard de Rochechouart in Paris and Eastern Parkway in Brooklyn are examples of boulevards that are similar in width to Fairfax Boulevard, but Rochechouart and Eastern Parkway are busy and full of life, and well connected to their surrounding neighborhoods. Unlike Eastern Parkway, Rochechouart is a local commercial center, but both boulevards have medians for walking and have stops for important subway lines below. In contrast, Fairfax Boulevard serves little but the car. To a great extent, the boulevard's commercial activity still reflects the car-happy era that produced it: car-oriented discount retailers, car dealerships, muffler shops, and garages dominate. Its separated land uses and haphazardly scattered commercial buildings only work well for cars, and residential buildings are mostly located away from the boulevard.

In 2008, Fairfax hired Dover, Kohl & Partners to design a new master plan for Fairfax Boulevard and its surroundings. The city has had an uneasy relationship with growth in recent decades, warily eyeing the real estate boom all around it in Northern Virginia. The tranquil suburban scenes of single-family houses flanking the corridor are in high demand, but the boulevard itself has languished, and Fairfax has missed out on some much-needed jobs, businesses, and housing variety.

Residential uses had not previously been a part of the mix on the corridor, but now a clear opportunity exists for Fairfax to retrofit the existing fabric, embrace growth, and build its way out of its problems. The real estate market has changed, and Fairfax Boulevard has become a prime location for mixed-use, walkable development. To succeed in that market, it will be critical to set appropriate limits for building size, adopt standards for architecture and landscaping, and require thoughtful transitions from the newly citified corridor to the suburban houses lying just beyond it (Figure 4.13).

Fairfax Boulevard is still a bypass that drivers use to get from one destination to another. However, creating a new boulevard that balances traffic capacity, safety, placemaking, and local character could turn it into a great street—a destination rather than a bypass (Figures 4.14 through 4.17).

Figure 4.15: Fairfax Boulevard, Fairfax, Virginia. Dover, Kohl & Partners, 2008. Computer Simulation. After: The corridor reimagined as a multilane, multiway boulevard. © 2008 Dover, Kohl & Partners / UrbanAdvantage

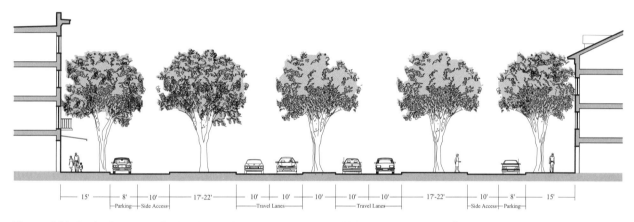

Figure 4.16: Fairfax Boulevard, Fairfax, Virginia. Dover, Kohl & Partners, 2008. Proposed section. © 2013 Dover, Kohl & Partners

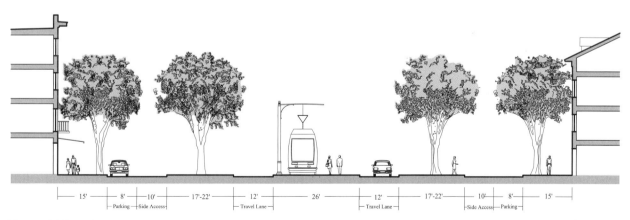

Figure 4.17: Fairfax Boulevard, Fairfax, Virginia. Dover, Kohl & Partners, 2008. Proposed section showing streetcar concept. © 2013 Dover, Kohl & Partners

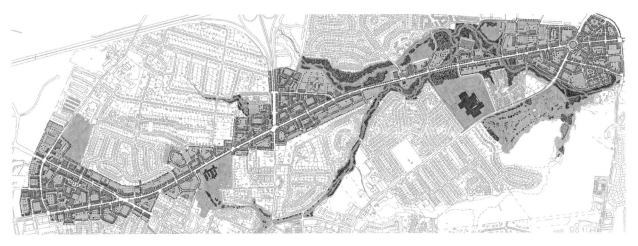

Figure 4.18: Fairfax Boulevard, Fairfax, Virginia. Dover, Kohl & Partners, 2008. Illustrative Plan. The plan proposes that redevelopment efforts should be focused in three distinct nodes, around Kamp Washington (left), Chain Bridge Road (center) and Fairfax Circle (right). © 2008 Dover, Kohl & Partners

Proposed Retrofit(s):

- Multistory, mixed-use buildings along the boulevard will step down to smaller, residential development closer to existing houses.

- Side access lanes with parallel parking will provide a comfortable pedestrian environment on the boulevard. Street trees in the medians between the side access lanes from the through-going lanes are a key part of the strategy.

- Two lanes of on-street parking in the side lanes will buffer the sidewalks from the traffic and provide convenient access to the stores.

- "Sharrow" markings—a street-painting technique that promotes sharing travel lanes with cyclists—will signal that cyclists are welcome, and help to calm traffic in the narrow side lanes.

- New public spaces, wide sidewalks, multiple transit options, and consistent tree lines will transform Fairfax Boulevard into a more productive, more pleasant place (Figure 4.18).

Boundary Street, Beaufort, South Carolina

Dover, Kohl & Partners, 2006

Retrofit: Arterial Strip to Multiway Boulevard

Multiway Boulevard

In 2006, the City of Beaufort hired Dover-Kohl to prepare a Master Plan for Boundary Street, a major transportation corridor that runs from the city limits to downtown Beaufort. A key street in Beaufort itself, Highway 21 also traverses the city's marshlands to points further east, and is used both for short local errands and longer regional trips. Dover-Kohl led a charrette for Beaufort that produced a community vision for transforming the corridor from a typical suburban strip (Figure 4.19) to an urban street suitable for more economically productive uses than fast-food chains and tire shops. With a design strategy that maintains traffic flow while improving safety and character, Boundary Street will stop being a road that is only used to get to another destination. It will become a destination itself, with its own memorable reputation.

Dramatic vistas across marshlands are a hallmark of South Carolina's Lowcountry. During the design and planning process for the Master Plan of Boundary Street and its surroundings, therefore, the team gave a lot of attention to the Battery Creek marshes next to the southern side of a long stretch of the corridor. Dover-Kohl proposed a continuous marsh-front park to showcase the marshes and reconnect natural places that had been divided by the construction of the highway. More marshlands lay just to the north, narrowing the landmass along the corridor; the master plan shows a new town square or village green at the narrowest point to reunite the divided landscape (Figure 4.20).

Figure 4.19: Boundary Street, Beaufort, South Carolina. Watercolor rendering, aerial view. Before: Existing conditions, circa 2006. At Jean Ribaut Square, one-story, single use retail buildings are set behind large parking lots in a typical strip shopping center configuration. © 2006 Dover, Kohl & Partners

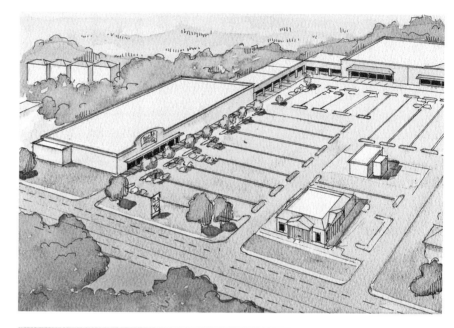

Figure 4.20: Boundary Street, Beaufort, South Carolina. Dover, Kohl & Partners, 2006. Watercolor rendering, aerial view. After: Redevelopment scenario for Jean Ribaut Square. A pattern of streets and blocks is to be established, creating addresses for new multi-story, mixed-use buildings, public spaces, and civic buildings; on-street parking will be combined with parking within the block. © 2006 Dover, Kohl & Partners

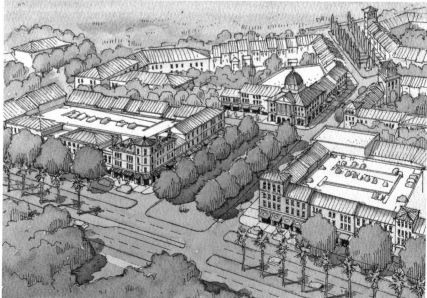

Figure 4.21: Boundary Street, Beaufort, South Carolina. Before: Existing conditions, circa 2006. © 2006 Dover, Kohl & Partners / UrbanAdvantage

Figure 4.22: Boundary Street, Beaufort, South Carolina. Dover, Kohl & Partners, 2006. Computer simulation. After: The north side of the corridor will eventually have the side access lane of a classic multilane, multiway boulevard. © 2006 Dover, Kohl & Partners / UrbanAdvantage

The overall concept for the master plan is to create a heightened sense of connectedness in this fragmented part of Beaufort. Therefore, in addition to unifying the long views and natural landscapes, it establishes a coherent network of streets. Boundary Street will eventually have a "slow lane," with adjacent on-street parallel parking (Figures 4.21 and 4.22). This establishes a pedestrian- and business-friendly environment without unduly sacrificing capacity for vehicles going through. Converting commercial shopping centers with large, ugly parking lots into town blocks will encourage local activity. The combination of new public space and the retrofit of the existing shopping centers on the strip will set up a new generation of economic opportunity.

A successful master plan begins a course of action that eventually creates a neighborhood with a distinct urban form—which is further defined by well-made streets. Walkable streets have travel lanes with narrow dimensions, large sidewalks, parking that is appropriately located, and buildings adjacent to sidewalks—qualities that encourage interaction and accessibility. A few simple changes in the placement of buildings, parking, and landscape can begin to transform the urban character of any outdated and placeless corridor (Figures 4.23 and 4.24).

A few defining elements help change a good road into a great street. Mature shade trees add comfort and protection to the street space, while awnings allow pedestrians to use the sidewalks consistently and conveniently.

At the intersections, small curb radii are proposed, and crosswalks appear frequently.

The architecture should act as a visual reminder of place. The drawings for the Boundary Street Master Plan reference a regional vernacular—one derived not just from tradition, but from the famously sticky Lowcountry weather, in which porches, verandas, awnings, overhangs, and breezeways make life more comfortable and help conserve energy. The hope is that Boundary Street will not only look as it should, but that it will also work with the local climate.

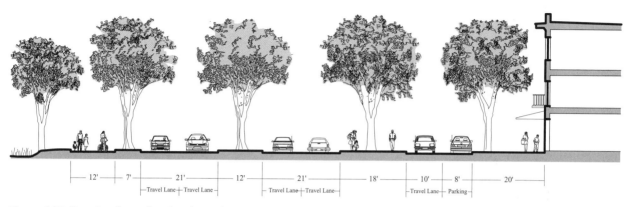

Figure 4.23: Boundary Street, Beaufort, South Carolina. Dover, Kohl & Partners, 2006. Proposed section. © *2013 Dover, Kohl & Partners*

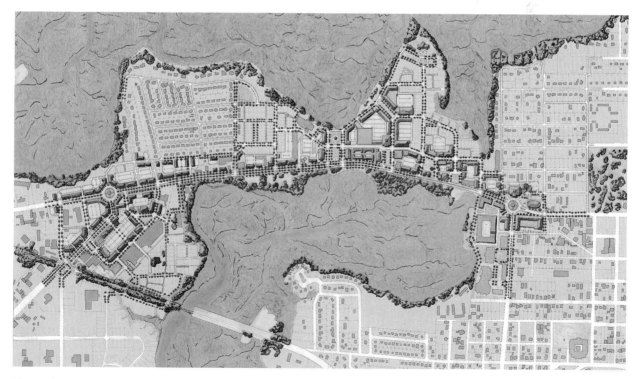

Figure 4.24: Boundary Street, Beaufort, South Carolina. Dover, Kohl & Partners, 2006. Illustrative Plan. In the central segment, the new buildings on the north side will face views of the Battery Creek marsh across the street. © *2006 Dover, Kohl & Partners*

Mesa Street, El Paso, Texas

Dover, Kohl & Partners, 2010

Retrofit: Right-sizing the Roadway

Main Street and Multiway Boulevard

As cities mature and grow, they can spread outward, reach skyward, or fill in the overlooked and poorly-used spaces already within their boundaries. The latter, called "infill development," is the most promising option today for many American cities. Mesa Street in El Paso, Texas—a wide thoroughfare flanked by urban land that feels half-built—is crying out for infill development. The six-lane route is the primary connection between northwest El Paso and downtown. As it approaches central El Paso, the road narrows to a four-lane street. This corridor invites large volumes of high-speed traffic and considerable economic activity in the aggregate, but the road is difficult to navigate as a pedestrian, cyclist, or transit user. Very little space is dedicated to walking.

Mesa Street's first generation of commercial developments, surrounded by large expanses of surface parking, failed to define the street's public realm. This condition prevails in many American cities and suburbs, resulting in an auto-centric atmosphere that misses out on the synergy of real towns. Ironically, a "sell-scape" meant to syn-

Figure 4.25: Mesa Street, El Paso, Texas. Before: Existing conditions, circa 2010.

Figure 4.26: Mesa Street, El Paso, Texas. Dover, Kohl & Partners, 2010. Computer simulation. After: In this segment, right-sizing the street will allow for wide sidewalks, street trees, on-street parking, and a cycle track. © 2010 Dover, Kohl & Partners / UrbanAdvantage

chronize with motoring and draw customers in becomes swamped with frustrating traffic and pushes customers away. Simultaneously, it effectively isolates businesses from any potential customers on foot, bikes, or public transit. A great commercial street is a *place*, full of people—browsing, shopping, dining—and accommodates all modes of traffic, not only car traffic. Retrofitting the right-of-way and implementing infill development with this in mind is the key to transforming Mesa Street.

Recently, the city initiated *Plan El Paso*, a comprehensive plan that targets the revitalization of specific neighborhoods and streets.[7] In an effort to grow the community in a smarter, healthier, and more sustainable way, the plan identifies specific areas for infill and redevelop-

ment. If it capitalizes on its strategic location, Mesa Street has the potential to become a dynamic public space under *Plan El Paso*. The road will become a destination for local patrons, as well as a through-going travel route.

The new design for one part of Mesa Street converts some of the existing road into a main street (Figures 4.25 and 4.26); the remaining stretch becomes a multiway boulevard (Figures 4.27 and 4.28). These street types—newly reintroduced to El Paso—accommodate large volumes of drivers but dedicate a sizable portion of the right-of-way to those walking, biking, or taking transit. Installed in a series of planned phases, this urban evolution will alter the character of the street, reactivating pedestrian life and turning Mesa Street into a vibrant public space.

Figure 4.27: Mesa Street, El Paso, Texas. Before: Existing conditions, circa 2010.

Figure 4.28: Mesa Street, El Paso, Texas. Dover, Kohl & Partners, 2010. Computer simulation. After: In this segment, the street can be reconfigured into a multilane, multiway boulevard with a Texas twist, using drought-tolerant native trees. © *2010 Dover, Kohl & Partners / UrbanAdvantage*

Creating a lively multiway boulevard for the majority of Mesa Street involves establishing a right-of-way that is approximately 150 feet wide and accommodates multiple lanes of through traffic; a lane for bus rapid transit and two side access lanes lined with on-street parking complete the boulevard cross-section. There are median spaces located in the center of the road and on either side of the access lanes. These spaces, especially when shaded by mature trees, will help to make the wide street maneuverable for the pedestrian.[8]

The climate-conscious retrofit of Mesa Street provides comfort and shelter from the sometimes harsh local weather with the use of awnings, arcades, and trees where appropriate. *Plan El Paso* seeks to redevelop key spots in the central city as walkable urban centers—several of which are directly on Mesa—connected by transit to other neighborhood centers along primary corridors. *Plan El Paso* is heavily illustrated with images showing how Mesa Street and other corridors will be transformed along their length, creating complete streets.

MAIN STREETS

Kensington High Street, London, England

Royal Borough of Kensington and Chelsea, 2004

Retrofit: Restoring the High Street

Main Street

By the mid-1990s, business owners and residents in the center of London had come to a consensus that the capital's roads were congested, ugly, and inefficient for cars and pedestrians alike.[9] Authorities had turned many of the main roads leading in and out of the city into auto sewers. Streets such as the Kensington High Street, which had been identified by the "London Plan" as one of the thirty-five most important centers in the city, had heavy iron railings along the side of the road that prevented citizens from crossing it except at widely dispersed crosswalks with staggered crossings (Figure 4.29). Here,

Figure 4.29: Kensington High Street, London, England. Before: Heavy iron railings lined the sidewalks and the High Street had degraded into an "auto sewer." *Property of the Royal Borough of Kensington and Chelsea*

Figure 4.30: Kensington High Street, London, England. Before: Excessive, auto-scaled striping, signs, and railings took the joy out of the street experience. *Property of the Royal Borough of Kensington and Chelsea*

more railings herded pedestrians into what Londoners disparagingly call "pigpens" to further control how they crossed the road. Traffic signs on the High Street were numerous and large, visually overwhelming both the road and the commercial signs. Most important, with almost no parked cars or errant parking to slow it down, traffic was fast, noisy, and polluting. (London had many diesel trucks, taxis, and private cars with few pollution controls.)

The railings along the sidewalks, the proliferation of signs, and the highway-scale striping and notices painted on the roadbed were all ugly and visually disruptive, weakening the pedestrian's experience of the space of the otherwise well-designed street, which boasted some of the most beautiful buildings in London (Figure 4.30). Daniel Moylan, a councilor for the Royal Borough of Kensington and Chelsea, led the fight to redesign and rebuild Kensington High Street. Moylan observed that the street had been designed "with the principal purpose of making it difficult for road accident victims to bring successful litigation against the highway authorities."[10]

Applying the K.I.S.S. Rule (Keep It Simple, Stupid)

Moylan coordinated a new design effort that aimed to balance the needs of cars, pedestrians, and cyclists (Figure 4.31). The road had a high traffic count (2,100 to 2,300 vehicles per hour), and local merchants wanted to keep that flow; at the same time, they wanted to make the street more attractive to the pedestrians coming from the affluent surrounding residential streets and the Underground stops on the street. Moylan said, "Some people find it difficult to get away from the idea that streetscape design is fundamentally an exercise in engineering that excludes enhancement of the visual experience."[11] Moylan, however, pragmatically pointed out that Kensington High Street was in competition with shopping malls. "Nobody designing an indoor shopping mall ever feels he has to justify making it attractive," Moylan said. "The idea is absurd. Yet, our critics talked as if paying serious attention to the attractiveness of the redesigned street was a form of guilty frivolity."

Figure 4.31: Kensington High Street, London, England. Royal Borough of Kensington and Chelsea, 2004. Compare with Figures 4.29 and 4.30: today, the railings are gone, the traffic markings and signals are minimal, and pedestrians are on an even footing with motorists. Bicycle parking in the median has proved extraordinarily popular.

> Nobody designing an indoor shopping mall ever feels he has to justify making it attractive. The idea is absurd. Yet, our critics talked as if paying serious attention to the attractiveness of the redesigned street was a form of guilty frivolity.
>
> —Daniel Moylan, Councilor, Royal Borough of Kensington and Chelsea

On the issues of safety and liability, the team followed practices already proven to work in the Netherlands and went to great lengths to ensure that they did not compromise safety when departing from Britain's design norms. Following an evidence-based approach, they left "plenty of opportunities for pulling back if need be—it is, after all, easy to add guardrailing later if absolutely necessary."[12] Since the work was completed, however, accident rates have significantly declined.

Before starting work, Moylan's team decided that they wanted "simplicity, quality, and elegance," and came up with a list of principles and goals that are worth repeating almost *verbatim*.

- No guardrails or bollards.
- The removal of all but the most necessary street clutter.
- Rectilinear footways, as far as possible.
- No pavement build-outs [bumpouts] other than to bring footways back to a true line.
- Improved north-south pedestrian crossings and, as far as possible, no staggered crossings.
- If crossings have to be staggered, then the central island should have no guard railing. (With no fences to stop them, pedestrians go straight across.)
- More pedestrian space but useful pedestrian space, where the pedestrians wish to be and to go.
- In practice, this means it should be on the south side, not on the north (where, on Kensington High Street, it would have been easier to accommodate).

- More bicycle parking (put in the center to avoid using pedestrian space).

- The detailed design of dropped curbs should be based on traditional vehicle crossovers rather than on contemporary models.

- Tactile blister paving should be replaced by a more attractive alternative. (In Kensington, stainless steel studs were used. See Figure 4.32.)

- The number of surface materials should be reduced to the minimum possible. (On Kensington High Street, they used only two for the sidewalks: York stone and granite.)

The final effect is underwhelming—which is exactly the point. It is the buildings and the space between the buildings that draw your attention, rather than busy details that pull our focus away from those (Figures 4.33 and 4.34). Moylan, with no training in design or even planning, had the wisdom and the confidence to oversee the design of what at the time was the best new road

> The final effect is underwhelming—which is exactly the point. It is the buildings and the space between the buildings that draw your attention, rather than busy details that pull our focus away from those.

Figure 4.32: Kensington High Street, London, England. Royal Borough of Kensington and Chelsea, 2004. A limited palette of materials and colors gives the street simple elegance. Stainless steel studs replaced the usual yellow tactile blister paving at crosswalks.

in London. Most elected officials are more influenced by the professionals whispering in their ear about standards and lawsuits. "In Britain the flat-earthers deny evidence and cry that the great god traffic would 'grind to a halt' if streets were shared and traffic lights were abolished," wrote Sir Simon Jenkins FRSL, journalist and Chairman of the National Trust. "Yet as Galileo told the Inquisition, *Eppur si muove*, and yet it moves."[13]

Figure 4.33: Kensington High Street, London, England. Royal Borough of Kensington and Chelsea, 2004. The center median in the busiest part of the High Street has different uses in different places: service parking, bicycle parking, pedestrian islands, and occasional turn lanes. The traffic lanes still handle large volumes of cars and trucks every day, but now they go more slowly.

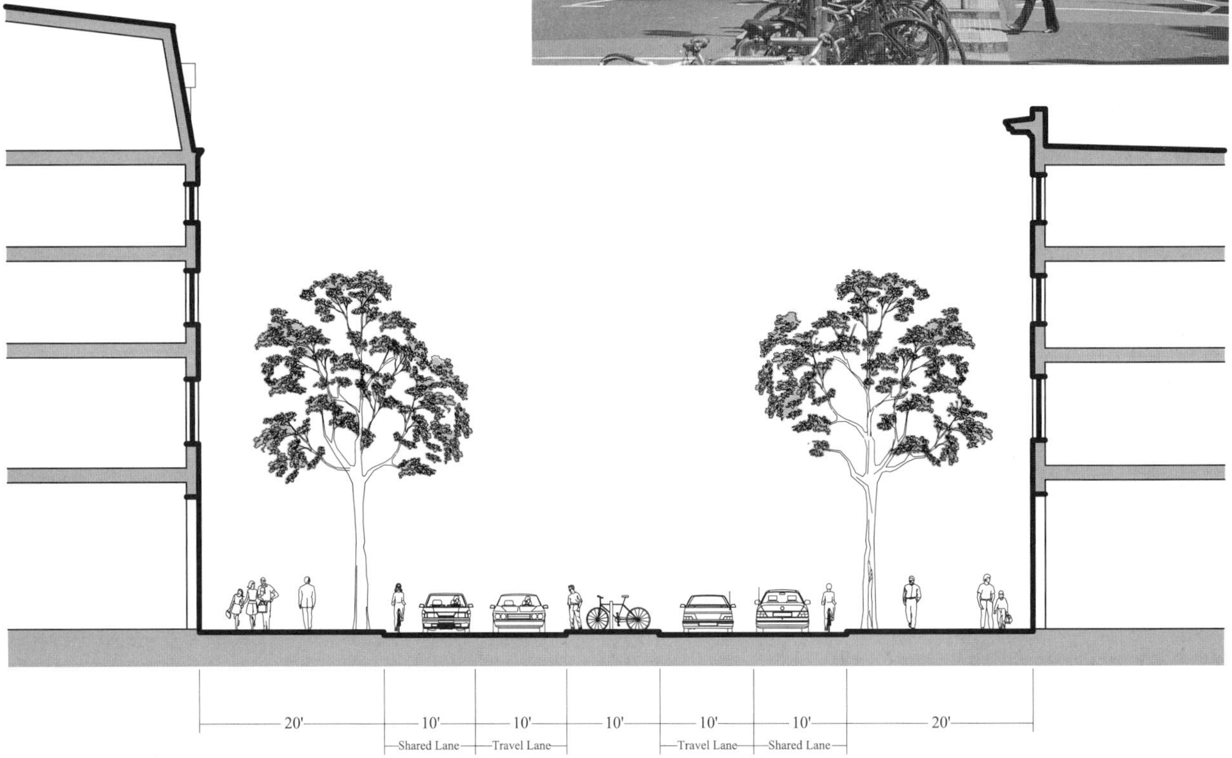

Figure 4.34: Kensington High Street, London, England. Royal Borough of Kensington and Chelsea, 2004. Section. © *2013 Dover, Kohl & Partners*

20'   10'   10'   10'   10'   10'   20'
Shared Lane — Travel Lane   Travel Lane — Shared Lane

ADA STANDARDS (CAMBRIDGE, MASSACHUSETTS, SIDEWALKS)

The ramps shown in Figures 4.35 and 4.36 illustrate the old and the new standards in Cambridge, Massachusetts. The new ramps were installed in the brick sidewalks of the college town to meet the guidelines of the American with Disabilities Act (ADA). It would be too strong to say they demonstrate that the sidewalks to hell are paved with good intentions, but they do show that the best intentions can lead to expensive and unnecessary changes that work against the principles of good placemaking. The changes were part

Figure 4.35: Massachusetts Avenue, Cambridge, Massachusetts. Sidewalk detail. Looking north towards Wigglesworth Hall and an entrance to Harvard Yard. The access ramp is simply made by sloping the bricks and tapering the granite curb.

Figure 4.36: Bow Street, Cambridge, Massachusetts. Sidewalk detail. Looking north towards Adams House (Harvard College) at Plympton Street. The Bow Street sidewalk formerly had a ramp detail identical to the one in Figure 4.35, which is one block away. The ugly and unnecessary new detail seen here was put in at considerable expense. Its odd geometry combines with similar details on the other corners and a pedestrian island between Bow Street and Mt. Auburn Street to call attention to the ramps in a jarring way that detracts from the streetscape. A holistic view of the street, rather than a specialist's narrowly focused view, would say the previous detail was both cheaper and better.

of an effort to make all streets in Cambridge Complete Streets.[14] They remind us that Complete Streets should be beautiful places where people want to be. That requires good design, not just the implementation of engineering standards. As we've said before, design is a way of solving problems—in this case, combining equal access for all, engineering, cost, and placemaking.

> It would be too strong to say they demonstrate that the sidewalks to hell are paved with good intentions, but they do show that the best intentions can lead to expensive and unnecessary changes that work against the principles of good placemaking.

The Federal Highway Administration has a set of ADA guidelines online at its website, fhwa.dot.gov.[15] These are presented as guidelines outlining possibilities, not as regulations, and they could not all be carried out, because some of the guidelines make others impossible. And yet state and local Departments of Public Works or Departments of Transportation frequently treat particular guidelines as rules that must be followed to prevent litigation—mandatory standards rather than principles or benchmarks for contextual design.

Elsewhere in the book we've questioned the DOT formula that sees multicolor, brick-pattern concrete combined with plain concrete strips as the best solution for most new work, suggesting that a less-expensive, good-quality but plain concrete sidewalk is frequently better. In the context of Cambridge, which historically has had many brick sidewalks with concrete or granite curbs, the situation is different. The red-brick sidewalks of Cambridge go well with the many red-brick buildings in the city, and the city has learned from its historic brick sidewalks and knows that bricks in the sidewalks look best when they're more muted in color than bricks on the adjacent buildings. As far as we've seen, Cambridge never uses imitation brick-pattern sidewalks in place of real brick sidewalks.

The city now goes to considerable expense to rebuild corner curbs with new concrete ramps containing bright red "domes" (textured pads next to the street). Bricks are easy to slope, and Cambridge already has many sloped corners. The bricks could have been placed on concrete pads that made sure the bricks did not settle unevenly, and there are bricks made with the tactile bumps. Instead, someone in the Department of Public Works decided that the ramps should contrast in color and texture with the bricks, and that the domes should contrast in color with the ramps.

The intent is good, but the ugly detail is unnecessary. While there is a paragraph in the FHWA guidelines that mentions the detail, the experience of most cities—including New York, London, Paris, *and* Cambridge—is that ramps that don't contrast with the sidewalk work well. Cambridge has many concrete sidewalks with concrete ramps in which all the concrete is the same, and New York City makes its new ADA compatible ramps from the same material as the sidewalk (usually concrete), because New York's experience is that the change in slope is enough of a cue for the disabled. Some might think that Cambridge substitutes the concrete for bricks because the concrete is less slippery, but that depends on the construction detail, and Cambridge has a number of much steeper slopes along many of their brick sidewalks that it does not plan to replace.

New York uses good-quality concrete, dark grey domes with texture, and granite curbs. In London and Paris, stone sidewalks get stone ramps that can be quite beautiful (see Color Plate 47). At London's Kensington High Street, the Royal Borough of Kensington and Chelsea specified natural-color metal domes, specifically to avoid red and yellow plastic domes.

The red domes Cambridge uses would be pleasant in brick ramps. The ramps they build instead are not the worst thing in the world, of course, but neither are they good. And when it comes to placemaking in the public realm, it's appropriate to quote Modernist master architect Ludwig Mies van der Rohe: "Less is more," and "God is in the details."

Worth Avenue and Hibiscus Place, Palm Beach, Florida

Sanchez & Maddux, Landscape Architects; Bridges, Marsh & Associates, Architects; 2010

Retrofit: Restoring Main Street

Main Street

Yes, Worth Avenue is a shopping street for the super-rich. We include it here because Worth Avenue is one of the best American examples of a redesigned street that is as simple as Kensington High Street, without the signs, stripings, warnings, multi-colors, multi-textures, and the like that dominate contemporary street design in the United States. Why should the rich get to have all the beauty? Of course, the rebuilding of the street was expensive, but that's not due to the lack of signs and striping.

Applying the Coco Chanel Rule to Main Street

The $15.8 million reconstruction (more than two-thirds of that for underground infrastructure) was spearheaded by the merchants on the street, who paid for much of the work with a bond (Figures 4.37 and 4.38).

Figure 4.37: Worth Avenue, Palm Beach, Florida. A view looking east on Worth Avenue before the renovation. Addison Mizner's apartment and studio were in the tall, arcaded building on the north side of the street. *Image courtesy of Sanchez and Maddux, Inc.*

Figure 4.38: Worth Avenue, Palm Beach, Florida. Sanchez & Maddux, Landscape Architects; Bridges, Marsh & Associates, Architects; 2010. Looking west on Worth Avenue, at Hibiscus Place.

Figure 4.39: Hibiscus Place, Palm Beach, Florida. Sanchez & Maddux, Landscape Architects; Bridges, Marsh & Associates, Architects; 2010. Looking west on Hibiscus Place, at Worth Avenue.

Figure 4.40: Hibiscus Place, Palm Beach, Florida. Sanchez & Maddux, Landscape Architects; Bridges, Marsh & Associates, Architects; 2010. Looking north on Hibiscus Place, from Worth Avenue.

One of the driving forces behind the work was the Chanel boutique on the corner of Worth Avenue and Hibiscus Street, where the block in front of the store was rebuilt in a simple and elegant way as Hibiscus Place (Figures 4.39 and 4.40). Perhaps the designers were channeling Coco Chanel, the icon of early twentieth-century fashion and design, who famously said, "Simplicity is the keynote of all true elegance." She advised every woman before leaving the house to "look in the mirror and remove one accessory."

Worth Avenue is a shopping street, and so another of the basic ideas was to support the merchants. The noted New Urban shopping consultant Robert Gibbs said of the simple sidewalks on Worth Avenue, "Remember, the store owners want you to look at their windows—not the sidewalk or the streetscape." That's a lesson all designers

> The experience of the public realm is what's important, not the streetscape or the new bumpout.

who work on Main Streets should remember. The same principle applies to the street space in general. The experience of the public realm is what's important, not the streetscape or the new bumpout.

In 1918, what is now Worth Avenue was a dirt road, with the private Everglades Club under construction at its western end. Standard Oil partner Henry Flagler had started to develop the island of Palm Beach approximately twenty-five years earlier, when he extended his Florida railroad as far south as West Palm Beach on the Florida mainland. The Everglades Club was designed by the architect Addison Mizner, who had moved to Palm Beach and become the architect of choice for the rich building winter houses there. He later designed a building diagonally across Worth Avenue for his own office and studio, and behind it the "Via Mizner" and the "Via Parigi," small, picturesque shopping passages in the center of the large block between Worth Avenue and the next street over (Figure 4.41). The pedestrian passages expand the retail area of Worth Avenue and provide a convenient way to walk through the middle of the long block. Today, the Via Mizner and the Via Parigi (named after the Singer Sewing Machine heir and Florida developer Paris Singer) supply less expensive smaller spaces than the buildings on Worth Avenue.

Mizner planted tall coconut palm trees on Worth Avenue. After these died in the lethal yellowing blight of the 1970s, they were replaced with shorter Christmas palms. Part of the recent renovation of Worth Avenue was to replace the Christmas palms with 32-to-40-foot-tall coconut palms. (This may sound strange to people from northern climes, but it's common practice in Florida and Southern California to plant fully grown palm trees that have been cultivated on tree farms.) At the same time, overhead power lines were buried and underground infrastructure was replaced.

The graceful trees are striking but restrained. Similarly, the tabby-shell concrete sidewalks may be more luxurious than plain concrete, but they are part of a muted palette that quietly works together (the tabby shell also feels good under bare feet). Other visually restrained design moves were a drastic reduction in the number of signs and the quantity of striping, well-designed bumpouts, and the decision by the clients to light the sidewalks during the evening with overflow light from the storefronts. At Hibiscus

Figure 4.41: Worth Avenue, Palm Beach, Florida. Sanchez & Maddux, Landscape Architects; Bridges, Marsh & Associates, Architects; 2010. Looking north, across Worth Avenue to the Via Mizner.

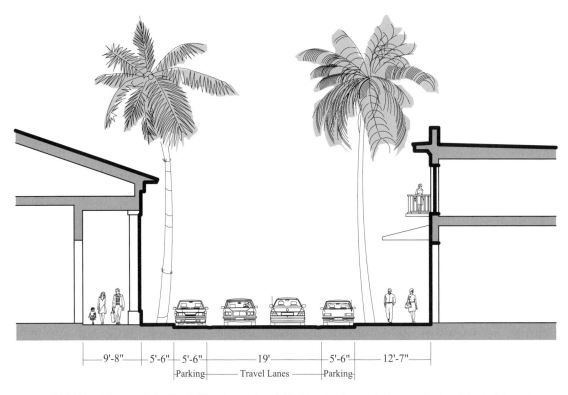

9'-8" — 5'-6" — 5'-6" — 19' — 5'-6" — 12'-7"

|Parking| —Travel Lanes— |Parking|

Figure 4.42: Worth Avenue, Palm Beach, Florida. Sanchez & Maddux, Landscape Architects; Bridges, Marsh & Associates, Architects; 2010. Section. *Image courtesy of Dover, Kohl & Partners with data provided by the City of Palm Beach*

Place, parking lanes were removed. A well-proportioned island with a coquina fountain and coquina bollards was put in the center of the street to slow cars as they approach Worth Avenue. Because the cars were going slowly, a single, discreet directional sign could be used to guide traffic, without bold Do Not Enter signs on the inbound lane.

The slow speeds on Worth Avenue allowed for other appealing choices that had fallen out of favor in downtown street design in America over the last few decades. The sidewalk curbs are very low, and the curbs around the grassy median are at the same level as the street and the grass as you approach from the north. At the other end of Hibiscus Place, a small planter extends into Worth Avenue at grade level. No curbs, bollards, signs, or striping prevent drivers from running over the planting (Figures 4.39 and 4.40). And yet people rarely do. Even if they do, the planting is easy to replace.

Since there are no parked cars buffering people on the sidewalk from the traffic on Hibiscus Place, palm trees and coquina bollards prevent cars from veering onto the sidewalks. But the slow speeds of the cars, the lack of highway-scale graphics, and the placemaking touches in the design turn the roadbed into a space comfortably shared by walkers, cyclists, and motor vehicles.

For the most part, Worth Avenue follows Robert A.M. Stern's first rule of design: "Line things up." Since its blocks are long, however, there are mid-block bumpouts to make pedestrians feel at ease crossing the street. One conveniently lines up with the Via Mizner (Figure 4.41). All are much wider than the ubiquitous, formulaic bumpouts we have become accustomed to in new street construction. They are well proportioned and planted, so that they are pleasing to look at, and they have benches where people can stop and rest without blocking the sidewalk.

Park Avenue, Winter Park, Florida

Dover, Kohl & Partners, 1998

Retrofit: Restoring Main Street

Main Street

In the 1880s, two northern businessmen bought a large tract of land in Orange County, Florida, where they platted the town of Winter Park. They slowly developed the town, which they sold in 1885 to the newly formed Winter Park Company, which, in turn, successfully promoted the town as a winter escape for wealthy northerners. Park Avenue was the Main Street, which from the beginning was meant to be urban. Even before the roadway was paved, the earliest buildings had a traditional, street-oriented relationship to the public space of the avenue and its adjacent Central Park.

Over time, the street was widened to accommodate diagonal parking (later removed), and its distinctive curvature was relaxed and broadened, to speed up traffic. Unlike many other main streets, which became virtually deserted in the mid-twentieth century, Park Avenue continued to occupy a place of importance to the people of the town as the central scene of civic life. Periodically, however, Park Avenue was threatened and further encroached upon. Serious proposals were floated to pave Central Park for more parking; a bland suburban-style City Hall was built on a key focal site, and, in the early 1960s, the big Winter Park

Mall opened just a few blocks away. Some predicted the mall would kill Park Avenue, but things turned out differently. The avenue hummed along and grew more beloved, while the mall began to languish within a decade. Customers chose the authentic main street.

Eventually, though, leaders of prosperous Winter Park decided to improve the quality of Park Avenue—to bring it into the class of what Allan Jacobs calls the "great world streets." The timing for reconstruction was right, because the century-old lateral sewer pipes under the avenue began to fail, one at a time. The new design needed to preserve the classic main street without overdoing it, restore features that had been lost over the years, and improve the experience for motorists and pedestrians.

The City of Winter Park hired Dover, Kohl & Partners, whose design team began building consensus for a careful refurbishment of the avenue, starting in 1994 with the "Winter Park in Perspective" conference and a subsequent charrette. Dover Kohl studied the existing conditions and decided to narrow the excessively wide travel lanes to accommodate widening the sidewalks and to slow down traffic. The team also judged the tree canopy along the avenue to be insufficient; the lack of shade made walking uncomfortable. Unsightly overhead wires ran along the avenue, and the poles for span-wire traffic signals in the sidewalks crowded pedestrians and seemed out of place (Figure 4.43). At the same time, it was clear that Winter Park wanted something better than another visually obnoxious,

Figure 4.43: Park Avenue, Winter Park, Florida. Before: Existing conditions, circa 1996.

Figure 4.44: Park Avenue, Winter Park, Florida. Dover, Kohl & Partners, 1998. After the retrofit, new rules for development were instituted, bringing the public effort to remake the street and private investment in new buildings into one, coordinated ensemble. An abrupt midblock crank (center left) replaced a swooping curve. *Image courtesy of Rick Hall, HPE*

Figure 4.45: Park Avenue, Winter Park, Florida. Dover, Kohl & Partners, 1998. Design process sketch showing the restoration of simple intersection geometry, with no bulbouts. Small corner radii and elongated tree wells are also introduced. © *1998 Dover, Kohl & Partners*

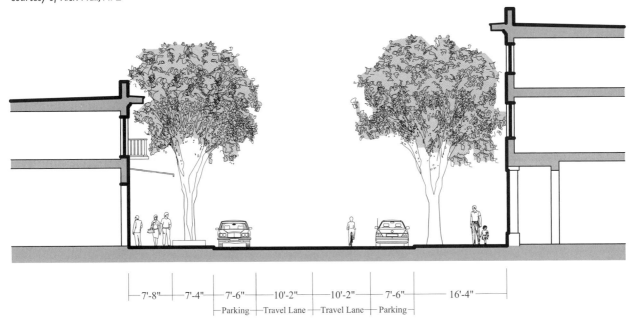

7'-8" | 7'-4" | 7'-6" Parking | 10'-2" Travel Lane | 10'-2" Travel Lane | 7'-6" Parking | 16'-4"

Figure 4.46: Park Avenue, Winter Park, Florida. Dover, Kohl & Partners, 1998. Section. © *1998 Dover, Kohl & Partners*

overcooked "streetscape" project with excessive amounts of the clichés Peter Katz calls the B's (benches, bollards, bricks, banners, and so forth).[16] The town's Community Development Director at that time, Don Martin, demanded instead a street design with "simple, understated elegance."

The reconstruction, largely completed by 1998, is considered a great success among local residents (Figure 4.44). First, the way Park Avenue changes in spatial character along its length, with a distinct beginning, middle, and end, was respected in the design (Figures 4.45 and 4.46). Each block was understood to be different, yet the corridor is still sufficiently united. The most challenging block was between Lyman Avenue and Comstock Avenue where, decades ago, engineers had reworked the street network to bend the alignment of Park Avenue into a high-speed curve. Here the geometry of the rebuilt street was significantly altered by changing that broad, swooping curve to a much more abrupt crank, tightening the scene visually, slowing the cars, expanding pedestrian space, and pulling new buildings into one's field of vision.

Sidewalks, intersections, and curb cuts were altered to meet ADA standards. The historic brick street surface, buried under generations of asphalt, was uncovered and restored, and new sidewalks poured with simple, easy-to-clean concrete. The old bricks in the roadway were combined with newer brick pavers in the crosswalks, with a very slight difference in color and a muted pattern change to visually define the crosswalk in a subtle way (Figure 4.45). To address the perennial local problems with older brick streets, where the bricks shift and sag over time as their sand base is compacted or eroded, a more stable base of lime rock, sand, and soil cement was made especially for Park Avenue.

Another perennial complaint about modern "streetscapes" is that the new trees do not grow to their proper height and full canopy; for Park Avenue, a customized tree-planting detail (copied from nearby Disney World, where the trees have thrived) should allow the new oaks to grow to their full size. The overhead utilities on the avenue were buried. Mast-arm traffic signals, modeled on a century-old design rediscovered and revived by the landscape architect Jay Hood, replaced the span-wires. These employ a cable-stay to hold the arms steady instead of using fattened tubes, and the result is a visually welcome alternative to the standard mast arms used in most streetscape projects. Pedestrian signals were integrated at several intersections.

The City of Winter Park adopted new design rules to go with the refurbished street, and infill development following those rules has further sewn the segments of the street together. Galvanized by the success on Park Avenue, local leaders completed a grand plan for the long-term revival of Central Park under the direction of landscape architect Forest Michael, and Rollins College installed a new monumental entrance and admissions hall to visually terminate one end of the avenue, both designed by architect Maricé Chael (Figure 4.47).

Figure 4.47: Rollins College entrance, Park Avenue, Winter Park, Florida. Dover, Kohl & Partners and Chael, Cooper & Associates, 1998–2002. *Image courtesy of Chael, Cooper & Associates, photograph by Corey Weiner*

Columbia Pike, Arlington, Virginia

Dover, Kohl & Partners and Ferrell Madden Associates, 2002–2013

Retrofit: Transit-Oriented Development with a Form-Based Code

Main Street

Columbia Pike is one retrofitted corridor where all the pieces are coming together. Among similar projects underway in the United States, it is also one of the farthest along in its transformation. Arlington County adopted a revitalization plan and form-based code for portions of the corri-

dor in 2002, after thirty years of disinvestment and decline. The plan and code cover a series of mixed-use nodes along the corridor where redevelopment will produce higher densities and walkable station areas, in anticipation of an improved public transit system with stops in these locations (Figures 4.48 and 4.49). Two years later, the county finalized public-space standards that will control the rebuilding of the Pike, and in 2010 it took over the road from the Virginia Department of Transportation. Five major private redevelopments have been completed, replacing low-slung stores, parking lots, and car dealerships with multistory, mixed-use buildings with housing, office space, and stores, including a full-size grocery store tucked within an urban

Figure 4.48: Columbia Pike, Arlington, Virginia. Before: Existing conditions in 2002 after decades of blight and disinvestment. The auto-only phase on the two-hundred-year-old corridor had run its course. © 2002 Dover, Kohl & Partners / UrbanAdvantage

Figure 4.49: Columbia Pike, Arlington, Virginia. Dover, Kohl & Partners and Ferrell Madden Associates, 2002. After: The form-based code facilitates redevelopment around the future transit station areas, in a series of mixed-use nodes distributed along the corridor. © 2002 Dover, Kohl & Partners / UrbanAdvantage

Figure 4.50: Columbia Pike, Arlington, Virginia. Before: Existing conditions between the "nodes" in 2011. © *2011 Dover, Kohl & Partners / UrbanAdvantage*

Figure 4.51: Columbia Pike, Arlington, Virginia. Dover, Kohl & Partners and Ferrell Madden Associates, 2011. After: The new Columbia Pike Neighborhoods Plan directs the redevelopment of areas between the mixed-use nodes, increasing residential density, converting the development pattern to street-oriented, transit-worthy urbanism. © *2011 Dover, Kohl & Partners / UrbanAdvantage*

block. The character of the corridor has changed rapidly from despair to optimism (see "Placemaking's Potential for Return on Investment" in Chapter 1). Interestingly, the Columbia Pike Streetcar—admittedly, an optimistic idea during planning sessions in 2002—gained considerable support and funding and should be operational within the decade. Installing the streetcar will require reconstructing the street, following the new design.

All of the progress on Columbia Pike can be attributed to elected officials and neighborhood leaders who got impatient and doggedly persisted until somebody listened. It is too early for them to relax and celebrate, however. The early-adopter developers of the first few new private buildings were made sufficiently confident by the county's commitments to get started, but if this commitment shows signs of flagging, private development will flag, too. So far, the opposite has been the case. In 2012, Arlington County reconvened the planning team and adopted their companion volume to the original revitalization plan, after an extensive process of research and public consultation. The new "Columbia Pike Neighborhoods Plan" addresses a much larger context—including the surrounding neighborhoods and the largely residential segments of the Pike between the original plan's nodes—and a wider range of topics, including mixed-income housing and sustained funding for the revitalization initiative (Figures 4.50 and 4.51). The county board now has a second form-based code under consideration, which will interlock with the original code and give the Neighborhoods Plan the force of law.

Main Street, Great Barrington, Massachusetts

massDOT, 2013

Retrofit: Rebuilding Main Street

Main Street

RETROFITTING A MAIN STREET THAT'S ALSO A STATE HIGHWAY: A CAUTIONARY TALE

In May 2012, *Smithsonian* magazine named Great Barrington, Massachusetts, the best small town in America.[17] We like it too. One of the reasons we like it is because we enjoy spending time on the town's Main Street, a still-functioning town center and shopping street that is one of the best and most beautiful in New England (for historic photos of the street, see Figures 4.52 and 4.53). By the time this book comes out that may be less true, because if all goes as planned the Massachusetts Department of Transportation (massDOT) will have cut down the Bradford Pear trees that line the street during a $5.5 million renovation (Figures 4.54 and 4.55).

Regardless of how that plays out, the reasons why Great Barrington's Main Street is threatened reflect the way most Departments of Transportation work, and how other professionals involved as consultants to DOTs frequently approach street design and tree planting. The proposed changes remind us that transportation and traffic engineers

Figure 4.52: Main Street, Great Barrington, Massachusetts. Historic photo from the nineteenth century. The brick building on the southwest corner of Main Street and Railroad Street is 304 Main Street, the oldest "commercial block" on Great Barrington's Main Street. The building is also visible in Figure 2.115. In the one-hundred-plus years between the two photos, the road has been paved and widened. *Image courtesy of James Mercer*

Figure 4.53: Main Street, Great Barrington, Massachusetts. Like Figure 4.52, a nineteenth century view of Main Street, this one looking south. Planted along the still-dirt road, the trees grew well, forming a beautiful canopy. *Image courtesy of the Special Collections Department / Iowa State University Library*

have become the default urban designers for a lot of America's public realm. Scenarios similar to this one in Great Barrington have been going on across America for decades.

Great Barrington's Main Street has all the elements necessary for making a street where people want to get out of their cars and walk. The central blocks are lined with three-story-tall, mixed-use buildings—mainly loft-style brick buildings from the late nineteenth and early twentieth centuries characteristic of New England, with stores on the ground floor. Perpendicular to Main Street is another retail street, Railroad Street (see Figures 2.115 and 2.118). Parking is on-street and in lots behind Main Street.

> Great Barrington's Main Street has all the elements necessary for making a street where people want to get out of their cars and walk.

Great Barrington is where the story of the Alice's Restaurant Thanksgiving "Massacree" began, and there is still a countercultural element in this part of the Berkshires, which has its own local currency, called BerkShares. Locals and tourists alike frequent many of the stores and

restaurants in the town, including a whole-wheat pizza place called Baba Louie's, a fancy cheesemonger with a slow-food café out back (Rubiner's and Rubi's, respectively), two excellent supermarkets (one a cooperative) that feature local produce, a great hardware store, and a regionally-important restored theater called the Mahaiwe. Matt Rubiner tells anyone who asks that one of the reasons he opened his shops in Great Barrington was the beauty of the downtown, which attracts customers the way it attracted him.

Main Street is also U.S. Route 7, which is why it comes under massDOT's jurisdiction. On its long passage from Long Island Sound in Connecticut to the Vermont–Canadian border, Route 7 has many different characters. In southern Connecticut it's a six-lane divided highway known locally as Super 7; in northern Connecticut it's a wide two-lane road that winds along the scenic Housatonic River; and in many places along the route it is the old Main Street in various cities and towns. In Great Barrington, Route 7 outside of the downtown is also an ugly modern arterial that attracts auto-centric shopping and development of the kind that has harmed many downtowns by taking away stores and services.

Figure 4.55: Main Street, Great Barrington, Massachusetts. Looking north from the corner of Main Street and Castle Street (opposite Bridge Street), in the spring of 2012. The road and the traffic lanes are wide, *too* wide visually unless there are mature trees. At this time, massDOT had announced its plans to cut down the Bradford Pear trees they had once planted.

MassDOT's first plan for Great Barrington followed its usual formula for downtown streets, as seen in a number of towns around Massachusetts. Fortunately, Great Barrington residents involved in local government committees eliminated a number of the formulaic elements in massDOT's design, like concrete sidewalks stamped with colored-brick patterns and ostentatious pedestrian crossings (Color Plate 52). Unfortunately, though, massDOT and its consultants have convinced the town that it will be best to cut down the Bradford Pear trees that were planted on their advice in the 1960s.

After all the problems of the demolition and messy reconstruction of Main Street are over—a process that will disrupt the businesses along the street and cost them sales—the result will be a place that in all meanings of the word will be less attractive: both locals and tourists will be less attracted to coming to Great Barrington and getting out of their cars. Keeping the pear trees and phasing in other trees over time would serve the town far better.

If the town *is* going to take the drastic step of cutting down all the mature trees at one time, then it should demand more from massDOT in return. All over the country, pro-

◀ **Figure 4.54:** Main Street, Great Barrington, Massachusetts. Looking north on the east side of Main Street in the spring of 2012, from Bridge Street. MassDOT had announced its plan to cut down the Bradford Pear trees, which are fuller when the green leaves are out.

gressive towns looking to the future and thinking about climate change are using the techniques of suburban retrofits to transform their arterials and transportation corridors into walkable places. Great Barrington could use some of those as well. We add a few ideas at the end of this essay.

Placemaking

In Chapter 1, we talked about techniques urban designers use to make streets like outdoor rooms, fashioning a public realm where people want to be. People enjoy being in these rooms when they are well-proportioned, comfortable spaces. If the space is wide and uncontained—as it is north and south of downtown on Route 7, where the road travels through sprawl and shopping centers—people are more comfortable in their cars than on foot.

MassDOT's plan for Great Barrington paid lip service to placemaking principles, and the state agency is more sensitive to the local importance of Main Streets than most state Departments of Transportation. Unlike the neighboring New York DOT, massDOT has rarely gone through small towns simply removing all the trees along main streets and reducing sidewalks to uncomfortably narrow strips. But their first priority in the Great Barrington plan is still traffic flow and infrastructure engineering. Like most DOTs, massDOT has developed an impressive ability to procure funding, even in times of recession like now. Once it has those funds, one of its highest priorities becomes to spend the money on what it does best. If push comes to shove in public meetings, massDOT is ready to change the aesthetic parts of the design but strongly resists compromising on what is important to it, which is traffic flow and controlling the roadbed.

A real Department of Transportation—as opposed to a Department of Auto Flow—might say the highest and best use of the funds in Great Barrington would be to rebuild the streetcar line that once ran along Route 7 from Canaan, Connecticut, to Pittsfield, Massachusetts, or to restart train service to New York City, a possibility that private investors are discussing. Instead, massDOT is saying that it is important to change the camber of the road from 1 percent to 2 percent, but urban designers or town planners with money to spend in Great Barrington would not begin by making a 1 percent change in the grade of the road, cutting down trees that are one of the town's greatest assets, or tearing up pleasant sidewalks, as massDOT plans to do in their Main Street reconstruction. They would recognize that the blocks between Town Hall and the Post Office are one of the town's greatest strengths and that the money would be best spent to the north and south, where the town fabric and walkability quickly fall apart. Great Barrington could use many more projects like the River Walk it built along the Housatonic River, where it flows downtown. It wouldn't be hard to find better uses for this money.

If engineers were poets, they would never write, "I think that I shall never see / a poem lovely as a tree." They dislike trees near roads for a variety of reasons, beginning with their preference to remove any "hazardous object" from the side of the road. They realize there will be things next to the road in the center of towns, so they compromise by accepting a small tree, which will do less damage to a speeding car than a larger one. Overlooked is that pedestrians behind large trees will suffer fewer injuries, and might actually escape unharmed. Engineers also want to control variables; they don't like messy trees that might interfere with power lines. Last but not least, they use modern construction and compaction methods that interfere with existing tree roots.

The tree mix proposed by massDOT's consultants can never grow to the height or the width required for a leafy canopy over the sidewalk or a "wall" of tall trees along the road (Figure 1.23). MassDOT uses consultants who think it's old-fashioned to use traditional street trees to shape a traditional American Main Street. The consultants use functional arguments about disease to support their preferences but frequently promote change for the sake of change.

The consultants will tell you that the Bradford Pear trees on Main Street are brittle, which is true. They won't tell you that there's no such thing as a no-maintenance, mature tree. And they won't tell you that the trees they advise planting will never grow as large as the Bradford Pears or that a number of small-town Main Street studies show mature trees have a significant economic value for shopping streets. That's particularly true for Great Barrington because its Main Street is unusually wide, and the buildings that line it are not big enough to comfortably shape and visually contain the space between the buildings. The mature Bradford Pear trees are just large enough to do that, however, as well as jobs like providing shade in the summer.

In their work with massDOT, the town committees have thus far been unable to get a simple row of street trees of the type Great Barrington needs and has traditionally had. The town's Department of Public Works weighed in, calling for trees that would not block the town's cherry picker from getting to the second and third floors of the buildings along the street. This stipulation ignores the fact that the trees make a better life for the people on the second and third floors, just as the tree selection ignores the economic value of trees for the town's merchants and the fact that the small trees will block the view of the storefronts. Has there been a cherry picker problem in the past, or is the DPW simply overthinking their part of the problem?

The DPW also complains about cracked sidewalks and places where the concrete slabs have been slightly raised by tree roots. Real bricks can alleviate that problem, as opposed to the brick-pattern stamped concrete panels that massDOT prefers. But traditionally, cracked sidewalks have not been a problem for New Englanders: in Nantucket, the town values what it has, so Nantucketers live with the uneven sidewalks instead of letting lawyers, engineers, and other specialists introduce monofunctional solutions. They balance function, construction, and beauty, and the result is one of the most beautiful and popular places in America.

In Great Barrington the specialists undervalue the beauty and diminish it. They might tell you that beauty is in the eye of beholder and that what's important is dotting all the i's and crossing all the t's in their limited criteria. With the new CNU ITE Street Design Manual, *Designing Walkable Urban Thoroughfares: A Context Sensitive Approach*, this should be less of a problem, because in the manual the ITE officially endorses transect-sensitive design and calls for mature trees in the right downtown contexts. Great Barrington's Main Street discussion shows that these changes can take time to trickle down to the field, however.

The Future of Main Street

New Englanders used to be known as frugal people. "If it ain't broke, don't fix it," was a New England motto. When they spent money on big changes, they demanded value. Since World War II, our road building and interstate highway program has been the most expensive public works project in the history of the world. DOTs have become used to doing whatever they want with our roads, as well as controlling the funding to do so. They like plans along the lines of massDOT's $22 billion Big Dig in Boston, where massDOT tore down a functioning highway to improve traffic flow, at tremendous cost. In the current economic state of America that doesn't work anymore, and it's not the best way to make our cities, towns, and neighborhoods more walkable.

Some say that all politics is local. All community design should be, too. When we look at the needs of Great Barrington, we can see ways to make the current plan better for the town, its citizens, and its merchants. The town's Main Street is a wide one that needs traditional street trees for its civic and economic well-being. Traditionally, new trees would have been phased in over time, because new trees grow slowly in New England. If the town decided to do that, the trees would have to be chosen so that they would make a harmonious streetscape with the Bradford Pear trees. Most of the trees in the massDOT plan have different shapes and sizes than the existing trees and will never form a canopy. They are chosen with the idea that they will be replaced again in ten or fifteen years.

If the town wants to go ahead with the DOT plan to dig up Main Street, then it should get a bigger bang for its buck. The money DOTs spend is our money, and we should put the needs of our communities ahead of a narrow focus on making spaces for cars. The time has come to build complete streets that put people, public transportation, bicycles, and placemaking back in the mix.

> One solution would be to dig a trench between the sidewalk and road so that one could grow healthy street trees there. If the trees were planted eight feet out from the sidewalks on both sides of the street, bike lanes with pervious surfaces could be put between the road and the sidewalk, the drains could be left where they are, the road would be shaped by a beautiful allée, and the roadbed would be sixteen feet narrower.

In Holland, the street would probably be made into a shared space, as welcoming and safe for pedestrians as cars. Massachusetts probably isn't ready for that (even though Harvard students at the other end of the state are famous for plunging into the traffic on Massachusetts Avenue without looking). But there are other things that could be done, once one starts thinking about the space between the buildings as the public realm, rather than as a vehicular thoroughfare. For example, the street is very wide, but one impediment to narrowing the street is the cost of moving the street drains along the curbs: cost wasn't mentioned when the road was widened, but DOTs do have less money these days. One solution would be to dig a trench between the sidewalk and road so that one could grow healthy street trees there. If the trees were planted eight feet out from the sidewalks on both sides of the street, bike lanes with pervious surfaces could be put between the road and the sidewalk, the drains could be left where they are, the road would be shaped by a beautiful allée, and the roadbed would be sixteen feet narrower. Since the road has two wide parking lanes and five wide traffic lanes, it would be improved by losing sixteen feet of vehicular space, the bike lanes would be protected from the traffic by parked cars and the trees (perhaps with bollards too), and even the water that goes into the drains and then into the Housatonic River two blocks away would be healthier. It's all good.

STREET TREES

The experience of revisiting great streets while writing this book confirmed many times over something we already knew: lining a street with parallel rows of classic street trees can be one of the easiest and most productive steps in making a great street. Look at the old photos here of the Main Streets in Nantucket and Great Barrington, with their glorious canopies made by classic elms (Figure 2.72). Or look at the contemporary photos of Queens Road in Charlotte, North Carolina, which has a forest of mature oaks planted in seven rows (see opening spread in the beginning of the book).

Here is a short description of how to make these beautiful allées today. First, select a tree species that will grow to a majestic height and form a canopy over the street. This generally means avoiding new hybrids. "On the whole, old species drawn from regional stock or old hybrids are better than the new hybrids for creating elegant canopies," landscape architect Douglas Duany says. "Many hybrids invented after 1950 right up to today develop problems over time, and—quite intentionally—few match the shapes of the old trees."[18] You can see these newer hybrids on roads all over America. Some grow tall but not wide. Others have dense balls of branches that never reach out across the road the way traditional street trees do. Some, loved by many current professionals, never grow tall or wide.

The new hybrids are sometimes recognizable by their names. This is not a hard and fast rule, but when a tree has a complicated and silly name like Espresso Kentucky Coffee Tree or Big Tooth Rocky Mountain Glow Maple (actual names chosen almost at random while looking at the list of trees at a tree farm), then it is a new hybrid that is likely to have an anti-traditional shape. Prewar hybrids have more straightforward names like Marshall's Seedless (a green ash that can be a good street tree).

We learn the characteristics of trees from long observation in the field. The problems and weaknesses of the newer hybrids are therefore unknown until we have had experience with them over time. That's why it is safer to choose more familiar hybrids—including ones like American sycamores, which are related to the London Plane trees we see in Great Britain and on the great boulevards of Paris and Barcelona. (The London Plane in turn is thought to be a sycamore hybrid that first appeared in Moorish Spain, where Middle Eastern sycamores and American sycamores were planted in close proximity. Another theory says they were developed in the royal gardens of England during the reign of Charles IV.) Time has taught us that among the trees that produce great canopies, the American sycamore and the London Plane are two of the heartiest (see Color Plate 46 for a view of London Plane trees in London).

> We learn the characteristics of trees from long observation in the field. The problems and weaknesses of the newer hybrids are therefore unknown until we have had experience with them over time.

Second, older street trees remain healthier and more resistant to disease if they are planted in groups. Therefore, they should be planted in ditches rather than tree boxes. In nature, most good street trees are flood-plain trees that grow together in what are called "single stands." Being flood-plain trees gives them the ability to survive periods when the oxygen supply to their roots is low. In the city, that helps them to resist the stress of compact urban soils. Equally important, though, is that in their single-stand natural habitat their roots intermingle, which helps the trees to communicate and protect one another against disease. This is done through a nutrient system produced by the stand that feeds a tree under attack by disease. The nutrient system is weakest directly under the tree, which means that the planting boxes we have used for the last few decades actively harm street trees in three ways: first, by restricting the spread of their roots and thereby limiting the amount of nutrients and water the trees can get from the earth below them; and second, by preventing them from getting nutrients from other trees. Last but not least, any large tree needs to be able to spread its roots over an area larger than the tree box as it matures, or the tree is vulnerable to toppling over during storms with high winds.

Because it's best—both aesthetically and ecologically—to think of street trees in forests rather than as individual trees, street trees should be planted in ditches that approximate their condition in the woods. Dig and loosen or "decompact" a ditch the length of the block, place the trees in the ditch on a stable foundation, and backfill it with local dirt as quickly as possible. Water and gently tamp the soil but never compact it. There are various methods for lining the sidewalls of the ditch to prevent the roots growing horizontally near the surface. That can prevent conflicts with utilities and roots raising the sidewalk, but may also limit the explorations of roots looking for water. There are construction details for preventing compaction around the tree, and devices such as Silva Cells may be used around the base of the tree trunks to prevent the roots from coming to the surface.

A community that wants an allée may find that the professionals involved in the street design oppose planting trees in a row or allowing street trees that make a canopy over the street, dismissing the idea as impractical and old-fashioned. Here, therefore, is a short summary of the benefits of a high deciduous canopy for an urban street.

On a wide road like Main Street in Great Barrington, Massachusetts, the trees are relied on to visually define a space that is too wide for the buildings to adequately contain. The high canopy also solves solar problems: in the winter, bare branches reduce glare and sharp winter winds; and in the summer, the leaves shade the asphalt, which is both climatically and aesthetically best. In addition, the high canopy shields the upper floors of buildings from the harshness of the street and its traffic, which is particularly beneficial for apartments on the street. Add to that the advice from retail experts like Robert J. Gibbs, who say to plant only trees that will rise above the storefronts, to avoid costing the merchants sales.

Unfortunately, the trees proposed by most engineers, arborists, and landscape architects today cannot solve those problems, nor can they make the classic American tree-lined street that we all picture in our mind's eye. It

is important to understand that when an engineer or an arborist proposes replacing a mature allée with an almost random mixture of popcorn trees and small ornamentals (Figure 1.23), they are proposing a radically different street. The justifications for such proposals vary, depending on the professional agendas of their authors, but the unfortunate fact is that most of the professions involved in street design today do not value the classic tree-lined street. If we agree with the urbanist's belief that these classic streets and their stunning canopies make great places, however, then we can weigh the criteria differently and we may arrive at very different conclusions.

Traffic and roadway engineers traditionally have not liked large trees, because speeding cars are damaged when they hit them. (This is starting to change: the CNU ITE Street Design Manual, sponsored by the Federal Highway Administration and the Environmental Protection Agency, says that in urban contexts large trees are contextually appropriate. Drivers should not be speeding on urban streets, and trees simultaneously have a traffic-calming effect and protect pedestrians from errant cars.) Engineers also know that there is more public interest in saving mature trees than smaller ones and that it's easier to rebuild streets if the drivers of the heavy equipment used to do so don't have to be careful about killing the trees in the process. Thus, the engineers can kill two birds with one stone by replacing trees whenever they do major roadwork. For all these reasons, they often periodically replace street trees before they have matured.

Trained to control variables, engineers prefer to place trees in concrete planting boxes, so that they can contain the roots. This method has the added advantage, from the engineer's point of view, of limiting the root spread and thus the size of the tree: beyond a certain size, the tree starts to fail. As we have seen, this approach also limits the trees' resistance to disease. Last but not least, if the trees are in a box, the engineers can specify their preferred method of compacting soil when they work around the tree.

Arborists have different reasons for opposing traditional allées. They typically argue for replacement on the basis of disease and blight—and now climate change—as the primary reasons for putting in new tree species. Urbanists resist this way of thinking for several reasons. As already pointed out, the mixture of trees recommended by many arborists will never produce the great canopied street that makes the risk worth taking. Second is the fact that the risk is often small. Older Americans remember the terrible effects Dutch elm disease had on our towns and cities, because the elm was our greatest street tree. But while these blights can be terrible, they are rare.

In the long run, all trees age and have to be replaced eventually, and in that process there is more than one way to introduce variety. The traditional method is to phase new trees in over time and, as discussed, to plant them in stands so that they can support each other. In the rare situation where disaster strikes, experienced gardeners will tell you that working with Mother Nature always involves dealing with problems and change. In the end, having a great stand of trees that has to be replaced is better than never having a great street.

Remember that the same professionals who say disease is a terrible problem may periodically recommend replacing all the trees for other reasons. Drastic tree-clearing is a philosophy that developed with Modernism. Modernist design frequently advocates the opposite of what was traditionally done and looks for a functional

basis on which to build a new approach: as a profession, arborists tend to share that attitude. The cynical point out that arborists make money by replacing trees, but you don't have to be cynical to acknowledge that while we have hundreds of years of knowledge about the old tree species, there is no significant body of knowledge about the new hybrids' problems over time. The dominant philosophy in contemporary landscape architecture is also a Modernist attitude that on principle opposes traditional design and placemaking. For thirty years, New Urbanists, who try to focus on what works rather than what is new or old, have been complaining that most landscape architects won't plant two trees in a row, because that is the traditional way of designing streets. Travel the world looking at our great tree-lined historic streets, and you will find that only a handful of them have a diversity of tree type, and that almost all have trees planted in parallel, symmetrical rows.

Some New Urbanists suggest introducing variety by using trees of similar size and shape on the same block, but that is not good for single-stand trees. Perhaps a greater number say it is better to introduce variety every other block or two rather than within each block, for both functional and aesthetic reasons. They value harmony and coherent unity and believe that a forced mixture of trees will never be as elegant as the great allées that were once the default standard for American street design.

Stone Avenue, Greenville, South Carolina

Dover, Kohl & Partners, 2011

Retrofit: From "Auto Sewer" to Neighborhood Main Street

Main Street

Just outside downtown Greenville, the city's North End streetcar suburb is a busy place again. A generation of new owners is restoring historic houses and starting up creative businesses.

The primary street in the North End, Stone Avenue, was historically a residential corridor, but it was widened in the late 1940s as a U.S. highway route. Over time, the avenue's auto-oriented design caused the corridor to decline; residential properties were retrofitted for office and low-level retail uses, and Stone Avenue became an auto sewer. In recent years, however, business owners and homeowners in the surrounding neighborhoods have begun incremental, grassroots efforts to reclaim the street as the centerpiece of the neighborhood.

The flaws in urban design that plague Stone Avenue are not unfamiliar. At a glance, it appears that it's unsafe to bike and walk along Stone Avenue and North Main Street, and it probably is. The street also has narrow sidewalks, overly wide traffic lanes, almost no appropriate street trees, a lack of building enclosure, a limited mix of land uses, and, most damaging of all, high-speed traffic. But by implementing just a few key physical changes, these existing conditions can be successfully ameliorated (Figures 4.56, 4.57, 4.58, and 4.59).

Figure 4.56: Stone Avenue, Greenville, South Carolina. Before: Existing conditions in 2011. Decades of flight to the suburbs and road widening left the North End with substantial vacant property ready for infill and revitalization. © 2011 Dover, Kohl & Partners

Figure 4.57: Stone Avenue, Greenville, South Carolina. Dover, Kohl & Partners, 2011. Watercolor rendering, aerial view. After: The intersection of Main Street and Stone Avenue would reclaim its role as a physical and economic hub for the city, with new buildings positioned to frame the street spaces. © 2011 Dover, Kohl & Partners

Creating a mix of housing, retail, office space, civic institutions, and public open space, all located within a short walk of one another, will be a good first step to making this part of the city more livable. Certainly these missing elements can be added on North Main Street and Stone Avenue. The second step is to ensure that an interconnected street system binds these addresses together, giving pedestrians easy access to their destinations. Narrowing the width of travel lanes to ten feet or less is another priority (Figure 4.60). This change will reduce traffic speeds and make the street easier to cross. Finally, the streets that connect these destinations must be designed for pedestrian use, with generous sidewalks, shade trees, protection from passing cars, and street-oriented buildings. Traffic speeds must be lowered to make pedestrians and bicyclists feel safe using the street.

Figure 4.58: Stone Avenue, Greenville, South Carolina. Before: Existing conditions in 2011. Curb cuts for driveways are nearly continuous, and the scene is discouraging to pedestrians. © *2011 Dover, Kohl & Partners/UrbanAdvantage*

Figure 4.59: Stone Avenue, Greenville, South Carolina. Dover, Kohl & Partners, 2011. Computer simulation. After: The plan calls for a step-by-step transformation of the street, converting to a narrower cross-section with onstreet parking, street trees, and proper sidewalks faced by storefronts. The center turn lane is designed as a textured "safety strip," which allows the turns and keeps the street wide enough for emergency vehicles to navigate around traffic when necessary, but keeps the ordinary motoring speeds slow on all other occasions. © *2011 Dover, Kohl & Partners/UrbanAdvantage*

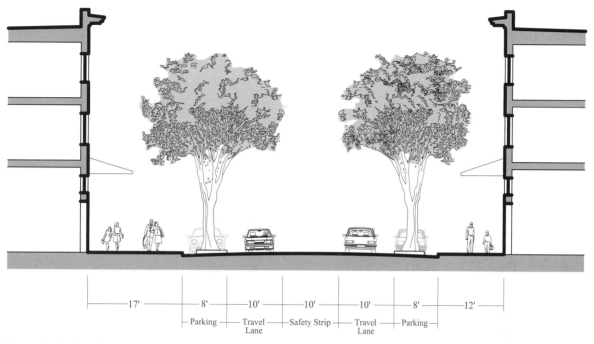

17'	8'	10'	10'	10'	8'	12'
	Parking	Travel Lane	Safety Strip	Travel Lane	Parking	

Figure 4.60: Stone Avenue, Greenville, South Carolina. Section. © *2013 Dover, Kohl & Partners*

ROUNDABOUTS AND SLOW-SPEED ROADS

Street design in our walkable cities, towns, and neighborhoods should begin and end with making places where people want to be. Ironically, many of the "Complete Streets" Americans are now building are incomplete when it comes to placemaking and beauty. Too many designers of Complete Streets still give the car top priority, on a road that is first and foremost about vehicle throughput, even if the roadway is shared with bicycles and buses. That's often appropriate in suburban environments where most people drive and few people walk. But today we have suburban-style traffic-calming techniques that don't work for the creation or restoration of walkable places being used in towns and cities in the name of Complete Streets. As a nation, we're still learning how to make real complete streets that promote walkability as much as traffic flow.

Figure 4.61 shows a roundabout in Okemos, Michigan, that Cleveland, Ohio's City Planning Commission uses to illustrate Traffic Calming in their Online Glossary. On the whole, the glossary is very good,[19] but there are a few reasons why the photo is not the best choice to illustrate traffic calming in the walkable parts of Cleveland.

■ There are many cars on the road today that could drive through the roundabout as designed and built at quite a high speed, and that's not traffic calming. The photo shows a design that puts the flow of cars above the comfort and well-being of the pedestrian. For the pedestrian crossing an urban street, the geometry of the corner radii should force the car to slow almost to a stop.

Figure 4.61: Okemos Roundabout, Okemos, Michigan. Aerial view. A shiny, new roundabout makes a strong impression—but it's not necessarily good for pedestrians and cyclists. *Image courtesy of the Ingham Country Department of Transportation and Roads*

- What differentiates the design of a modern roundabout from old designs for traffic circles is that the "splitter island" at the entrance to the circle should narrow the lane and direct the driver to the right, slowing the car. "Slowing" is relative, however.

- The traffic lanes are very wide: that's good for speeding cars, bad for pedestrians crossing the roads, and bad for making the street a space where pedestrians feel comfortable.

- The yellow striping is visually aggressive—much more appropriate for highway traffic than urban speeds.

- The large signs can be read at fifty-five miles per hour, alerting the pedestrian that he or she is not in a pedestrian space.

- The sheer number of signs warning us of hazardous road conditions for cars also tells us we are in auto-dominated space.

- Things that people like, such as trees, have been removed.

- It is better for placemaking if the circle is not a perfect circle and has something more interesting to look at than dying grass.

- It is better for placemaking if the pedestrian islands are shaped for people rather than cars—rectangles rather than deformed triangles, for example.

- The curves on the outside of the traffic circle have no visual relationship to the circle at the center because the traffic engineer was thinking about moving cars rather than shaping a place. One goal should be shaping space: the simplest way to do that with circles is to make concentric circles. But the shapes don't have to be circles. What's important is that the shapes define and make comfortable spaces for the pedestrian as well as the car.

As a photo, Figure 4.61 can make a good first impression, particularly when it's seen in color. Everything is shiny and new, the design is orderly, and the grey of the asphalt goes well with the white concrete and the green grass—and, at this scale, with the white and yellow striping. But for the pedestrian standing on a splitter island, the auto-based geometry of the island subtly tells that person that he's standing in a place made for cars rather than humans. Add the bold striping and the bold signs, and the message is no longer subtle, even if we're so used to auto-dominated design that we don't consciously have that thought.

In the way we build today, traffic engineers are among the most important urban designers, always given great authority by towns and cities. But traffic engineers think about engineering rather than design. If they are going to retain this power, they need to understand placemaking and civic art as well as vehicular capacity.

Conventional traffic circles have stop signs or stoplights on entry roads perpendicular to the circle. Looking into the history of roundabouts, one discovers that the primary reason Departments of Transportation and Departments of Public Works all over America are reflexively putting them in is because we have a lot of bad drivers who roll through stop signs and cause accidents. If a roundabout is substituted for a stop-sign system at a circle or a regular intersection, T-bone and rear-end accidents go from significant numbers to almost zero. Auto accidents become angled collisions, usually at low speed, that are less serious than the T-bone and rear-end accidents. In addition, throughput rises, and cars don't have to stop and start, which is good for increasing gas mileage.

Roundabouts, in other words, are installed primarily for the benefit of cars and their drivers. Roundabouts can be uncomfortable for inexperienced or cautious cyclists, however, and pedestrians are moved away from the circle for crossings. This is because drivers approaching the circle and in the circle are usually looking to their left rather than in the direction of pedestrians crossing on their right. For the engineer, the priorities of pedestrians are secondary to the free flow of traffic.

Traffic Circles & Civic Art

There was a time before the era of Organized Motordom when traffic circles and roundabouts served everyone. Columbus Circle was built in Manhattan in 1905, when cars and pedestrians still shared the roads. The center of the circle was reserved for streetcars, their riders, and other pedestrians, while cars circled around the perimeter. The first modern roundabout in England had a center island that was a refuge for pedestrians. Designed by the noted town planners Parker & Unwin and built in Letchworth Garden City in 1909, it was a response to increasing traffic. Today, as we've seen, pedestrians are banned from crossing the circle, while pedestrian crossings are pushed away from the circle.

The quiet, flat backstreets of Coral Gables, Florida, can be good places for walking. Recently, however, the city has built roundabouts there that—while some of the best looking roundabouts in the country, with low, planted islands; few or no signs; and subtly-colored splitter islands—simultaneously seem to speed up the cars and make the roads slightly less pleasant for walking.

Many of these streets have no sidewalks because they have such low levels of traffic that they were shared spaces before Hans Monderman[20] was born. With long allées of live oaks and banyan trees that form canopies over the street and keep the harsh sun at bay, the streets in the flat landscape have long, lovely vistas that highlight the slight topographical changes where they do exist. Even here, though, the scale is for the car. New bumpouts interrupt the vistas and hide the streets on the other side, while the splitter islands and traffic engineer geometry make the streets' intersections feel like a place where the pedestrian is not welcome. The change can appear very subtle, but one effect is that when a pedestrian at one of the roundabouts sees a car approaching, he or she knows that the driver probably will not see him or her until the car is exiting the roundabout. And these, the roundabouts of Coral Gables, are among the simplest and most low-key in America.

The old streets in Coral Gables show how differently designers approached these issues one hundred years ago. Most of the planned new town was built at the scale of the car, and some of the roads are very wide. A traffic circle at De Soto Plaza, for example, has a large, stone fountain with a tall obelisk in the center (Figure 4.62). It appears to have been intended as a shared space when the city was designed in the 1920s, because the fountain is attractive in both meanings of the word, and it has a space around it where pedestrians may once have felt welcome to venture. Now cars fly through the plaza, however, and it can be hard for pedestrians to reach the fountain.

In the quieter, shared-space streets nearby, there are sometimes large grassy medians with no curbs that calm traffic the way roundabouts do but that also work as Civic Art, making beautiful places where walkers feel comfortable. They give variety and richness to the plan and varied experiences to the pedestrian. Occasionally there are even trees planted in the middle of the road. Drivers manage to avoid hitting them or suing the city over them, despite the worst fears and warnings of traffic engineers of what will happen if you expect intelligent behavior from drivers.

Figure 4.62: De Soto Plaza / Fountain, Coral Gables, Florida. Denman Fink, 1925. *Image courtesy of Kenneth Garcia*

When a roundabout is used for beauty and placemaking rather than just as a traffic control instrument, it can be a welcome addition. But while modern roundabouts can be appropriate in some circumstances, they are often created where they shouldn't be. After being banned for decades for the wrong reasons, roundabouts have recently become the embodiment of the old adage that if the only tool you have is a hammer, everything looks like a nail. A well-designed, modern roundabout with minimal striping and signs and a strong sense of Civic Art should be in every urban designer's toolkit, but it should be used sparingly.

> Many of the perils of monuments in the road go away if we just slow cars down when they're in walkable areas—which has the extra benefit of letting the pedestrians live longer. A driver going twenty miles per hour doesn't need striping, signs, splitter islands, or a fence to understand that hitting a five-ton piece of granite would be a bad idea.

In the nineteenth century it was common to put monuments in the middle of roads, and many of them are still standing in the twenty-first century (Figures 2.79 and 4.63). Lawyers and engineers require that we give them more protection today, in the form of fences, wide foundations, bold striping, and signs. But many of the perils of monuments go away if we just slow cars down in walkable areas—which has the extra benefit of letting the pedestrians live longer. A driver going twenty miles per hour doesn't need striping, signs, splitter islands, or a fence to understand that hitting a five-ton piece of granite would be a bad idea. Alternatively, it's a good idea to learn which drivers don't understand that, so that we can get them off the road.

In our current world of Happy Motoring, ubiquitous traffic engineers, and overzealous lawyers, that approach might seem dangerous. Like so many other factors in making better streets and places, it depends on slowing down the car. But places like Seven Dials show that that can be done (Figure 3.27).

Figure 4.63: Court Square Fountain, Montgomery, Alabama. Frederick MacMonnies, sculptor, 1885. *Image courtesy of Dover, Kohl & Partners. Photograph by Peter Fouts, Fouts Commercial Photography*

DOWNTOWN STREETS

Madison Square, New York, New York

NYC DOT, 2008

Retrofit: Tactical Urbanism and Reclaiming Pedestrian Space

Intersection Redesign

New York City's Commissioner of Transportation, Janette Sadik-Khan, is a modern-day American hero. She was the first big-city DOT boss in the United States to take the virtually absolute power of the DOTs over our public realm and use that power to make things better for the pedestrian and cyclist rather than the car. That seems like common sense in Manhattan, where 80 percent of the residents do not own cars and only 20 percent of the workers commute by car. And yet until Sadik-Khan came along the city's DOT was little different than other DOTs. Like practically everywhere else in the United States since World War II,

New York City gave the car primacy over the avenues of Manhattan and virtually all other streets in all five boroughs. In the 1950s and 1960s, sidewalks were narrowed, streets were made one-way with wider lanes and staggered traffic lights, and many streets became high-speed auto sewers. Sadik-Khan frequently reversed that policy—most notably by closing parts of wide New York streets to cars and setting up tables and chairs so that people could claim the former roadbeds as public space.

At 11 p.m. one night in 2008, work crews started putting out bollards and chairs to create new pedestrian plazas for Madison Square, where Fifth Avenue awkwardly meets the diagonal of Broadway (Figure 4.64). They painted the street brown where it was closed to cars, added some striping to warn cars away, and by the time the morning traffic came all the work was done. New Yorkers started using the spaces and chairs immediately. Even when the DOTs were at the height of their power to widen roads and remove pedestrians, they didn't act that quickly. But that raises important points

Figure 4.64: Madison Square, New York, New York. NYC DOT, 2008. Satellite view. Tactical urbanism at its best. *Image courtesy of Google Earth*

as we move away from the auto-centric planning and street design of the last few decades. First, we should remember that all the DOTs that gravely say, "We must be slow and cautious about change" acted quickly fifty years ago, when the national program was to widen roads and it suited them to act quickly. Second, we should take advantage of what has come to be known as Tactical Urbanism, which tries out and tests change with paint and other inexpensive materials.

Most of the changes made by the New York City DOT have been popular—not that you would always know that from the press. "There are not only 8.4 million New Yorkers, but at times 8.4 million traffic engineers," Sadik-Khan once said. "And we're, you know, very opinionated." [21] Under Sadik-Khan, the DOT has also built over 250 miles of bicycle lanes, with one of the lanes in front of the Brooklyn building where Sadik-Khan's DOT predecessor lives with her husband, U.S. Senator Charles Schumer. The former commissioner was very active in the efforts to have the offending lanes removed, but the

campaign ended unsuccessfully in court. Meanwhile, the work completed in Madison Square raised property values in an already rising market.

The pedestrian crossing at the intersection of Broadway and Fifth Avenue on the north side of 23rd Street was the longest in the city. The length of two football fields, it was an ugly and hostile environment for walkers, with exhaust-stained, delaminating white and yellow plastic sticks marking traffic lanes, and highway-scale striping that assaulted the pedestrian's senses. The DOT's overnight transformation was an immediate and enormous improvement. Those ugly plastic sticks are still there in the new arrangement, but they're not as dispiriting when you know they're temporary and in the service of the public good.

All the NYC DOT's pedestrian plazas began as similar tactical interventions. Temporary elements were put in so that the neighborhood could visualize the benefits of change. Inexpensive materials, like brown epoxy paint with gravel that covers the closed portion of the street, were used. Boulders the city had stored from public-works excavations were often brought in to serve as bollards and temporary seating. Lightweight folding chairs and tables like the ones used in Parisian parks were set up, so that individuals and groups could arrange the furniture as they liked—in a circle, or perhaps two alone, in the sun. The plaza immediately became a popular place to sit.

When Tactical Urbanism Becomes Permanent

Taking street space from the car and giving it back to the people was a radical step after sixty-plus years of Happy Motoring. Presenting the changes to the public as a temporary *fait accompli*—a done deal, but reversible—was a brilliant maneuver, because from the moment New Yorkers had a chance to use the spaces, it was clear they loved them. The inevitable criticism from some quarters was overwhelmed by public acclaim. The DOT perhaps took the strategy from Tactical Urbanism, which used short-term actions to evaluate long-term change before Sadik-Khan took office. In the case of the pedestrian plazas at Madison Square, we can see not only that they were a good idea but also that—by correcting a few problems illuminated by the test run—the permanent solution can be even better.

A big improvement could be made by moving the plaza, which is now "attached" to the Flatiron Building. This plaza is not a rectangle, because of the "flatiron" shape made by Broadway slicing diagonally through the New York grid; therefore the eastern side of the Flatiron Building and the western side of the building across the street are not parallel. Because of that, the old roadbed was wider at 23rd Street than at 22nd Street.

The DOT's new plan reduces Broadway to just two lanes, which halves the number of lanes it has just a few blocks north. The temporary plaza built by the DOT attached to the Flatiron fills more than half of the old, very wide roadway, and the eastern side of the plaza is parallel to the building on the eastern side of Broadway, rather than to the angle of the Flatiron Building. But the Flatiron Building is triangular precisely because it was custom-fit to the intersection of Fifth Avenue and Broadway, and the test plaza visually takes away its reason for

being (Figure 4.65). Moreover, a plaza attached to the new building on the east side of the street would focus the view of people sitting in it on the Flatiron Building, rather than on the boring new building.

Moving Broadway back toward the Flatiron Building would mean that the test lanes between 25th Street and 23rd Street would have to be redesigned, but that's a virtue rather than a vice, as we see when we visit the site. In the current plan, the DOT put a large island on the northern side of 23rd Street between the new roadbeds for Broadway and Fifth Avenue, cutting up the widest crossing in Manhattan into comfortable pieces. They also narrowed it to two lanes, with a turn lane at 23rd Street that becomes a parking lane south of 23rd. That is all for the good, but the particulars of the new design caused several unnecessary problems. Specifically, the DOT engineers designed one set of large curved lanes for the cars going south on Broadway, and another set of large curved lanes for cars going east on 24th Street. Between the two large curves, is an oddly shaped left-over space (Figure 4.66). Although it is painted brown

Figure 4.65: Madison Square, New York, New York. NYC DOT, 2008. Tactical urbanism at its best. Looking south on Broadway from the north side of Twenty-third street. Overnight, boulders were placed in the roadbed to close large parts of the roadbed to cars, closed sections of the road were covered in sand-colored, textured paint, and light-weight, outdoor furniture was scattered around. New Yorkers responded immediately and enthusiastically.

Figure 4.66: Madison Square, New York, New York. NYC DOT, 2008. Looking south from 23rd Street and Broadway. A temporary solution. The very wide traffic lane, the bold reflective signs, the high-speed striping, and the broad, fast curve—alien to the Manhattan grid—create an area where the pedestrian feels unwelcome.

Figure 4.67: Madison Square, New York, New York. Sketch of concept for a permanent, simpler solution, discussed in the text. © 2012 Dover, Kohl & Partners / Massengale & Co LLC

and there are the same boulders there as in the other pedestrian plazas, this space—surrounded by garish striping and bold warning signs for the traffic—is a DMZ where few would intentionally sit. All in all, it's a suburban-style place designed for cars, not people. But with a simple redesign, there's no reason why 24th Street couldn't end with a T-intersection and a stop sign or a stop light, like a normal New York intersection.

A simple redesign for the permanent roadway could lead to another big improvement (Figures 4.67 and 4.68). In the test design, a pedestrian plaza floats between Fifth Avenue and Broadway, a less than ideal solution. The plaza would be better if it were attached to Madison Square, which is a well-used park in a neighborhood with a shortage of parks. Keeping Broadway on the west side of the plaza, instead of swinging it to the east, would make a simpler, more straightforward experience for drivers, and a better urban experience for the pedestrian. That design also maintains the vista down Broadway and along the diagonal of the Flatiron Building.

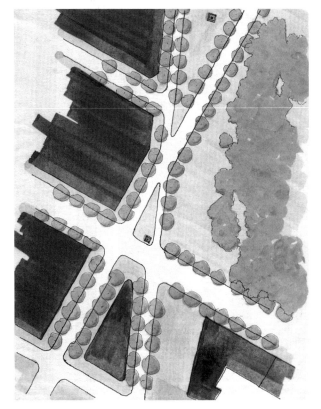

Figure 4.68: Madison Square, New York, New York. View looking south on Fifth Avenue and Broadway (on the left), circa 1910. Zooming in on the large digital image at the Library of Congress, one can see barriers in the road made with lightweight stanchions and thin cables. These closed the east side of Fifth Avenue above 23rd Street to traffic, much as our proposed redesign in Figure 4.67 does. At the time, people waiting for the cable cars going up and down Broadway could wait behind the cables. In the center of the photo, between Fifth Avenue and Broadway, is the Flatiron Building, designed by Daniel Burnham and completed in 1902. For another historic photo of Madison Square, see Figure 4.82. *Library of Congress, Prints and Photographs Division, Detroit Publishing Company Photograph Collection, LC-D4-15953*

> Tactical Urbanism is praised for making changes at low cost. It gives people the chance to see what the changes will produce, tests the design, and allows improvements in the final product.

Weaving car lanes with lots of large warning signs are inappropriate for Manhattan. Designed by traffic engineers like a curved pipe for throughput, the lanes are separated from the grid, and their highway-scale signs and striping are machine scale, rather than for the pedestrian. Taking them out and putting in normal urban streets would make a wider crossing at 23rd Street that would still fall well within the norm for Manhattan while providing a more usable plaza attached to Madison Square.

Until Commissioner Sadik-Khan started her bold land grab, all of Manhattan's existing "squares" were green parks, like Union Square and Madison Square. Her department's Tactical Urbanism has shown conclusively that New Yorkers are also eager for paved squares like the ones we see in other parts of the world.

Tactical Urbanism is praised for making changes at low cost. It gives people the chance to see what the changes will produce, tests the design, and allows improvements in the final product. The rise in value in the surrounding neighborhood is a good reason to make the changes around Madison Square permanent.

JANE JACOBS SQUARE, NEW YORK, NEW YORK

Massengale & Co LLC and Dover, Kohl & Partners, with H. Zeke Mermell, 2011

Jane Jacobs Square was a proposal for a competition organized by the Institute for Urban Design called *By the City / For the City*.[22] Entrants could pick their own site in New York City and suggest an improvement. We chose an interesting fissure in the Manhattan grid where Bleecker Street crosses Christopher Street and West 10th Street in Greenwich Village. Before the New York City Commissioner's Plan of 1811 platted a single, unifying grid over most of the island, the rural hamlet of Greenwich Village had a few small grids and individual roads laid out by various landowners as they thought best. Two of the grids come together in this block of Bleecker Street, making a comfortable triangular space that's unusual in Manhattan. Today the space is dominated by the cars speeding down Bleecker Street. Jacobs Square reclaims it as a shared space for cars, bikes, and pedestrians.

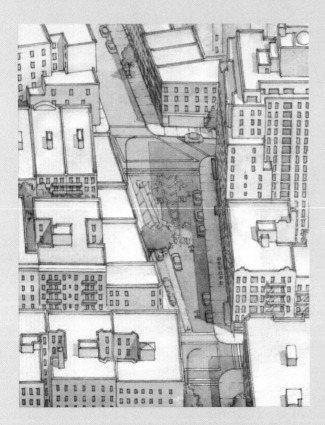

Figure 4.69: Jane Jacobs Square, New York, New York. Dover, Kohl & Partners / Massengale & Co LLC, 2011. Watercolor rendering, aerial view. Before: Highway-scale striping and speeding cars currently dominate the potentially lovely space. © 2011 Dover, Kohl & Partners / Massengale & Co LLC

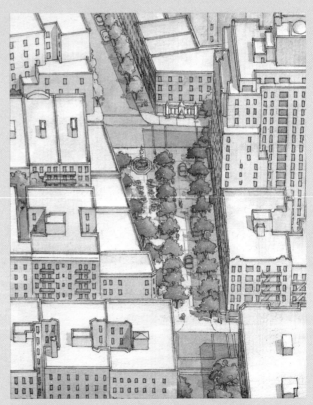

Figure 4.70: Jane Jacobs Square, New York, New York. Dover, Kohl & Partners / Massengale & Co LLC, 2011. Watercolor rendering, aerial view. After: Showing one option. This version has the attached plaza on the east side of the square. © 2011 Dover, Kohl & Partners / Massengale & Co LLC

The intersection of Bleecker and Christopher streets marks one of the original centers of the old village, where a public well once stood. It is still one of the centers of Village life, but there are narrow sidewalks and ugly highway-scale stripings on the street that clearly claim the space for cars while telling people to stay over on the sidewalk where they belong (Figure 4.69). Anyone who walks through it can see its potential to be one of the great public places in New York—if we simply do away with its present 1960-style, auto-dominated design.

The proposed redesign (Figure 4.70) uses principles of placemaking to create a square shared by walkers, cyclists, drivers, and diners:

- The sidewalk on the east side of the square is expanded to the west, forming a triangular "attached plaza" that covers the majority of the square.

- The roadbed, now parallel to the buildings on the west side of the square, is reduced to a narrow traffic lane and a lane for parking and loading for the stores on the square.

- A speed table[23] on the south side of West 10th Street raises the roadbed to the level of the sidewalks and the rest of the plaza.

- Trees along the sides of the road act like bollards, defining the boundaries of the street.

- A fountain on the north side of Christopher Street reduces ambient noise and recalls the eighteenth-century well once on the site.

- Bleecker Street no longer goes straight through: cars either stop and then turn right on Christopher Street or stop at Christopher before turning left. In that scenario, Christopher either becomes a two-way street, or a one-way, eastbound street.

- A monument to the Commissioners' Plan of 1811 on the blank wall of the building on the southwest corner of Christopher and Bleecker streets visually terminates the view down Bleecker, while the fountain on axis with the southern leg of Bleecker points to the continuation of the street.

- Tables and chairs in the square, along with the new shade trees and programming for the public (restaurant and café tables, chess boards, and so on), encourage people to use the space.

Some of the tables and chairs would be like those used in Bryant Park and by the New York City DOT in outdoor spaces—lightweight furniture the public can easily rearrange. The plan would go a step further by embracing the storefronts lining the square to involve them in the "programming" of the space: two parts of the square would be reserved for a restaurant and a café, each with tables.

Cars passing by would be tamed by the speed table, the narrow roadbed, the trees bordering the road, the cars and trucks entering and leaving from the short-term parking spaces, and—most important—by the shared-space roadbed, now jointly used by cars, trucks, cyclists, and walkers.

New Yorkers are ready for spaces like the new Jacobs Square. They have small apartments and live much of their lives in public space and Third Places.[24] Their enthusiasm for the Tactical Urbanism pop-up squares recently built around the city by the New York City DOT demonstrates their desire for more outdoor spaces that aren't dominated by cars.

Jacobs herself lived nearby at 555 Hudson Street, and we like to think she would have embraced our idea. Innovations like the Citi Bike bicycle share program are transforming her old neighborhood. Compare busy Bleecker Street, which has a bike lane, with the parallel street, West 4th Street. They run in opposite directions, making one of the "two-way couplets" beloved by transportation engineers. West 4th has no bike lane, and it has become a popular sharrow street. That in turn has made customers waiting for tables at the sidewalk cafés along the narrow street more comfortable standing in the street while they talk and wait. Drivers accordingly adjust their speed to accommodate the pedestrians and cyclists. Filling Bleecker Street with a public space where it crosses Christopher Street is a logical next step in redressing the balance between pedestrians and cars in the neighborhood.

Giralda Avenue, Coral Gables, Florida

Jaime Correa, Charles Bohl, and Jennifer Garcia, 2009

Retrofit: Right-Sizing the Road

Downtown Street

Giralda Avenue is too wide and too barren (Figure 4.71). An analysis of the existing urban condition yields a clear conclusion: too much of the street space has been taken over by too many automobiles. Motor vehicles get sole possession of over 75 percent of the right-of-way, while the pedestrian gets only 25 percent of the space.

Nevertheless, Giralda Avenue is a downtown street that still attracts a good deal of business, due to its many restaurants. For most of the year, Coral Gables' subtropical climate allows diners to eat outside if shade is provided; so many of

them have gravitated to Giralda that the avenue has earned the name "restaurant row." About once a month, an entire block is closed off to car traffic, and the restaurants extend their sidewalk dining into the street space. In an effort to consistently replicate this festive atmosphere, Charles Bohl, Jaime Correa, and Jennifer Garcia designed a retrofit that will make the street more usable and comfortable.

The proposed retrofit of Giralda Avenue (Figures 4.72, 4.73, and 4.74) provides ample space for outdoor dining by making sidewalks wider and adding shade trees to the urban space. To accommodate the expanding pedestrian realm, central travel lanes would be narrowed and parallel parking adjusted. (Today, the traffic lanes are more than twelve feet wide, which is too wide for this intimate neighborhood street. The recommended approach would keep parking on the street while also extending the sidewalks on both sides of the road in order to allow restaurants to have more outside space for dining.)

Figure 4.71: Giralda Avenue, Coral Gables, Florida. Before: Existing conditions, 2009. *Image courtesy of Jennifer Garcia*

Figure 4.72: Giralda Avenue, Coral Gables, Florida. Jaime Correa, Charles Bohl & Jennifer Garcia, 2009. After: In Option 1, the street would be narrowed and sidewalk dining expanded, including open-air pavilions perfectly suited to the subtropical weather. *Image courtesy of Jennifer Garcia*

Figure 4.73: Giralda Avenue, Coral Gables, Florida. Jaime Correa, Charles Bohl & Jennifer Garcia, 2009. After: In Option 2, street trees could be introduced between parking spaces. *Image courtesy of Jennifer Garcia*

Figure 4.74: The "Giralda Under the Stars" monthly street closure, Coral Gables, Florida. *Image courtesy of Kenneth Garcia*

In this proposed scenario to retrofit Giralda, as much as 60 percent of the right-of-way would be for shoppers, diners, and strollers, while 40 percent would be allocated to cars and trucks. Worth noting is the fact that the number of travel lanes stays the same, despite the sharp increase in size of the pedestrian realm.

An easy retrofit for any oversized street, narrowing travel lanes provides more space for people who are not in their cars. More people walking by restaurants and shops on the sidewalks is simply better for business (see also the "Economic Benefits of Complete Streets" in Chapter 1).

Dorn Avenue, South Miami, Florida

Dover, Kohl & Partners, 1993

Retrofit: Right-Sizing the Road

Downtown Street

Dorn Avenue was one of the first roads in Florida to be *narrowed* in modern times; its retrofit was an early step in South Miami's citizen-driven Hometown Plan for its downtown. Unattractive and excessively wide (Figure 4.75), Dorn Avenue also had a prominent location,

visible from South Miami's Metrorail platform and the town's two most important streets: Sunset Drive (its Main Street) and the South Dixie Highway (U.S. 1). Because it had the makings of a dramatic before-and-after sequence, Dorn Avenue was chosen in 1992 as a small "100 percent model" project to demonstrate what was possible on the neglected side streets of downtown.

Dorn Avenue is a key pedestrian link between the transit station and nearby multifamily housing, yet its narrow sidewalks, blank walls, and lack of shade made walking along it in 1992 unpleasant. South Miami had prohibited outdoor dining by ordinance, and high parking requirements and deep setback rules discouraged infill and redevelopment.

In a reconstruction of the street (Figure 4.76), Dover Kohl narrowed the travel lane and shifted the parking to parallel spaces, which allowed significant widening of the sidewalks. The City installed pedestrian-scaled lighting and planted street trees in rows. The road surface and sidewalks were paved in bricks (which in hindsight have not weathered well and have been difficult to maintain, but which did achieve the effect of visually unifying the carriageway and the sidewalks). Six-inch-wide trench

Figure 4.75: Dorn Avenue, South Miami, Florida. Before: Existing conditions circa 1992. It seemed less a street than a wide, barren alley, faced by blank walls. However, the scene is very visible from the Metrorail station platform (top center) so it was selected as the pilot street-transformation project.

Figure 4.76: Dorn Avenue, South Miami, Florida. Dover, Kohl & Partners, 1992. After: Today the street is the social center of the town. Informal sidewalk cafés line the narrowed street. *Image courtesy of Kenneth Garcia*

Figure 4.77: Dorn Avenue, South Miami, Florida. Dover, Kohl & Partners, 1992. After: The least possible amount of space is devoted to circulating cars; speeds are slow. *Image courtesy of Kenneth Garcia*

drains between the parking spaces and the travel lane were used to eliminate the need for both gutters and striping, minimizing the glare of concrete in the bright subtropical scene (Figure 4.77).

The local chamber of commerce, the downtown merchants association, property owners, and the City collaborated to press for the reconstruction of the street. To pay for the improvements, the City matched the privately raised funds with revenue from a local-option gas tax—

meaning that motorists helped pay for improvements benefiting pedestrians and transit riders.

Today the street trees seem crucial to the scene, but they almost got scratched off the plans during construction. Once demolition began, city crews discovered an unexpected but crucial water pipe running under the sidewalk on one side, right where one of the new tree lines was to be aligned. There was no budget for relocating the line. City officials were prepared to eliminate the trees,

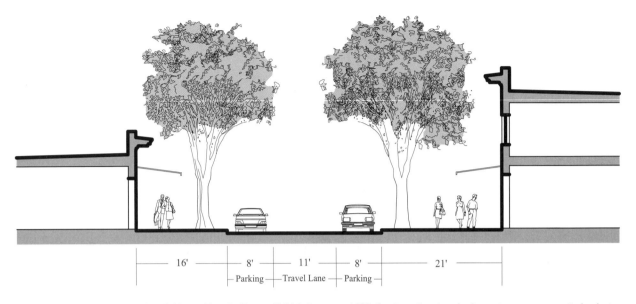

16'   8'   11'   8'   21'
    Parking — Travel Lane — Parking

Figure 4.78: Dorn Avenue, South Miami, Florida. Dover, Kohl & Partners, 1992. Section, showing the last-minute asymmetrical solution that allowed for street trees. © 2013 Dover, Kohl & Partners

but Dover-Kohl convinced them to realign this segment of the street instead, creating an asymmetrical cross-section, so the trees could be planted after all (Figure 4.78).

The reconstruction of Dorn Avenue was big news. Although the local authorities had plenty of experience with road-widening projects and shopping-center parking lots, this was the first time that *traditional* urban street dimensions and details had been used in greater Miami since the 1920s. In the learning process that followed, they transformed an anonymous and forgotten dead zone into the social center of the town. Eventually, Sunset Drive itself was also reconstructed following the Hometown Plan (which narrowed it from five lanes to three), and several more downtown streets have been remade since.

The physical changes were matched with an overhaul of the land-development regulations. A new form-based code supplanted the conventional zoning, replacing setback rules with build-to lines, reducing parking requirements, and repealing the prohibition on outdoor dining. Owners and merchants responded immediately, extending awnings, knocking windows into formerly blank walls, and eventually building new mixed-use buildings in the traditional main street format for the first time in seventy years.

The economic story was as profound as the bricks-and-mortar tale. In 1992, annual retail rents hovered around $6 to $7 per square foot, historic buildings were slated for demolition, and there were boarded-up storefronts around downtown. Ten years later, rents topped $60 per square foot, historic structures had been rehabbed, and cafés with white tablecloths had sprouted up on the sidewalks.

Twenty years on, the progress in South Miami continues, albeit with imperfections and occasional reversals. Spurring the rehabilitation of existing retail buildings has proven easier than attracting the new housing and offices needed in the downtown, at least so far. The parking-policy reforms have been unwound, reworded, reinstated, and de-reinstated as the local political pendulum has swung from year to year. The popularity of the renewed Dorn Avenue and Sunset Drive with cyclists was underestimated at the time of the Hometown Plan, and work is now underway to boost the amount of bike parking and upgrade the overall cycling experience.

THE TWENTIETH-CENTURY STREET

"When you come to a fork in the road, make it wavy." That was James Howard Kunstler's first reaction when he saw the prize-winning competition drawing for *A Twenty-First Century Street for New York City* (Color Plate 50).[25] Its over-the-top reinvention of the wheel seems strictly twentieth-century, just like its emphasis on vehicular throughput instead of urban design.

The retrofit is for Fourth Avenue in Brooklyn, New York, a large, underdeveloped street between the high-rent Park Slope neighborhood and a low-rent area with low-rise buildings from an era when the area had a lot of manufacturing. Every firm and individual that entered the competition made their designs special and "different," following the twentieth-century architecture ideal of reinventing form, with formal invention based on functional elements like the turn lanes. Instead of using placemaking principles to create outdoor rooms between the intersections, each design focused on the traffic lanes and the intersections themselves. This misplaced focus created intersections where pedestrians would probably not feel comfortable crossing the street—even though, or perhaps because, so much effort went into making the crossing special.

> It reflects the specialist's understandable effort to make the part he's focusing on Special—which attracts too much attention to the intersection, and detracts from the experience of being on the street.

Surrounded by speeding cars, pedestrians on Fourth Avenue don't want jazzy pavement patterns with swerving vehicles in the turn lanes. The trees drawn are awkward, the decorative poles are too slight and minimal in their detail to be visually interesting, and the striping of the traffic engineer is picked up and made into a cacophonous pattern. Many of the design elements in the competition came from a fashionable school of architectural thought in New York City that says architecture and urban design should express "confrontation and complication."[26] This particular design, however, was designed by a bicycle specialist rather than an architect. It reflects the specialist's understandable effort to make the part he's focusing on Special—which attracts too much attention to the intersection, and detracts from the experience of being on the street.

That says more about late-twentieth-century architectural ideology and specialization than about what New Yorkers want today; most people going to Fourth Avenue are looking for less confrontation and complication rather than more. That's one of the reasons Park Slope, which has some of the most pleasant streets in New York, is among the most in-demand neighborhoods in the city, whereas the former manufacturing district, which has empty lots on treeless streets that people avoid, had turned Fourth Avenue into a DMZ at the edge of Park Slope. The way to improve it is to make it more beautiful and harmonious, like the great Parisian avenues of similar width. Urban renewal tends to go a block at a time, but for more than thirty years Fourth Avenue has been an obstacle to the expansion of "the Slope."

All of this reflects the suburban roots of many of the ideas we see in street design today. These started in the early 1990s when Federal legislation funded transportation specialists to improve the lot of cyclists and pedestrians on American streets. Most of the work was done on the placeless suburban arterials where pedestrians and cyclists were worst off, and placemaking was not an option. Just making a space on the road for the bicycle was an achievement, and the specialists worked within the transportation engineer's preference for dividing the street into parts, usually with paint. Most Road Diets slow cars down and make a place for bicycles, but they rarely make a place where people want to get out of their cars and walk. The favored elements like bumpouts make it easier to cross the intersection where they're installed, but they don't give a reason to cross the intersection. The designs focus on the roadway and the intersection, where cars cross, rather than the spaces next to the streets, where people meet.

PROMENADES

Yorkville Promenade (Second Avenue), New York, New York

Massengale & Co LLC, Dover, Kohl & Partners, with H. Zeke Mermell, 2011

Retrofit: Reclaiming Street Space

Promenade Street

The following description is adapted from an entry in the competition *The Unfinished Grid: Design Speculations for Manhattan*, organized by the Architectural League of New York and the Museum of the City of New York.[27]

For so many reasons, we must reduce auto use in New York City. Studies completed for Mayor Bloomberg's administration showed that living on a high-traffic avenue in Manhattan is unhealthy, particularly for children. To add insult to injury, 80 percent of Manhattan residents do not own cars, and only 20 percent of out-of-town commuters drive to work. The city's ugly, unhealthy avenues are more for the benefit of others than Manhattan's workers and residents.

Most Manhattanites live in small apartments and spend a great deal of time in public life. When the weather is nice, they spend lots of money to dine next to noisy, smelly streets made so that suburbanites can quickly and easily drive in and out of the city. The roads are one-way, the lanes are wide, and frequently there is no parking at rush hour, so that the speeding cars and trucks are sometimes just inches from the sidewalk. It doesn't make much sense.

The New Yorkville Promenade

The Yorkville Promenade (Figures 4.79, 4.80, and 4.81) is an idea for a new way to rebuild Second Avenue, after the completion of the new subway being built beneath it. Inspired by the famous Ramblas of Barcelona, the design gives the center of the wide avenue to a new promenade for walking, biking, sitting, dining, and

people-watching. Cafés and restaurants along Second Avenue would be licensed to have tables on the center island. Narrow traffic lanes and short-term parking lanes to each side would let cars and deliveries come and go while eliminating speeding traffic from Second Avenue.

Construction would take advantage of the fact that work on the new subway line has Second Avenue dug up between 96th Street and 63rd Street (where the Second Avenue subway will initially connect with the Q train, an existing line that runs from Queens to Coney Island, via Manhattan). The Promenade would be a special place that enlivens the Manhattan grid, like Broadway on the Upper West Side and Park Avenue on the Upper East Side, but with a vibrant street life unlike staid Park Avenue, where stores and trucks are prohibited.

West of Third Avenue on the Upper East Side, the introduction of Madison and Lexington avenues into the normal city grid produced shorter blocks that made the grid more interesting for pedestrians and thereby increased the value of the real estate. Yorkville is east of Third Avenue. Its long blocks are less pedestrian-friendly, and Second and Third Avenues both used to have that New York oxymoron–the elevated subway–which depressed real estate values and building quality for decades. But the El was taken down in the 1950s, and more recently the area has boomed. The Yorkville Promenade would give it a linear neighborhood center unique in New York City, and the new subway line would also make it more accessible for tourists and other New Yorkers.

New York Congestion Zone

Mayor Bloomberg and the New York City DOT proposed a congestion zone for the city, modeled after one in London. New York's zone was initially going to cover all of Manhattan south of 86th Street (later changed to 60th Street). Under the proposed plan, anyone other than Manhattan residents living within the zone would have to pay a daily fee to drive a car into it between 6 a.m. and 6 p.m. The U.S. DOT gave the city a $354 million grant to start the program and increase express

Figure 4.79: Yorkville Promenade, New York, New York. Massengale & Co LLC, Dover, Kohl & Partners, with H. Zeke Mermell, 2011. Second Avenue today is a suburban-style arterial, encouraging suburbanites to drive into the city instead of taking the train, subway, or express bus. © *2011 Dover, Kohl & Partners / Massengale & Co LLC*

Figure 4.80: Yorkville Promenade, New York, New York. Massengale & Co LLC, Dover, Kohl & Partners, with H. Zeke Mermell, 2011. After reconstruction, Second Avenue could be a unique street in the New York grid, adding variety and claiming a local role. © *2011 Dover, Kohl & Partners / Massengale & Co LLC*

Figure 4.81: Yorkville Promenade, New York, New York. Massengale & Co LLC, Dover, Kohl & Partners, with H. Zeke Mermell, 2011. Section. © *2011 Dover, Kohl & Partners / Massengale & Co LLC*

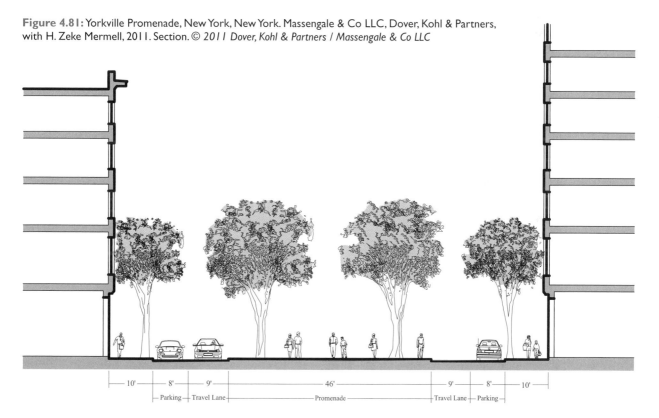

bus and ferry service, but unfortunately the plan had to be approved by the New York State legislature in Albany. So many legislators from upstate, New York's suburbs, and the city's outer boroughs were against the congestion zone that the proposal was never voted on, forcing the city to give back the $354 million.

Despite having been denied the right to create a congestion zone, New York City can still achieve similar effects with a few fundamental changes. Until the 1950s, almost all Manhattan streets, including cross-streets, were two-way, and there is nothing to prevent the city from doing that again. Second, the NYC DOT has started a program of giving select neighborhood streets twenty-miles-per-hour speed limits. In New York State, drivers are never ticketed for going slightly less than ten miles per hour over the limit, so that makes an effective speed limit of thirty. This would make the city much safer: the only way to save more pedestrian lives in Manhattan would be to ban traffic altogether. And finally, New York could turn some of its avenues into Rambla-like boulevards and others into Parisian-style multiway boulevards, while continuing the work of simply taking street space for pedestrians begun by NYC DOT Commissioner Janette Sadik-Khan. If all those things—two-way streets, low speeds, and taking back parts of the roadway—were done, traffic in New York City would decrease. Today, Second Avenue, and most of New York's avenues, are suburban-style arterials: very wide, one-way with staggered lights, no parking in places at rush hour, and with large signs and bold graphics

> Despite having been denied the right to create a congestion zone, New York City can still achieve similar effects with a few fundamental changes.

on the roadbed. Roads like that encourage suburbanites to drive into the city instead of taking a train, the subway, or an express bus. It's quite common to be in a New York taxi driving over fifty miles per hour on these roads, simply rolling with the traffic. The legal speed limit is thirty, but New York City police rarely give speeding tickets on the avenues.

The avenues the cars are speeding on are some of the most important places in New York's public realm. Second Avenue and Third Avenue are the main outdoor dining spaces for the Upper East Side. They should be treated like neighborhood streets, but instead they are arterials for out-of-towners, New Yorkers rich enough to have cars with drivers, and people who routinely take taxis instead of taking the subway or walking. All together it's a surprisingly small number of people causing traffic jams. Make the streets slower and less convenient and you would have a natural congestion zone, with a healthier and more pleasant public realm for the majority. Perhaps the U.S. DOT would give a grant for that.

These sound like radical steps, but that's only because most Americans alive today have grown up during a period when the car was king. We're so familiar with auto sewers that we think they're normal—but America is starting to change. We don't need to build more suburban roads, because we probably have a hundred-year supply. The problem will be paying for the maintenance of the millions of miles of roads in low-density areas, where property taxes don't come close to covering the cost of maintaining them. The federal government paid a large percentage of the original construction costs, but they pay nothing for ongoing upkeep. Where we need to spend money is in retrofitting urban roads made for drivers rather than pedestrians.

THINGS IN THE MIDDLE OF THE ROAD

Figure 4.82: Madison Square, New York, New York. The Dewey Arch at the intersection of Broadway and Fifth Avenue. Looking north from below Twenty-third Street, circa 1899. *Library of Congress, Prints and Photographs Division, Detroit Publishing Company Photograph Collection, LC-D4-12490*

Before Organized Motordom claimed control of the public realm in our towns and cities, there was a popular tradition of putting monuments in the roadway. Baroque planners particularly liked them (see Figures 2.8 to 2.10), but long before the Baroque there was an ancient tradition of fountains, obelisks, and triumphal arches in the road in Europe, and we liked them here in America, too (see Figures 2.73 and 2.79, as well as Figures 4.62 and 4.63). New York City developed a tradition of elaborate but temporary monuments and memorials, like the Dewey Arch and colonnade (Charles Robinson Lamb, 1898), built to commemorate Admiral George Dewey's victory in the Battle of Manila Bay. Like the more politically correct Washington Arch erected on Fifth Avenue in 1889 to commemorate the centennial of President George Washington's New York inauguration, the Dewey Arch was built of "staff," a plaster mixture that could be molded or troweled on, but that looked like stone when it dried. The Washington Arch was later rebuilt in marble, and Fifth Avenue passed through it for many years. The Dewey Arch, which had contributions from a number of well-known sculptors, lasted less than two years.

CORNER CONDITIONS

Figure 4.83: Worth Avenue, Palm Beach, Florida. Sanchez & Maddux, Landscape Architects; Bridges, Marsh & Associates, Architects; 2010. Looking south at the intersection with Golfview Avenue.

An important difference between new streets and historic streets is that we now want corner ramps for wheelchairs, disabled access, and even luggage with wheels. The formulaic, poorly designed and narrow ramps we build today can be both ugly and inconvenient. In their renovation of Worth Avenue, Sanchez & Maddux sloped the entire corner, a detail that works best with wide sidewalks. On the opposite side of Worth Avenue, where there is no cross street, they put an attractive bumpout, which visually breaks down the long block, reassuring the pedestrian that he or she hasn't been forgotten. Design solves problems. Formulaic design, like the placement of a poorly proportioned bumpout at every corner, commonly creates problems.

BUMPOUTS

Our respective offices are in Manhattan and South Miami. All the sidewalks in the intersections on Broadway near the New York office have 7½-foot corner radii: that is, where the sidewalks come together at the corners they are rounded off with a quarter-circle with the 7½-foot radius used throughout most of Manhattan. In South Miami, the office is near the intersection of Sunset Avenue and Red Road. In Bob Gibbs's terms (See "Secrets of Successful Retail"), that's the local Main and Main corner, at the heart of South Miami's downtown. The corner radii there are approximately 25 feet. They're big so that large trucks can easily turn the corner there, even though the road is very wide. The effect of the large corner radius is to make the already wide street even wider. Standing on the corner, the other side of the street looks a long way off, and you understand why street specialists working on bad suburban streets want to use bumpouts, also known as bulbouts, pork chops, and curb extensions (Figures 4.84 and 4.85). Unfortunately, this suburban solution has become both formulaic and ubiquitous in urban situations.

There is a place in good street design for bumpouts. For example, a bumpout might be appropriate when there is a midblock pedestrian crossing on a long block (as in Figure 4.41. Another type of problem is solved with the bumpout in Figure 2.117). The way they get pasted onto every wide intersection for "pedestrian improvements," however, is poor design. Most of the time, bumpouts are like lipstick on a pig—cosmetic efforts that don't address the real problem, which is that the street is too wide and dominated by cars and trucks (Figure 4.84). The balance on American streets between walking, driving, and other forms of transportation like bicycles and streetcars must be recalibrated.

A problem with bumpouts is that when they are pushed out into the street the traffic engineer wants to make the corner radius even larger, because a bumpout now intrudes into the area where the trucks turn. That's good for trucks and lazy auto drivers and bad for pedestrians. If the entire roadway is narrowed without bumpouts, the corner radius can be kept small, because the roadway is still available for turning.

In keeping with the KISS Rule of Good Placemaking (Keep It Simple, Stupid), the public realm is usually most harmonious and comfortable when the curbs line up with the buildings. Talented designers like Camillo Sitte and Léon Krier can play with this (Figure 5.20). Visually, ordinary bumpouts tend to take on a life of their own, disrupting the continuity and unity of the space. Throw in multi-color bus lanes, bike lanes, and pedestrian crossings and the effect is magnified. Without exception, the beautiful streets of the world do not have this cacophony of elements.

In the redesign of Worth Avenue in Florida, one of America's most successful shopping streets (Figure 4.38), care was taken to make the street visually harmonious. The city removed most road signs, chose a limited color palette, carefully aligned the new palm trees, and used a light concrete rain gutter that visually lines up the bumpouts—particularly when the parking spaces are full, as they usually are. These bumpouts were also designed to be a visually pleasing width, unlike the formulaic, narrow bumpout we usually see (Figure 4.85).

> No walkable city or town should need bumpouts "taming" the streets, because the streets shouldn't need taming. Streets in cities and towns need narrow traffic lanes, slow speeds, drivers afraid of hitting pedestrians—and whatever it takes to make streets where people want to get out of their cars and walk.

In the end, the Transect has to be included in discussions about bumpouts. Worth Avenue was once a small-town Main Street, but it is now a luxury shopping street for aging, wealthy Boomers—and they might appreciate the comfort of a well-designed bumpout like the one in

Figure 4.84: El Camino Real, Santa Clara, California. The road is wide, the buildings alongside the road do not enclose the space, and the scale of the auto-centric road is boring for the pedestrian. In this situation, the bumpout may make it psychologically easier for the occasional pedestrian to cross the street. But why would the pedestrian even be on the street here? This is not a detail that entices people out of their cars, and it is not a detail that would improve a walkable street. *Image courtesy of the City of Los Altos*

Figure 4.85: Worth Avenue, Palm Beach, Florida. Sanchez & Maddux, Landscape Architects; Bridges, Marsh & Associates, Architects; 2010. In context, this bumpout works well. It is for an upscale shopping street most people will drive to, it marks a place to cross in a long block, it functions well with the arcaded sidewalk, it breaks the monotony of a long block, and it works visually with the design of the rest of the avenue. In other words, it is an example of a good designer solving problems with good design.

Palm Beach. Watch pedestrians in walkable places like Boston and New York, and you will see that they don't wait on the sidewalk, and that they certainly don't need bumpouts. Even though the New York City DOT turned many of New York's avenues into fast-moving suburban arterials in the 1950s and 1960s, New York pedestrians think the public realm belongs to them, and they wait out in their road for the light to change. Thank- fully, the city is once again trying to give New Yorkers roads worthy of their ambitions. No walkable city or town should need bumpouts "taming" the streets, because the streets shouldn't need taming. Streets in cities and towns need narrow traffic lanes, slow speeds, drivers afraid of hitting pedestrians—and whatever it takes to make streets where people want to get out of their cars and walk.

PEDESTRIAN AND SHARED SPACE

Exhibition Road, London, England

Dixon Jones, 2012

Retrofit: Experimenting with Shared Space

Shared Space

Exhibition Road is another radically rebuilt street in the Royal Borough of Kensington and Chelsea. It is a broad street lined with institutional buildings, including the Victoria and Albert Museum, the Science Museum, the Natural History Museum, the Royal Geographical Society, and Imperial College London. Like Kensington High Street, it had too much traffic, but the borough tried a different experiment on Exhibition Road than they had on the High Street, dividing most of the street down the middle. It gave one side exclusively to pedestrians and the other to both pedestrians and cars. The result is a mixed success (Figures 4.86 and 4.87).

Exhibition Road runs from the South Kensington Tube Station north to Hyde Park, where the 1851 Great Exhibition of the Works of Industry of All Nations was held in the famous Crystal Palace. A lack of coherence on the street and in the surrounding area led to ambitious plans in the late twentieth century by Norman Foster, Daniel Libeskind, and others—which all foundered. In 2003, the borough organized a competition to improve the design of Exhibition Road. The architecture firm Dixon Jones won the competition with a plan that reduced traffic and gave more space to the pedestrian.

The scheme begins at the intersection of Thurloe Street and Exhibition Road. The rebuilt road changes character as it goes north. First, it crosses two busy streets, Cromwell Road (the A4, one of the main routes in and out of London) and Thurloe Place (the A3218). In between these two streets is a short transitional block, where almost everyone is just passing through. North of Cromwell Road, the wide road runs straight as an arrow to Hyde Park. This long stretch is now one of the best-known shared spaces in England.

The innovations at the southern end of Exhibition Road have been more successful than the primary stretch between the museums and other institutions. Thurloe Street and the adjacent plaza are small-scale, comfortable spaces that are well used by the public. Both are lined with attractive storefronts that have been revived by the popularity of the new design, now filled with several cafés with outdoor dining, a bookstore for the Victoria and Albert Museum, and other shops. Cars can enter the Exhibition Road space here, but it feels more like a piazza than shared space. Low ventilating stacks for the tube station and a tunnel leading to it poke up in the middle of the space, helping the spatial definition. Built-in benches attached to the stacks are frequently occupied by those who don't want to have to spend money to spend time people-watching, and the few cars and vans that park in the square tend to cluster around them, giving some visual order to the parking. On the street itself, bold striping in light and dark grays clearly sets the space off from the through traffic on Thurloe Place.

The effect of these paving techniques on the long, wide piece of Exhibition Road to the north is less pleasing, because here the street feels vast and poorly shaped. The bold diagonal striping is visible for many blocks, and since there are no sidewalks, the supergraphic bumps into the institutions lining the road in an almost random and uncomfortable way. On the small piazza to the south, on the other hand, the paving pattern seems less repetitive and is more broken up by the ventilation shafts and the benches around them, the parked vehicles, and the number of people in the space. The outdoor tables on the southern block of Exhibition Road also cover the supergraphics at the edges, softening their effect.

A smaller pattern north of Cromwell Road would bring a more human scale to the vast space, and breaking it into smaller parts would help, too. A more traditional design would make borders along the edge and break the long space into smaller parts. Cars park in the center of the road, which has traffic on one side and pedestrians on the other. "Only the parked cars look comfortable," says Hank Dittmar, the Chief Executive of the Prince's Foundation.[28]

An allée of London Plane trees would have been an effective way to shape and modulate the space, but Dixon Jones instead went for tall metal pylons down the center of the street. This out-of-scale and minimally-detailed choice brings to mind two contrasting short passages into the Mount Street Gardens, a lovely midblock park a short distance away in Mayfair. One is a short block treated as a normal street, with building entrances, parked cars, and now, a Barclays Cycle rental station. Even without trees, it's a beautiful small block. At the other end of the park is a short block of about the same size that terminates Carlos Place. Now closed to traffic, it has an austere, minimalist design that is close to sterile. This block has a certain cerebral charm but little of the human scale that makes the street at the other end of the gardens so charming. If its small, scrawny trees grow to a mature height, it may be a very good space, eventually. But the trees are in raised planters that may prevent them from growing, and for now, like Exhibition Road, the place suffers from too much fashionable ideology and too little placemaking.

A theme of this book concerns the perils of specialists making their designs too special, according to the criteria of their specialty. Engineers may overengineer, pedestrian specialists draw special crosswalks that attract too much attention, and bicycle specialists design brightly-colored cycle lanes that look like the most important thing on the street. The problem of the architect can be overdesign: reinventing the street in a way that yells, "I'm special," even when it's austere and minimal.

By contrast, one of the greatest achievements of the other new road in the borough, the Kensington High Street, is that borough Councillor Daniel Moylan made sure that everyone worked toward the common goal of a better Complete Street. Its clean, modern details are always understated, in the service of a simple street design, rather than for the purpose of making an architectural statement. Architectural expression can serve placemaking, but that's rarely the emphasis in fashionable contemporary design.

▲▲ **Figure 4.86:** Exhibition Road, London, England. Before: Home to some of the most important cultural institutions in the city, Exhibition Road was dominated by the car. *Property of the Royal Borough of Kensington and Chelsea*

▲ **Figure 4.87:** Exhibition Road, London, England. Dixon Jones, 2012. After: The supergraphic hyperstriping shouts, "Look at me." A row of London Plane trees could have divided the pedestrian space on one side from the shared space on the other, but the architects opted for thin metallic pylons instead. *Property of the Royal Borough of Kensington and Chelsea*

HANS MONDERMAN AND SHARED SPACE

> If you want vehicles to behave like they are in a village, build a village.
>
> —Hans Monderman, as quoted by Fred Kent[29]

Hans Monderman (1945–2008) was a Dutch traffic engineer who saw that excessive signage, stripings, traffic signals, and specialized space were all intended to improve safety but, ironically, served instead to lull motorists into unsafe complacency. He pioneered modern concepts of shared space and reduced traffic-control markings.

Monderman was a conventional planner when he started his career, but as his experience grew, he became concerned that many of the engineering "improvements" that the government was making in the interest of safety actually made some road segments more dangerous. Monderman believed that there were many places in Dutch cities and towns where the best way to control traffic would be to remove curbs, signs, and markings, thereby forcing the driver and the pedestrian to look each other in the eye when negotiating the right-of-way. This may be easier to do in the rather homogenous, communal, and bike-riding culture of the Netherlands than in most other places, but the world nevertheless seems to be slowly catching up to Monderman.

Lincoln Road, Miami Beach, Florida

Morris Lapidus, 1960

Retrofit: Experimenting with Pedestrian Space

Pedestrian Street

In a very short time (urbanistically speaking), the character and function of Lincoln Road were profoundly transformed. What began as a dense grove of mangroves at the beginning of the twentieth century was swiftly cleared by the visionary developer Carl Fisher for the construction of Lincoln Road. In the 1920s, the wide, auto-oriented street flourished (Figures 4.88 and 4.89).[30] Saks Fifth Avenue, Harry Winston Jewelers, and other tony retailers there catered to well-heeled socialites; many of the Beach's VIPs were enthusiastic about motorcars and had ties to the rapidly growing transportation industries, so they were known at the time as "the Gasoline Society." The success of the shopping street continued until the middle of the century, when it experienced a rapid decline in popularity among tourists

and locals. Much of the previously vibrant retail began to leave the road for other, more up-to-date locations, including shopping malls.

In a radical move for the time, famous architect Morris Lapidus proposed to close Lincoln Road to car traffic, "pedestrianizing" the commercial street (Figures 4.90 and 4.91). Lapidus's design for an unusually wide pedestrian mall, slightly more than one hundred feet across, was completed in 1960.[31]

At first, eliminating cars did more harm than good; Lincoln Road went from financially struggling to financially moribund. The attempt to compete with suburban malls by being more like them backfired, and Lincoln Road went from bad to worse. By the mid-1980s, vacant storefronts were the norm, and every night Lincoln Road became a dark, eerie ruin. Gradually, artists took up low-rent space on the street and a gallery scene emerged, catalyzed by the presence of the South Florida Arts Center. During this period, the rest of South Beach and the Art Deco District became a mecca for fashion photographers and the area came back one block at a time. Tourists soon followed.

Figure 4.88: Lincoln Road, Miami Beach, Florida. View looking east, circa 1936. The street was open to traffic and lined with tall palms. The asymmetrical Mediterranean Revival silhouette of the Van Dyke Building (1924) is visible in the background, at center right. *Image courtesy of HistoryMiami, Archives and Research Center*

Figure 4.89: Lincoln Road, Miami Beach, Florida. View looking east, circa 1936. *Image courtesy of HistoryMiami, Archives and Research Center*

Figure 4.90: Lincoln Road, Miami Beach, Florida. Morris Lapidus, 1960. After languishing for thirty years, Lincoln Road sprang back to life, with one of the highest concentrations of pedestrian activity to be seen anywhere in the American Sunbelt. © 2013 Stephen A. Mouzon, Photographer

Figure 4.91: Lincoln Road, Miami Beach, Florida. Morris Lapidus, 1960. The staid Gasoline Society finally gave way to hip café society; Lincoln Road was overhauled a second time by the City of Miami Beach, taking the kitschy "boomerang moderne" image up a further notch by restoring Lapidus' pavilions (center), adding even more glitzy fountains and pavements, and luring artists with subsidized rents. © 2013 Stephen A. Mouzon, Photographer

Economically, Lincoln Road continued to struggle, but the street's edginess slowly attracted a following among the creative class. The City of Miami Beach toyed with the idea of reopening the street to traffic but backed off, opting instead to overhaul the finishes, fountains, and kitschy pavilion structures designed by Lapidus. After nearly forty years, when the surrounding neighborhoods were thoroughly revived, Lincoln Road finally took off. Instead of being a dim, forgotten nowhere, it is now a bright social center of the city. Crowds stroll and dine there every night, even in the off-season. The essential framework of the urban form (including building frontage lines and lot dimensions) has not changed much, but infill happened through the decades, reinforcing the street facade and the definition of the space.

Española Way, Miami Beach, Florida

Savino & Miller, 2002

Retrofit: Right-Sizing Pedestrian Space

Shared Space

Also known as the Historic Spanish Village, Española Way is the only street on Miami Beach with a style of architecture and urban form that resembles what one might find in a Mediterranean city. Conceived as an artist colony, early on it took on notoriety for gambling and as a red light district.

Today Española Way is a prized address. It is mostly a pedestrian environment, although cars can come in on a limited basis. The design of the outdoor space has seen multiple iterations, but the buildings have mostly been preserved.

In 2012 Española Way was selected as the Best Block in South Florida in a *Miami Herald* competition.

During the initial building boom on Miami Beach in the 1920s, the vehicular right-of-way on Española Way was nearly twice the size it is now (Figure 4.92). Today, it's a pedestrian passage (Figures 4.93 and 4.94). The sidewalks have more than doubled in size, trees have been planted, and the historic facades are restored. The street is often closed to car traffic via the use of movable planters at its eastern end. Unlike neighboring pedestrian passages, however, Española Way tolerates vehicles: slight widenings at specific intervals accommodate a small amount of on-street parking for local residents.

Like Aviles Street in St. Augustine, Florida, or Tweede Tuindwarsstraat in the Jordaan District of Amsterdam, Española Way is skinny, with a single central travel lane that measures 13 feet 4 inches (Figure 4.95). Large, 13-foot-wide sidewalks on both sides of the street are typically full of patrons dining, shopping, or walking to their apartments.

Figure 4.92: Española Way, Miami Beach, Florida. Before: Existing conditions in 1928. *Image courtesy of the Matlack Collection, HistoryMiami*

Figure 4.93: Española Way, Miami Beach, Florida. Savino & Miller, 2002. Wider sidewalks permitted trees and ornamental landscaping, and now the scene feels lush. *Image courtesy of Jason King*

Figure 4.94: Española Way, Miami Beach, Florida. Savino & Miller, 2002. The widened sidewalks have been filled with tables from the restaurants, and most pedestrians walk in the center lane.

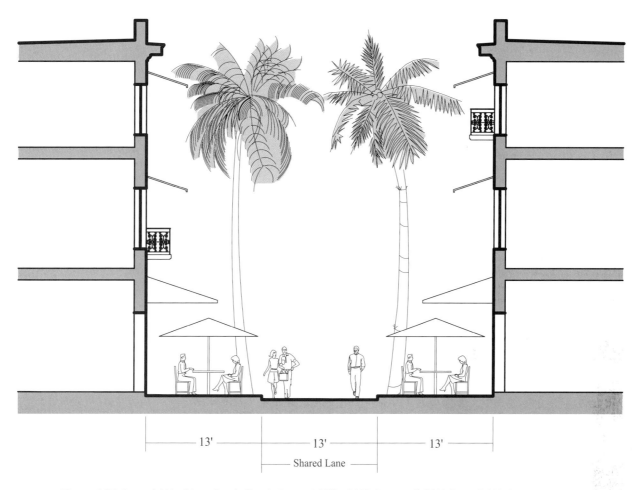

Figure 4.95: Española Way, Miami Beach, Florida. Savino & Miller, 2002. Section. © 2013 Dover, Kohl & Partners

The Alley, Montgomery, Alabama

2WR / Holmes Wilkins Architects, 2008

Retrofit: Opening the Alley

Pedestrian Passage

The Alley was a service lane that opened onto Tallapoosa Street in the center of a block in downtown Montgomery. The sides of brick buildings line the alley—remnants from a time when even the most utili-

tarian structures were built in a way that added texture and character to urban life. The city and local investors saw the opportunity to leverage that character and add a bright spot to downtown nightlife in Montgomery. The narrow passage—conveniently located between Biscuit Stadium and parking along Bibb Street—began as a place for a beer after the game, and a small portion of it was initially set aside for outdoor seating at the bar. Gradually, this forgotten space became the Alley (Figure 4.96), the liveliest part of the downtown pedestrian network. Initially shaped like an "L" and opening

Figure 4.96: The Alley, Montgomery, Alabama. 2WR/Holmes Wilkins Architects, 2008. *Image courtesy of the City of Montgomery*

An old, humble rooftop water tower was rescued and installed by the Tallapoosa Street entrance; the Alley's boosters then creatively lit the water tower and turned it into a unique combination of a signpost and a conversation piece, raising eyebrows among some preservationists and delighting others. Now the water tower is considered an iconic feature of the street and appears in most photographs of the Alley.

Today, The Alley is surrounded by three downtown hotels. The Entertainment Express rubber-tire trolley now circulates from the Old Cloverdale streetcar suburb and from Maxwell Air Force Base to the Downtown Entertainment District. The recent opening onto Coosa Street is very important, because Coosa Street is an underused, two-sided architectural gem that is now attracting pedestrians for the first time in a long time—and a new restaurant is scheduled to open there as of this writing.

Stone Street, New York, New York

RBA Group and Signe Nielsen Landscape Architecture, 2000

Retrofit: Opening an Alley

Pedestrian Street

Stone Street is an old street in downtown Manhattan, near Wall Street. It has been called the oldest paved street in the city, although that seems to be an urban legend.[32] The original name was Brouwerstraat (Brewers Street), but it was renamed Stone Street in 1660, when it was paved with cobblestones. In the 1980s, the construction of a new headquarters building for Goldman, Sachs & Company split the street in two. A general level of unhappiness with that decision led to the present requirement that the closing of any street in downtown Manhattan must be approved by the city's Landmarks Preservation Commission.

In 1996, the Commission designated the derelict street part of a new Stone Street Historic District and

onto Tallapoosa and Commerce Street, the Alley now extends to connect Commerce and Coosa Street with a "T" configuration.

According to Deputy Mayor Jeff Downes, the city and county have invested a combined $1.6 million in the common space at The Alley, while the private sector has invested a combined $25 million. This investment has paid off. Now the heart of downtown Montgomery's historic entertainment district, The Alley contains four restaurants, two bars, and an art gallery. Each opens to the alley space itself. The AlleyBar contains the "BackAlley" concert hall, a 5,000-square-foot party room and music venue.

Figure 4.97: Stone Street, New York, New York. RBA Group and Signe Nielsen Landscape Architecture, 2000. Looking northeast on Stone Street. The former alley has become the main gathering spot for young Wall Street workers whenever the weather is warm enough after work.

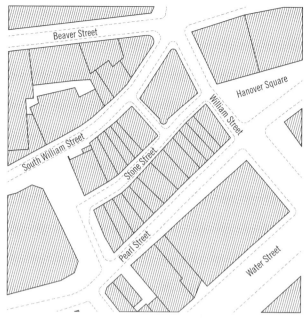

Figure 4.98: Stone Street, New York, New York. Figure-ground.
© 2013 Dover, Kohl & Partners

worked with the Alliance for Downtown New York to transform it. "This street has such historic consequence," said Carl Weisbrod, president of the Alliance. "But it was really a back alley filled with graffiti, a garbage pit, used for low-level drug dealing."[33] The ensuing streetscape renovation, which was spearheaded by the Alliance, cost $1.8 million (Figures 4.97 and 4.98).

From building to building, Stone Street is approximately thirty feet wide. In the center of the block, the highly restored buildings are fifty feet tall, and there are taller buildings at each end. The north end of the street is visually closed by the twenty-three-story Cotton Exchange (now apartments), designed by Donn Barber in 1923, that sits at 3 Hanover Square. Across William Street on the northeast corner of Stone Street is a tall 3½-story brownstone palazzo that was the original home of the Hanover Bank. The opposite corner of Stone Street has an interesting eleven-story private-banking building designed in a Renaissance Revival style by Francis H. Kimball in 1906, with a postmodern addition by Gino Valle: for many years this was the home of Lehman Brothers. Near the southern end of Stone Street is a pair of Dutch Colonial facades designed by the architect C.P.H. Gilbert in 1906.[34] Looming over the street is the ungainly behemoth designed by Skidmore, Owings & Merrill for Goldman Sachs. The RBA Group and Signe

Nielsen Landscape Architecture designed the Stone Street renovation.

With the buildings on Stone Street taller than the street is wide, the space between them makes a comfortable outdoor room. The street and the sidewalks are stone, and the building facades are mainly stone and brick. The buildings have traditional vertical punched windows with deep shadows that emphasize the solidity of the walls and firmly contain the space. Most of the lots are narrow, so that the horizontal repetition of the vertical building facades sets up a pleasing rhythm. There are a variety of building heights, and the styles are eclectic, but the double-hung windows used in most of the buildings other than the Goldman Sachs headquarters add some unity and harmony.

"They've put the stone back in Stone Street," the *New York Times* said in December 2000, referring to the cobblestones and bluestone sidewalks that replaced the cracked asphalt roadbed and concrete sidewalks.[35] Lampposts that look like gaslights were also installed. Before the renovation, the landlords of the buildings along this street—all of which also face on neighboring streets in better conditions—treated their Stone Street frontages as backs. Today, Stone Street is perhaps the most successful "restaurant row" in the city.

Seventeen of the twenty-one restaurants on the block are owned by the Poulakakos family, and a few by Goldman Properties (which has no connection to Goldman Sachs). Harry Poulakakos led a renovation featuring all-new storefronts along the alley. He had to argue with the New York City Department of Transportation, which expected the outdoor dining to fail and therefore wanted a street that could easily revert to traffic. But the Poulakakoses are kings of the street for as long as their restaurants succeed, and they were right that the street would become popular. Today, Stone Street is closed to traffic and has one of the liveliest bar and restaurant scenes in lower Manhattan, with many outdoor tables filling the space. On a nice afternoon or evening, the street is overflowing with people taking a break after work. Few of them probably realize that the historic-looking storefronts have been built since 1996.

Winslow Homer Walk, New York, New York

Massengale & Co LLC and Dover, Kohl & Partners, with H. Zeke Mermell, 2011

Retrofit: Opening an Alley

Pedestrian Passage

The long blocks of midtown Manhattan are uncomfortable for pedestrians. Manhattanites know midblock building lobbies go through centers of the blocks, giving significant shortcuts for some trips. As Jane Jacobs pointed out, pedestrians like frequent intersections, so they can look ahead and see a variety of routes and choices.[36] Midtown has a tradition of places like Shubert Alley that open the middle of the block, and a newer tradition of using the bonus plazas given by New York City's 1961 zoning plan for pedestrian cut-throughs at buildings like the Equitable Building on Seventh Avenue. For the *By the City / For the City* competition in 2011,[37] we looked at a midblock passage between 56th and 57th streets that's closed in the middle and poorly used by most passersby (Figure 4.99).

Directly opposite the Art Students League on West 57th Street, our proposed Winslow Homer Walk (Homer once taught at the school) brings the passage down to ground level and removes the high fence between the raised "Hooters Plaza" on 56th Street and the more formal raised plaza on 57th Street, which is connected to the building at 888 Seventh Avenue (Figure 4.100). Decades of studies have shown that raised plazas are less used than spaces at ground level, and the formal plaza at 888 is not welcoming.[38]

The existing plazas on 56th and 57th streets are both fifty feet wide, but there is a jog in the middle of the block, where the fence separates the two spaces (Figure 4.101). In our design, we moved the diner in front of 888 on 57th Street around the corner, so that it would face Homer Walk. The 56th Street side of the Walk is quieter, and we made that side wider, with more trees and more outdoor tables. A narrow two-story addition to 211 West 56th Street on the west side of the Walk gives a beautiful face to a boring utilitarian design from the 1960s and opens to the tables in the

Figure 4.99: Winslow Homer Walk, New York, New York. Before: Existing conditions, 2011. Rendering looking south from West 57th Street. The plaza on 57th Street is raised, which discourages use, and there is a wall between it and the outdoor space for Hooters on 56th Street. © 2011 Dover, Kohl & Partners / Massengale & Co LLC

Figure 4.100: Winslow Homer Walk, New York, New York. After: Rendering shows the passage brought down to grade, opened to 56th Street, planted with trees, and lined with restaurants and food carts. © 2011 Dover, Kohl & Partners / Massengale & Co LLC

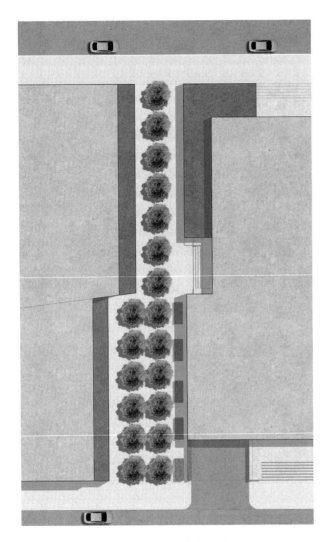

Figure 4.101: Winslow Homer Walk, New York, New York. Plan of proposed intervention. The diner that was moved to 57th Street when the office building was built is placed along Homer Walk. The office building gains a more important entrance on 57th Street, but also has an entrance at the middle of Homer Walk. © 2011 Dover, Kohl & Partners / Massengale & Co LLC

quiet places like Homer Walk. The most-used of these, like Bryant Park or the paved plaza where Occupy Wall Street encamped, have food vendors, free Wi-Fi, and benches and tables that can be moved by the users.

In the end, the plan removed thirty-seven top-level parking spaces from the garages at 888 Seventh Avenue and 211 West 56th Street in order to bring the plaza down to ground level. At the same time we added thousands of square feet of public and commercial space. That is the type of trade we need more of as we move away from the auto-centric planning of the last fifty years. Luckily, the New York City DOT is leading the way. Less than a year after we drew our imaginary Winslow Homer Walk, the DOT put up street signs, stoplights, and mid-block crosswalks for something they call 6½ Avenue.[39] The mini-avenue marks a series of bonus plazas in the middle of the blocks between Sixth Avenue and Seventh Avenue, and between West 51st and West 57th Streets. The next step would be to work with the owners of the lots and buildings 6½ Avenue passes through, because these "public plazas" can be quite barren. Some are next to popular restaurants, but the landlords don't let the restaurants put tables in the spaces.

In terms of density and transportation, New Yorkers live in the most walkable city in America, with carbon footprints similar to Europeans. In terms of streets, squares, and places like Homer Walk and 6½ Avenue, New Yorkers need more places and more variety in the public realm, appealing places where people want to congregate. New York City residents and workers, unlike the politicians in Albany, wanted the Congestion Zone. When the city reduces the number of cars in the city, it will be able to make more places like Homer Walk.

The Most Important Factor for Retrofits: Political Will

In 2009, Ellen Dunham-Jones and June Williamson wrote a book entitled *Retrofitting Suburbia*.[40] "The American suburb as we know it is dying," *TIME* said in response to the book in a special issue entitled *10 Ideas Changing the World Right Now*: "The suburbs need

passage. On the opposite side, a new marble wall similar to the one on the other side of the garage entrance for 888 makes a backdrop for a row of New York food carts with outdoor seating. New Yorkers love to take lunch breaks in

to be remade, and just such a transformation is under way in regions that were known for some of the worst sprawl in the U.S. Communities as diverse as Lakewood, Colo., and Long Beach, Calif., have repurposed boarded-up malls as mixed-use developments with retail stores, offices, and apartments. In auto-dependent suburbs that were built without a traditional center, shopping malls offer the chance to create downtowns without destroying existing infrastructure, by recycling what's known as underperforming asphalt." Many Americans will still prefer the space of the suburbs—including the parking spaces. "People want to balance the privacy of the suburbs with more public and social areas," says Dunham-Jones.[41] But the result will be a U.S. that is more sustainable—environmentally and economically.

Dunham-Jones is right. Many Americans will prefer suburban sprawl—if they can afford it. But many will also want greater walkability, and many will want places where they can live more sustainably. Good streets will be a crucial element in suburban retrofits.

In many cases, though, designing retrofitted streets may be the easiest part of getting them built. Even when a community has made the decision to change and has garnered the necessary political will, NIMBYs and professionals in the field may protest vehemently.

In recent years, public planning discussions have become more heated. Perhaps contemporary resistance is partly due to the fact that we are still living with so many of the disasters of the twentieth century; the high-handed results of urban renewal fifty years later remain scars in many of our cities. At the same time, in a rapidly expanding country like the United States, development is inevitable, and it is in all of our interests for that process to be democratic, engaged, and compassionate.

In the 1980s the New Urbanism movement met the then-current antigrowth situation with new tools and techniques: a revival of visualization, so that people could see what proposed growth would look like; a revival of design, which demolished the idea that all growth is bad, because well-designed growth could be shown to be smart growth; and the evolution of charrettes—multiday gatherings with a wide variety of stakeholders and massive public participation.[42] Urbanists began to gain ground by declaring their opponents their partners, and working to build consensus. The engagement was real, the compromises were real, and the trust built up from the process was real.

Now, however, a new group of roving interlopers is shadowing planning efforts at many levels, actively working to thwart them. Many charretters (including the authors) have run into organized protesters who repeat rumors that New Urbanism and Smart Growth[43] are part of a murky United Nations conspiracy to force a New World Order on America, under the aegis of something called Agenda 21.[44] Labeling those who promote Smart Growth or New Urbanism "socialists" or "communists," these activists are part of a well-organized, well-funded effort to perpetuate sprawl. Rightwing groups maintain websites about how to disrupt charrettes and other consensus-building processes to prevent Smart Growth policies; single-issue extremists are now routinely allowed to hijack public meetings while elected leaders sit by helplessly, unable to keep discipline.

We don't need to abandon visuals, design, or charrettes, but new methods are called for. As citizens, we need to elect leaders who can do what we want them to do: lead. As urban designers, we must concentrate on reaching out to public officials and citizens alike on matters of growth and retrofitting urbanism, so that they understand the issues under discussion and participate in these debates from a position of knowledge rather than fear.[45] City-building must remain a public act, dependent on decision-making that is transparent and fair, and all of us must take responsibility for keeping it so. This book is a small part of that effort.

NOTES

1. But how convenient is it walking through rain-soaked or sun-drenched parking lots at the regional malls where the outer edge of lots are more than a quarter mile from a mall entrance?

2. Chester Liebs, *From Main Street to Miracle Mile* (Baltimore: Johns Hopkins University Press, 1995), 10–15, 54. Liebs says the term strip is shortened from "taxpayer strip," which meant a "temporary" row of development on the road leading away from town, where businesses popped up once cars began to pass that way in numbers. The scale of development was supposedly just intensive enough to generate sufficient income to pay the taxes on the land, while its owners waited for the town proper to grow out to that distance so they could redevelop at a profitable city scale. The "taxpayer" part of the term lost its meaning once sprawl accelerated so fast and the assumptions switched around: now it was assumed the real profits were to be had in the suburbs and the city was dying, so the owners dropped their plans to ever redevelop the temporary one-story development, skipping over that to chase the new motorists' dollars that were by then moving ever farther out.

3. Greg Konar, "Lancaster Showcases 'Living Street," *San Diego Planning Journal*, May 19, 2012, http://sdapa.org/go/lancaster-showcases-model-living-street/. Kaid Benfield's essay originally appeared on his NRDC blog. See "How retrofitting a California suburb for walkability is spurring economic development," Switchboard, http://switchboard.nrdc.org/blogs/kbenfield/how_a_california_suburban_retr.html.

4. Allan B. Jacobs, *Great Streets* (Cambridge, MA: MIT Press, 1995).

5. See official correspondence of the Association pour la Protection des Demeures Anciennes et Paysages Aixois (APDAPA), La "requalification" du Cours Mirabeau; Projet municipal et Contre-project, http://apdapa.free.fr/pages/cours/cours_projet_fr.htm and http://bit.ly/mirabeautranslate.

6. See the website of architect and urban designer Antoine Grumbach, http://www.antoinegrumbach.com/atelier/fiche/fiche.asp?projetid=50.

7. *Plan El Paso* is available online at http://www.planelpaso.org/.

8. See the Case Study on Gran Via de les Corts Catalanes in Barcelona, in Chapter 2.

9. Daniel Moylan, "Committed to the Cause," *Green Places* (June 2004): 32–34.

10. *Ibid.*, 32.

11. *Ibid.*, 33.

12. *Ibid.*, 34.

13. Simon Jenkins, "Rip Out the Traffic Lights and Railings," *The Guardian*, February 29, 2008, 36.

14. City of Cambridge, Massachusetts, Department of Public Works, "Five Year Sidewalk and Street Reconstruction Plan," http://www.cambridgema.gov/TheWorks/OurServices/Engineering/FiveYearPlan.pdf.

15. United States Department of Transportation, Federal Highway Administration, "Designing Sidewalks and Trails for Access." The first paragraph of the FHWA guidelines says, "Without sidewalks, public rights-of-way are inaccessible to all pedestrians." The short sentence sums up the attitude of most DOTs towards shared space. http://www.fhwa.dot.gov/environment/bicycle_pedestrian/publications/sidewalks/chap4a.cfm.

16. See also Peter Katz, *The New Urbanism: Towards an Architecture of Community* (New York: McGraw-Hill, 1994).

17. Susan Spano and Aviva Shen, "The 20 Best Small Towns in America," *Smithsonian*, May 2012, http://www.smithsonianmag.com/travel/The-20-Best-Small-Towns-in-America.html.

18. In conversation with John Massengale.

19. City Planning Commission, City of Cleveland, "Glossary of Terms," http://planning.city.cleveland.oh.us/cwp/glossary/glossary.php.

20. Hans Monderman (1945–2008) was a Dutch traffic engineer who pioneered modern concepts of shared space and reduced traffic-control markings, after seeing that excessive signage and specialized space were intended to improve safety, but ironically served to lull motorists into unsafe complacency. See "Hans Monderman and Shared Space" in this chapter.

21. Frank Bruni, "Bicycle Visionary," *New York Times*, September 10, 2011, http://www.nytimes.com/2011/09/11/opinion/sunday/bruni-janette-sadik-khan-bicycle-visionary.html.

22. The results of the competition were published in Anne Guiney and Brendan Crain, eds. *By the City/For the City: An Atlas of Possibility for the Future of New York* (New York, Multi-Story Books, 2011). Jane Jacobs Square is on page 192.

23. A speed table is a speed hump with a long, flat section in the middle, used for traffic calming. Cars crossing a speed table slow less than for a speed bump, because the flat "table" is longer than the wheelbase of the average car. Speed tables can be used anywhere along the street, but a current trend is to use them at the intersection with side roads along wide or heavily trafficked roads. In that location, the striped

pedestrian crossing runs across the speed table, signaling the entrance to a slower, less trafficked road.

24. Ray Oldenburg, *Celebrating the Third Place: Inspiring Stories about the "Great Good Places" at the Heart of Our Communities* (New York: Marlowe & Company, 2000), *passim.*

25. James Howard Kunstler, personal communication, March 17, 2012.

26. Justin Davidson, "The Greatest Building: 'If I Had To Pick One Tower, It Wouldn't Be The Empire State Building,'" *New York* (January 9, 2011), http://nymag.com/news/features/greatest-new-york/70475/.

27. The Architectural League of New York, "The Unfinished Grid, Design Speculations for Manhattan." http://archleague.org/2011/11/the-unfinished-grid-design-speculations-for-manhattan/.

28. In conversation with John Massengale, December 2012.

29. Gary Toth, "Where the Sidewalk Doesn't End: What Shared Space has to Share," *Project for Public Spaces*, Aug 17, 2009, http://www.pps.org/shared-space/. Also see "Can a Street Be a Place?" PlannersWeb, plannersweb.com/2010/05/can-a-street-be-a-place/.

30. See also Allan T. Shulman, ed. 53, *Miami Modern Metropolis: Paradise and Paradox in Midcentury Architecture and Planning* (Glendale, CA: Balcony Press, 2009), 233.

31. *Ibid.*, 238–39.

32. Albert Ullman, *A Landmark History of New York* (New York: D. Appleton & Co., 1901): 19. Also Wikipedia article "Stone Street, (Manhattan)" and "Lower Manhattan Streets and the Stories They Tell, lowermanhattan.info, http://www.lowermanhattan.info/news/downtown_street_names_and_44900.aspx.

33. David W. Dunlap, "Turning an Alley into a Jewel," *New York Times*, December 6, 2000, http://www.nytimes.com/2000/12/06/nyregion/commercial-real-estate-turning-an-alley-into-a-jewel.html.

34. Christopher Gray, "A Nod to New Amsterdam," *New York Times*, December 27, 2012, http://www.nytimes.com/2012/12/30/realestate/streetscapes-on-south-william-street-a-nod-to-new-amsterdam.html.

35. Dunlap, *op. cit.*

36. Jane Jacobs, *The Death and Life of Great American Cities* (New York: Random House, 1961), 178: "Condition 2: Most blocks must be short; that is streets and opportunities to turn corners must be frequent."

37. Guiney and Crain, 347.

38. For example, see William H. Whyte, *The Social Life of Small Urban Spaces* (New York: Project for Public Spaces, 2001): *passim.*

39. Matt Chaban, "Meet Me on 6½th Avenue: DOT Planning Public Promenade Through Middle of Midtown Towers," *New York Observer*, March 26, 2012, http://observer.com/2012/03/meet-me-on-6%C2%BDth-avenue-dot-planning-public-promenade-through-middle-of-midtown-towers/.

40. Ellen Dunham-Jones and June Williamson, *Retrofitting Suburbia, Urban Design Solutions for Redesigning Suburbs* (Hoboken: Wiley, 2009).

41. Bryan Walsh, "Recycling the Suburbs," *TIME*, March 12, 2009, http://www.time.com/time/specials/packages/article/0,28804,1884779_1884782_1884756,00.html.

42. "A charrette is a multiple-day, collaborative design workshop that harnesses the talents and energies of all interested parties to create and support a feasible plan that represents transformative community change. A charrette is five to nine consecutive days, allowing at least three design feedback loops. It is an open process that includes all interested parties and is focused on producing a feasible plan with minimal rework." National Charrette Institute, www.charretteinstitute.org.

43. Smart Growth America's website says, "Smart growth is a better way to build and maintain our towns and cities. Smart growth means building urban, suburban and rural communities with housing and transportation choices near jobs, shops and schools. This approach supports local economies and protects the environment." http://www.smartgrowthamerica.org/what-is-smart-growth.

44. Wikipedia describes Agenda 21 as a nonbinding, voluntarily implemented action plan of the United Nations with regard to sustainable development. Agenda 21 was signed by President G. H. W. Bush, even though it contains language that would be anathema to most Americans, including a statement against the appropriateness of private property ownership. http://en.wikipedia.org/wiki/Agenda_21.

45. The Mayors Institute on City Design, an activity of the Design Arts Program of the National Endowment for the Arts, may be seen as one of the most effective efforts to prepare elected officials for the task of leading retrofits. According to MICD founder Mayor Joe Riley of Charleston, South Carolina, "The mayor is the chief urban designer of every city."

CHAPTER FIVE
NEW STREETS

TWO VERY DIFFERENT DEVELOPMENTS from the early 1980s are important landmarks in the recent history of urban design and street design. Battery Park City, a ninety-two-acre extension of Manhattan in the Hudson River that was built on landfill from the construction site of the World Trade Center, has office towers, mid-rise and high-rise apartment buildings, and stores. Seaside, Florida, an eighty-acre development on the Florida panhandle, is a resort built in the form of a town. What the two places have in common is that their streets were designed with many of the placemaking principles outlined in this book. Both projects were a radical departure from conventional practice of the time. The histories of both demonstrate how auto-centric regulations across the country hinder the making of good streets.

It wasn't that people didn't understand the principles; by the early 1980s, they had been talked about and praised for at least two decades. Jane Jacobs wrote the enormously popular *The Death and Life of Great American Cities* in 1961, Bernard Rudofsky published *Streets for People*[1] (also very popular) in 1969, and William H. "Holly" Whyte had been publishing his influential studies of how people use urban space since the late 1960s.[2] Despite professional acceptance of the theories, however, most of the sprawl in America was built after the publication of *Death and Life*. Many planners endorsed these works, but the American Planning Association and its members continued to promote regulations based on an auto-centric separation of uses, with road standards established by the engineering profession's anti-urban Functional Classification system. "The pseudoscience of planning," Jacobs wrote, "seems almost neurotic in its determination to imitate empiric failure and to ignore empiric success."[3]

◀ Glenwood Park, Atlanta, Georgia. See Color Plate 34.

303

> Despite professional acceptance of Jane Jacobs' theories, most of the sprawl in America was built after the publication of *The Death and Life of Great American Cities*.

In the design world, many architects and urban designers quoted Jacobs as though she were a New Testament prophet, but the manifestation of her ideas in built works was slow in coming. A landmark event was New York Mayor John Lindsay's creation in 1966 of a municipal Urban Design Group, staffed with young architects who later went on to become important urban designers, like Robert A.M. Stern, Jaquelin Robertson, Jonathan Barnett, and Alex Cooper. Working in the context of America's largest and densest city, they chipped away at New York's 1961 Zoning Resolution, which institutionalized Le Corbusier's paradigm of making the building more important than the street.

Nevertheless, the city regulations affecting street design continued almost unchanged, favoring cars over pedestrians. When Cooper and his partner Stan Eckstut designed Battery Park City, New York's auto-centric regulations still required overscaled streets that were wider than the most common streets in the city's grid. The designers at Cooper Eckstut Associates knew how to design good streets and make good urbanism, but when it came to the size of the streets, their hands were tied.

They couldn't ignore city law, but their design was often innovative, paying little attention to many of the conventional planning standards of the day. It was customary then for a single architect and one developer to plan and build the entire project, usually by beginning with the design of the buildings and then putting in streets as necessary—a method of planning sometimes called Big Architecture. In fact, Battery Park City had an earlier tower-in-the-park plan designed that way, but Cooper Eckstut instead began with the street plan rather than the building or buildings, as urban designers should.

They brilliantly extended adjacent city streets through the site, giving long views to the Hudson River and the open sky over it. Using those through streets as a framework, they made a pattern of streets that produced normal New York City blocks, the antithesis of the super blocks that were still in vogue with most architects and planners at the time. On top of that, they laid a simple form-based code over the plan, so that the Battery Park City Authority could sell building lots to different developers with some confidence about what would be built.

The Seaside Community Development Corp. started construction of the resort on the Panhandle several months after the Battery Park City Authority began building. The development benefited from a trend in architectural education that was perhaps the biggest change in the twenty years between the publication of *Death and Life* and the parallel achievements of Battery Park City and Seaside. During that brief period in the late 1970s and much of the 1980s when Postmodernism and Modernism peacefully coexisted in the world of architecture (particularly in architecture schools), a renewed appreciation for the design of traditional cities and streets was somehow floating in the air. Practitioners like Stern, Cooper, Robertson, and Eckstut were teaching as well as practicing, and from 1973 on, students in schools around the country seemed to find their way to books like *Civic Art*[4] that had been literally gathering dust on the library shelves.

Occasionally, a new book made a strong impression. The bilingual *Rational Architecture Rationelle*[5] from Maurice Culot's Archives d'Architecture Moderne was treasured, particularly for its glimpses of the work of the architect Léon Krier. Although Krier had no built work at that time, his entry in a French competition to design a new neighborhood called La Villette came in second, behind a plan by Bernard Tschumi. For students poring over texts like *Civic Art*, Tschumi's scheme seemed like conventional planning of the time dressed up with French intellectual conceits, but Krier's design was eye-opening. It had some of the most beautiful drawings in the recent history of architecture and urbanism, but the ideas it illustrated were even better. Krier's entry was a fresh design for a normal European neighborhood, with streets and squares and a public realm with civic monuments. The concept was simple, but it was executed with an astonishing richness and invention unlike any other work being published at the time. It gave encouragement and inspiration to students who went on to become New Urbanists, Classical architects, or both.

At least part of the reason these students were open to studying old models was that they were one of the first generations to grow up in a world of cul-de-sacs and suburban arterials. They had personally experienced the old and the new, and they frequently found the latter lacking. Plus, there were the cases where the new models were proving to be just plain bad: the highly acclaimed and award-winning Pruitt Igoe, a textbook tower-in-the-park housing project in St. Louis, was such a disastrous social experiment that the city had to demolish it in 1972.

It was the students of that generation who designed Seaside a few years later in 1981, under the leadership of Miami developer Robert Davis and architect Andrés Duany. Davis was a little older than the others, but the entire team had three advantages that helped them design Seaside: no one on the team had designed a new town; the county on the Florida panhandle where they built Seaside had virtually no planning or building regulations; and although the market was in a recession when Davis started planning Seaside, he had inherited the land debt-free, so there was time to ponder what to do. Fate gave the team a *tabula rasa* to work on, and they designed a place on the Gulf Coast where they would enjoy spending time. Davis wanted a place where generations of families would come for the summer year after year, as he had with his grandparents. And there was talk of building Seaside so simply and reasonably that even architects would be able to afford a second house there.

When Davis revisited the site on the Gulf Coast, where he had been many times as a child, he was appalled to discover that the paradise he remembered was overrun with Miami-style condominium high-rises behind large parking lots. So Robert and Daryl Davis took Duany and his partner Elizabeth Plater-Zyberk touring in southern Alabama and on the Panhandle to look at local small towns and building types that Davis admired (Figure 6.27). Eventually, they came up with a plan that was essentially the program for a large resort hotel broken down into small parts. Instead of hotel rooms, they planned small houses arranged in the pattern of a small town, on normal streets. The spa was placed at the back of the town and called The

Country Club. The public meeting rooms and shops were the downtown, and so on.

A model for the streets of Seaside came from a nearby beach town called Grayton Beach, where Davis had spent many happy boyhood summers. Grayton had unpaved sandy roads and occasional boardwalks. Most of the time, people on foot shared the narrow roads with the cars. Davis was also influenced by *Streets for People*, calling Bernard Rudofsky one of his heroes.[6] And Duany, who had recently met Krier, brought him onboard as a consultant.

The Seaside streets they designed were narrow: there was a hierarchy of streets with different widths, but the most common width was eighteen feet. Outside of the downtown and a few other places, the streets had no sidewalks and no signs other than stop signs here and there and an occasional speed-limit sign. Davis experimented with various ideas before he settled on some of the details. The first road was paved with clay, but clay had wash problems in a hard rain, and it could be messy in a light rain as well. In the second year Davis switched to compacted oyster shells for the roadbed. The oyster shells could also have wash problems when it rained, and they were dusty when it was dry in the hot Florida sun. Davis settled on tinted concrete bricks, leaving the oyster shells by the side of the road where there were individual parking spaces.

Just as in Grayton Beach, walkers, cyclists, and cars shared the road, creating one of the first purpose-built "shared spaces" in America in many decades. As much as possible, the plan followed traces on the land of things like paths through the dune grass to the beach. On the highest point in Seaside, the plan had a small traffic circle with a gazebo in the center (Figures 5.61, 5.62, and 5.64).

The team took great care to make the streets comfortable places to be. In place of minimum setbacks for buildings, there were build-to lines, placed so that the buildings would shape the street. In other words, rather than saying that a house could be no closer to the street than twenty feet, the Seaside code specified that all houses on a particular street must be exactly ten feet from the street's edge, and no more. The build-to line for the downtown buildings was on the front lot line, and no downtown building could be set farther back.

After construction started in 1981, Seaside developed slowly. Davis set up a stand where he sold shrimp, sangria, and lots, and in the beginning he sold more sangria than land. But, as the market has proven time and again, because Americans in recent years have not made enough good *places*—places where people want to be—the law of supply and demand drives prices up for those smart enough to strike out on their own to meet an unfilled demand. Within a few years, the price of lots had gone from $11,000 to $100,000, and the last few of the four hundred or so lots sold for almost $4,000,000. Davis wanted to limit the number of houses simultaneously under construction, and every year there were too many buyers. So once he sold the number he wanted, he raised the prices in the fall or the winter to a point of sales resistance—but in the spring the buyers always came back, willing to pay that much more. It quickly became clear that Seaside would not be a place for impoverished architects. (Even the charrette members who received lots in lieu of cash or checks did not foresee Seaside's phenomenal success and most sold too early in the process, thinking they were making a good deal for themselves.)

With success, came problems. Impressed by Seaside, officials from the local county (Walton County) talked to Davis about how to spread the good fortune around. Davis sponsored some charrettes for critical pieces of land along the coast, and Walton County decided that planning was the secret to Seaside's success. Contacting the American Planning Association, it was given names of planning firms in and around Walton. To make a long story short, the Alabama firm hired by the county came up with a plan that immediately made many of the standards at Seaside illegal—including its distinctive street widths. Making matters worse, Davis was only partway through building Seaside when the rules were changed: in order to finish the rest as originally designed, he had to get a variance for each new section as he went along.

By the standards of the new countywide code, the streets were too narrow, and the way they "lay lightly on the land" didn't meet construction standards. Being designed to let water pass through the road and into the ground, the roads didn't have the required gutters and drains. Instead, the bricks were laid with pervious joints,

and the oyster-shell parking spaces were also pervious. The wider streets near downtown had a pipeless drainage system that directed the water to a large, grassy bowl in the center of town that fills with water in hard rains. The rest of the time, it serves as an open-air amphitheater.

Seaside was the first "New Urban" design to be built, and it garnered a lot of praise. In *TIME*, Kurt Andersen wrote that it was one of the best designs of the 1980s, calling Seaside "one of the most influential projects of the decade, and, hopefully, decades to come."[7] Around the country, similar projects began to appear. Not because they were copying Seaside, but because the time was right. The designers and builders of these projects quickly discovered that planning and zoning rules made it difficult or even impossible to build walkable, mixed-use places. Most of America by that time had regulations that prohibited anything other than arterial roads, collector roads, or cul-de-sacs, usually with engineering standards that required wide roads, clear-cut areas on both sides of the roads, and one-size-fits all requirements for drainage, on-site water retention, location of electrical supply boxes, and the like.

In 1993, Duany, Plater-Zyberk, Davis, Krier, and approximately two hundred others (including the authors) met in the Athenaeum in Alexandria, Virginia, at what was planned to be the first annual meeting of a new organization called the Congress for New Urbanism. The mission of the CNU was the advancement of walkable, sustainable cities, towns, and neighborhoods. Perhaps half the original membership was made up of architects who had rejected most of the planning principles they had been taught in school. One requirement for membership was a pledge not to contribute to sprawl. Many of the participants were passionate about their desire to create great streets, and there were many war stories about how difficult it was to do that.

So when you see a new street or a new retrofit that isn't quite right, remember that what you are looking at may not be what the designer wanted. The trailblazing new streets required the painful upending of two generations of entrenched bad practices, and many arguments about them were lost. Slowly, however, examples have emerged that prove Americans can again make civilized streets. The work is improving, and the evidence is mounting.

MAIN STREETS

Main Street, Rosemary Beach, Florida

Duany, Plater-Zyberk & Company, 1995

Main Street

Rosemary Beach is one of two resorts designed by Duany Plater-Zyberk & Company (DPZ) on the Florida Panhandle after the success of Seaside, where Robert Davis multiplied the value of his land more than a hundred times. Less than ten miles to the east, Rosemary Beach was developed by Leucadia National, a large holding and investment company. Their first plan for the site was more conventional than Seaside's, without a town center and with less emphasis on walkability. But after Leucadia learned that comparable houses in the area were selling for less than a third of the price of Seaside houses, the company hired Duany-Plater Zyberk & Company to develop a town plan for their site.

Selling exclusively to the rich was not Davis's intention when he started Seaside. Leucadia National, on the other hand, wanted to maximize the return on its investment,

and market analysis convinced the company that building its development in the form of a town would give it the highest returns. The scarcity of placemaking in American development during the last few decades means that many of our best designed places—new as well as old—get a significant sales premium.

By the time Leucadia hired DPZ in 1995, many developers and house builders had copied what they thought was the Seaside style of architecture. None of the new site plans, however, were designed for walkability. The developments repeated the conventional Florida model, with prominent garages on the street, direct access to the houses from the garages, and little or no emphasis on creating a comfortable public realm or making places to socialize. It was assumed that instead of walking downtown for dinner, people would get in their cars and drive a few miles to a restaurant.

The DPZ plan for Rosemary Beach made a downtown on both sides of the main road through Rosemary Beach, with restaurants, stores, offices, and public meeting places. The streets in the resort were designed to encourage walking to the town center and to the beach. The first

Figure 5.1: Main Street, Rosemary Beach, Florida. Duany, Plater-Zyberk & Company, 1995. The vertical facades of the two buildings that deflect the vista (and their lack of balconies) visually focus attention at the end of the vista.

block of Main Street, which leads down to the Gulf from the main square, is shown in Figure 5.1. Both at the top of the block and the bottom of the block the land is flat, which visually accentuates the slope of the street in between. Where the slope of the street changes, the angle of the street and the individual buildings along it do so as well, drawing one's attention to their decreasing height as they go down the hill, and thus drawing attention to the fall of the hill itself. The deflected vista at the end of the street means that no one seeing the street for the first time knows if the slope continues beyond the guesthouse that terminates the view. In fact, there is a flat lawn there, which makes a nice place to gather by the Gulf.

Northgate Street, El Paso, Texas

Dover, Kohl & Partners, 2010

Main Street

Once the largest shopping center in El Paso, the Northpark Mall opened in 1960. Like most "modern" malls constructed during that era, Northpark was designed to reflect the new auto-dominated culture of suburban America (Figure 5.2). A radically experimental landscape (that quickly became obsolete) emerged across the continent, one giant parking lot at a time. So, like most standard-issue malls, Northpark had a central megabuilding surrounded by parking fields, with land set aside for smaller commercial establishments along the adjacent highway. But retailing changed, El Paso changed, and the mall—like so many others—faded. After a few decades of steady decline, Northpark closed and was left unoccupied. The City of El Paso recently purchased the property, with plans to demolish the derelict building and redevelop most of the site. The new proposal for Northpark and the nearby Northgate transit stop could become a showcase for reinvigorating suburbia with mixed-use and transit-oriented development. Most important, a street pattern anchored by Northgate Street will be set up in place of the mall (Figure 5.3).

The mall was an isolated place for shopping and little else. The new design will change the property into a more complete, livable community with considerable amounts of housing and other uses that complement the retail. Located at the northern terminus of one of the city's new bus rapid transit (BRT) corridors, the site is an ideal candidate for new development. The complete, walkable neighborhood that will replace the mall is designed around the BRT transfer station, placing public transportation at the center of daily life.

Figure 5.2: Northpark Mall, El Paso, Texas. Existing conditions in 2010. The sprawl experiment eventually led to spectacular commercial failures like this one, all over North America.

Figure 5.3: Northgate Transit-Oriented Development, El Paso, Texas. Dover, Kohl & Partners, 2010. Aerial view of proposed retrofit of the Northgate Mall. A network of blocks and streets will replace the single super-parcel of the dead mall. © *2010 Dover, Kohl & Partners*

Figure 5.4: Northgate Street, El Paso, Texas. Dover, Kohl & Partners, 2010. A watercolor rendering of the proposed redesign of the Northgate Mall. Where the former mall was introverted, Northgate Street's buildings will be extroverted, facing the street with storefronts, windows, and balconies. © *2010 Dover, Kohl & Partners*

Northgate may no longer be able to support an oversized shopping complex, but a significant number of shops and businesses can nevertheless thrive in an urban neighborhood. Northgate Street (Figure 5.4) will become the main street for northeast El Paso, with mixed-use buildings that have retail on the ground floor and apartments or offices above. Wide sidewalks lined with shade trees will provide ample room for outdoor dining.

Awnings and arcades along the storefronts are designed to create shelter from the elements.

In addition to the on-street spaces, most parking will be in the center of the block, to avoid large parking lots facing the streets. As the spine of the neighborhood, Northgate Street will be the route of choice for connecting the surrounding community to the rapid transit system.

CENTRAL BRANDEVOORT, THE NETHERLANDS / Paul Murrain

KK Architects and Paul van Beek landschappen BNT, 1996–Present

Main Street & Neighborhood Streets

Brandevoort is a new town on the outskirts of Helmond in the Dutch province of Brabant. When completed, it will house 17,000 residents on a 365-hectare (900-acre) site. A project from the studio of Rob Krier and Christophe Kohl, Brandevoort is emblematic of their belief in acknowledging and celebrating the familiar, modifying where necessary, innovating in many ways, but always remaining firmly embedded in the traditions of place that have evolved over many centuries (Figure 5.5). The community of the town of Helmond specified its desire for this type of design. Both Krier and Kohl studied the typologies of other local towns, and characteristics of Dutch facades were catalogued. Street, block, plot, and type are the tools of their trade.

The Urban and Architectural Codes: Working in Tandem

In so far as it is feasible today, Brandevoort manifests the New Urbanist dictum of "one code, many hands."

So, in both product and process, the fine-grained adaptation of the building stock is a striking feature of its streets. There are never two adjacent buildings by the same architects, exceptions only being made for important sites—for example, where Krier and Kohl required specific compositions for the termination of a vista. The other architects were at ease with this, aware that they were designing for a place where creativity was channeled towards a common language.

> In so far as it is feasible today, Brandevoort manifests the New Urbanist dictum of "one code, many hands."

It is the common language of the code that gives the "variety within a pattern" that typifies most places people find desirable. The street codes in Brandevoort are produced for different locations within the central area, including the primary streets that meet at its heart (and adapt an old country road), a secondary street system, and a specific type that runs around the perimeter, overlooking drainage canals and native vegetation.

Figure 5.5: De Plaetse, Brandevoort, the Netherlands. KK Architects, 1996–Present. A view of a typical residential street in 2009. *Image courtesy of Paul Murrain*

Street Composition

After the elements of the code were established, the crucial stage of composing full street elevations by manipulating these elements in peer review was arguably the most unusual aspect of the project. Krier and Kohl referenced traditional Dutch townhouse facades for inspiration; the three-bay elevation is dominant on the three-story buildings in central Brandevoort that have dormers in the roof (Figures 5.6, 5.7, 5.8, and 5.9). Traditionally, two-story dwellings and narrower plots have two bays, but, again, symmetrically composed with immense variety. On occasion, the gable faces the street. Within this underlying pattern the possibilities for variety are many.

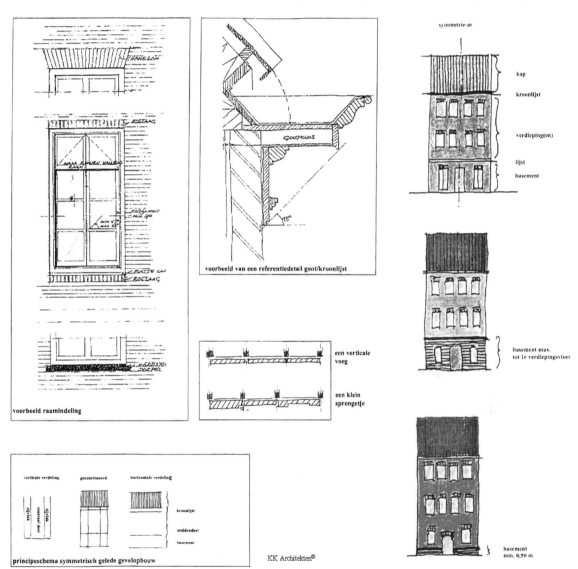

Figure 5.6: De Veste, Brandevoort, the Netherlands. KK Architects, 1997–Present. Urban codes for the rowhouse facades defined in the "image quality plan." *Archives KK Architects, Berlin*

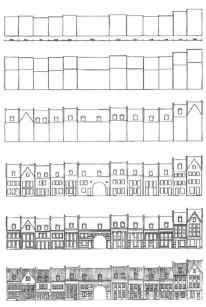

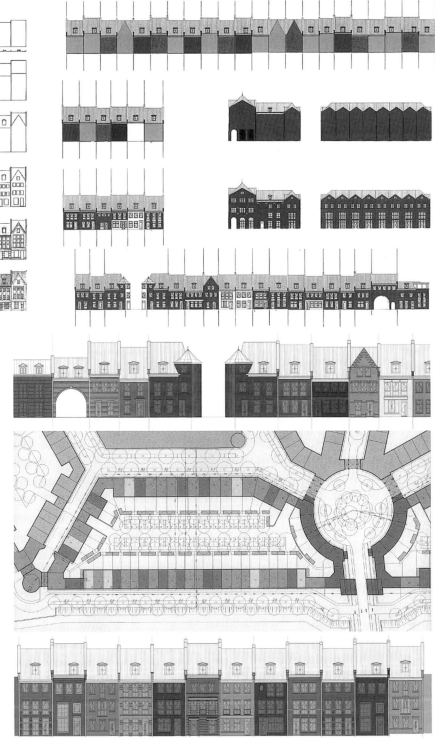

Figure 5.7: De Veste, Brandevoort, the Netherlands. KK Architects, 1997–Present. Sketch made during the facade design process for the groups of rowhouses. Within a subtle range, designers vary heights, widths roofs, dormers, fenestration, materials, and ornament. *Archives KK Architects, Berlin*

Figure 5.8: De Veste, Brandevoort, the Netherlands. KK Architects, 1997–Present. Drawings made for the coordination of plan and elevation during the rowhouse design process. *Archives KK Architects, Berlin*

Figure 5.9: De Veste, Brandevoort, the Netherlands. KK Architects, 1997–Present. Study sketches. The underlying pattern permits immense variety despite the repetition of the type, using subtle manipulations of a few basic elements. *Archives KK Architects, Berlin*

Characteristically, the greatest freedom of expression is in the fenestration, which is again held together compositionally by the underlying patterns (Figures 5.10, 5.11, 5.12, 5.13, and 5.14). The Dutch are at ease with displaying the interior of their dwellings to the street outside, even with the smallest unfenced privacy strip (Figure 5.15). Historically, the proportion of window to wall is significant, particularly on the first two floors of the three-story types. But this often involves the use of mullions and fine-grained glazing bars that operate as a filter when compared with sizeable, single panes of glass.

The higher density streets of apartment buildings in the heart of central Brandevoort break these underlying patterns to a greater extent, being different and more

recent building types (Figure 5.16). And yet even here it is evident that street composition played a significant role. Corners are afforded more freedom in order to allow building continuity at a variety of angles in the deformed grid, resulting in a number of prominent hipped roofs. (These at times can appear a little contrived.)

For the pedestrian, the streets of central Brandevoort serve up a superb urban experience because the horizontality of the street perspective is arrested by the powerful vertical emphasis expressed in the narrow plot subdivision. There are vertical proportions in facades and a subtle variety of reveals behind a relatively consistent frontage line. The ordered visual richness and overall permeability invites the pedestrian forward.

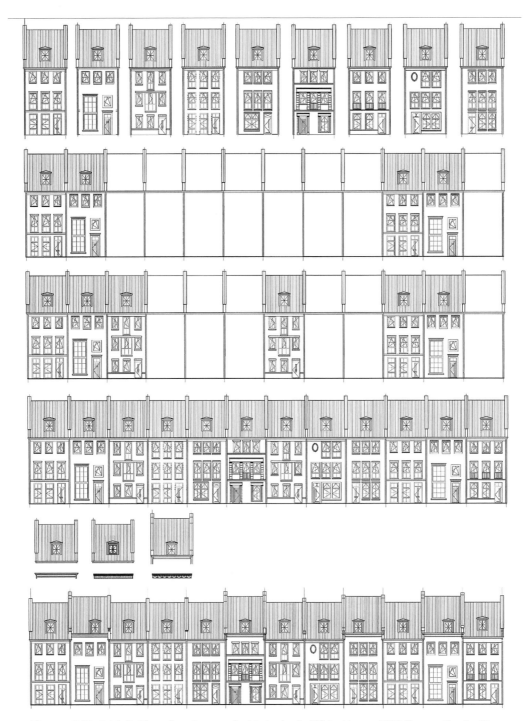

Figures 5.10–5.14: De Veste, Brandevoort, the Netherlands. KK Architects, 1997–Present. Studies illustrating the process of designing the rowhouse facades. *Archives KK Architects, Berlin*

Figure 5.15: De Veste, Brandevoort, the Netherlands. KK Architects, 1997–Present. Completed facades. *Archives KK Architects, Berlin*

Figure 5.16: Biezenlann / Koolstraat, Brandevoort, the Netherlands. KK Architects, 1997–Present. A street with a mixture of apartments and rowhouses. *Image courtesy of Paul Murrain*

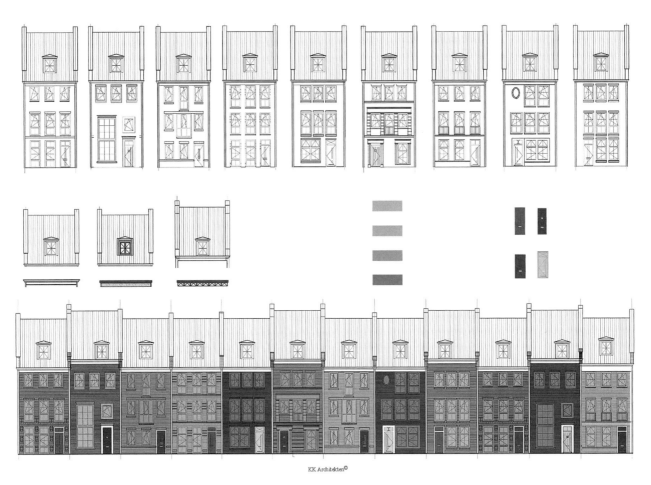

KK Architekten©

Figure 5.17: Central Brandevoort, the Netherlands. KK Gesellschaft von Architekten, 1997–2017. Composition of facades: subtle variations create an ordered visual richness down to the doors and windows. *Archives KK Architects, Berlin*

LONGMOOR STREET, POUNDBURY, ENGLAND / Léon Krier

Léon Krier, 1998

Main Street

Longmoor is one of the six radial streets of Middle Farm Quarter fanning out from its center, Middle-marsh Square. It is 250 meters long, between 7 and 12 meters wide, and rises on a low gradient towards Burraton Square, the western gate to the Quarter (Figures 5.18 and 5.19). This first quarter of Poundbury is so named because of the old Duchy of Cornwall farm, which for two centuries dominated the rolling countryside with its majestic beech-tree crown. Half-moon shaped, the quarter nestles into a natural topographic bowl, the market square occupying the bottom. The Village Hall and the Market Tower[8] form the visual foci for the radiating streets. They also dominate the long prospect of the preexisting Cambridge Road, the suburban road linking Middle Farm eastwards to the historic center of Dorchester, seat of the regional government. Longmoor Street is, in fact, the continuation of the Cambridge Road axis. The Market Square has thus become an urban heart not just for Middle Farm but for the neighboring Cambridge Road suburb as well.

The West Dorset District Council and the residents of the suburb refused initially all vehicular or pedestrian connections with the new Middle Farm urban quarter. We designed and built connections, nevertheless, erecting bollards to checkmate the opposition. When, after years of refusal, Cambridge Road residents expressed the wish to be linked, the Middle Farm Residents Association refused the offer. The bollards still stand as monuments to the motorized-cul-de-sac-attitude. Indeed, the urban network of Poundbury is at various points absurdly blocked by bollards to this day, totem poles of an immoderate "Health and Safety" cult. In fact, we control speed ranges by design and geometry rather than by signage and obstacles. There has not been an accident in nearly twenty years.

The street-section of Longmoor is of variable widths, and the facades are at times interrupted by garden walls, allowing large trees to spread their leafy crowns into an otherwise rather narrow public space. The setting back of some houses articulates at once the street and mews frontages, avoiding the excessive repetition of house or garage alignments. A subtle curving of the street axis allows for a dramatic sequential deployment of private and public buildings. The nonparallel runs of facades, curbs, and sidewalks caused the planning authorities the same anxieties as my refusal of cul-de-sacs.

The sheer countless versions of the master plan of this phase resulted not from design indecision but from the necessity to overcome unrelenting bureaucratic chicanery, eager to enforce strict obedience to suburban design guidelines, while realizing a piece of true city. At some point my line-drawing perspectives caused such hand-wringing despair amongst authorities and consultants that my clients had them redrawn by graphic artists from the development and real-estate milieu. The little horrors still adorn the office walls of the Duchy of Cornwall. Now only surviving in a poor 35-mm slide, Carl Laubin's beautiful original oil painting based on my sketch (Figure 5.20 and Color Plate 18) was meticulously dissected by a palace-crisis-committee. It then issued a painstakingly detailed report instructing Carl on how to edulcorate his masterpiece or face its extinction.

The same committee replaced my open Market Hall by the Village Hall, whereas we had envisioned the latter on a different square on higher ground dominating Ashington Street, another major radial street overlooking the open countryside. The monumental gable and perron would have created another civic magnet for this quarter, marking a prominent symbolic articulation on the public park at the town edge.

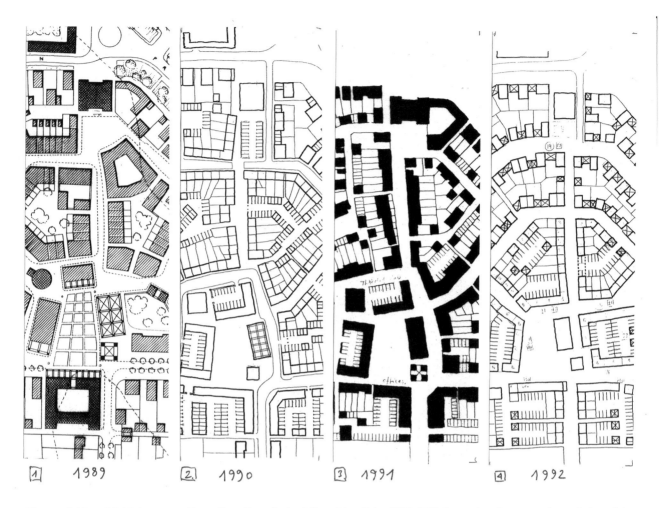

1989   1990   1991   1992

Figures 5.18 and 5.19: Longmoor Street, Poundbury, England. Plans. Léon Krier, 1989-1992. Successive plans trace the evolution of the Longmoor Street design. *Images courtesy of Léon Krier*

The character of the street and two squares is decidedly urban, while both public and private buildings are held in a vernacular tone; more formal architecture and paving are reserved for the Civic Center of the New Town of Poundbury, Queen Mother Square, now under construction. The architecture of the Tower and Village Hall and the Burraton House Employment Center, on Burraton Square, are without rhetoric or figural adornments, their monumentality being achieved by sheer size of whole and detail, creating a strong contrast with the modest

shopfronts, houses, and garden walls (Figure 5.21). The master plan premise of variously sized, shaped, and used lots has been generally followed on Longmoor; however, the ground floors of the entire street were originally to be occupied by shops. The West Dorset District Council opposes the idea of commercial high streets in Poundbury for fear of unwanted competition with the Historic Center of Dorchester. We are therefore only allowed to have continuous commercial frontage on the quarters' main squares (Figures 5.22 and 5.23).

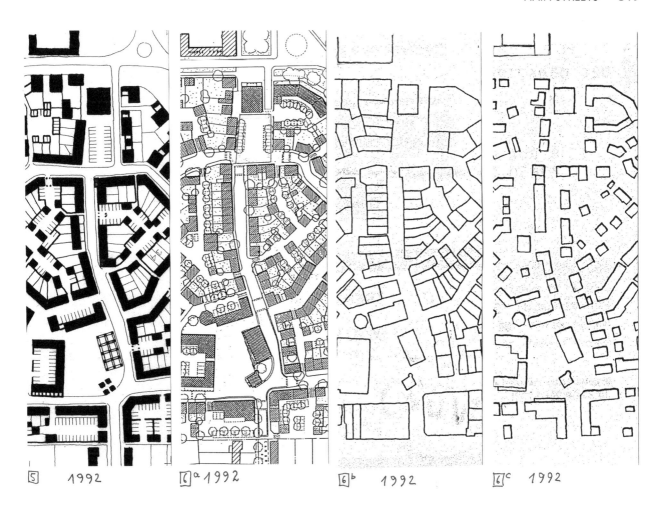

5   1992   6ᵃ 1992   6ᵇ   1992   6ᶜ   1992

Only natural building materials and lime-based render are used for building elements. Curbstones are
of local Purbeck stone and laid in unequal lengths
and widths. At the time our builders were able to
buy local stone more cheaply than international
products. Roads are paved in blacktop, sidewalks
and mews in a clear gravel. Market Square and Burraton Square are paved as "shared spaces." Given
the fact that the varied lot shapes, sizes, and uses,
the vernacular urban geometry, and the volumetric
compositions by themselves ensure a rich formal
articulation, I had desired a greater uniformity

in building materials than what actually became
policy. After nearly twenty years of aging, however,
the effects of weathering and planting have attenu-
ated the impression of an initially too-rich palette of
color and materials. This is a quality we are able
to achieve now at once, thanks to the lessons
learnt.

Only natural building materials and lime-based render
are used for building elements.

Figure 5.20: Longmoor Street, Poundbury, England. Perspective. Léon Krier, 1922. Study sketch looking east. Perspective shows the more open market hall and tower originally envisioned for the focal point of the village. *Image courtesy of Léon Krier*

Figure 5.21: Longmoor Street, Poundbury, England. Léon Krier, 1989–1992. Study sketch looking west. *Image courtesy of Léon Krier*

Figures 5.22 and 5.23: Market Square, Poundbury, England. Sketches. Léon Krier, 1992. Studies showing the public and private buildings framing the square. *Images courtesy of Léon Krier*

Figure 5.24: Longmoor Street, Poundbury, England. Comparative study—Traditional. Léon Krier, 1992. The architectural language matters; in this depiction, an immersive environment is created from traditional forms in harmony. *Image courtesy of Léon Krier*

Figure 5.25: Longmoor Street, Poundbury, England. Comparative study—Modernist. Léon Krier, 1996. In this sketch, Krier illustrates the same spaces shaped into another kind of immersive environment—still consistent, but now one of dissonant, individualized forms. *Image courtesy of Léon Krier*

Figure 5.26: Longmoor Street, Poundbury, England. Comparative study—mixed styles. Léon Krier, 1996. In this version, Krier combines the two into an absurd mixture; "anything goes" is not an adequate instruction for placemaking. *Image courtesy of Léon Krier*

Figure 5.27: Poundbury, England. Aerial perspective. Léon Krier, 1989. *Image courtesy of Léon Krier*

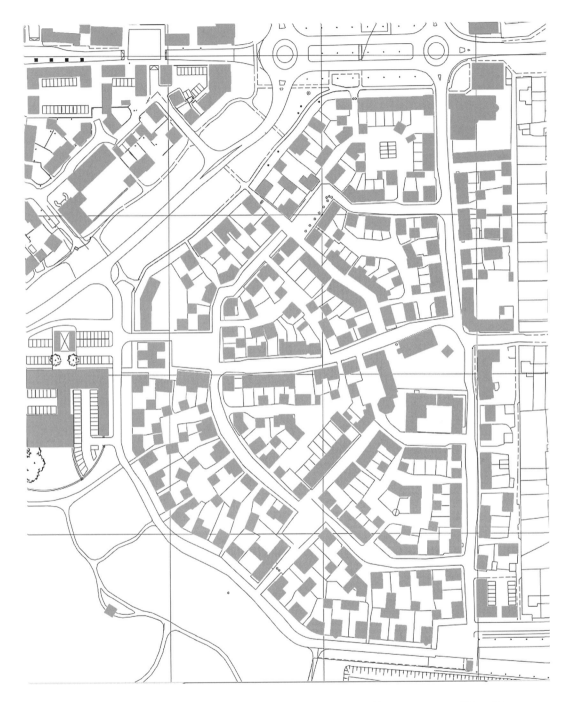

Figure 5.28: Middle Farm Quarter, Poundbury, England. Plan. Léon Krier, 1992. *Image courtesy of Léon Krier*

MARKET STREET, HABERSHAM, BEAUFORT, SOUTH CAROLINA / Thomas Low

Duany Plater-Zyberk & Company, 1997

Main Street

Adapted in part from the *Light Imprint Handbook,* New Urban Press, 2008

With a sizable town center, the new town of Habersham will serve as an urban hub for surrounding villages.

Market Street and Le Chene Circle are located in the heart of the town center and contain a post office, a fire station, restaurants, and a few dozen live–work units that provide living space above street-level commercial space (Figures 5.29 and 5.30). Together, Market Street and Le Chene Circle help to distinguish Habersham as a community that values sustainable development.

Figure 5.29: Market Street, Habersham, Beaufort, South Carolina. Duany Plater-Zyberk & Company, 1997. Looking north.

Figure 5.30: Le Chene Circle, Habersham, Beaufort, South Carolina. Duany Plater-Zyberk & Company, 1997. Looking southwest.

Initiated in 1997, the design and construction of Habersham can be seen as a case study for Duany Plater-Zyberk & Company's Light Imprint initiative. The initiative is designed to provide a framework for the design of sustainable neighborhoods based on New Urban planning principles. Some of the infrastructure is based on low-tech practices for providing good environmental design. By approaching each site as a unique entity, a Light Imprint system of stormwater management creates compact, walkable neighborhoods. Habersham has over thirteen thousand linear feet of marsh frontage, making the site especially sensitive to pollution from stormwater runoff and yet an ideal candidate for showcasing Light Imprint strategies.

The 283-acre site is crossed by a number of small creeks that drain into the Broad River marshes. Seventy-three acres of the site have been preserved for parks, common areas, and natural drainage basins.

Mature vegetation along the marsh edge has created a natural windbreak and an inviting habitat for wildlife. Extensive ecological analysis and tree surveys were conducted at the beginning of the design process; as a result, wetland preservation and marsh buffers became an important part of the master plan.

Additional Light Imprint techniques found on Market Street and Le Chene Circle include narrow streets with sidewalks on one side, pedestrian spaces constructed with pea gravel (Figure 5.31), and large medians planted with trees. Because these pervious surfaces and their arrangement help to slow down, percolate, and cleanse the runoff on rainy days, they assist with proper stormwater management and drainage patterns. Such initiatives are present throughout Habersham but are adjusted according to context—whether in the center of town, where development is most dense, or at the suburban edge, where development is characteristically less dense (Figures 5.32 and 5.33).

Figure 5.31: Le Chene Circle in Habersham, Beaufort, South Carolina. Duany Plater-Zyberk & Company, 1997. Looking southwest, showing pervious pea gravel path. The "Light Imprint" approach at Habersham does not call attention to itself as stormwater infrastructure, because it looks and feels like traditional Lowcountry placemaking.

Figure 5.32: Harford Street, Habersham, Beaufort, South Carolina. Duany Plater-Zyberk & Company, 1997. Looking west, towards townhouses in the center of Habersham.

Figure 5.33: St. Phillips Boulevard, Habersham, Beaufort, South Carolina. Duany Plater-Zyberk & Company, 1997.

LIGHT IMPRINT URBANISM / Thomas Low

Green Infrastructure and Community Design

Low Impact Development (LID) and Light Imprint both offer systems for greener, more environmentally friendly stormwater infrastructure. However, LID adopted through standard ordinances can promote sprawl, since its primary solutions are to push apart the impervious surfaces cities always have and wrap buildings with more (albeit smaller) ponds and trenches. This occupies more land for the same amount of development and disrupts walkability. Light Imprint uses many of the same tools found in LID, including a range of more pervious surfaces, but Light Imprint is a system of treatments that are context-sensitive. By approaching each site as a unique entity, a Light Imprint system of stormwater management creates compact, walkable neighborhoods.

Light Imprint addresses these issues through a transect-based stormwater management system that integrates community design with tools found in LID. Light Imprint introduces a tool set for stormwater runoff that uses natural drainage, traditional engineering infrastructure, and infiltration practices. These tools are to be used collectively at the sector, neighborhood, and block scale. Light Imprint offers context-sensitive design solutions that work together on the community level. These design solutions highlight tools that are appropriate from the rural to the urban condition.

In the *Light Imprint Handbook*, a transect-based matrix organizes over sixty tools and resources in a simple, useful form. The right Light Imprint tools to use in a given situation are identified using the matrix, based on variables. These variables include soil hydrology, slope condition, climate, initial costs, long-term maintenance factors, and Urban to Rural Transect zones. Once these variables have been analyzed, a customized palette of tools specific to the project's needs emerges.[9] Since Habersham is located near the Atlantic Ocean, heavy squalls can produce a large amount of rain there in a short time. The region is also prone to rainfall accumulations from tropical storms and hurricanes, making storm-

water management a key consideration. Most of the street paving in Habersham is asphalt. It is a relatively cost-effective and readily available material. However, the impervious surfaces are minimized by keeping each street as narrow as is practical given its function.

Light Imprint: Materials and Configurations at Habersham

- Paving
  - Wood Planks
  - Crushed Stone/Shell
  - Asphalt
  - Concrete
  - Pea Gravel

- Channeling
  - Vegetative/Stone Swale
  - Slope Avenue
  - Shallow Channel Footpath
  - Concrete Pipe
  - Gutter

- Storage
  - Retention Basin with Sloping Bank
  - Retention Pond
  - Landscaped Tree Wells

- Filtration
  - Wetland/Swamp
  - Filtration Ponds
  - Shallow Marsh
  - Surface Landscape
  - Natural Vegetation
  - Constructed Wetland
  - Green Finger

NEIGHBORHOOD STREETS

Grace Park Way, Habersham, Beaufort, South Carolina

Duany, Plater-Zyberk & Company, 1997

Neighborhood Street

In the center of Habersham, lots are small and streets are edged with curbs. Away from the center, at the neighborhood edge, lots for the single-family houses are bigger and the streets gently become more suburban and rural near the marshfront. Grace Park Way (Figure 5.34) is in this section of the Traditional Neighborhood Development. It is notable that, even here, streets remain in a connected pattern, and a strong building-to-street relationship is legible, while lot sizes and the scale of houses vary.

Grace Park Way has a series of cottages on fourteen medium-sized building lots with shallow front yards. The street is narrow, without curbs, and shady. The pavement has an approximate width of eighteen feet, which allows two-way traffic to pass but discourages fast driving (Figure 5.35).

Even from the suburban areas within its range of Rural to Urban Transect zones, Habersham is walkable (Figures 5.36, 5.37, and 5.38). A range of businesses and neighborhood institutions is within walking distance, so a car isn't mandatory for every errand. Grace Park is less than half a mile away from the center of Habersham.

Figure 5.34: Grace Park Way, Habersham, Beaufort, South Carolina. Duany Plater-Zyberk & Company, 1997. Looking northeast toward Mum Grace Park. The cottages and the curbless street are in the T3, or Suburban, transect zone.

Figure 5.35: Grace Park Way, Habersham, Beaufort, South Carolina. Duany Plater-Zyberk & Company, 1997. The developer chose an unusual number for the speed limit so that people would notice it and remember.

Figure 5.36: St. Phillips Boulevard, Habersham, Beaufort, South Carolina. Duany Plater-Zyberk & Company, 1997. Looking north across St. Phillips Pond.

Figure 5.37: Mum Grace Park, Habersham, Beaufort, South Carolina. Duany Plater-Zyberk & Company, 1997. The lower-density edge.

Figure 5.38: South Park Way, Habersham, Beaufort, South Carolina. Duany Plater-Zyberk & Company, 1997. At the neighborhood edge, the Light Imprint street is curbless and winding, saving mature trees.

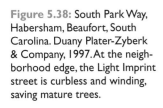

Crystal Lake Drive, Hammond's Ferry, North Augusta, South Carolina

Dover, Kohl & Partners, 2005

Neighborhood Street

Hammond's Ferry is an infill development in the heart of downtown North Augusta, South Carolina. A new neighborhood on the Savannah River, the planned area has two hundred acres that stretch one mile along the river, directly across from Augusta, Georgia. Eventually Hammond's Ferry will have shops, offices, and apartments in mixed-use buildings, and 800 to 1,500 attached and free-standing houses. It is being built by the North Augusta Riverfront Company, an affiliate of Leyland Alliance.

Crystal Lake Drive (Figures 5.39 and 5.40) is emblematic of the attitude the neighborhood founders adopted for Hammond's Ferry. It is a traditional neighborhood street, designed to show the houses well and constructed around a sequence of pedestrian experienc-

Figure 5.39: Crystal Lake Drive, Hammond's Ferry, North Augusta, South Carolina. Dover, Kohl & Partners, 2005. Section. © 2013 Dover, Kohl & Partners

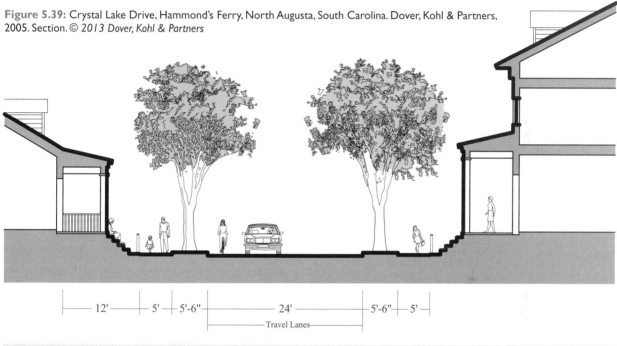

Figure 5.40: Crystal Lake Drive, Hammond's Ferry, North Augusta, South Carolina. Dover, Kohl & Partners, 2005. Elevations along Crystal Lake Drive. © 2005 Dover, Kohl & Partners

Figure 5.41: Crystal Lake Drive, North Augusta, South Carolina. Dover, Kohl & Partners, 2005. Aerial view. *Image courtesy of Pictometry International Corp. Copyright 2013*

Figure 5.42: Hammond's Ferry, North Augusta, South Carolina. Dover, Kohl & Partners, 2005. In the past, downtown North Augusta was cut off from its riverfront; Hammond's Ferry unites the two. *© 2005 Dover, Kohl & Partners*

es. During the planning process, Dover-Kohl visualized the experience of walking from Georgia Avenue, across the new trail that girds the historic downtown, through the neighborhood to the riverfront park, along the esplanade, and back again. Crystal Lake Drive literally follows that sequence as it makes the crucial connection between the older neighborhoods of downtown North Augusta and the new settlement on the riverfront. In the past, downtown North Augusta was cut off from its riverfront. The idea for Crystal Lake Drive was to rein-

force the new, direct connection between the two in a memorable way.

For most of its length, Crystal Lake Drive is lined with a range of different types of housing—some houses grand and large, others small and modest, as well as rowhouses and apartment buildings (Figures 5.41 and 5.42). Small businesses are taking root within the growing neighborhood, and this becomes evident as the street intersects with Railroad Street. Subtle "cranks" or turns in the street tame traffic and create a village character by closing and opening the vista. For example, at one point the street takes a substantial Z-turn and the space widens out into a small neighborhood green. The green is unusually shaped, almost like two guitar picks placed back to back. This has the effect of giving the whole set of adjoining houses unique addresses and views.

Although much of Hammonds Ferry will take a generation or more to build out, this street already feels "grown in"; it does not look like just another housing subdivision (Figures 5.43, 5.44, 5.45, and 5.46). This is an example of what can be done with brand new streets to establish both community character and a market position early on. The first phase of construction is complete, and the sequence of experiences along the street showcases two key ideas about Hammonds Ferry. First is the pleasant new connectedness between the river

Figure 5.43: Crystal Lake Drive, Hammond's Ferry, North Augusta, South Carolina. Dover, Kohl & Partners, 2005. Front porches, not garage doors, face the street space. *Image courtesy of Joseph Kohl*

Figure 5.44: Crystal Lake Drive, Hammond's Ferry, North Augusta, South Carolina. Dover, Kohl & Partners, 2005. Mixing businesses, houses, and apartments feels natural at Hammond's Ferry, but it is rare today in newly developed neighborhoods. *Image courtesy of Joseph Kohl*

Figure 5.45: Crystal Lake Drive, Hammond's Ferry, North Augusta, South Carolina. Dover, Kohl & Partners, 2005. Informal on-street parking means drivers going in opposite directions occasionally have to yield, keeping speeds down. *Image courtesy of Joseph Kohl*

Figure 5.46: Crystal Lake Drive, Hammond's Ferry, North Augusta, South Carolina. Dover, Kohl & Partners, 2005. Where sizable houses face Crystal Lake Drive at Arrington Street, the other side of the same block has a grouping of modestly-sized cottages. The street designs lend themselves to variety in households and building types. *Image courtesy of Joseph Kohl*

and the rest of the town. Second is the neighborliness. Most homes have porches, stoops, balconies, and verandas within "conversational distance"[10] of the sidewalk. Everywhere, doors and windows face the public spaces, supplying "eyes on the street"[11] for a sense of safety and community.

The roadbed is generally twenty-four feet wide. When cars park in the informal, unmarked spaces on both sides, drivers going in opposite directions occasionally have to yield. The street widens into a slightly splayed form just before reaching the riverfront park and esplanade, opening sight lines to and from the waterfront.

Newpoint Road, Newpoint, Lady's Island, South Carolina

Vince Graham, Robert Turner, and Gerald Cowart, 1991

Neighborhood Street

Newpoint Road was the first street built in the breakthrough development of Newpoint—an early neo-traditional neighborhood across the Beaufort River from Beaufort's historic Old Point (Figure 5.47). Designed and largely developed before the term "New Urbanism" had been widely adopted, Newpoint Road has several important physical qualities that make it a model alternative to typical suburban streets of the time. First, great care was taken to save the trees on the property; the street was threaded in between particularly impressive oaks. Second, the architecture along the streets in Newpoint was largely inspired by the Lowcountry coastal vernacular style seen, for example, on nearby Craven Street in Beaufort. Together, the big trees and traditional architecture made Newpoint Road seem especially natural in its setting, to the point where it seemed almost instantly as if it had always been there. Locals started calling Newpoint Road the neighborhood's "historic district" about two years after the houses were built.

Third, although the house lots at Newpoint were not platted in an especially compact size because of local regulatory requirements at the time, some visual sleight of hand makes the scene feel neighborly and close; the lots are deep and narrow, with the narrow side along the street, and the houses are pushed forward on their lots and close to one another. In one stroke this design decision made the backyards more spacious and brought the houses within what developers Bob Turner and Vince Graham called "conversational distance from the sidewalk" (Figure 5.48).

Fourth, the calm visual impression and slow traffic speed on the street result from some simple, clever detailing. There is a moderate curb-to-curb width, an

Figure 5.47: Newpoint Road, Lady's Island, South Carolina. V. Graham, R. Turner, and G. Cowart, 1991. Looking west. The developers carefully built around the old trees, so that Newpoint Road looks like an old street, even in person. In reality, the new street looks better than the old, second-growth woods that covered much of the flat site.

Figure 5.48: Newpoint Road, Lady's Island, South Carolina. V. Graham, R. Turner, and G. Cowart, 1991. The porches on Newpoint Road are within "conversational distance" of the sidewalk.

eight-foot planting strip, and a five-foot sidewalk. But the pavement surface is an old-school, exposed-aggregate asphalt that is slightly rough and matte-textured, unlike the shiny butter-smooth paving used in most residential subdivisions. This has the effect of discouraging speeders, yet it also makes Newpoint seem older and more natural.

Last, since Newpoint Road is long and straight, the developers interrupted the straightaway with a small diversion around a gazebo (Figure 5.49). The gazebo itself is architecturally understated but highly visible, with its red roof and white columns silhouetted against the green backdrop. Urbanists familiar with the Lowcountry will immediately recognize the precedent, at St. Philips Church in Charleston; the radically different scale and level of monumentality in these two examples shows how some design ideas are adaptable independent of scale and transect zone (Figures 2.136 and 2.137). Motorists see the gazebo from far down the street and slow down to go around it. When the developers were first requesting permits to build Newpoint, engineers and inspectors weren't sure what to call this unconventional feature. Turner and Graham settled on "horizontal speed bump"; that sounded familiar enough, and they got their permits.

Newpoint became an influential prototype for a revamped vision of suburbia, one in which the character of the public spaces between buildings mattered more to home buyers than the quantity of space inside the house or the acreage of the lot.

Bartram Street & Brasfield Square, Glenwood Park, Atlanta, Georgia

Dover, Kohl & Partners and Tunnell-Spangler-Walsh & Associates, 2001

Neighborhood Street

Glenwood Park broke with the development industry's old habits and introduced the Atlanta region to new ways of doing things. Lots of things. It's a brownfield reclamation project, a traditional neighborhood, an infill development, a green-building trendsetter, a transit-ready development, a mixed-use/mixed-income/mixed-tenure neighborhood center, a small-is-beautiful business model—and an exemplar of walkable streets (Figures 5.50, 5.51, and 5.52).

The twenty-eight-acre site, formerly home to a concrete plant, was organized into a neighborhood around an elliptical park. It was developed by Green Street Properties. The urban form of the neighborhood reflects the developers' goal to "maximize the mixing" of daily activities. Unlike every other local example of production building at the time, dwelling types, small businesses, and recreation were blended together in a fine-grained way.[12] The project emphasizes walkability, diversity, quality over quantity, and the importance of the public realm.

Figure 5.49: Newpoint Road, Lady's Island, South Carolina. V. Graham, R. Turner, and G. Cowart, 1991. Traffic calming as a byproduct of placemaking: drivers have to slow down to go around the gazebo that interrupts the straight street and terminates the vista.

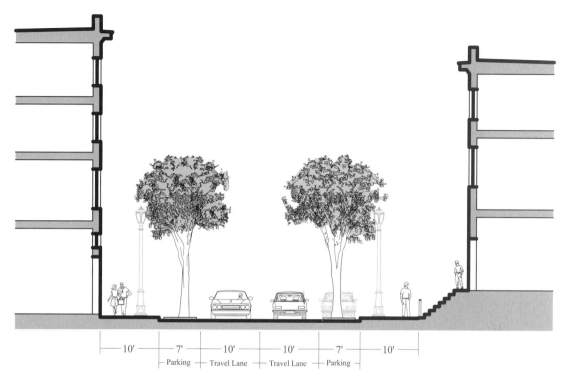

Figure 5.50: Bartram Street, Glenwood Park, Atlanta, Georgia. Dover, Kohl & Partners and Tunnell-Spangler-Walsh, 2001. Section. © 2013 Dover, Kohl & Partners

Figure 5.51: Brasfield Square, Glenwood Park, Atlanta, Georgia. Dover, Kohl & Partners and Tunnell-Spangler-Walsh, 2001. Rendering of the concept for the square. © 2001 Dover, Kohl & Partners

Figure 5.52: Bartram Street, Glenwood Park, Atlanta, Georgia. Dover, Kohl & Partners and Tunnell-Spangler-Walsh, 2001. Detail of overhead view, showing the elliptical park at the end of Bartram Street. © 2001 Dover, Kohl & Partners

Figure 5.53: Bartram Street interrupted by Brasfield Square, Atlanta, Georgia. Dover, Kohl & Partners and Tunnell-Spangler-Walsh, 2001. *Image courtesy of James Dougherty*

Figure 5.54: Brasfield Square, Atlanta, Georgia. Dover, Kohl & Partners and Tunnell-Spangler-Walsh, 2001. Upright, urbane live/work units face the square. *Image courtesy of Justin Falango*

The developers of Glenwood Park set out to accommodate vehicular traffic, but not to be oppressed by it. It was, primarily, to be a place for people. This meant they had to wage a protracted and expensive technical battle with government officials over street details and dimensions. Eventually, Green Street Properties was permitted to build narrower streets and smaller turning radii at the intersections. The result is that motorists navigate slowly and carefully within the neighborhood—as they should.

Bartram Street serves as the main north–south axis of the community, connecting the elliptical park to Glenwood Avenue. The intersection where Bartram Street crosses Garrett Street—essentially Glenwood Park's main street—is really the psychological center of the neighborhood, and here Brasfield Square terminates Bartram Street in a formal, but small, civic space (Figure 5.53). Brasfield Square itself is faced by mixed-use and live/work buildings on narrow lots. The high degree of spatial enclosure and the varied building facades make Brasfield Square the neighborhood's most memorable address. Note that here, too, is one part of Glenwood Park that demands a great deal of care and

requires motorists to remain alert. Around the square the dimensions are tight and the turns are challenging (although few European motorists would be fazed by them). If you look closely enough at some of the corners, you will occasionally find black tire-marks on the curbs. Those marks are worn proudly by Glenwood Park; they indicate that some speeder got a gentle reminder that this is a neighborhood where kids are playing and seniors are strolling, so they'd better slow down and drive through on the neighbors' terms.

North of the Square, Bartram Street necks down and is lined by row houses modeled after the building type and architecture in Chicago's Lincoln Park neighborhood. Parking is on both sides of the street, flanked by planting strips, sidewalks, stoops, and dooryards. Farther along, the view suddenly opens up to the roomy, slightly sunken ellipse, producing a contrast between the narrow space and the wide one that effectively dramatizes both. Connected yet varied spatial sequences like this one engender a genuine sense of the significance of the public realm in Glenwood Park (Figure 5.54).

INCLUSIVE STREETS

The street designer has roles to play in achieving social inclusiveness, with indirect control over factors that affect whether the goal of mixed-income, diverse communities will be realized. These include:

- containing costs by avoiding the use of oversized streets that consume excessive amounts of land and material.

- making medium- and high-density housing desirable, thereby lowering the per-unit land cost.

- lowering household transportation costs by making walking, biking, and transit feasible.

The physical design must aim for excellence and walkability, irrespective of the luxury or modesty of the surrounding real estate.

GALT HOUSE DRIVE, THE NEW TOWN AT ST. CHARLES, MISSOURI /
Laura Lyon

Duany Plater-Zyberk & Company, 2002

Neighborhood Street

The New Town at St. Charles is a New Urban development far enough across the Missouri River from St. Louis that it is outside the metropolitan center. What was once an old sod farm began to come to life as a town in 2003. Today, New Town is ten years old, and it is also my home. I have been lucky enough to have arrived after plantings from the tree farm have grown in and are bountifully in tune with all four seasons. With undulating soils and Big Muddy nearby, streets were drawn and plowed, cut and filled. Then, each street was framed so carefully, down to inches, to ensure a deep relationship to its users.

In New Town, the pattern of development gradually shifts from urban to rural. If you wander too far from the town's center, you will find agricultural crops growing within platted blocks, waiting for their future. But in the core, the inner sanctum, there is a framework of streets carefully and thoughtfully built out by the Town Architect and Town Founder. This net of roads and drains and sidewalks, pervious and not, all works like a siphon—gathering people from their homes, cars, and parks, while also moving water, wildlife, and seasonal color throughout the town.

I have grown fond of one street in particular: Galt House Drive. It is long in view but not in length (Figures 5.56, 5.57, and 5.58). It reaches for all to be enveloped in its cross-section, but it is not wide

Figure 5.56: Galt House Drive, New Town, St. Charles, Missouri. Duany Plater-Zyberk & Company, 2002. View towards the southeast, overlooking New Town Lake. *Image courtesy of Lawrence Duffy*

Figure 5.57: Galt House Drive, New Town, St. Charles, Missouri. Duany Plater-Zyberk & Company, 2002. The streets in New Town are the backdrop for homegrown seasonal celebrations. *Image courtesy of Lawrence Duffy*

in girth. It is stately and welcoming. It rises and falls from the tallest homes to the deepest fountains. In its proudest moments it carries children to play, fishermen to the rocky piers, teens to sun on the banks of the canal, and mothers to the market, all while awaiting the community celebrations that each season brings. The proud townhomes (recalling an eighteenth-century era of dignity) cast reflections in the grand fountains. The chapel peers from across the amphitheater, stealing the vista high and low, while the pedestrian is enveloped in a topologically whimsical cross-section. As the land reaches its highest point, the porches loom over, softened by cascades of ivies and blooms billowing out of garden walls and stairwells. The fountains bend to the windbreak of the view. In high rains, the waters lap at the walk. But this street also comes alive as the spine of the community, its social network. It is the prized place of honor for any parade-watcher. In winter, its bollards coated in ice and snow, this street waits quietly, majestically. Then its trees fill with blossoms and birds, and it awakens all the neighbors from their icy slumber and leads them back into spring. This is welcome. This is home.

Figure 5.58: Galt House Drive, New Town, St. Charles, Missouri. Duany Plater-Zyberk & Company, 2002. *Image courtesy of Lawrence Duffy*

Tupelo and West Grove Streets, Seaside, Florida

Duany, Plater-Zyberk & Company, 1981–Present

Neighborhood Street

Urbanism takes time. Fifty years might pass before the last streets, parks, or buildings drawn in a master plan are completed. Or, during those fifty years, there might be two new master plans. Most of us involved in urban design will be dead before any of our plans are fully built out.

> Urbanism takes time.

The Seaside plan was drawn in 1981. When *Progressive Architecture* visited in 1984, forty buildings had gone up, which is less than 10 percent of the final number.[13]

As we write this in 2013, there are still a few lots that haven't been built on, and the downtown is less than half complete.

The *Progressive Architecture* critic Daralice Boles was impressed by the urbanism of Seaside, although it has to be said that in 1985 there was more *promise* of urbanism than the real thing. It's noticeable that not one of the photos in the seven-page article is a street view. In

Figure 5.59: Tupelo Street, Seaside, Florida. Duany Plater-Zyberk & Company, 1981. Looking south on Tupelo Street in 1983. There were a number of experiments carried out on Tupelo Street, the earliest street at Seaside. In the first year, seen here, there were palm trees and a clay roadbed. An unusually harsh winter killed many of the palm trees (which normally can grow on the "Redneck Riviera"), and the clay roadway was bad once the traffic from buyers and potential buyers picked up. © *Steven Brooke Studios*

Figure 5.60: Tupelo Street, Seaside, Florida. Duany Plater-Zyberk & Company, 1981. Looking north on Tupelo Street in 1984. In the second year, Robert Davis first planted tupelo trees and then sycamores as street trees, but eventually settled on the same oaks that had originally covered the site. In 2014, the Seaside Community Development Corp. will plant new palm trees downtown. © *Steven Brooke Studios*

fact, although there are a few photos taken from the first street built—Tupelo Street—the street has been carefully cropped out of every photo that included any part of it.

One reason for the lack of street views was that Tupelo did not yet have any continuous streetwalls shaping it. The trees were too small, and the houses were so scattered that there was only one place where there were three houses in a row, and only one place where there were two houses across the street from each other, even though Seaside was built one street at a time. Another view in the magazine shows Tupelo Street from behind, looking east over the scrub that covered the site. When that photo

was taken, individual, freestanding houses rose above low scrub oaks that were barely higher than the level of their raised floors, built on wooden pilings in the sand.

When the developer Robert Davis (Figure 6.27) inherited the land, his grandfather had already clear-cut most of the site to build summer housing for the employees of the Pizitz Department Stores in Alabama. Many years later, the land had no plants or trees taller than three feet. These were buffeted by salt air and winter winds off the Florida Gulf, so that in some years the oaks would grow an inch or two, but in other years they shrank.

Seaside's landscape code, one of the first xeriscape plans in the United States, emphasized the preservation of existing oaks and only allowed the planting of a few tree types that could withstand the climate without high maintenance. Eventually, the hundreds of houses and other buildings built for the resort buffered the wind and concentrated the rainwater on the site. Over time the trees grew significantly, so that narrower east–west streets like Forest Street developed a natural tree canopy from the old scrub. Today, the streets can be quite lush, but they took decades to get to that stage.

In the two early pictures by the photographer Steven Brooke, one can see the original palm trees (in Figure 5.59) and the oyster shell roadbed (Figure 5.60).

Figure 5.61: Forest Street, Seaside, Florida. Duany Plater-Zyberk & Company, 1981. Looking east on Forest Street, towards Savannah Street, in 2011. Helped by the houses on the land breaking the wind and concentrating the rainwater, the Sand Live Oaks and shrub oaks grew rapidly. The oyster shell road surface seen in Figure 5.62 was replaced by bricks in 1985, because the oyster shells were too dusty in the summer when cars drove over them.

Figure 5.62: Tupelo Circle, Seaside, Florida. Duany Plater-Zyberk & Company, 1981. Looking east on West Grove Avenue in 2011. As the trees matured, they began to conceal some of the houses, reminiscent of tropical hammock street scenes in Coconut Grove, Miami, Florida.

There are palm trees on the Florida Panhandle, but the first winter after the palm trees were planted at Seaside was a particularly hard one, and several of the trees died. New Sand Live Oaks replaced the palm trees in 1983, and today, some of the houses on Tupelo and the surrounding streets are completely hidden from the street by the live oaks (Figures 5.61 and 5.62). The effect is similar to the tropical hammock ecosystem that Davis knew from his former home in Coconut Grove, Florida, when he was a developer in Miami.

344

Boathouse Close, I'On, Mount Pleasant, South Carolina

Duany, Plater-Zyberk & Company and Dover, Kohl & Partners, 1995

Close

The notorious cul-de-sacs in suburbia aggressively disconnect and isolate people from their town. The bulb-shaped spaces at their ends fill no placemaking purpose but are simply vehicle turnaround areas. The overuse of the cul-de-sac pattern in America has given us too many dead-end streets and too few connecting routes to school, work, and stores.

On the other hand—although this is one of those medicines that should only be taken in small doses, once in a while—a dead-end street can be a useful feature in a plan. This is particularly true when site constraints make a fully connected street impractical. Traditional urbanism offers a range of solutions preferable to the suburban cul-de-sac, including the occasional close and the pedestrian court.

Figure 5.63: Boathouse Close, I'On, Mount Pleasant, South Carolina. Duany Plater-Zyberk & Company and Dover, Kohl & Partners, 1995. Aerial view. *Image courtesy of Pictometry International Corp. Copyright 2013*

Figure 5.64: Boathouse Close, I'On, Mount Pleasant, South Carolina. Duany Plater-Zyberk & Company and Dover, Kohl & Partners, 1995. View looking west.

Figure 5.65: Boathouse Close, I'On, Mount Pleasant, South Carolina. Duany Plater-Zyberk & Company and Dover, Kohl & Partners, 1995. A Neoclassical house (B. J. Barnes, 2001) on Eastlake Road concludes the space.

Closes have buildings arranged around a small square or green, with a lane or road fronting the houses. The central space, faced by the fronts of the buildings, is a "socially useful" public space (unlike the cul-de-sac's asphalt bulb).[14] The close itself is usually sized to accommodate the turning radii of fire trucks and moving vans, but the result does not look like automotive space.

The close can be a valuable addition to a neighborhood plan layout, for several reasons. First, it offers a way to insert additional lots in what would otherwise be lost space in an irregular, oversized, or inefficient block, maximizing frontage and therefore lots; maneuvers of this sort that add interest and valuable curb appeal can be important in making the overall plan more financially feasible. Second, given its low traffic volume, the drive lane in the close can be designed to the lower-cost standards of driveways. Third, groupings of residences on a close lend themselves particularly well to varying lot sizes, unit sizes, and levels of luxury within the group.

Most of the streets in the new village of I'On are part of an interconnected web, without dead-end streets, but Boathouse Close is an exception to that rule (Figures 5.63, 5.64, and 5.65). The close opens to Eastlake Road, on an otherwise unusually long block that gains a vista to the lake and some spatial relief from the close. At the opposite end, the close is anchored by a small but iconic civic building— the boathouse itself—and a view to the lake. The view is framed by three houses, each of which has a front porch oriented toward the space. The result of this window to the view is that there is a practical and psychological connection to the lake for residents who might live a block or several blocks away from the actual waterfront. The central space of the close is slightly splayed, eighteen feet wide at one end and thirty-four feet wide at the other. The tapering of the close as it moves away from the lake improves the view of the lake for the houses farthest from it, and the foreshortened perspective makes the space seem larger than it actually is. Facing the eastern end, a neoclassical house designed by B. J. Barnes on Eastlake Road formally concludes the space.

RULE OF FRONTS AND BACKS

> Street-oriented architecture is crucial to livable, walkable cities, and it is not difficult to achieve.

Like humans, buildings have faces and backsides with different purposes. In the real world (no matter what creative protests architects may offer to the contrary), buildings almost always have a front and back. A public facade naturally belongs to the public space, and a private facade usually faces the rear.

Street-oriented architecture is crucial to livable, walkable cities, and it is not difficult to achieve. The architectural grammar of this building-to-street relationship is both recognizable and flexible. The front should speak to the community and shape the public realm (Figure 5.66). For example, the front should have the primary entry door or doors, and openings that allow occupants to overlook the space and provide natural surveillance. In this way, the organization of the building is legible at a glance to passersby, and the individual building communicates with the larger community. Dan Camp[15] calls this "the presentation face" of the building. In a Main Street building, the front may be expressed with storefronts, awnings, signs, perhaps galleries or arcades over the sidewalk, perhaps balconies extending from upper floors. In a residential building or a house, the front may be expressed with a porch, stoop, dooryard garden, verandah, or the like. In a civic building, a main portico could be positioned on the front to communicate the relationship of the building to the street. There are hundreds of ways to design buildings that let the front facade do its job of establishing the public space, so the creative architect is not unduly burdened or constrained. But without these features, a building that turns its face away from the public space sends a message of disrespect. At a minimum, placemaking suffers, and one might also end up with one of those buildings in front of which people stare in confusion or pace up and down, looking for the door.

The right place for certain service and messy utilitarian functions is the back of the building and its lot, in the most private outdoor spaces (Figure 5.67). Away from public view, this is where necessary but unsightly features belong, like garage doors, garbage cans, loading docks, drive-through lanes, parking lots, and parking structures. When at all possible, backflow preventers,

Figure 5.66: Glenwood Park, Atlanta, Georgia. Dover, Kohl & Partners and Tunnell-Spangler-Walsh, 2001. Rowhouses designed by Historical Concepts in 2006 face the public space with their fronts. *Image courtesy of James Dougherty*

Figure 5.67: Glenwood Park, Atlanta, Georgia. Dover, Kohl & Partners and Tunnell-Spangler-Walsh, 2001. The garage doors and midblock parking areas for the row-houses designed by Historical Concepts are on the alley side. *Image courtesy of James Dougherty*

air conditioning compressors, and the myriad boxes and meters needed by telecommunications companies and electric and water utilities should also be positioned away from the important spaces of the public realm. This is easiest when the master plan provides alleys or rear service lanes. In some other cases, where blocks are sufficiently small and streets plentiful, certain streets can be identified as what Andres Duany and Elizabeth Plater-Zyberk call the "A" streets and be kept free of the back-of-house functions that are relegated to the "B" streets or alleys. Either way, the thinking about the Rule of Fronts and Backs best begins when the streets, blocks, and lots are first laid out, long before the individual building architect appears on the scene.

CHUCK MAROHN'S TAKE: THE DIFFERENCE BETWEEN A STREET AND A STROAD / Chuck Marohn

The highway system was a replacement for the railroad, and the railroad (as its name implies) is a road on rails—an efficient system for connecting one place to another. When highways were roads that connected two places, they also functioned well. The problem is that we've changed what a road is. We don't build roads or streets anymore. We've introduced elements of streets into roads, and vice versa. So our roads are no longer efficient connections, and our streets are financially unproductive. A street should be part of a network that allows you to get around in a place. Streets not only move cars, they also accommodate parking, walking, biking, people in wheelchairs, people roller-skating. They serve as a framework for capturing taxable value from businesses, houses, office buildings, and hotels. But when we reconfigure our streets to have the characteristics of roads—as *stroads*—we are no longer able to capture the value or share the space. A modern stroad (Figure 5.68) is about the least safe traffic environment you could be in, too, with high-speed designs mashed up with turning traffic, stop-and-go traffic, sudden lane changes, and obnoxious signage. This ridiculously unsafe design is accepted as "normal" just because it was allowed to become ubiquitous.

Figure 5.68: Stroad, Any-where, USA. © 2012 Andy Boenau, used with permission

STREETS, ROADS, AND THOROUGHFARES

Linguistically, engineers put streets and roads into narrower boxes than the general public does. Chuck Marohn's point about the difference in character between streets, roads, and what he calls "stroads," is a valuable one, but it's important to remember that it relies on definitions of the words "street" and "road" that are not necessarily understood by the general public.

The traditional dictionary definition says that a road goes from one place to another, like one of the oldest roads in America, the Boston Post Road, which goes from New York to Boston. The dictionary also tells us that streets are roads that are in towns or cities—it follows, therefore, that all streets are roads (but... see below). That goes along with Marohn's point, but many people are unaware of the city / country distinction, and roads like the Boston Post Road can start in cities and pass through towns along the way as the Main Street—which means that many towns and cities have downtown streets with "road" in their name. Moreover, in the nineteenth century, many developers and municipalities gave urban streets names ending in "road," to give them cachet for commuters. Shepherd's Bush,

in London, has a large area with block after block of terrace houses (rowhouses) in which every street name ends with "Garden," "Gardens," or "Road."

The dictionary also tells us that the space between the curbs on a street is the road (engineers call it "the roadway"), while the space between the buildings, including the sidewalk and the road, is the street. These precise definitions are not widely known, but it's not uncommon for someone in the city to say the sidewalk is "next to the road," or for someone in the country to think of walking out to the mailbox on the street. The ambiguous character of nature and public space in the suburbs further blurs the distinctions.

New Urban engineers and SmartCode writers, on the other hand, want us to think streets are only in the city, while roads are only in the country. Rather than saying all streets are roads, they say all streets and all roads are "thoroughfares," an archaic name that strikes many as jargon. In other words, at the same time that the design of our streets and roads is evolving, so is the way we talk about them.

Swift Street, Buena Vista, Colorado

Dover, Kohl & Partners and Peter Swift, PE, 2004

Neighborhood Street

There's irony in the name of Swift Street because it is among the *slowest* new streets in the United States. It was named after transportation engineer Peter Swift, a tireless advocate of safer, saner streets where pedestrians are welcome.

Swift Street and the adjacent Swift Circle are part of the thirty-eight-acre South Main neighborhood in Buena Vista, Colorado (Figure 5.69). Dover-Kohl designed South Main for the developers Jed and Katie Selby as an extension of the small town's historic main street, which was lengthened to reach the new whitewater park, a regional recreation destination. The plan for the neighborhood reconciles the two existing street grids

Figure 5.69: South Main, Buena Vista, Colorado. Dover, Kohl & Partners, 2004. Aerial rendering of the neighborhood. © 2004 *Dover, Kohl & Partners*

of Buena Vista, joining them at a new square on the Arkansas River.

This is a narrow and intimate street. It was designed to contrast with the wider, more formal Main Street. For its part, South Main Street frames long axial views of the surrounding peaks and gives the neighborhood legible orientation, rooting it in the town's larger context of mountain, valley, and river. Swift Street, on the other hand, is all about the short close-up views across the skinny space and the experience of being within it. Swift collaborated on the design of all the thoroughfares in the South Main neighborhood and calls them his "proudest achievement," crediting the town staff and fire officials for their open-mindedness and "can-do attitude." The street was originally conceived as a *woonerf*, or pedestrian-dominated shared space,[16] but later plans were simplified to a more straightforward and traditional street, albeit a narrow one. The result is a street that could be an example for many other American towns.

Swift Street intersects with South Main Street, creating a convenient location for a corner store, local restaurant, and live/work units (Figure 5.70). In order to accommodate some informal parking for the mix of uses emerging in the neighborhood, Swift Street briefly becomes wider and two-way where it crosses South Main Street (Figure 5.71). The street section then shifts, narrowing to a total curb-to-curb width of twelve feet in order to establish an ultra-slow-speed outdoor room that is quiet, safe, and easy to navigate (Figure 5.72). The roadbed is paved with hand-set local glacier stones, giving the street a visceral connection to its rugged surroundings (Figures 5.73 and 5.74). The choice was intended to keep the speed down—pedestrian advocate Dan Burden says seven miles per hour feels about right there—but the rough stone road surface also creates a kind of local distinctiveness to boot. Striping, signage, and other traffic-control devices are practically moot at these slow speeds and are kept to an absolute minimum. A narrow strip of flat, smooth concrete is incorporated in the wider section, to keep the stones in place, with the added benefit of a few seconds of smooth riding for cyclists.

Figure 5.70: Swift Street, South Main, Buena Vista, Colorado. Dover, Kohl & Partners and Peter Swift, PE, 2004. The street is flanked by mixed-use buildings at S. Main Street; a small turret on the house where Swift Street bends in the distance is a focal point. *Image courtesy of Justin Falango*

Figure 5.71: Swift Street, South Main, Buena Vista, Colorado. Dover, Kohl & Partners and Peter Swift, PE, 2004. Section with parking. © 2013 Dover, Kohl & Partners

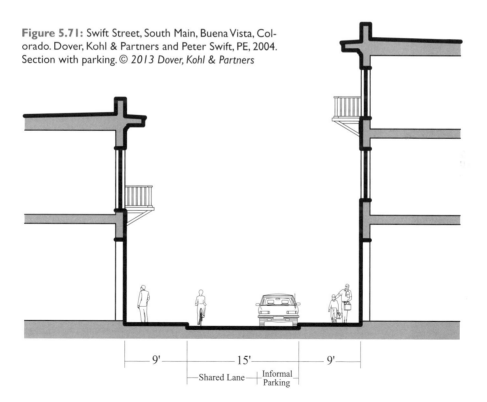

9'

15'
Shared Lane — Informal Parking

9'

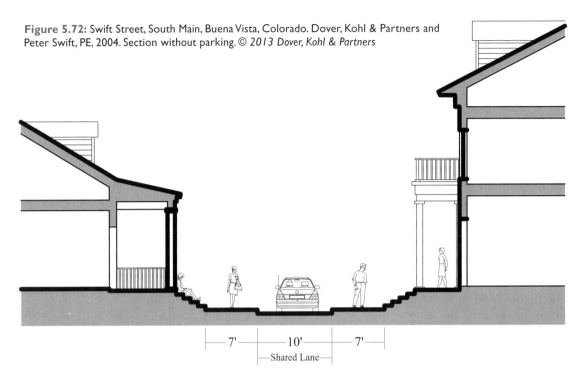

Figure 5.72: Swift Street, South Main, Buena Vista, Colorado. Dover, Kohl & Partners and Peter Swift, PE, 2004. Section without parking. © 2013 Dover, Kohl & Partners

7'   10'   7'
Shared Lane

Figure 5.73: Swift Street, South Main, Buena Vista, Colorado. Dover, Kohl & Partners and Peter Swift, PE, 2004. A form-based code controls both the streets and the buildings. © *South Main*

Sound environmental design was a high priority for the extension of downtown Buena Vista, where water is at a premium. In addition to implementing limited and water-efficient landscaping standards, the Selbys carefully considered other aspects of the local climate. The overall design corresponds with the building traditions of the region by responding and adapting to wind and weather patterns. The architecture maintains the sense of place with the Western mining-town vernacular but also shows adaptations of the traditional building types; the local architectural style is cross-pollinated with influences from that of other dry, high-altitude places. Materials such as adobe and stone provide insulation, high floor-to-ceiling heights promote air circulation, and shaded exterior spaces encourage outside activity.

The quality of the street space results from the combination of the architectural design and the details within the right-of-way. To get this ensemble right, a form-based code carefully controls both the street and the buildings (Figure 5.74). Every lot has build-to lines or zones that determine when stoops or porches are required. On the regulating plan, a "Privacy Side" symbol

Figure 5.74: Swift Street, South Main, Buena Vista, Colorado. The roadbed is paved with local glacier stones, a connection to its rugged surroundings. *Image courtesy of Kennley M Selby*

designates the side of the building where windows must be at least six feet above the average ground elevation, providing a measure of privacy for neighboring buildings. The primary roof-ridge orientation for each lot is also predetermined in the code, to optimize sun exposure and allow buildings to capitalize on the potential use of solar energy. These building regulations are accompanied by tight instructions from the urban designers on the configuration of the thoroughfares, via the Street Standards in the form-based code.

Twain Avenue, Davidson, North Carolina

Dover, Kohl & Partners, 1997

Neighborhood Street

The St. Albans neighborhood[17] is an infill development near Davidson College, devised in response to the form-based Land Plan and code adopted by the town in the 1990s. The neighborhood has generous park space, civic buildings, live/work units, large houses, cottages, and rowhouses.

Twain Avenue is a gently sloping street that connects a small neighborhood center to the formal Faulkner Square, another landmark in the new neighborhood (Figures 5.75, 5.76, and 5.77). It is faced with rowhouses that terrace down the slope. Although the rowhouses appear to resemble one another from the street—like facing like—they are actually different in plan, size, and cost. On one side of the street, the row of houses serves as a "liner" that screens the church parking lot, with semidetached garages on the alley. On the other side, the rowhouses are smaller park-under units that fit on shallower lots.

The street itself is as narrow as regulations would permit. It is a "give-way" or "yield street," meaning in this case there is two-way traffic but only one travel lane shared by motorists going in both directions. Drivers must sometimes pull aside to let oncoming cars pass, so they stay alert and go slowly. A travel lane and parallel parking on one side of the street have a combined width of twenty feet curb-to-curb, reflecting current fire regulations. Keeping the carriageway narrow saved enough room for street trees in a five-and-a-half-foot planting strip. Sidewalks are five feet wide, flanked by dooryards and stoops.

Figure 5.75: Twain Avenue, St. Albans, Davidson, North Carolina. Dover, Kohl & Partners, 1997. The street is framed by rowhouses that vary in size, cost, and floor plan. *Image courtesy of Dover, Kohl & Partners, Photograph by Douglas Boone*

Figure 5.76: Faulkner Square, St. Albans, Davidson, North Carolina. Dover, Kohl & Partners, 1997. The square is an elongated rectangle with narrow, tree-lined streets on each side.

Figure 5.77: St. Albans Lane, Davidson, North Carolina. Dover, Kohl & Partners, 1997. The St. Alban's Parish steeple anchors two streets that intersect to make a small neighborhood center.

The neighborhood was created in an uneasy union of high-minded New Urban principles with the old habits of corporate builders more accustomed to suburban subdivisions. On balance, it proved that this can be done successfully, but there are a handful of compromised details that would have turned out better had the builders been willing to follow tradition more closely. For example, the porches on Twain Avenue are oddly tucked within the building envelope behind the front facade, ultimately an unsatisfying experiment on the builders' part. One wishes the rowhouses had more traditional projecting stoops and porches like many in Savannah.

Another unfortunate detail is that the dooryards are not individualized in the way they would be in Savannah, Alexandria, or Georgetown. The streetscape that creates, with exceedingly consistent plantings, gives the faint scent of common management (Figure 5.75). Something about the lack of spatially defined side property lines betrays the dooryard space as condo-complex common area—which, of course, it is. The planting "strip," while green, subtly disengages the houses from their street. These criticisms aside, Twain Avenue and the other streets in the St. Albans neighborhood represent proof that the basic recipe of combining street-oriented buildings, street trees, and restraint in the amount of space given to the car can make streets that unify communities instead of isolating them.

PEDESTRIAN COURT AND ALLEY STUB

▲▲ **Figure 5.78:** Pedestrian Court, Juniper Point, Flagstaff, Arizona. Dover, Kohl & Partners, 2006. Computer model. The scenic view can be shared with the whole neighborhood, and the street and park are spatially united. © 2006 Dover, Kohl & Partners

▲ **Figure 5.79:** Conventional Layout for Comparison, Juniper Point, Flagstaff, Arizona. Computer model. This form increases impervious surfaces, produces less real estate value, and hides the view so that it can be enjoyed by only a few households. © 2006 Dover, Kohl & Partners

Like a close, a pedestrian court is a street type that can reconcile challenging block geometry with the principles of good placemaking. Urban designers use pedestrian courts to add variety and value to a neighborhood by extending the public realm, lot frontages, and street connectivity. The pedestrian court is a short, semi-public space for pedestrians only, in which the primary access to the front of the buildings is from walkways in the courtyard rather than from streets.

Houses on the court face onto it, and the court is paired with a parallel alley stub that gives vehicular access and keeps garage doors and service areas away. This allows adherence to the Rule of Fronts and Backs (see "The Rule of Fronts and Backs" in this chapter) and promotes "like facing like" (discussed in Chapter 1),[18] even where block size or topography might otherwise conspire against it. Used judiciously, the pedestrian court can also offer an opportunity to connect sidewalks and bike paths where for one reason or another a full-blown street cannot go through.

In the example shown here, the outer rank of houses in the Juniper Point neighborhood in Flagstaff, Arizona, abut a "wash," a steep, wooded valley that was preserved as a natural park (Figures 5.78 and 5.79). There are spectacular long views across the wash, but under a conventional layout only the houses on the outer layer would enjoy the view. The other households would have no psychological connection to the open space, and front-loaded lots would have to be wider and fewer in number. On the other hand, with a combination of alley stub and pedestrian court kept open at the end closest to the wash, the view is shared with the whole neighborhood. Driveways can be eliminated or consolidated, and higher density is feasible without any negative consequences. The sidewalks of the street network within the neighborhood are seamlessly, spatially connected to the system of trails within the park.

Variations on the pedestrian court street type lend themselves to concepts like cohousing[19] and "pocket neighborhoods."[20]

SEA GARDEN WALK, ALYS BEACH, FLORIDA / Marieanne Khoury-Vogt and Erik Vogt

Duany Plater-Zyberk & Company, 2003

Pedestrian Passage

Located in Alys Beach, Florida, Sea Garden Walk is a pedestrian street that integrates architecture and landscape into a harmonious whole and delineates the transition from an urban to a rural environment along its passage.

It is one of several main north–south passages that run through the community and connect it to the beach at the south and a woodland preserve along the northern edge.

The design was overseen by the Office of the Town Architect, and it began with a strict urban and architectural code provided by the Town Planner, Duany Plater-Zyberk & Company (DPZ). The primary residential building type is the attached courtyard house, with frontages that form a continuous and solid street wall. The street was designed to achieve two related goals. The first was to extend into town the relationships of solid and void, of public and private space, formed by the residential courtyards and their *zaguans* (the traditional entries into the courtyards that are found in Spanish colonial towns). The second was to establish the primacy of a harmonious streetscape over individual architectural expression. To that end, the house designs contributed by over a dozen architects were collected and assembled into overall street elevations, which were then edited and synthesized to form a coherent whole.

The resulting space of the street was conceived as a long public room, to be furnished with paving, landscaping, lighting, and amenities composed to work both as an overall urban composition and as a response to local architectural conditions. Street trees mark entryway axes, urns are positioned so as to balance adjoining facades, and benches or fountains animate places of gathering.

An additional requirement of the design was to work in concert with the urban-to-rural transect code instituted by

DPZ. As embedded in the master plan, the transect decreed a more urban character to the town on its southern half, which gradually changes to a more rural, naturalistic character at its northern edge. Lot sizing, building disposition, and house types all follow suit, to be reinforced by all elements of the streetscape, designed or selected to fit appropriately within its transect zone.

Figure 5.80: Sea Garden Walk, Alys Beach, Florida. Duany Plater-Zyberk & Company, 2003. At its southern end, the Walk has continuous paving in a tighter, more urban space. *Image courtesy of Kurt Lischka*

Figure 5.81: Sea Garden Walk, Alys Beach, Florida. Duany Plater-Zyberk & Company, 2003. At its northern end, the Walk opens up into less tightly wound space. (Construction photo.) *Image courtesy of Kurt Lischka*

At its southern end (Figure 5.80), the street is a continuously paved surface, house-wall-to-house-wall, punctuated by elements of an urban landscape—formal tree groupings, overscaled planted urns, climbing vines on wall and roof trellises, contained planters built into the house facades. As one moves north, the paving gradually narrows down to a broad walk bordered by landscaped swales containing more informal groupings of native plantings that weave into the existing scrub.

Finally, the northernmost end of the walk opens up to a man-made lake, designed as a picturesque landscape. Native oak, pine, and cypress trees blend into the backdrop of the woodland preserve. The walk divides into a narrow paved path that circumscribes the lake edge and joins up with a boardwalk that snakes through the preserve.

Here, the architecture becomes episodic, subordinate to the predominant landscape. A pedestrian bridge and fountain work together to mark the southern edge of the lake and connect with an east–west path through the town (Figure 5.81). A terrace in the form of an exedra juts into the lake, its built-in wall benches shaded by a willow tree. The vehicular bridge spanning the lake is marked by a tower, its form inspired by the simple gabled houses of the town. From here, a prospect can be taken southward of the path, walk, and street that lead to the sea.

STREET DESIGN, HIGH PRICES, AND HOPE VI

Good streets should be a basic ingredient in all community design, not just a special feature for wealthy neighborhoods. The fundamentals of good streets can be achieved on a reasonable budget, and good streets inevitably help to create or sustain a neighborhood's economic and cultural value. Judging by the market, people prefer to live on attractive and functional streets, and so prices on them rise. America simply does not have enough good streets to meet the demand for them.

> Good streets should be a basic ingredient in all community design, not just a special feature for wealthy neighborhoods.

In 2012, Brookings Institution researchers Christopher Leinberger and Mariela Alfonzo established a list of five criteria for measuring walkability, then classified sixty-six places in the Washington, DC, area according to the criteria. The researchers found an astonishing degree of correlation between walkability and economic performance. They concluded, "Considering the magnitude of influence that walkability has on economic performance, a one-level (or approximately 20-point) increase in walkability (out of a range of 94 points) translates into a $8.88 value premium in office rents, a $6.92 premium in retail rents, an 80 percent increase in retail sales, a $301.76 per square foot premium in residential rents, and a $81.54 per square foot premium in residential housing values" [in 2012 dollars].[21]

One dismaying risk of this book is that some may get the impression that good streets are only for the rich. They are not. Certainly the solution to creating mixed-income neighborhoods and insuring social inclusiveness is not to design grim, repellent streets— we built too large an inventory of those in the twentieth century. We need to increase the supply of decent, economically produced streets and to address the need for long-term affordable housing and affordable commerce with the array of financial and legal tools now available to government and developers.[22]

In the 1990s, the U.S. Department of Housing and Urban Development (HUD) set out to remake hundreds of the miserable public-housing projects across the country with the HOPE VI initiative. Most of the old projects used the tower-in-the-parking-lot model promoted by Le Corbusier. They had superblocks that usually required closing city streets, because as we saw in Chapter 1, Corb didn't like the street, which he thought was old-fashioned. The "projects" were also for low-income tenants only.

HOPE VI replaced the public housing tracts with mixed-income, mixed-use neighborhoods, and leaders of the Congress for the New Urbanism collaborated with HUD to integrate principles of traditional neighborhood design into HOPE VI housing policy. At the core of the initiative was the notion that good street design is integral to thriving neighborhoods. Well-designed streets connect communities, link residents to public transport, and provide safe and healthy places for people to gather. They can also revitalize neighborhoods by introducing a mix of housing types and a convenient mix of land uses.

HOPE VI infill and retrofit projects like the Laurel Homes Revitalization in Cincinnati, Ohio, and College Park in Memphis, Tennessee, demonstrate the role that effective design can have in the transformation of depressed neighborhoods (Figures 5.82 and 5.83). Both projects aimed to reestablish a network of streets that accommodate walking, cycling, and transit as well as driving.

At Laurel Homes (now known as City West), public policy and a master plan with affordable housing have begun to connect previously unconnected streets, making the neighborhood walkable, safe, and interesting. The retrofit focuses on the renovation of existing housing and infill development in order to further define the new street network while also introducing a mix of new housing types. A community center and live/work retail space on Linn Street integrate commercial uses into the neighborhood. This puts daily destinations like the

Figure 5.82: City West, Cincinnati, Ohio. Torti Gallas & Partners, 1999. HOPE VI buildings are designed to face the streets, unlike the campus-style public-housing projects that turned away from streets. *Image courtesy of Torti Gallas and Partners, Inc. Photograph by Steve Hall © Hedrich Blessing*

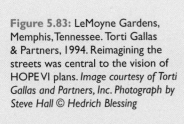

Figure 5.83: LeMoyne Gardens, Memphis, Tennessee. Torti Gallas & Partners, 1994. Reimagining the streets was central to the vision of HOPE VI plans. *Image courtesy of Torti Gallas and Partners, Inc. Photograph by Steve Hall © Hedrich Blessing*

grocery store within walking distance for the residents, allowing them to become less dependent on cars.

The retrofit of the College Park public housing project in Memphis used HOPE VI funds to change the character of the place and construct new development better connected to the surrounding neighborhoods. Reimagining the streets was central to the vision of the plan, which linked College Park to a local college campus, parks, and an adjacent neighborhood comprised of

mostly single-family houses. Multifamily housing and duplexes, designed to face the street, are close to the street and one another, in contrast to the mid-twentieth-century, campus-style public-housing projects that eschewed streets and pushed buildings apart.

The street designer has roles to play in achieving social inclusiveness.

NOTES

1. Bernard Rudofsky, *Streets for People* (New York: Doubleday & Company, 1969).

2. Whyte's keen social observations on modern corporate culture and cities spanned from *The Organization Man* (New York: Simon & Schuster, 1956) to *The Social Life of Small Urban Spaces* (Washington: The Conservation Foundation, 1980, and New York: Project for Public Space, 2001) to *City: Rediscovering the Center* (New York: Doubleday & Company, 1988).

3. Jane Jacobs, *The Death and Life of Great American Cities* (New York: Random House, 1961), 183.

4. Werner Hegemann and Elbert Peets, *The American Vitruvius: An Architects' Handbook of Civic Art* (New York: The Architectural Book Publishing Company, 1922). In the 1980s, a mail-order bookstore that specialized in remaindered books fortuitously sold copies of *Civic Art* for $1 each.

5. Maurice Culot, ed., *Rational Architecture Rationelle: The Reconstruction of the European City* (Brussels: AAM Edition, 1981).

6. Robert Davis, in conversation with John Massengale, October 2012.

7. Kurt Andersen, "Design: Best of the Decade," *TIME*, January 1, 1990. Andersen also wrote two other *TIME* articles about Seaside: "Design: Building a Down Home Utopia," *TIME*, April 18, 2005, http://www.time.com/time/magazine/article/0,9171,1050544,00.html and "Oldfangled New Towns," *TIME*, May 20, 1991, http://www.time.com/time/magazine/article/0,9171,972988,00.html.

8. The Market Tower is both the only unbuilt structure from Poundbury's first phase, as well as the only building designed by Léon Krier for the first phase.

9. This section on Light Imprint is taken in part from the *Light Imprint Handbook* (New Urban Press, 2008) by Thomas Low. For a further description of the Urban to Rural Transect see "Context Matters" in Chapter 1.

10. We first heard the term "conversational distance" used by Vince Graham and Bob Turner, the developers of Newpoint (*q.v.*).

11. Jane Jacobs, *The Death and Life of Great American Cities* (New York: Random House, 1961), 269.

12. Neighborhood founder Charles Brewer used a fictional town from an animated children's cartoon—Busytown from *The Busy World of Richard Scarry*—to explain his ideal development program: a bustling place where neighbors from all walks of life are in frequent contact and come to know one another.

13. Daralice D. Boles, "Robert Davis: Small Town Entrepeneur," *Progressive Architecture* (July 1985): 111–118.

14. Duany Plater-Zyberk & Company, *The Lexicon of the New Urbanism*, 2002, http://www.dpz.com/Research/Lexicon.

15. Dan Camp is the founder, designer, and builder of the Cotton District infill development in Starkville, Mississippi, and former mayor of Starkville. See http://www.cottondistrictms.com.

16. A *woonerf* is "a street, also known as a home zone, shared zone, or living street, where pedestrians have priority over vehicles and the posted speed limit is no greater than 10 miles per hour. Physical elements within the roadway, such as shared surfaces, plantings, street furniture, parking, and play areas, slow traffic and invite pedestrians to use the entire right-of-way." Definition from the USGBC's LEED-ND rating system: http://www.usgbc.org/search/woonerf.

17. It was originally called simply "the new neighborhood in Old Davidson," breaking with the convention among developers that each new subdivision is given its own annoying brand name, e.g., "Arcadia Ridge at Hunter's Glen" or "Fawn Creek at Farmers Run." (A favorite parody: Jerry's parents on *Seinfeld* live in "Del Boca Vista Phase III.") Eventually, neighborhood founder Doug Boone agreed to make a new sanctuary for St. Albans Episcopal Church, the landmark centerpiece of what has since become become known informally as the St. Albans neighborhood.

18. Pedestrian courts and variations on the idea are employed to good effect in New Urban neighborhoods including The Waters, Montgomery, Alabama, and Rosemary Beach, Florida. The benefit of a public pedestrian space facing an important view is also vividly illustrated at Newpoint Green, Beaufort, South Carolina (*q.v.*).

19. Kathryn M. McCamant, Charles Durrett, and Ellen Hertzman, *Cohousing: A Contemporary Approach to Housing Ourselves* (Berkeley, California: Ten Speed Press, 1988).

20. Ross Chapin, *Pocket Neighborhoods, Creating Small-Scale Communities in a Large Scale World* (Newtown, Connecticut: Taunton Press, 2011).

21. Christopher Leinberger and Mariela Alfonzo, "Walk this Way: The Economic Promise of Walkable Places in Metropolitan Washington, D.C." *Walkable Urbanism,* http://www.brookings.edu/research/papers/2012/05/25-walkable-places-leinberger.

22. Emily Badger, "Why We Pay More For Walkable Neighborhoods," *The Atlantic Cities*, May 28, 2012, http://www.theatlanticcities.com/jobs-and-economy/2012/05/why-you-pay-more-walkable-neighborhoods/2122/. Also see: Peter Katz, "Hope VI and the Inner City," Better! Cities and Towns, May 7, 2012, http://bettercities.net/news-opinion/blogs/peter-katz/17943/hope-vi-and-inner-city; Melinda J. Milligan, Kevin Fox Gotham, and James R. Elliott, "HOPE VI, New Urbanism, and the Utility of Frames: A Reply to Melendez and Coats," http://www.urbanconservancy.org/library/pdf/framing_the_urban_response_to_uc.pdf; and Henry G. Cisneros and Lora Engdahl, eds., *From Despair to Hope: Hope VI and the New Promise of Public Housing in America's Cities* (Washington DC: Brookings Institution, 2009).

CHAPTER SIX
CONCLUSION

> An individual only has one life, and if during it he has no great environment, no community, he has been irreparably robbed of a human right.
>
> —Paul Goodman, *Growing Up Absurd*[1]

CHAPTER 1 opened with a quotation saying that when you degrade the public realm, you degrade the common good. In the last sixty years, Americans *have* degraded the public realm—so is it just coincidental that our nation is now terribly divided? Studies like those in *Bowling Alone: The Collapse and Revival of American Community* suggest there is a connection.[2] That's hardly surprising, because we are social beings, and for thousands of years our wise men and women have been saying that we achieve the good life by venturing out into the *res publica*.

For many of us, Happy Motoring stopped being a happy experience a while ago.[3] Research in *Time* magazine shows that the four most significant sources of happiness for Americans involved spending time with others,[4] while our cars isolate us and rob us of our free time. Commuting times doubled in 20 years, and the phenomenon of Road Rage developed from America's new way of life.[5] "Data strongly suggests that real community and real friendships are important keys to happiness," says Stephen Post, coauthor of *Why Good Things Happen to Good People*.[6] "Some cities make that possible in ways that others don't."[7] "Towns too," he could have added, because this is not about big city versus small town, but about meeting our friends and neighbors in the public realm.

Good cities and towns require good streets. Streets are the public realm glue that holds the polis together. To be that glue, they must be places that make people want to get out of their cars. Once upon a time, making streets

◄ First Avenue, New York, New York. See Color Plate 51.

363

where people wanted to be was easier than it is today, because humans didn't have to compete with their own machines for a piece of the space. Now, the time has come to fight back against the pride of place we gave the car. So where do we go from here?

Virtually everyone alive today in America has grown up in an era so dominated by the car that we frequently see simple steps to address the imbalance as too radical or impractical. But the standard solutions used today to slow or reduce traffic—narrowing the traffic lanes a little, adding bumpouts at every intersection, and slowing the cars from fifty miles per hour to forty—do not and cannot create good, walkable places.

PUTTING THE PROBLEM IN CONTEXT

A simple yet powerful idea could change the way we design streets in America. Because the Functional Classification System throws up roadblocks that make the design of great, walkable streets difficult, in 2013 John Massengale, Victor Dover, and Rick Hall proposed to the U.S. DOT a change in the FHWA and AASHTO design guidelines.

The crux of the idea is to introduce new criteria for street design in cities and town centers. That sounds simple, but it's difficult when working in the context of the Functional Classification System, because for purposes of road design, the FHWA and AASHTO divide the world into two "Area Types," "Rural" and "Urbanized." In that very simple transect, exurban arterials and big-city boulevards have almost the same regulations: the boulevard must conform to standards appropriate for auto-dominated suburbs, and the city suffers. Therefore, the authors and Hall proposed a more sophisticated transect, with three Area Types instead of two: Urban, Suburban, and Rural.

Discussions about patterns of living and making changes to our streets are always politically charged, so it's important to understand that the proposal does *not* mean that all Americans would have to change the way they live. A large percentage of the area now classified Urbanized would be reclassified Suburban, but despite the name change the Suburban road standards would have little change from the current Urbanized Functional Classification system. Care would be taken, however, not to impede progress towards Complete Streets legislation in all areas across the country.

On the other hand, the areas reclassified Urban would not only be the places that are currently walkable, but also the communities where the citizens decide they want to introduce walkability and compact development. Some of the greatest benefits would come in formerly walkable

FLEXIBILITY

In August 2013, the FHWA took a different step towards producing more walkable urban streets when it endorsed the CNU ITE Manual, *Designing Walkable Urban Thoroughfares: A Context Sensitive Approach*.[8] The CNU ITE manual tackled the problem by introducing context-sensitive design, which seeks to balance the movement of vehicles with other objectives, like promoting active transportation and fostering retail businesses. Engineers using the manual have a lot of freedom to decide what that means and whether or not they agree with the manual's solutions. As a result, an engineer who wants walkable places may design streets to support that context, while a conventional traffic engineer can still design streets like the suburban arterials and collector roads he has always designed. That freedom is sometimes called "flexibility," which theoretical and academic engineers like. But most engineers in the field like to control variables, valuing clarity and specificity over flexibility.

The CNU ITE Manual is evolving, and the next edition will be more specific about urban design and placemaking, with fewer suburban-style elements than it has now. It also needs states and municipalities to adopt it, as Texas and the Texas city of El Paso have.

Figure 6.1: Place François Spoerry, Le Plessis-Robinson, France. François Spoerry, 1993. When Philippe Pemezec was elected Mayor of le Plessis-Robinson in 1989, three-quarters of the city's residential stock was dilapidated, twentieth-century public housing. With designs by Spoerry, Xavier Bohl and Breitman Architectes, Pemezec reintroduced traditional streets and buildings to le Plessis-Robinson. The slow speeds in these narrow streets allow the introduction of traditional civic elements like fountains without the need for bold striping and reflective warning signs. *Image courtesy of Gabriele Tagliaventi*

places that have suffered from the recent construction of suburban-style roads, a description that unfortunately fits most old towns and cities in America.

The new road standards would turn many of the current Functional Classification standards on their head. Two-way streets, narrow traffic lanes, slower speeds, bicycle sharrows, and a prohibition on slip lanes and turn lanes would be the norm. In large cities, faster urban routes might be limited to broader streets like Brooklyn's Ocean Parkway (Figure 2.28). Drivers coming into areas like Manhattan, where there are no streets that wide except for the limited-access highways along the rivers, would have to accept that city streets do not have suburban standards. But we're not just talking about urban roads; small-town residential streets and Main Streets also need to be redressed. If the DOT and the FHWA approve this simple idea, there will be a radical change in the way we build streets in cities and towns.

> The new road standards would turn many of the current Functional Classification standards on their head. Two-way streets, narrow traffic lanes, slower speeds, bicycle sharrows, and a prohibition on slip lanes and turn lanes would be the norm.

SLOW DOWN—SPEED KILLS

An important step in making better streets is simply to slow cars down when they enter walkable areas. If we slow cars down enough, then we can replace a lot of the traffic engineer's detritus that give streets an auto-based scale with human-scaled elements. The principle is simple: drivers of speeding cars need lots of warning to steer them away from things they might hit, but drivers in slow-moving cars do not, because they clearly see what is in front of them and have time to react (Figures 6.1 and 6.2). Pedestrians naturally feel more comfortable in a human-scaled space that has not been disfigured by bold striping, large reflective signs, and cheap, ugly elements like white plastic sticks. A fundamental principle in the design of shared space is to take away all the signs and markings that make the speeding driver feel comfortable while making the pedestrian feel like an intruder in an unsafe space. Even when urban streets are *not* shared space, however (which is most of the time), pedestrians should feel comfortable crossing the street. Most of suburbia is free-range auto space, but most of the public realm in our towns and cities should feel like free-range pedestrian space.

SLOW = SAFE

15 mph

20 mph

25 mph

30 mph

Figure 6.2: Cone of Vision Simulation. NACTO, 2010. The diminishing circles show how much small increases in speed decrease what a driver sees. The combination of reduced vision, the increased distances required for stopping, the greater amount of time needed for the driver to react to an obstacle, and the increased harm from impact as speeds go up show why speed kills. *Image courtesy of NACTO*

LEXINGTON
AVENUE:
BEFORE AND
AFTER

Figure 6.3: Lexington Avenue, New York, New York. Before: The northwest corner of Lexington Avenue and 89th Street in 1913. Photographed during the construction of the East Side IRT subway line, which explains why parts of the sidewalk have wooden planks rather than concrete. *Image courtesy of the New York Transit Museum*

Figure 6.4: Lexington Avenue, New York, New York. After: The northwest corner of Lexington Avenue and 89th Street in 2013. Lexington Avenue was widened twice, most drastically in 1960, when the DOT converted the road to one-way traffic and widened the roadway to speed up traffic. A comparison of Figures 6.3 and 6.4 reveals that the sidewalk was narrowed so much that the houses along Lexington lost both their stoops and the window wells for the basements. Underneath the avenue is the busiest subway line in America, and one block away are three commuter train lines that run north from Grand Central to Connecticut and Westchester County. The attitude behind the road widening is why we burn twice as much gas per person as the residents of Middle Eastern oil-producing countries, and why we have such ugly streets.

Last but not least, slowing cars down saves lives: experience shows that reducing the urban speed limit from 30 to 20 miles per hour will lead to a 40 percent reduction in the number of casualties.[9] If a car going 20 mph starts to brake and hits a pedestrian while traveling 15 mph, most pedestrians will survive the crash, frequently with only minor injuries. At 25 mph, almost all accidents result in severe injuries, with roughly half of the crashes fatal: at 40 mph, the pedestrian will die 90 percent of the time.[10]

Twenty miles per hour feels slow in a modern car, but the injury and fatality statistics for accidents at higher speeds are as dramatic as the numbers for drunk driving accidents. Because of this, it will be surprising if the majority of cities and towns don't have 20-mph speed limits on most residential and many downtown streets in the future. Hoboken, New Jersey, and New York City are already testing 20-mph speeds on what they call "neighborhood streets," but the U.S. lags far behind Great Britain and the rest of Europe in creating these slow streets. Thanks to a popular campaign called 20s Plenty for Us,[11] more than eight million Britons now live on 20-mph streets, and 60 percent of the nation supports 20-mph limits in built-up areas.[12]

COMPLETER STREETS

The National Complete Streets Coalition has been phenomenally successful. Now a part of Smart Growth America, the Coalition has brilliantly and effectively written and promoted policies for the guidance of transportation planners and engineers in the design and operation of "the entire roadway with all users in mind," including cyclists, public transportation riders, and pedestrians of all ages and abilities.[13] And it has overseen the successful adoption of Complete Street legislation in more than 500 "US jurisdictions," including twenty-three states and counting. Legislators and policymakers are not placemakers or urban designers, however, and on the ground Complete Streets are still in a transitional phase, from policy to construction.

One way the policymakers achieved success was by allowing street designs that met all the functional requirements to fall under a big Complete Streets umbrella. In the eyes of placemakers and urban designers, that led to

too many streets that were not good places, particularly as suburban-style Complete Street techniques like painted Road Diets started to make their way into urban settings.[14] A Google search for Complete Street photos and renderings shows this problem. The next step for Complete Streets is the creation of beautiful places where people want to be.

> Unfortunately, its primary purpose is to move vehicles (now including bicycles) *through* the city, and little or no thought is given to being *in* the city, on a particular block. It is good engineering, in other words, but weak urban design and poor placemaking.

When discussing the design of Complete Streets and urban road standards in context, it is worthwhile to bring New York City into the discussion for several reasons. First, some of the most interesting innovations in American street design are going on there (see *Tactical Urbanism and Reclaiming Pedestrian Space* in Chapter 4). Second, New York City is our greenest and densest city, where the argument for auto-centric street design is weakest, so the fact that suburban-style streets are still being built in Manhattan illustrates the stranglehold that Organized Motordom continues to have on the American public realm. Last but not least, prime examples of nationally-promoted Complete Streets are currently under construction in Manhattan, and these illustrate both exciting progress and notable flaws in contemporary practice.

The new design for First Avenue in Manhattan shows both the good and the bad (see Color Plate 51 and the opening photo in this chapter). Similar designs are used on most avenues in the borough, sometimes without a bicycle lane but still with the left turn lane and the concrete pedestrian island. The configuration does some things well: it promotes traffic flow, it allocates space on the road for bicycles and buses, it establishes protected bike lanes that allow people to ride around the city more safely, and it reduces auto accidents. Unfortunately, its primary purpose is to move vehicles (now including bicycles) *through* the city, and little or no thought is given to being *in* the city, on a particular block. It is good engineering, in other words, but weak urban design and poor placemaking.

What are the problems with this Complete Street paradigm? First, the one-way layout, staggered traffic lights, and boldly marked turn lanes encourage fast driving. The posted limit is 30 miles per hour, but in New York State that means one can legally drive 39.9 miles per hour, and the New York City police rarely target speeders in Manhattan, while they boast about targeting cyclists.[15] Sadly, speeds of 50 miles per hour and above can be quite common on Manhattan's avenues. Second, in the latest iteration of the design, the express bus lane on the right side of the avenue removes the customary lane of parked cars that buffers the pedestrian from the noise and potential physical harm of a runaway car. Third, the highway-scale markings that buffer the parked cars and announce the turn lanes are psychologically uncomfortable for anyone on foot. Stepping out onto the street, people unconsciously understand that they are in an alien, dangerous space created for moving machines. That is a problem Complete Streets should fix in our walkable places, not perpetuate. But while this new version of Second Avenue will have bicycle and bus lanes, the bicycle lane is the engineer's version of the lane: efficient but ugly, with specific, well-defined places on the road for each type of user. In the center, still dominant, is the automobile. To one side, in a protected lane that still gives too much priority to vehicle flow, is the bicycle. The pedestrian is assigned a rather meager space on the side, where his or her experience walking along the avenue was better before the new design. In that way, it's almost the antithesis of the DOT experiments going on south of Times Square and in South Brooklyn.

In a borough where 80 percent of the residents don't own cars and only 20 percent of the workers commute by car, what is the justification for making a suburban-style arterial for use primarily by suburbanites? We designed the Yorkville Promenade (Figure 4.80) for Second Avenue because of all the streets on the Upper East Side, Second Avenue has the most sidewalk dining, and it's as important for shopping as any street in the large neighborhood. After the new subway is completed, that will become even more true. But instead of being treated as an important public space, the majority of the avenue will have an unfriendly scale, and the amount of unhealthy pollution that will be spewed out by the speeding cars is well documented. Even in our most walkable city, in the midst of exemplary experimentation elsewhere on the island, we see a political climate that places the convenience of those driving in and out of Manhattan over those who live there. This Complete Street retrofit shows how unbalanced America remains—even as it attempts to remake the public realm.

New York's avenues are shared by cars, trucks, buses, cyclists, and pedestrians, but when you compare the number of users with the amount of the public realm given to each, it's clear that the division of the space is not proportional to the percentage of users—and particularly the percentage of residents and local workers. Organized Motordom did its job very well.

Another problem with the design is that the proposed bicycle lane runs along the east side of the avenue, thereby pushing the parked cars out towards the middle of the street and giving the avenue an out-of-kilter appearance. This is not an effete aesthetic quibble: many of the harshest critics of New York's bike lanes have objected to this attention-grabbing element in the design, and their complaints on this point meet with knowing nods from many New Yorkers who support the construction of bicycle lanes. The unwillingness of bicycle advocates who are understandably worried about losing the bike lanes to address the merits of this particular argument unnecessarily strengthens doubts about the lanes, which is unfortunate.[16] Pedestrians crave beauty, and this engineering solution is ugly.[17]

Before we export the same problems to other communities that want to be more walkable and have more Complete Streets, there are some easy fixes to look at that are no more expensive than the current model and are just as efficient. The first step is to move the bicycle lanes from the east side of the avenue to the west side (facing the direction of the traffic flow, that's from the left side to the right side). The bus lane can then move to the outside of the bike lane, separated from it by a low, narrow concrete barrier that broadens into a platform where bus riders can wait. That allows the parking formerly separated from the curb by the bike lane to move back to the curb on the east side of the road, where it's less disruptive for the visual harmony of the street. And it gives a psychological buffer from the traffic on the road back to the pedestrians on the west side. Pedestrians on both sides of the road are better off.

Turning Second Avenue and other avenues in New York back into two-way streets could have far greater gains. Virtually all Manhattan streets were two-way until the 1950s, when they also had wider sidewalks. During the current mayor's administration, the city applied to the state for permission to make a "Congestion Zone" that would have sharply reduced the amount of traffic in Manhattan by charging drivers for bringing cars into the city. The resulting drop in demand might have led naturally to the return of two-way avenues, which inherently slow traffic. Having been turned down by New York State, New York City could reverse-engineer the process and create a *de facto* congestion zone by instituting two-way streets again. So, far, politicians have deemed that idea too hot to handle.

The new New York avenue makes an interesting comparison with the old New York street in Figure 6.26. The 1908 photo shows Broadway, looking north from Herald Square towards Times Square (the *New York Herald* building, designed by McKim, Mead & White is on the right in the foreground, while the *New York Times* tower is the tall building in the distance). Taken before the coronation of the car, the photo shows no traffic signs, traffic lights, stop lights, or striping. People wait in the middle of the street for the cable cars that run up and down Broadway, and while most pedestrians are on the wide sidewalks next to the street, they look comfortable stepping out into the street. Organized Motordom told us this was dangerous and that there were many fatalities, but there's good reason to think what made it dangerous was drivers wanting to go faster and faster. In 1908, when the population of the United States was approximately 89 million, there were 751 motor vehicle deaths, while last year we had 32,367, from a population of a little under 315 million people. No one is proposing that New York City take out its traffic lights (although Amsterdam has done that), but the walkability and livability of our towns and cities would increase enormously if our street designs went more in the direction of Broadway in 1908 than Second Avenue today.

COMPLETER STREETS WITH BICYCLE LANES

Money spent on bike lanes generates more than twice the number of jobs than money spent on car lanes.[18]

Ten bikes can park in the space of one car, and the typical bike lane handles five to ten times the traffic volume of a car lane that is double the bike lane's width.[19]

If every American biked an hour per day instead of driving, the U.S. would cut its greenhouse gas emissions by 12 percent, meeting the Kyoto accords.[20]

—Jeff Speck, *Walkable City: How Downtown Can Save America, One Step at a Time*[21]

Bicycle lanes are an essential element of the design for Second Avenue and an important part of Complete Streets. They are good for both our health and our carbon footprints. To quote Jeff Speck, the author of *Walkable City*, "You can't spell 'carbon' without 'car.'"[22] But like Complete Streets, bicycle lanes are in a transitional phase in which weak, monofunctional designs are frequently touted as best practices.

The protected lane shown in Figure 6.5 is sometimes referred to in America as a Copenhagen Lane. That means that the street-level lane is sandwiched between the sidewalk and a buffer lane that runs along a row of parked cars. In Copenhagen, where 36 percent of the population commutes to work or school by bicycle every day, the form is better: the cycle track is raised above street level, with a curb separating it from the street. The track is usually attached to the sidewalk, which is often slightly higher still, so that there is another low curb between the bicycle space and the pedestrian space. Cars may or may not be parked next to the cycle track, depending on the width of the street. But when there are no parked cars, the cycle track provides a buffer between the pedestrians and the cars. Because the cycle track is attached to the sidewalk, the odd appearance of cars floating in the street is avoided, and the parking lane is

Figure 6.5: Eighth Avenue, New York, New York. NYC DOT, 2009. Looking north at the intersection with 17th Street. A few good pictures can be worth a thousand words: please compare this photo with Color Plate 51 and Figure 6.26. In Manhattan, most public life takes place on the wide north-south avenues, but this design still gives most of the public realm to cars and throughput. Like East Broadway in Long Beach (Figures 6.6 and 6.7), a significant amount of space is given to the bicycle, but this is the engineer's version of the bike lane, weak on urban design and placemaking. The avenues are one way, have turn lanes (which were previously rare in Manhattan), and traffic moving at a speed that makes lots of striping necessary, making these feel more like suburban-style arterials than city streets. The ugly pedestrian island sitting asymmetrically in the street and the white plastic sticks are more appropriate for suburban traffic-calming than urban placemaking, while the turn-lane signals mean that cyclists have to stop every 400 feet to wait for cars to turn left, and then wait through another light cycle while cars on the side streets cross the avenue. Newer designs on other avenues have "mixing zones" that allow bicycles to take priority, but inexperienced riders almost always give way to the two-ton vehicles bearing down on them.

not encumbered with the auto-scaled turn lanes, striping, and concrete pads.

The bicycle lane is wider in New York than most places (so that garbage trucks with snow plows mounted can clear the lane when it snows), and bold striping more appropriate for a freeway than a city street surrounds it. The usual delaminating plastic sticks are used in New York, too, and the crosswalks have an ungainly concrete pad in the street where pedestrians can wait to

cross. Like the formulaic suburban bumpouts, this ugly island is unnecessary in New York City: New Yorkers rarely stand on the curb while waiting to cross. Instead they wait by the corner of the parked cars, knowing that the car will prevent drivers from straying into the space where they wait.

Even cyclists have some problems with New York's Copenhagen Lanes. Earlier designs, like the one shown in Figure 6.5, have lights for left turn lanes. When the

Figure 6.6: East Broadway, Long Beach, California. Looking east, near the intersection with Long Beach Boulevard. In the center of Long Beach, the car is still king of the road. The engineer has allocated space for a bicycle lane, but the design priorities are clearly vehicular throughput (with bicycles included), rather than making a public realm where people want to get out of their car. The one-way street and the turn lanes help cars move rapidly, so lots of striping and warnings are necessary, which marks the street as a place for machines and gives it a scale unfriendly to humans. The protected bicycle lane is not a place where parents would let young children ride, because of the way the lane crosses over left turn lanes for cars. Making the road two-way, widening the sidewalks, and slowing the cars down would eliminate the need for bold striping and give the street a more human scale.

cars have a green light for turning left, bicycles have a red light. The timing on those means that cyclists have to stop every 400 feet (two New York City blocks) and wait for two light cycles: first the turn lane light, and then the light for the cars going across the avenue. Later designs got rid of the left-turn lights, substituting "mixing zones," where bold diagonal triangles alert drivers to watch out for bicycles. In reality, few duffers (and there are many of

those now that New York City has bike sharing) are going to cross in front of the two-ton gorilla behind them on the road, and the mixing zones add another level of machine-scale ugliness to the streetscape. New York had few turn lanes before these new Complete Streets, because they are anti-urban elements that favor the car and traffic flow.

Unfortunately, many engineers, bicycle advocates, and even pedestrian specialists have adopted America's

Figure 6.7: East Broadway, Long Beach, California. Looking east, from a vantage point half a block west of the view in Figure 6.6. The narrow sidewalk, the red curb, the parked cars visually floating in the middle of the street, and the accompanying striping all add up to an uncomfortable place for pedestrians on an important downtown street.

so-called Copenhagen Lane as Best Practice. Long Beach, California, a walkable city that sometimes promotes itself as the Brooklyn of Los Angeles, has been one of the most proactive American cities in the construction of bicycle lanes, and it adopted new auto-centric streets like Second Avenue in the heart of its downtown. But as in New York City, the one-way streets, staggered lights, turn lanes, and aggressive striping clearly show that the primary purpose of the Long Beach streets is to smoothly move traffic through the downtown. Very little is done to make the sidewalks attractive places to walk (Figures 6.6 and 6.7).

That serves many of the residents of Long Beach badly. Almost 40 percent of the residents in car-crazy Southern California (and the rest of the country) don't drive, because they are too young, too old, too poor, have a disability that prevents driving, or simply choose not to own a car or get a driver's license. In the long run, there will be better, more holistic solutions than these transitional Copenhagen Lane streets. It's not too early to start looking at better solutions, as long as we acknowledge the understandable tensions in the conversation.

OPTIONS (A STREET IS A TERRIBLE THING TO WASTE)

The worst bike lanes are the most ubiquitous: a narrow painted lane in the street, next to parked cars. If there is no buffer between the rider and the parked cars, people getting out of their cars sometimes "door" the cyclist as they exit. In addition, cars and delivery trucks frequently double park in the lane, forcing cyclists to swerve into the road, in front of traffic behind them and thus out of their view. Two virtues of the Copenhagen Lane as seen in New York are that there is a painted buffer zone between the parked cars and the bicycle lane that prevents dooring and that double-parkers don't block the lane.

Like bicycle lanes, bicycle riders come in many forms. There's the old-style, hard-core rider, who enjoys sparring with traffic and might wear latex bike clothes, have a fast, light bicycle, and weave in and out of the traffic. At the opposite end of the scale are the riders whom transportation expert Enrique Peñalosa (also a former Mayor of Bogotá, Colombia) is thinking of when he says, "A true bicycle network is one that can be used by a child."[23] These different users are not well served by a one-size-fits-all solution.

Bike lanes for young children should be separated from traffic. Here again, European practice is often ahead of standard practice in America. The cycle tracks in Munich and Berlin have an ideal form for children. The cycle track is a bike lane integrated with the sidewalk, but within a well-defined area identifiable by the pedestrians and protected from the road by trees and parked cars. There are important differences between the cycle track in Munich and the Copenhagen Lane as it is used in New York. The lane in Munich is part of the sidewalk, rather than the roadway; the sidewalk on the other side of the two-way street is the same, a symmetrical condition; and the lane has its own set of traffic lights, at a height where they are easy for cyclists to see. In the year 2013, very few places in America have bicycle networks in which all lanes are suitable for young children. A safe network is a worthwhile goal, but this is another area where the design and the form are still evolving. Children and duffers alike need what we might call Peñalosa Zones.

> A true bicycle network is one that can be used by a child.
>
> —Enrique Peñalosa, former Mayor of Bogotá

The best solutions are context-sensitive. The best bicycle lane for most adults is a slow, lightly trafficked street marked with the sharrow symbol that reminds drivers that the driving lane is also a bike lane (Figures 6.14 and 6.15).[24] When traffic is congested or going over 20 or 25 miles per hour, separated lanes are better. In Paris, there are many examples of single lanes reserved for buses and bicycles, separated from other lanes by low, narrow concrete strips on the road that are easily seen or felt through the steering wheel (Figures 6.11 and 2.59). In Barcelona, the city uses reflective "cat's eyes" to mark the space. But in snowy climates snowplows tear up the reflectors. The need to hyper-mark the road dissipates when cycling becomes ubiquitous; Stockholm's bike lanes and cycle tracks continue to function well even when snow covers the street and the lane markings (Figure 1.45).

Some cities are beginning to put two-way bike lanes or cycle tracks in the center of two-way streets (Figures 2.27 and 6.13). Riders in these can feel insecure when surrounded by fast or heavy traffic if the lanes are only defined by paint, but with the raised cycle tracks, they work well and look good. Great lanes can be made on boulevards and avenues with wide medians like Pike Street in Manhattan or the boulevard de Rochechouart in Paris (Figures 2.60 and 6.8), where there is room for the cycle track in the promenade section of the road. Cycle tracks can also be raised and attached to the outside of medians.

BICYCLE LANES & CYCLE TRACKS

Figure 6.8: Boulevard de Rochechouart, Paris, France.

Figure 6.9: Cours la Reine, Paris, France.

Figure 6.10: Urbanstraße, Berlin, Germany. *Image courtesy of Gianni Longo*

Figure 6.11: Boulevard St.-Germain, Paris, France.

Figure 6.12: Rue Robert Esnault-Pelterie, Paris, France.

Figure 6.14: Sharrow, Miami, Florida.

Figure 6.13: Pennsylvania Avenue, Washington, D.C. *Image courtesy of Richard Layman*

Figure 6.15: Tradd Street, Charleston, South Carolina.

EXPERIMENTATION AND DESIGN

Design can solve problems. Stanford Business School teaches what they call Design Thinking as a problem-solving technique, and urban designers use public charrettes to work out with stakeholders and local residents solutions to perennial planning issues. The general public today usually dislikes most recent development in their area and has a hard time envisioning something better. A good urban designer creates images that show something better is possible, demonstrating how specific problems can be overcome through design. A drawing of a bad downtown intersection everyone thinks of as blight might show how it could be transformed into a good urban place, for example. In the future, as we decrease traffic in our cities, we can apply bolder design thinking than simply narrowing roadbeds and widening sidewalks. We are still in an experimental phase in the design of streets, and we have to be careful about standardizing engineering solutions that emphasize throughput over more holistic solutions. An important goal is to design streets where activity can flourish and people want to walk.

ASYMMETRICAL STREETS

Figure 6.16: Rue Saint-Sulpice, Paris, France. Looking east on the rue Saint-Sulpice between rue Bonaparte and rue des Canettes. The broad, shady sidewalk is as wide as the street in front of it. *Image courtesy of Michael Ronkin, Designing Streets for People*

Figure 6.17: Brabantse Turfmarkt, Delft, the Netherlands. Looking south on Brabantse Turfmarkt from Burgwal. Traffic on the two-way street is so light that it is easy to imagine the street divided down the middle like Exhibition Road (Figure 4.87).

Figure 6.18: Mount Vernon Street, Boston, Massachusetts. Looking east on Mount Vernon Street, near the top of Beacon Hill. Setting the houses back on one side gives them more sun in the cold New England winter.

Design can solve problems.

Streets like the ones in Chapter 2, the streets that convinced the authors they wanted to be urban designers, can be copied quite literally or used to spark the invention of something new and different. The Yorkville Promenade was inspired by the Rambla de Catalunya; if the Promenade were built, the details might be quite similar to those in Barcelona (Figures 2.53 and 4.80). The experimental plan for Exhibition Road in London divided the street down the middle, putting shared space on one side, pedestrians on the other, and parked cars in the middle, with mixed success (4.87). Similarly, one of the problems with contemporary use of the Copenhagen Lanes in America is the visual imbalance caused by pushing the parked cars and heavy infrastructure out towards the middle of the street. But if we are going to follow experiments like the one in Madison Square, in which large parts of the road are taken away from use by the car, the layouts of several historic streets can suggest ways to visually divide the street successfully. As on Exhibition Road, one side of the street might be for cars, and the other side for pedestrians, but if we plant trees in the center, rather than insubstantial pylons, the character of the street would be very different (Figures 6.16 and 6.17). Filling one side with street furniture and a café also alters the visual effect. The experience of walking on a street divided down the middle in either of those ways would be very different than the experience of walking down one of the many streets around the country with overscaled Copenhagen Lanes and parked cars to one side. A good design can make a beautiful asymmetrical street (Color Plate 9).

Two experimental street designs for New York—one breaking ground in 2013 and the other a proposal—show possibilities. Hudson Boulevard will be the first new boulevard in New York in almost a century, built as part of the development of the Hudson train yards on the west side of Manhattan (Figure 6.19). Michael van Valkenburgh's design for the street has a broad median with a style of landscape architecture known as Land-

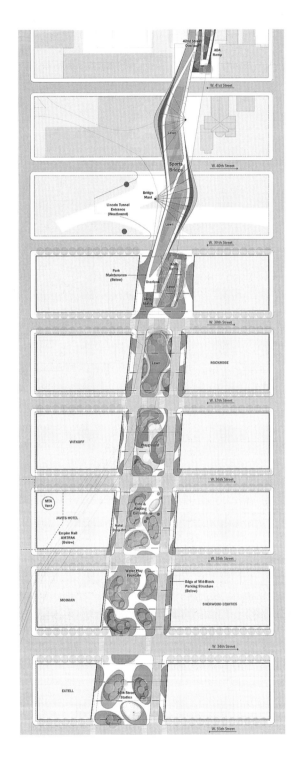

◀ **Figure 6.19:** Hudson Boulevard, New York, New York. Plan. Michael Van Valkenburgh Associates, 2013. The design features Mid-Century Modern "Googie" curves rather than traditional placemaking. *Image courtesy of Hudson Yards Development Corporation, New York City Economic Development Corporation, and Michael Van Valkenburgh Associates, Inc*

Figure 6.20 Park Avenue, New York, New York. Looking north on Park Avenue in 1920 at 50th Street, showing the wide median constructed over the train tracks after Grand Central Terminal was built. *Image courtesy of SHoP Architects / CURE*

Figure 6.21: Park Avenue, New York, New York. Computer simulation. SHoP Architects / CURE, 2012. Looking north from 51st Street, showing one of the blocks without left-turn lanes. © *2012 SHoP Architects / CURE*

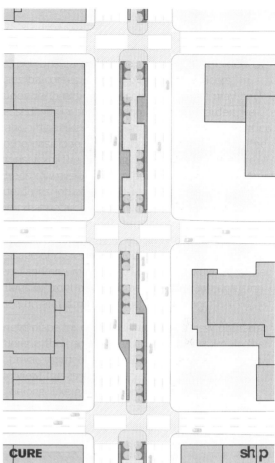

Figure 6.22: Park Avenue, New York, New York. Plan. SHoP Architects / CURE, 2012. © *2012 SHoP Architects / CURE*

scape Urbanism. In the hands of van Valkenburgh, Landscape Urbanism frequently emphasizes neo-1960s geometry and "narrative" rather than the placemaking advocated here.[25] When built, Landscape Urbanism can be surprisingly reminiscent of bland suburban gardens and 1960s office parks.

The *experience* of visiting another of van Valkenburgh's designs in Manhattan, Teardrop Park in Battery Park City, is neither very bad nor very good: the design illustrates intellectual concepts and generally ignores traditional park design.[26] The drawings for Hudson Boulevard similarly bypass placemaking principles and emphasize Mid-Century Modern curves reminiscent of what is known as "Googie" design. This was a futuristic style developed in 1949 by the architect John Lautner for a coffee shop in West Hollywood named Googies. America was falling in love with nuclear power and space travel, and Lautner's invention became a popular style for suburban drive-in restaurants that needed to attract the attention of motorists speeding by. For architects, the space-age curves were a way to break with traditional design, because their geometry is artificial in character and appears machine-made. They are popular today with Landscape Urbanists for similar reasons. When used "in plan," they are more about two-dimensional pattern making than placemaking.

The proposal by Vishaan Chakrabarti and SHoP Architects to rebuild Park Avenue from 46th Street to 59th Street harks back to the original plan for Park Avenue, which was built with a very wide median (Figure 6.20). Chakrabarti brings to the design a Modernist aesthetic *and* left-turn lanes. The broad median seems like a better idea for Manhattan than the suburban-style left-turn lanes, which regularly narrow the median with an unpleasant auto-based geometry (Figure 6.22). But like the NYC DOT experiments in places like Madison Square (Figure 4.68), the Park Avenue and Hudson Boulevard plans are a big step forward for the state of New York City streets—and probably more expedient politically than a design that takes away traffic or parking space without adding turn lanes.[27]

HUMAN HABITAT DIVERSITY

In any flourishing biohabitat, diversity and "species richness" are key indicators of health. When naturalists think of wildlife habitat, they think of a place's potential to attract a given species to nest, forage, or hunt, find a mate, engage in its rituals, and safely nurture its young. A place that allows all this for numerous fauna is considered the prime and most sensitive habitat. This principle applies to the human habitat as well. Cities use their menu of varied streets and building types to offer nurturing habitats for our widely varying households, businesses, and institutions. There are big businesses and small ones, with differing needs for corporate grandeur or for creative comfort in their addresses. We have households of all sizes, types, and income levels, each needing dignified housing; most are drawn to detached houses and low-rise or mid-rise buildings, while a few others—the ones Frank Lloyd Wright called "cliff dwellers"—are attracted to high-rises. Similarly, human beings also crave different kinds of street addresses and experiences, some narrow, some wide, some with views long and straight, others cranked or curved and revealed as we go. A diverse society in a modern city like Barcelona can find all these, in the twisting streets of the medieval quarter or the formal streets of the city's nineteenth-century extension. The ideal is for these diverse habitats to be connected via streets and public spaces that nurture them in turn. Streets can do this by encouraging convenient daily travel, helping commerce, speeding the flow of ideas, and increasing the opportunities for interaction among people. A high-quality street is psychologically uplifting as well, affording us a sense of communion with those around us that extends beyond our daily concerns.

The most productive, safest sort of street habitat is also busy at all times of day: the tree-lined, main street outside of our South Miami office, for example, is a prime habitat for runners and bicyclists on their morning fitness routine; drivers heading to work on their daily commute; workers walking to a café or bookstore during lunch; mothers taking their children for afternoon errands; transit riders waiting at the bus stop at the day's end; couples out for an evening meal and a movie; and singles walking home late after a night at the bar. Efficiently used, resilient space like this not only keeps neighborhoods safe and thriving, but also ultimately conserves land and energy resources.

HEALTH IMPACT ASSESSMENTS FOR STREET DESIGNS

We know that people who have to spend a lot of time driving are likely to be heavier and less healthy than those who live and work in walkable places. Now research suggests that they're also more vulnerable to mental health problems than we might suspect. One medical study found that the "form, scale, and speed of the environments we inhabit" can affect our mental well-being—or lack of it. The stress inherent in a rush-hour commute in suburbia is obvious, but the more subtle discomfort that arises while standing in large seas of parking in an overscaled commercial strip is just as real. Doctors found a likely link between the postwar growth of sprawl and an increase in mental illness, most specifically depression, anxiety, and attention deficit disorder.[28] The lack of beauty, physical activity, and human interaction characteristic of sprawl contributes to these conditions.[29]

Health Impact Assessments (known as HIAs) empower decision-makers to consider the well-being of humans when weighing the costs and benefits of urban design projects, making HIAs a possibly important tool for guiding new street design practice and policy. The World Health Organization defines an HIA as "a combination of procedures, methods and tools by which a policy, program, or project may be judged as to its potential effects on the health of a population, and the distribution of those effects within the population."[30]

According to the Centers for Disease Control and Prevention, the major steps in conducting a Health Impact Assessment include:

- Screening (identifying projects or policies for which a Health Impact Assessment would be useful).
- Scoping (identifying which health effects to consider).
- Assessing risks and benefits (identifying which people may be affected and how they may be affected).
- Developing recommendations (suggesting changes to proposals to promote positive or mitigate adverse health effects).
- Reporting (presenting the results to decision-makers).
- Evaluating (determining the effect of the HIA on the decision).

HIAs are still a relatively unregulated tool that can be used in a variety of ways, from quick, desktop analyses to multiyear, intensive research projects. Although new, HIAs have been used to assess projects as varied as citywide transportation plans, corridor plans, neighborhood rezoning projects, and housing development designs, from San Francisco to Decatur. HIAs could become a powerful tool for evaluating street designs, provided designers engage in an effort to refine the technique.

Figure 6.23: Motcomb Street, London, England. Looking southwest from the intersection with Kinnerton Street. Motcomb Street is a human habitat where healthy life flourishes.

STREETS MATTER

Mental health, physical health, societal health, planetary health—streets figure in all of them. The network of highways, arterials, collectors, and cul-de-sacs that America built in the second half of the twentieth century was the largest and most expensive building project in the history of the world, and it fostered an auto-dependent, suburban way of life that was perhaps our largest and most expensive social experiment in history. Now we find ourselves the first generations whose decisions about how to build will determine the future of our planet, for better or for worse—and streets are at the center of that too. Americans are 5 percent of the world's population, but we use almost 25 percent of the world's energy because of the way we planned our roads and buildings.

The good news is that the two biggest American consumer groups, the baby boomers and their millennial children, both want to live in walkable cities and towns, which will be good for them and good for the planet. Boomers no longer need large houses for their children, who have left the nest, while the share of miles driven by Americans in their twenties has dropped from 20.8 percent to just 13.7 percent since the late 1990s.[31] There is evidence that the trend is growing among teenagers, part of what Richard Florida calls "the Great Car Reset": "Younger people today . . . no longer see the car as a necessary expense. In fact, it is increasingly just the opposite: not owning a car and not owning a house are seen by more and more as a path to greater flexibility, choice, and personal autonomy."[32]

Figure 6.24: Germantown Avenue, Chestnut Hill, Philadelphia, Pennsylvania. Looking southeast from the Chestnut Hill SEPTA station. A classic American Main Street. © 2006 Sandy Sorlien

IF YOU KNOW IT IS USEFUL, AND FEEL IT IS BEAUTIFUL, REPEAT IT.

To close, we offer a simple idea: When you find something useful, and feel it is beautiful, use it in your own designs, either literally or for inspiration. That is how all the great streets in this book were created. We have included many photos and descriptions of them, knowing well that most of them cannot be replicated without special exemptions from the layers of rules and stacks of manuals that regulate street design and construction—but that doesn't mean they're not useful. We have illustrated both new streets and retrofitted streets that go beyond conventional contemporary practice, and while some are bold and others are just small first steps, they are all important steps. Nothing loosens up a deep-rooted paralysis in officialdom like a picture of an idea that's already been proven to work. Even if the street isn't built, the design might lead to other, better ideas that will be built.

In an article about the future of architecture, the former Dean of the Architecture School at Princeton University wrote, "What is required to comprehend globalism today are not tired generalizations, but close study of specific places, cities and cultures."[33] We have had almost a century of design that emphasized change and pure invention. The result in architecture and urbanism has been some great buildings, but many more bad ones. We've had Minoru Yamasaki's Pruitt-

Figure 6.25: Dauphine Street, New Orleans, Louisiana. Looking northeast towards Ursulines Avenue. A beautiful residential street in one of our most beautiful cities. There is nothing in this photo that cannot be easily and economically repeated today.

▲ Figure 6.26: Broadway, New York, New York. Looking north towards Herald Square and Times Square from the IRT Sixth Avenue Elevated, circa 1908. Before the coronation of the car, Broadway had no traffic signs, no stop signs, no stop lights, and no striping. People waited in the street for the cable cars, and one can see in the photo that they felt comfortable stepping out into the street. Cropped from a famous view taken by the Detroit Publishing Company. *Library of Congress, Prints and Photographs Division, Detroit Publishing Company Photograph Collection, LC-D4-90241*

◄ Figure 6.27: Grayton Beach, Florida. Circa 1981. Daryl and Robert Davis in the "land yacht" they used for touring towns on the Florida Panhandle and southern Alabama with Andrés Duany and Elizabeth Plater-Zyberk. The trips helped them envision what they wanted to build at Seaside, which led to a development *TIME* called "one of the most influential projects of the decade, and, hopefully, decades to come."[34] © *Steven Brooke Studios*

Igoe housing project and Richard Serra's Tilted Arc, both of which had to be torn down. Like New Coke and the Edsel, they reflect a thoughtless drive towards change for the sake of change, which is not the same thing as progress. "Western society has accepted as unquestionable a technological imperative that is quite as arbitrary as the most primitive taboo," Lewis Mumford wrote. "Not merely the duty to foster invention and constantly to create technological novelties, but equally the duty to surrender to these novelties unconditionally, just because they are offered, without respect to their human consequences."

The best architectural design of the last half century was almost always more concerned with making objects than making places. The public realm suffered badly, and now many people want it back, along with walkable towns and cities. This is not an idealistic dream, but a simple, practical solution to many of the complex problems we face as a society, problems that undermine our nation's economic competitiveness, environmental sustainability, and public welfare.

We present the case studies here with the hope that professionals, activists, and leaders will be emboldened by them and that they will use the images to win arguments and get street design back on track. Once we have reclaimed our streets for their original users—ourselves—who knows what evolutionary leaps might happen. Go out, look at our great streets, find your own, and make even better ones. The next generation of streets might just be the best yet.

To get where we want to go, we have to ask the right questions. Instead of asking "How do we make traffic flow better?" or "What is effective traffic calming?" we need to ask, "How do we make our streets and cities places where people want to get out of their cars and walk?" and "How do we make our cities and towns great places where people want to be?" Then we will have more liveable towns and cities. History and experience have shown us how to make great places and great streets. All that remains is to do it.

> What is the city but the people?
>
> —William Shakespeare, *Coriolanus*, Act 3, scene 1

NOTES

1. Paul Goodman, *Growing Up Absurd: Problems of Youth in the Organized System* (New York: Random House, 1956), 97.

2. Robert Putnam, *Bowling Alone: The Collapse and Revival of American Community* (New York: Simon & Schuster, 2000), *passim*.

3. There is no pleasure in driving on suburban arterials or getting stuck on the highway on the daily commute. Fifty years ago, driving around the suburbs could be a wonderful experience, because the roads were empty and often beautiful. But now our cars are where we develop road rage, flipping off the guy who had the audacity to slip in ahead of us. Cars are our five-thousand-pound, gas-guzzling cocoons, insulating us from contact with strangers and neighbors alike. And we haven't even mentioned climate change, peak oil, the price of gas, or the fact that on the whole our allies in the world are not the ones with large oil reserves. Andrés Duany, who loves fast cars, often says that New Urbanists

are trying to make driving fun again. The way to do that is to make us less dependent on driving on arterials and crowded highways.

4. Claudia Wallis, "The New Science of Happiness," *TIME*, January 9, 2005. http://www.time.com/time/magazine/article/0,9171,1015902,00.html.

5. According to John De Graaf, President of the public policy organization Take Back The Time. http://www.timeday.org. Recent neurological research indicates that face-to-face socializing increases happiness, while a lack of face-to-face time decreases not only our happiness, but also our ability to empathize with others and our physical health: "When you share a smile or laugh with someone face to face, a discernible synchrony emerges between you, as your gestures and biochemistries, even your respective neural firings, come to mirror each other. It's micro-moments like these, in which a wave of good feeling rolls through two brains and bodies at once, that build your capacity to empathize as well as to improve

your health. If you don't regularly exercise this capacity, it withers. Lucky for us, connecting with others does good and feels good, and opportunities to do so abound." Barbara L. Frederickson, "Your Phone vs. Your Heart," *New York Times*, March 23, 2013, http://www.nytimes.com/2013/03/24/opinion/sunday/your-phone-vs-your-heart.html.

6. Quoted by Lisa Farino, "How Happy Is Your City?" *msn healthy living*, http://healthyliving.msn.com/diseases/depression/how-happy-is-your-city-1. Post also says, "Forty years ago, neighborhoods had sidewalks, front porches, and parks—geographical opportunities for people to be socially engaged. In many communities today, we are lacking these things. We don't know our neighbors anymore. We just get into our car pods and never see anyone. We no longer have the opportunity to stumble upon happiness by being good neighbors in our communities." As mentioned, Post is the author of *Why Good Things Happen to Good People* (New York: Broadway Books, 2007).

7. *Ibid.*, http://healthyliving.msn.com/diseases/depression/how-happy-is-your-city-1.

8. Angie Schmitt, "FHWA Endorses Engineering Guide for Walkable Urban Streets," *Streetsblog DC*, September 13, 2013, http://dc.streetsblog.org/2013/09/13/fhwa-endorses-engineering-guide-for-walkable-urban-streets/. The CNU ITE Manual was funded by the FHWA and the EPA. Also see Institute of Transportation Engineers, *Designing Walkable Urban Thoroughfares: A Context Sensitive Approach,* 2010, http://ite.org/bookstore/RP036.pdf. The manual can be difficult reading for anyone but engineers, but in essence it uses the design criteria set by AASHTO for road design to argue that streets in walkable areas should have a "target speed" appropriate for the activities lining the road, i.e., for example, that downtowns require slow traffic speeds to function well as downtowns.

9. Jonathan Brown, Andrew Grice, and George Arnett, "The 20 mph Revolution: Millions of Drivers Face Lower Speed Limits as New Laws Sweep the Country," *The Independent*, December 31, 2012. http://www.independent.co.uk/news/uk/home-news/the-20mph-revolution-millions-of-drivers-face-lower-speed-limits-as-new-laws-sweep-the-country-8434292.html. Also, 20s Plenty for Us, the website of the British group, http://www.20splentyforus.org.uk/.

10. "20 MPH Zone," Wikipedia, http://en.wikipedia.org/wiki/20_mph_zone.

11. 20s Plenty for Us, http//www.20splentyforus.org.uk/.

12. Brown, Grice, and Arnett, *op. cit.*

13. From the National Complete Streets Coalition website at http://www.smartgrowthamerica.org/complete-streets: "Instituting a Complete Streets policy ensures that transportation planners and engineers consistently design and operate the entire roadway with all users in mind – including bicyclists, public transportation vehicles and riders, and pedestrians of all ages and abilities."

14. In addition, many policymakers will tell you that they are more interested in the means (getting legislation passed) than the ends (the final result, i.e., the quality of what gets built). Urban designers, on the other hand, care most passionately about the character of the Complete Street. Not only is God in the details, as in Mies van der Rohe's famous aphorism, but it is the character and quality of the street that determines whether or not the street is a place where people want to be. Broad sidewalks and safe bicycle lanes are useless if people don't use them.

15. John Doyle and Todd Venezia, "All Out to End the 'Cycle' Bike Crackdown," *New York Post*, January 24, 2011. http://www.nypost.com/p/news/local/all_out_to_end_the_cycle_woLvONH7WNzl5pjSLAYMuO?CMP=OTC-rss&FEED-NAME=

16. Lawsuits have been brought against the city by politically important figures and impassioned, derogatory stories have appeared in newspapers and magazines—sometimes met by equally derogatory defenses from the city's bicycle community. A sampling of articles for and against, beginning with Second Avenue and including a *New York Times* poll that says two-thirds of New Yorkers support the city's bike lane program: Ben Fried, "Bin Laden Is Dead, But the Second Avenue Bike Lane Lives On," *Streetsblog*, July 8, 2011, http://www.streetsblog.org/2011/07/08/bin-laden-is-dead-but-the-second-avenue-bike-lane-lives-on/; Ethan Kent, "Ciclovia, Is NYC Ready?," *Streetsblog*, June 6, 2007, http://www.streetsblog.org/2007/06/06/ciclovia-bogota/; Brian Paul, "Copenhagen Comes to New York?," *Remapping Debate*, February 9, 2011, http://www.remappingdebate.org/article/copenhagen-comes-new-york; John Cassidy, "Battle of the Bike Lanes," *The New Yorker*, March 8, 2011, http://www.newyorker.com/online/blogs/johncassidy/2011/03/battle-of-the-bike-lanes-im-with-mrs-schumer.html; Matt Chaban, "Bike Lames! Straw Men on 10-Speeds in New York's Last Culture War," *New York Observer*, March 9, 2011, http://observer.com/2011/03/bike-lames-straw-men-on-10speeds-in-new-yorks-last-culture-war/; Aaron Naparstek, "The New York City Bike Lane Backlash is Completely Irrational," *Naparstek Post*, March 9, 2011, http://naparstek.com/2011/03/

bike-lane-backlash-makes-no-sense/; Matthew Shear, "Not Quite Copenhagen, Is New York Too New York for Bike Lanes?," *New York*, March 20, 2011, http://nymag.com/news/features/bike-wars-2011-3/; Steve Cuozzo, "Murder on Broadway, Pedestrian Lanes Blighting Biz," *New York Post*, July 14, 2011, http://www.nypost.com/p/news/opinion/opedcolumnists/murder_on_broadway_HrAAmNfUqmTwQVVYL5zW3L; Brad Aaron, "In the Tortured Mind of Steve Cuozzo, Even Street Trees Are a Threat," *Streetsblog*, July 15, 2011, http://www.streetsblog.org/2011/07/15/in-the-tortured-mind-of-steve-cuozzo-even-street-trees-are-a-threat/; Adam Sternbergh, "'I Was A Teenage Cyclist,' or How Anti-Bike-Lane Arguments Echo the Tea Party," The 6th Floor Blog, *New York Times*, March 9, 2011, http://6thfloor.blogs.nytimes.com/2011/03/09/i-was-a-teenage-cyclist-or-how-anti-bike-lane-arguments-echo-the-tea-party/; Ben Fried, "Bin Laden Is Dead, But the Second Avenue Bike Lane Lives On," *Streetsblog*, July 8, 2011, http://www.streetsblog.org/2011/07/08/bin-laden-is-dead-but-the-second-avenue-bike-lane-lives-on/; Michael M. Grynbaum and Marjorie Connelly, "Bicycle Lanes Draw Wide Support Among New Yorkers, Survey Finds," *New York Times*, August 21, 2012, http://www.nytimes.com/2012/08/22/nyregion/most-new-yorkers-say-bike-lanes-are-a-good-idea.html; Steve Cuozzo, "The bike-lane cancer Metastasis on Columbus," *New York Post*, December 12, 2012, http://www.nypost.com/p/news/opinion/opedcolumnists/the_bike_lane_cancer_K9pLTd5ap3Vl-H7fDOYqSKM; Ben Fried, "Help Make Sense of Crazy Steve Cuozzo," *Streetsblog*, December 13, 2012, http://www.streetsblog.org/2012/12/13/help-make-sense-of-crazy-steve-cuozzo/; Noah Kazis, "The NBBL Files: PPW Foes Pursued Connections to Reverse Public Process," *Streetsblog*, December 20, 2012, http://www.streetsblog.org/?s=The+NBBL+Files%3A+PPW+Foes+Pursued+Connections+to+Reverse+Public+Process; Noah Kazis and Ben Fried, "The NBBL Files: Weinshall and Steisel Manufactured Anti-Bike Coverage," *Streetsblog*, December 20, 2012, http://www.streetsblog.org/?s=The+NBBL+Files%3A+P-PW+Foes+Pursued+Connections+to+Reverse+Public+Process; Denis Hamill, "'I Hate Bike Lanes and Support the Mayoral Candidate Who Will Put the Brakes on Them," *New York Daily News*, January 29, 2013, updated January 30, 2013, http://www.nydailynews.com/opinion/hamill-hate-bike-lanes-article-1.1250744#ixzz2JTqJEWDf; Christopher Robbins, "Daily News Columnist: 'Big Crashes' Await Cyclists Who Use Bike Lanes. *Gothamist*, January 30, 2013, http://gothamist.com/2013/01/30/daily_news_columnist_big_crashes_aw.php; Matt Flegenheimer,

"Anxiety over Future of Bike Lanes," *New York Times*, February 13, 2013, http://www.nytimes.com/2013/02/13/nyregion/new-york-bike-lane-advocates-fear-new-mayor-will-roll-back-gains.html. On June 23, 2013, the *New York Times* reported that following a June 2012 lawsuit filed against the New York City Police Department over a pedestrian death in Brooklyn, "the Police Department has quietly moved to examine more of these crashes, focusing new attention and resources on another manner of violent death in the streets—the victims walking, riding bicycles or in a vehicle." See J. David Goodman, "Police Unit Taking Closer Look at Deadly Crashes," *New York Times*, June 23, 2013, http://www.nytimes.com/2013/06/24/nyregion/police-unit-taking-closer-look-at-deadly-crashes.html. But in early July 2, 2013, soon after the Citi Bike bikeshare began in New York City, *Streetsblog* reported that, "NYPD precincts in Manhattan wrote nearly twice as many tickets to cyclists in the month after the launch of Citi Bike than they issued to speeding motorists in the first five months of 2013, according to data from NYPD and the Daily News." See Ben Aaron, "NYPD Speed Enforcement Uptick Dwarfed By Bike-Share Area Ticket Blitz," *Streetsblog*, July 2, 2013, http://www.streetsblog.org/2013/07/02/nypd-speed-enforcement-uptick-dwarfed-by-bike-share-area-ticket-blitz/.

17. Even cyclists prefer attractive routes to faster ones: "In the case of cyclists: a minute of cycling along a comfortable, pleasant and diversified cycling route will seem to pass much faster than the same minute spent cycling along a busy, and boring main road." See "Cyclists prefer comfortable routes over fast ones" at Fiets Baraad: http://bit.ly/14AZIS8. The website refers to an unpublished study at Dutch Railways that shows many activities went more quickly in attractive and interesting surroundings. For studies about the pedestrian preferences that include a number of factors, including the visual experience, see: E. Leslie, B. Saelens, L. Frank, N. Owen, A. Bauman, N. Coffee, and G. Hugo, "Residents' perceptions of walkability attributes in objectively different neighbourhoods: a pilot study," *Health & Place* (2005), 11:3, 227-236; P. Bovy and S. Hoogendoorn-Lanser, "Modelling route choice behaviour in multi-modal transport networks." *Transportation* (July 2005), 32:4, 341-368; E. Cerin, B. Saelens, J. Sallis, and L. Frank, "Neighborhood Environment Walkability Scale: Validity and Development of a Short Form," *Medicine and Science in Sports and Exercise* (2006), 1682-1691; S.L. Handy, "Understanding the link between urban form and nonwork travel behavior." *Journal of Planning Education and Research* (April 1996), 15:3, 183-198. For a similar study about bikeability, see L. Wahlgren,

and P. Schantz, "Exploring bikeability in a metropolitan setting: Stimulating and hindering factors in commuting route environments," BMC Public Health (2012), 12, 168.

18. Jeff Speck, *Walkable City: How Downtown Can Save America, One Step at a Time* (New York: Farrar, Straus & Giroux, 2012), 191.

19. *Ibid.,* 191.

20. *Ibid.*

21. *Ibid.*

22. *Ibid.,* 52.

23. Peñalosa is interviewed in the film *The Case for Separated Bike Lanes in NYC*, StreetFilms. http://www.youtube.com/watch?v=ONS2ptAR4mo.

24. "Sharrow" combines the words "share" and "arrow," and refers to the symbol painted on the street to indicate the shared lane. The lane itself is now commonly called a sharrow, however.

25. Hudson Boulevard will cover the Amtrak tunnel that runs from Pennsylvania Station to Long Island and points north. The boulevard is described on the website of the Hudson Yards Development Corporation, at http://www.hydc.org/html/project/hudson-park.shtml.

26. Although Ethan Kent disagreed with that assessment in his article "Hall of Shame, Teardrop Park," http://www.pps.org/great_public_spaces/one?public_place_id=869. Van Valkenburgh is the Charles Eliot Professor of Practice in Landscape Architecture at the Harvard Graduate School of Design (GSD). The department is a center of Landscape Urbanism, which has rapidly become both influential and an academic alternative to New Urbanism: see Charles Waldheim, *The Landscape Urbanism Reader* (New York, Princeton Architectural Press, 2006). Since 2006, Landscape Urbanists have been increasingly successful at winning urban design competitions. One example is Stoss's winning entry in the Movement on Main competition to "reimagine" the design of Main Streets like Wyoming Street in Syracuse, New York. This experiment is published in Daniel Jost, "Stoss's Winning Syracuse Street," *Landscape Architecture Magazine*, April 17, 2013, http://landscapearchitecturemagazine.org/2013/04/17/stosss-winning-syracuse-street/. For a contrasting view of Landscape Urbanism, see Andrés Duany and Emily Talen, Editors, *Landscape Urbanism and its Discontents: Dissimulating the Sustainable City* (Gabriola Island, BC: New Society Publishers, 2013).

27. Chakrabarti is a partner at SHoP Architects, director of the Center for Urban Real Estate (CURE) at the Graduate School for Architecture, Planning, and Preservation, Columbia University, and the former director of the Manhattan Office at the Department of City Planning. For his Park Avenue proposal, see Matt Chaban, "Pedestrians at the Gates: Pathway Plan for Park Avenue Could Turn Class Into Mass," *The New York Observer*, November 27, 2012. http://observer.com/2012/11/a-high-line-for-the-east-side-plan-for-park-avenue-could-turn-class-into-mass/. One of the developers to whom the Fund for Park Avenue might look for funding for the plan says in the story, "Nobody on Park Avenue walks." He's quoted again later: "'I stopped walking a decade ago,' said [the forty-year-old] Mr. Shvo nonchalantly, a statement of success rather than disability." This highlights that the "1%" who frequently get Mayor Bloomberg's ear are among those who often complain about Commissioner Sadik-Khan's more radical plans for New York City streets, because they travel around New York in limousines with drivers. The wife of another developer quoted in the story says, "That's ludicrous. What if you're coming here? Where would your driver stand the car?"

28. Dr. Howard Frumkin, "Urban Sprawl and Public Health," *Public Health Reports*, May–June 2012, 207, http://www.cdc.gov/healthyplaces/articles/urban_sprawl_and_public_health_phr.pdf.

29. Greg Lindsay, "Driving Makes You Fat, Urban Sprawl Bankrupts You, Other Life-Saving New Urbanist Epiphanies," *Fast Company*, May 21, 2010. http://www.fastcompany.com/1650173/driving-makes-you-fat-urban-sprawl-bankrupts-you-other-life-saving-new-urbanist-epiphanies.

30. "Definition of Health Impact Assessment," World Health Organization, http://www.euro.who.int/en/what-we-do/health-topics/environment-and-health/health-impact-assessment/definition-of-health-impact-assessment-hia.

31. Speck, 19.

32. Richard, Florida, "The Great Reset," *The Atlantic*, June 3, 2010. http://www.theatlantic.com/national/archive/2010/06/the-great-car-reset/57606/. Florida cites statistics from Nate Silver, "The End of Car Culture." It's not just erratic gas prices and a bad economy that's hurting automakers. It may be that Americans are changing," *Esquire*, May 6, 2009. http://www.esquire.com/features/data/nate-silver-car-culture-stats-0609. And Jack Neff, "Is Digital Revolution Driving Decline in U.S. Car Culture? Shift Toward Fewer Young Drivers Could Have Repercussions for All Marketers," *Ad Age | digital*, May 31, 2010, http://adage.com/article/digital/digital-revolution-driving-decline-u-s-car-culture/144155/.

33. Stan Allen, "The Future That Is Now," *Design Observer*, March 12, 2012, http://places.designobserver.com/feature/architecture-school-the-future-that-is-now/32728/. Allen continued, "It is worth remembering that architecture remains rooted to place, even in an age celebrated for global culture; what circulates are images, ideas, expertise and architects themselves." Political philosopher Kwame Anthony Appiah has written about the need to cultivate a cosmopolitan attitude in the face of global culture today, neither artificially preserving "authentic" local traditions, nor giving in mindlessly to the forces of globalism.* Instead, he advocates paying close attention to the necessary hybridity of a contemporary culture that works with elements of history and tradition just as it takes full advantage of new technologies and the opportunities of global exchange. Something similar will be required in architecture and education to take account of the issues discussed here as well as others impossible to anticipate." * Allen included this citation: Kwame Anthony Appiah, *Cosmopolitanism* (New York: Norton, 2006).

34. Kurt Andersen, "Design: Best of the Decade," *TIME*, January 1, 1990.

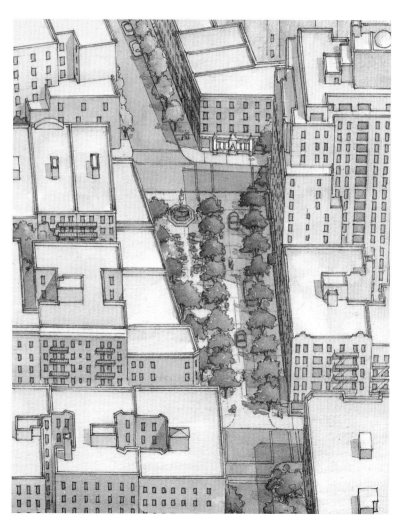

Figure 6.28: Jane Jacobs Square. New York, New York. See Figure 4.70.

AFTERWORD

James Howard Kunstler

FOR THE LAST QUARTER-CENTURY, a debate raged across this land between the people who delivered the suburban living arrangement (home builders, DOT engineers, zoning officials) and a small band of reformers calling themselves the New Urbanists. It was about whether the quality of the human habitat in America would continue to be the same horrifying, dehumanized, monotonous, formulaic, commoditized fiasco ordained by single-minded econometrics and an obeisance to Happy Motoring or a return to the sounder premise that, above all, the places we design and assemble must be worth caring about.

At the heart of this debate was the design of America's streets, the hierarchy of arteries that are supposed to keep any given civic organism alive. They were a perfect metaphor for the fantastically destructive way of life that was physically ravaging the very bodies of so many of our citizens. Our streets had become clogged and disfigured by the progression of a flamboyantly visible disease—the endless, ghastly, groaning panoramas of strip malls, hamburger sheds, muffler shops, chain stores, and one-story, tilt-up service effluvia, with all the clownish signage, stacked turning lanes, and free-parking wastelands—that pointed straight to cultural and economic sclerosis. The New Urbanists labored mightily to begin the daunting job of recovery.

Those arguments are now pretty much settled by default because the conditions of resource and capital scarcity we now find ourselves in have determined that the suburban project is over. We're done building things that way. Most of America does not realize it yet—particularly the home builders, the realtors, the DOT commissioners, et al. They are all hanging back, waiting for the housing bust to reach bottom, with the expectation that sooner or later they will resume their previous behavior. But they wait in vain. You can stick a fork in them: they're done. It's over.

We've entered a phase of history that will be characterized by a comprehensive contraction of human activity, especially of the magic elixir called economic growth—in the sense that we can expect to have ever more of everything. It must be obvious that there are many things we would benefit from not having more of, starting with human population and wholesale destruction of the only planet that is available for us to live on. The kind of economic growth I refer to—the financial manifestation of industrialism—is intimately dependent on the energy resources available to us. Peak oil (and peak many other natural resources) guarantees that we will have far less energy. Despite the monumental techno-narcissism reigning in a fearful and wish-beset society witnessing the first tremors of this epochal reset, so-called *alternative energy* will not compensate for the losses of oil, coal, and methane gas in the sense that no combination of wind, solar, nuclear, biodiesel, ethanol, algae secretions, or recycled fry-o-lator grease will allow us to run Walmart, Walt Disney World, suburbia, the Interstate highway system, the U.S. military, and all the rest of our kit as it was designed to run. This discovery will be hugely disappointing.

By the way, none of the above should suggest the end of the world—just the end of one phase of history and the beginning of a new one. Human life can go on and the project of civilization can continue, but surely at a different pitch than the frantic cavalcade of reckless techno-triumphalism we are used to. The effect on the places where we dwell will be stunningly transformative. First, of course, is the question of what happens to the stuff that is on the ground already. Eighty percent of everything ever built in America was built after the Second World War, and most of it was not designed for the ages, to put it nicely. As I see it, it has three destinies, none of them mutually exclusive: slums, ruins, and salvage yards. Most of the suburban fiasco does not lend itself to

◀ Market Street, Charleston, South Carolina. See Figure 3.8.

391

retrofit. Obviously, some places have more intrinsic value than others in terms of geography, proximity to resources, food production, et cetera, and some have the capacity to be improved. Our ability to do this will be constrained by the aforementioned capital and resource shortages. In fact, one of the reasons that suburbia will have so much salvage value is that many fabricated and modular materials that we now take for granted will probably be quite scarce in the decades to come—everything from aluminum truss-work to concrete blocks.

The real action will take place in our existing towns and cities, though I maintain that our gigantic metroplex megacities will have to contract substantially and that the smaller ones already scaled to the resource realities of the future will be the more successful places—especially those cities that are located on inland waterways, since the economy will be more internally focused in North America as globalism withers. One thing we can be sure of: the age of mass Happy Motoring will draw to a close, and with it the age of a public realm degraded by it. There is a connection between the tyrannical presence of cars moving at speed and the astounding lack of decorum in the everyday world of recent decades. When you are passing quickly by buildings very little registers—except, perhaps, a simplistic advertising message such as "Hamburgers Within." It has, therefore, been unnecessary, even futile, to furnish any detail or ornamentation, except of the most cartoonish kind—and, anyway, the architecture profession has militated against the decoration of buildings for a century for a variety of reasons, ranging from the ideological to the mendacious.

Believe me, we are about to slow down. We are once again going to start walking around the places we live, and as that occurs and becomes normal, we will rapidly redevelop a demand for higher quality in building at the human scale. We are also about to witness the obsoles-

cence of skyscrapers and tall buildings generally, not just because of energy issues—heating, cooling, et cetera—but for the more profound reason that in a resource- and capital-constrained future, they will never be renovated. The ones most recently built will prove to be one-generation buildings. This is unfortunate, and it is one of the reasons that our biggest cities will get into trouble, but life is tragic and sometimes whole societies make bad choices. However, if we can accommodate ourselves to this reality, we can free ourselves to put our remaining resources into rebuilding an everyday environment at a scale more congenial to human physiognomy and neurology, which will surely amount to places more comfortable to spend our lives in.

Finally, there is the question of artistry in the design and assembly of the human habitat. For several generations now we have endeavored to do without it, resorting instead to the false measures of statistical analysis and econometrics, neither of which have even any remote association with certain qualities of excellence that make us grateful to be alive. In doing so, we have starved and even deformed our souls. The result, naturally, has been a degraded culture. We are very fortunate, therefore, to have collided, finally, with the limits now imposed by our circumstances. We can't continue living the way we have been, and the future now compels us to do things differently. As this reality asserts itself, I think we will look back at the turn of the twenty-first century agog with regret not for what we had to let go of but for the fantastic squandering of untold wealth that it represented. And when we're done with the pity party, we will enjoy the consolation of having to do things better. This fine book by Massengale and Dover is a treasure map to the long-buried trove of knowledge, skill, and principle needed to build better places for the human project to dwell in.

INDEX

If you enjoyed this book, you may also like these:

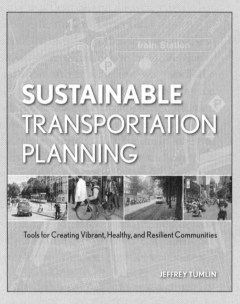

Sustainable Transportation Planning: Tools for Creating Vibrant, Healthy, and Resilient Communities by Jeffrey Tumlin ISBN: 9780470540930

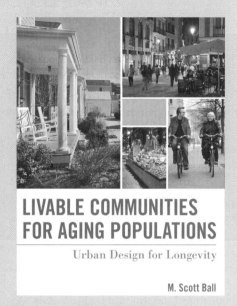

Livable Communities for Aging Populations: Urban Design for Longevity by M. Scott Ball ISBN: 9780470641927

Living Streets: Strategies for Crafting Public Space by Leslie Bain, Barbara Gray, Dave Rodgers ISBN: 9780470903810